The Street Where You Live

The University of Minnesota Press

gratefully acknowledges

financial assistance provided by

the St. Paul *Area Association of Realtors*

for the production of this book.

The Street Where You Live

A GUIDE TO THE PLACE NAMES OF ST. PAUL

Donald L. Empson

Foreword by Don Boxmeyer

With Wit,
Color, and Editing
by Kathleen M. Vadnais

University of Minnesota Press
Minneapolis • London

An earlier edition was published in 1975 by Witsend Press.

First University of Minnesota Press edition, 2006

Design and composition by Yvonne Tsang
at Wilsted & Taylor Publishing Services

Published by the University of Minnesota Press
111 Third Avenue South, Suite 290
Minneapolis, MN 55401-2520
http://www.upress.umn.edu

Library of Congress Cataloging-in-Publication Data
Empson, Donald, 1942–
    The street where you live : a guide to the place names of St. Paul / Donald L.
Empson; with wit, color, and editing by Kathleen M. Vadnais; foreword by Don
Boxmeyer.—1st University of Minnesota Press ed.
        p. cm.
    Originally published: St. Paul : Witsend Press, 1975.
    Includes bibliographical references and index.
    ISBN-10: 0-8166-4729-1 (pbk. : alk. paper)
    ISBN-13: 978-0-8166-4729-3 (pbk. : alk. paper)
    1. Street names—Minnesota—Saint Paul. 2. Saint Paul (Minn.)—History.
I. Vadnais, Kathleen M. II. Title.
    F614.S4E46 2006
    977.6'581—dc22   2006018610

Printed in the United States of America on acid-free paper

The University of Minnesota is an equal-opportunity educator and employer.

31 30 29 28 27 26 25 24 23 22   14 13 12 11 10 9 8 7 6 5 4

Dedicated to the CURIOUS:

of whatever size, shape,

color, sex, or age.

CONTENTS

FOREWORD

Don Boxmeyer

ST. PAUL'S NOT EASY. It takes some work, some effort to find one's way around on the city streets that one of our more or less enlightened leaders once claimed were laid out by tipsy Irishmen. This is a river town limited but also enhanced by its topography. St. Paul really is the city of Seven Hills so described by the late St. Paul newspaper columnist Gareth Hiebert.

And those charmingly irregular bumps in the ground, from its West End to its East Side and from its West Side to the North End, may have helped spare the city the ignominy of being reduced to a rectangular grid on which streets are numbered 1 to 150, or 250, or on and on into stratospheric digits. Imagine living at a five-digit address on a street named for an equal number of digits! You'd never want to get home! But in St. Paul we have Battle Creek Road, and White Bear Avenue, and Crocus Hill. We have Snowshoe Lane and Sterk Road, Neiderhoffer Street, Nina Street, and Nagasaki Road. How great would it be to live on Mystic Street?

Is there rhyme or reason to all this? To a certain extent, perhaps, but our founders didn't dwell on orderliness. There are a decent number of streets and avenues named for the presidents, but we never went overboard on the old guys, and certainly not in endless alphabetical or chronological succession, as you'll find in some la-di-da metropolises. You're far more likely in St. Paul to find streets named for the women in the various developers' lives.

One of the first to celebrate St. Paul's streets, and the often-quirky origin of their names, is historian Don Empson, who has researched his city quite literally from end to end. The first edition of *The Street Where You Live* was published in 1975 by Witsend Press, and the highest compliment I can pay it is to say the book virtually disappeared from newsroom libraries across the metropolitan area as reporters found it to be, along with a good dictionary and a fairly up-to-date almanac, a volume they could not personally do without. I managed to keep my purloined and dog-eared copy of Don's book, under lock and key, for almost thirty years. A friend of mine in the television news business rejoiced noisily when he found a copy in a used bookstore. *The Street Where You Live* remains one of my must-have books.

So I was overjoyed when I learned that Don was updating and expanding his work to include neighborhoods, parks, lakes, streams, caves, and other landmarks as well as streets and avenues. At the same time I was hopeful that he would not be discouraged from exercising his considerable wit and punacious penchant for whimsy. A careful read of this book will reveal delightful secrets of the city that might even bring a smile to the face of that erstwhile governor who so callously lambasted the street engineers of St. Paul. Then again, that might be too much to hope for.

PREFACE

LOCAL HISTORY HAS ALWAYS BEEN MY PARTICULAR FASCINATION: it is the ether of our existence, the lake in which we swim. The intimacy of local history makes the answers more obtainable: Why is my house where it is? Why are my neighbors who they are? How come downtown is over there, and the factories over here?

Local history provides a context for the space around our lives; it gives us a perspective on who we are and how we relate to those who lived here before us and those who will occupy our house and place in the next generations. Local history is an antidote to our ego that would have us assume—particularly on the daily level—that history begins and ends with us.

There are many evidences of the past in our day-to-day lives, but perhaps none is so obvious—yet so unremarked—as the place names of the city, especially the names of the streets and the parks. Thirty years ago, as a young reference librarian at the Minnesota Historical Society, I conceived the idea of researching and writing about the street names of St. Paul. The task proved to be more daunting than I anticipated, requiring more than three years of often mind-numbing detail and persistence, and many tedious hours in the vault of the Ramsey County courthouse. Poor health and personal adversities further hindered my work. Finally, in 1975, I self-published the first modest edition of this book.

Thirty years later, the University of Minnesota Press offered to reprint my book—by then long out of print. Knowing the continuing interest in the subject, I readily agreed, with the proviso that I add all the geographic place names of St. Paul, including early streams, lakes, and other features that have long since disappeared. I spent the better part of a year, working full-time, to expand the information included in the first edition.

I hope you will enjoy the book.

ACKNOWLEDGMENTS

MANY PEOPLE CONTRIBUTED TO THIS BOOK, and it is with great appreciation that I give them some due here. First is my intrepid wife, Kathleen Vadnais, who traipsed every mile and word of this urban project with me; I hope her sharp eye and wit are credited adequately on the title page.

Pat Igo, with his persistence and enthusiasm, deserves special mention for his efforts in obtaining a grant from the St. Paul Area Association of Realtors. Thanks, Pat.

Karen Swenson, a resident and community activist on the East Side as well as the one-time executive director of the North East Neighborhoods Development Corporation, spent three days introducing Kathy and me to the special features and delights of the East Side. Without her help, the book would have been much diminished. Likewise, the dynamic Ella Thayer, with her insider perspective, greatly enhanced our appreciation and knowledge of the colorful and diverse West Side. Cathy Kirby and Gloria Chesshir graciously showed us around the Highwood area and introduced us to Lynn Johnston, a wonderful gentleman and keeper of Highwood and Pigs Eye history.

The reference librarians of the St. Paul Public Library answered my innumerable questions. John Larson was particularly helpful, as were Kathy Castillo and Erin Zolotukhin-Ridgway.

Linda Murphy, chief supervisor of Maps and Records of the St. Paul Public Works Department, was always available to answer my questions; she also shared my curiosity and delight in finding obscure and arcane facts about the streets and parks. Her colleague Terri Vasquez also took time from her many official duties to look up information for me. Mike Murphy, historian and chief surveyor of the St. Paul Public Works Department, was very helpful in sharing his knowledge with me; most of the information on the islands of the city originated with him. Kevin Nelson, the cordial city bridge engineer, enhanced several of the book entries. Ron Mundahl orchestrated things for me at the public works garage. Others in the public works department who assisted were Mike Klassen, Larry Lueth, Tom Stadsklev, Bill Vos, and Dan Haak. And a special thank you to the director of public works, Bob Sandquist, who provided me with an entrée to the rest of the department.

The Ramsey County recorder's office went to extraordinary lengths to allow us access to the original plat books. Susan Roth (the county recorder), Lou Paul, and Stephanie Iverson (the supervisor of abstracts) deserve particular thanks.

Fellow historians generously gave of their knowledge. Greg Brick, the expert in underground St. Paul, graciously shared his knowledge of caves, creeks, and geology. I anxiously await the publication of his reference book. Jane McClure, a community journalist and prolific historian, unselfishly shared her many contacts and sources. Steve Trimble, venerable historian of St. Paul and Dayton's Bluff, contributed a number of facts that percolated their way into several entries. John Wickre supplied detailed material on the railroads. Kevin Kittilson greatly added to and confirmed my knowledge of Frogtown. Paul Nelson assisted with details about Central Park and the surrounding area. David Riehle gave me some great labor history entries, including the one for Rice Park. Jay Pfaender vetted the facts on Stonebridge and added pertinent details. Rhoda Gilman enlivened the entry on Henry Sibley. Stew Thornley kept me from striking out on the baseball entries. Karin DuPaul, long-time community organizer for the Dayton's Bluff Community Council, helped sort out some of the more obscure aspects of that delightful neighborhood. Brian McMahon introduced me to Alan Altschuler. Benton Hummel apprised me of her thesis on cemeteries. Nancy Goodman helped with her encyclopedic knowledge of early Minnesota. Janell Norman supplied history of her ancestor Pig's Eye Parrant. Roger Barr suggested several place names I did not know. Nancy Tracy pointed out unique features of the Summit-University area.

Special thanks to Michael Mischke, second-generation publisher of the *Villager* and *Avenues* newspapers, for his suggestions and encouragement. Andy Jenks, my neighbor and friend, plotted my course through countless maps. Neal Gosman offered his usual esoteric knowledge. Paul Mandell, principal planner of the Capitol Area Architectural and Planning Board, helped with the entries within the Capitol area. Cliff Aichinger of the Ramsey–Washington Metro Watershed District clarified a number of East Side wetlands issues. Mike McMahon provided some East Side place names. Hokan Miller of the Upper River Barge Service set me straight on Monkey Rudder Bend.

Other contributing folks include Emily Slowinski, Gale Frost, Chuck Lennon, Tom Raschke, Art Boeltl, Angelo Vruno, Ann Kenne, Sister Margery Smith, O.S.B., Bernae Gunderson, Micheal Danielson, Angela Anderson, Michael Marzitelli, Lloyd Burkholder, Linda Jungwirth, Jon Kerr, John Kerwin, Carla Hanson, Jim Berg, Barbara J. (Ide) Nelson, Sharon Born, Aaron Isaacs, Richard Faricy, Olive Taylor, Marilyn Deneen, Karlyn Eckman, Peggy Lynch, Jean M. Dick, Merf Dawkins, Harriet Ballian, Sylvia Carty, and Mrs. Nicolas Castillo.

This book could have been even better had the St. Paul and the Ramsey County parks departments, the St. Paul Planning and Economic Development Department, and the St. Paul Port Authority responded to my inquiries and questions.

And last, but certainly not least, let me thank my affable editor at the University of Minnesota Press, Pieter Martin. He had—to my way of thinking—the good sense to appreciate my sometimes idiosyncratic entries and slightly twisted sense of humor. His enthusiasm for reprinting the 1975 book and his consistent support are gratefully appreciated.

INTRODUCTION

What's in a Name?

ST. PAUL IS AN ENTRANCING COMBINATION OF THE PAST AND PRESENT. Neighborhoods well over a century old, like Dayton's Bluff, coexist with the latest beige townhomes in the Frost Lake neighborhood; the suburban lifestyle and architecture of Battle Creek contrast with the nineteenth-century mansions and brick streets along Summit Avenue. From the first hovel to the latest condominiums, the city has accommodated change.

To the knowledgeable person, every St. Paul neighborhood offers a surprising kaleidoscope of the past, present, and prospects for the future. By exploring the city's place names, its secrets are revealed: vanished neighborhoods can be seen again in the mind's eye; lakes long since drained can be contrasted with the landscape today; and people, forgotten for decades, come alive again. I hope this book will serve as your portal into the mysteries of St. Paul.

I have attempted to provide the origin and significance of as many St. Paul place names as possible, including every street name and park name in the city. "Ghost parks" and "ghost streets" have been noted, as well as the many public triangles and squares that go largely unnoticed and unused. When they are unique, I have also given the origin of the names and boundaries of many St. Paul neighborhoods. Thus, you will find the mysterious neighborhood name Horseshoe Bend in the book, but you will not find the self-defined Selby-Dale neighborhood. When it seemed at all plausible, I defined the borders of neighborhoods by the original plat boundaries. For example, in the case of that very loosely defined neighborhood Crocus Hill, I gave the borders of the original plat. In those cases where there was no plat, I have—with great trepidation—tried to specify some rough boundaries for that neighborhood. I know with absolute certainty that fully half my readers will feel I defined the neighborhood too large, while the other half will feel I made it too small. My greatest fear is that the reader, finding my definition of a neighborhood at odds with his or her own, will dismiss the rest of the book as equally erroneous.

I have also included the derivation of names for many geographic features of the city, both past and present. Thus, the reader will find both Fish Creek, which flows in the southeastern part of the city, and Cascade Creek, which once flowed through the West End. I have noted—when they have distinctive names—St. Paul's wetlands, many of which now serve as detention ponds to capture the overflow from the storm sewers. When found, I added the names of hills and bluffs. Historic lakes, long since filled and graded over by streets and neighborhoods, are mentioned alongside present-day lakes.

Making a New Street in Suburbs of St. Paul, Minnesota, a wood engraving by William Allen Rogers from *Harper's Weekly*, October 25, 1890. The earthmovers in the print are scrapers on wheels, probably made by the Western Wheeled Scraper Company of Mt. Pleasant, Iowa. The operator used a lever to lower the scraper, which would collect a thin layer of dirt into the rear of the box. When the box was filled, the horses were led to where the dirt was to be dumped, and the lever was raised to drop the dirt. This equipment was also used extensively for grading railroad beds and farm fields, and for other earthmoving tasks. This scene might depict the grading of the Bourne Avenue hill in St. Anthony Park. Courtesy of the Minnesota Historical Society.

I have not given names that exist as part of an institution. Thus, you will find Toni Stone Field in the book because it is a freestanding city facility, but you will not find the adjacent Griffith Stadium, because it is part of Central High School. Trying to give the significance and origin of the namesakes in all the public and private institutions of the city was far beyond the scope of this book, and certainly beyond the patience of the writer.

This is the most complete inventory of public spaces in St. Paul. There are over a thousand entries in this book and, as you might imagine, the task of compiling all this detail became rather tedious (even boring!) on occasion. To help speed the task along, my witty wife suggested we invent a character, the intrepid urban traipser, to entice you, the reader, to visit some of the more remarkable parts of the city. In that sense, I like to think of it as a pedestrian history, meant to collect information you can get only by walking around and talking to people. We hope you find the suggestions rewarding.

To amuse ourselves even further, Kathy and I added wordplay to some of the entries, hoping to evoke a giggle or two and otherwise add a touch of levity to what could be a humorless compendium.

To demonstrate similarities that would not otherwise be obvious, we introduced many "see also" references at the end of entries. For example, you can find groupings for all the streets and parks named for St. Paul mayors or the various attempts at an alphabetical street name sequence. In short, we hope these references help the reader detect the many interconnecting threads of St. Paul's history hiding in plain view.

HOW PLACES ARE NAMED

There are two types of names in this book. One is the informal names given without any official sanction. Most of the neighborhoods fall into this category, as do the early streams, lakes, and hills. Usually these names originate from some characteristic of the property or with the owner. Within each entry of this type is an elucidation. The second type is the official names: the names of streets and parks that have been approved by the city council. What follows is a description of the various ways in which these formal names originate.

Streets and parks have traditionally been named by the developer of the property on which they occur. Typically, a developer would purchase several acres to divide into building lots. Streets must be provided to allow access to each building lot. In the 1880s, a park also had to be provided. This division of unimproved acreage into building lots and streets—and sometimes parks—is known variously as a *development*, a *subdivision*, or an *addition*. The official map of this divided property—kept in the county recorder's office—is called a *plat*. For purposes of this book, the four words *development*, *subdivision*, *addition*, and *plat* are used interchangeably.

The developer is at liberty to bestow any name upon the streets and parks within the property as long as that name is not obscene, overly long, difficult to spell or pronounce, a duplicate of another name already used within the city, or will not in any way be confused with another name already in use. If the developer's new street happens to fall in a line with another street already named, the older name must be used within his property. All plats, with their building lot dimensions and street names, must be approved by the city council. Occasionally the city itself will act as the developer of publicly owned property. In that case, someone within the city offices will supply names they feel are significant—often those of other city officials or dutiful politicians.

In a few instances, particularly in past years, a private developer will not label street names on his plat. This void has often been filled by someone with the department of public works or a member of the plat commission, who slipped in the name of his wife, daughter, friend, or whomever. Names applied in this manner, such as Leone Avenue or Jayne Street or David Street, are very elusive to trace.

WHY STREETS ARE RENAMED

In the early decades of St. Paul, each developer, free to purchase property anywhere in the growing city, laid out the building lots and streets without a master plan or regard for what the adjacent developer might be doing. As the city grew and one development came to border another, the streets often had different names every few blocks. Many streets were not aligned, and intersected each other at peculiar angles. In general, various developers' eccentricities flummoxed the poor resident intent upon traveling from one part of the city to another.

The city council could do little to fix street alignment, and every St. Paul resident can think of instances where they have come to the end of one block and had to jog left or right to continue on that same street. However, the council could ensure that the streets running along more or less the same line would have the same name. For example, what was once St. Clair Street between Western Avenue and West Seventh Street, and Ludwig Avenue between West Seventh Street and Lexington Parkway, and Reserve Street between Snelling Avenue and Fairview Avenue, were eventually all brought under the original name: St. Clair Avenue.

The first streets in St. Paul, those of the downtown area, were named in 1847 and legally accepted in 1849. The first adjustment came nine years later, in July 1858, when the city council changed the name of Bench Street to Second Street; and St. Anthony Avenue, between Wabasha Street and Seven Corners, became Third Street (later Kellogg Boulevard).

In 1872, the first major renaming of streets within the city occurred. At that time there were a number of duplicate street names: three John streets, for example, and four College streets. The impetus for change came from the U.S. Post Office, which in instituting the home delivery of mail insisted there be only one street of each name within the city. It was also in May 1872, perhaps for this same reason, that the city made the first concerted effort to post street name signs.

In 1874, the second extensive renaming of streets occurred when the West Side, previously a separate village in Dakota County, was annexed to St. Paul and Ramsey County. This annexation brought a number of duplicate street names to the city map; all had to be changed to adhere to the policy of having only one street of each name.

In 1940, the third substantial renaming took place when the city planning department made another concerted effort to eliminate duplicate or duplicate-sounding names and to ensure the whole length of a street had the same name. The planning department also tried to mandate that all east-west streets would be designated "avenues," that north-south streets would be designated "streets," and that diagonal streets would be designated "roads." Traditional usage, however, created so many exceptions to this rule that the pattern is barely discernible—and certainly not to be relied upon.

While those particular years saw the renaming of dozens of streets, hardly a year has passed in which a few street names have not been changed. Unfortunately, not all the changes have been in the public's interest or even necessary. The city council, in acting on street name changes, has catered to individuals (Aida Place), to companies (Wall Street), and to organizations (Grand Hill). At best, these changes only perpetuate confusion and proliferate records; at worst, they replace a truly significant name with one of little or no meaning. In the past few years, the city council has taken to giving "co-names" to a few of the streets. For example, part of Dale Street is co-named Tiger Jack Street. This practice has the advantage of garnering political capital without effecting any actual change.

THE QUALITY OF OUR PLACE NAMES

Names do not necessarily have significance, aptness, originality, aesthetics, history, or any other aspect resulting in a meaningful street or park name. We have such misnomers as College Avenue with no college, Palace Avenue with no palace, Ocean Street with no ocean, and Hunting Valley Road with no valley or hunters. The selection of place names has often been, almost without exception, careless. Yet these names constitute, after a person's name, an important element of an individual's identity. In addition, place names greet every visitor and are used daily in myriad ways by every resident of the city.

The street names of St. Paul, like those of most cities, are generally lacking in creativity. With a couple of notable exceptions like John E. Warren's Mt. Ida Street and John Wann's Saratoga Street, the street names are common, predictable, and without humor. There is no Easy Street to grace the city, no Intercourse Avenue to stimulate commerce, no What Street (What Street do you live on?) to foster giggles. Where was the developer with the creativity to name his addition the Urinary Tract, with streets such as Kidneystone Lane, and Prostate Drive? Why did the city banish the name of Teepeola Avenue (a word indicating many tepees), and why has Argue Street vanished from the city records? Why are there no streets named for birds, herbs, colors, or zodiac signs?

Let there be a common sentiment between developers and city officials that place names, if possible, have some basic relationship with the land they occupy, acknowledging either the name of some individual associated with the property, or as a reminder of some striking and unusual geographic feature. If that is not possible, let the names be creative and different from those in other cities. Let there be an official policy that the merest suggestion of any place name containing the words *oak, hill, view, fair, pine, mont, wood, ridge, dale, crest, grove, hurst, land, park, edge, glen, high,* or *valley* will automatically incur a fine of not less than $100 and at least a month in the workhouse.

Finally, we must remember that most of the people whose names grace our street signs and neighborhood markers used to walk the streets of the city. They had children and spouses, heartache and sorrows, as well as moments of joy—just like you. They worried about their jobs, repaired their houses, grew older, and had health problems—just like you. They lived in your houses, visited over your back fences, traded garden produce, and sometimes had spats; in short they lived in your place then just as you live in your place today. Will there be someone tomorrow to chronicle the people and places of today?

A Guide
to St. Paul
Place Names

A

A STREET The forgotten village of Montville, an 1856 plat of residential lots among the Battle Creek bluffs, named streets A through K. However, it would be another century before any houses were built in these rolling hills, and only streets A, B, and C remain. This was the first of several attempts in St. Paul at an alphabetical series of street designations. Those of you who grumble about the deplorable disorder of our city's street names will be heartened to know—we did try! See also *Battle Creek, Berland Place, Greenwood Avenue, Montville.*

ABELL STREET William and Mary Abell were among the developers of this land near Oakland Cemetery in 1882. According to the directories, he was a railroad clerk who lived in St. Paul from 1881 to 1883. See also *Oakland Cemetery.*

ABOUT ROUND WAY See *Way Round About.*

ACADEMY TRIANGLE This small triangle on the southwest corner of Marshall and Western Avenues was originally a short diagonal allowing Marshall Avenue a jog to the south. It takes its name from the former St. Joseph's Academy, a Roman Catholic girls' school housed in the limestone buildings on the northeast corner of the intersection. See also *Western Avenue.*

ACKER STREET Captain William H. Acker (1833–62), a bookkeeper by profession, served as the adjutant general of Minnesota in 1860-61 before he was killed in the Civil War battle of Shiloh. This street near Oakland Cemetery was named in 1870 by his brother-in-law, Edmund Rice, a local developer. See also *Edmund Avenue, Oakland Cemetery.*

ADA STREET Previously Washington Street, the name was changed in 1876 to avoid duplication when the West Side was annexed by St. Paul. Several of these new names were those of women who remain unidentified. The Dunedin Terrace Apartments are at 469 Ada Street. See also *Dunedin Terrace, Eva Street, West Side.*

ADRIAN STREET This was most likely a personal name when the street was platted in the West End Addition in 1881. See also *West End.*

AGATE STREET Acknowledging the fine-grained rock that is now the state gemstone, this street near Oakland Cemetery was named in 1870 by Edmund Rice. The intersection of Agate and Granite Streets is a hard place to find. See also *Edmund Avenue.*

AIDA PLACE The other streets within Como Park were officially named by the city council in 1967 for past park managers. This street, however, was named for Aida, the mother of Victor

Tedesco, a park commissioner and longtime city council member. See also *Antonio Drive, Tedesco Street*.

AIRPORT ROAD A private road within the St. Paul Downtown Airport. See also *St. Paul Downtown Airport, West Side Flats*.

ALABAMA STREET Platted as Second Street, the name of this West Side Flats street was changed by the city council in 1876. At that time, there were several streets within this area named for states; today most of those streets have been vacated for an industrial park. See also *Colorado Street, Florida Street, Kentucky Street, West Side Flats*.

ALAMEDA STREET The name of this street near Como Park, previously Langtry, was changed by the city council in 1940 as part of a citywide renaming of streets. *Alameda* is Spanish suggesting a park or grove of trees. There are several places with this name, most notably a city and county in California. See also *Englewood Avenue*.

ALASKA AVENUE Previously Fulton Avenue, this West End street name was changed by the city council in 1886, digging the discovery of gold on Fortymile Creek in Alaska that year. Anyone who rushes to Alaska Avenue today will discover house numbers that do not correlate to any nearby streets. See also *Juno Avenue, West End*; see also "Equating Your House with Its Number."

ALBANY AVENUE Originally named Villard Avenue (for Henry Villard, president of the Northern Pacific Railroad), the name of this street between Como Park and the Minnesota State Fairgrounds was switched by the city council in March 1886 to avoid confusion with another Villard Avenue. Albany is a short name, easy to spell and pronounce, making it a good street name. See also *Villard Avenue*.

ALBEMARLE STREET Originating in Borup and Payne's Addition, this North End street was named in 1857 for a county in Virginia honoring an early governor of that state. Fauquier and Greenbrier were names of other Virginia counties given to St. Paul streets at this same time. See also *Fauquier Place, Greenbrier Street, Payne Avenue*.

ALBERT STREET John Wann, an Englishman and early landowner and developer in the Summit Hill area, named this street in 1874 for Prince Albert (1819–61), husband of Queen Victoria of England. See also *Lexington Parkway, Woodland Park*.

ALBION AVENUE In 1881 this name—part of the West End Addition—was in vogue; it evokes the mythological name for England. See also *West End*.

ALDEN SQUARE A romantic gazebo is at the heart of this small, one-third-acre park at the corner of Brewster Street and Gibbs Avenue in St. Anthony Park. Originally what is now Brewster Street had been Alden Street and Alden Place. John Alden was married to Priscilla (the name of an adjacent street) Mullens. Their names are immortalized in *The Courtship of Miles Standish* (also an adjacent street name) by Henry Wadsworth Longfellow, a popular poem when this park was platted in 1885. See also *Priscilla Street, St. Anthony Park, Standish Street*.

WHY ST. PAUL IS MORE SQUARE THAN YOU THINK
The Public Land Survey

There is an invisible web inlaid in the city of St. Paul, a subtle pattern we tacitly acknowledge without being aware of it, a form of organization around which we mold our daily lives without question. We owe it all to Thomas Jefferson.

In 1784, just after the Revolutionary War, the U.S. government had debts estimated at 40 million dollars, but an income of 4.5 million dollars. The new country had a valuable asset—land, lots and lots of "empty" land west of the Ohio River. How and to whom would it be sold? Land speculators wanted huge chunks, creating the equivalent of medieval fiefdoms. But others, led by the intellectual Thomas Jefferson, believed the broadest possible ownership of land made for the most democratic society. With Jefferson's guidance and inspiration, the decision was made in the Land Ordinance of 1785 that all the land "in the western territory" would be divided into units—called townships—six miles square. Each thirty-six-square-mile township would be further divided into one-square-mile units called "sections." Each section consisted of 640 acres, which could be further subdivided to halves (320 acres), quarters (160 acres), eighths (80 acres), and so on. This has become known as the Public Land System.

This township method of land measurement, based on the number four, originated in medieval England. "Foure graines of barley make a finger," was the rule of Queen Elizabeth I, "foure fingers a hande; foure handes a foote." The amount of land that could be worked by one person in one day was four square perches, or one daywork. An acre, the amount of land a team of oxen could plow in one day, equaled forty dayworks. The twenty-two-yard-long Gunter's chain used by surveyors to calculate the miles was the equivalent of four perches, but the Gunter's chain also worked in the decimal system. Ten chains in length and ten chains in width would contain ten acres.

The thirty-six sections in each township were numbered in a boustrophedon sequence: having alternate lines written in opposite directions; literally "as the ox ploughs."

A crucial element of land measurement was, in Jefferson's eyes, the square. In the early colonies, land measurement had been a complicated and complex process, requiring a surveyor—who could easily be bribed. Jefferson felt the simplicity of the square made it democratic; rectangular land boundaries made it possible for any settler, using even the most rudimentary tools, to verify his land purchase. It would be difficult to cheat the common man out of "a square deal."

With these dimensions as tools, using Gunter's chain, government surveyors were sent out to divide the vast landscape—regardless of topography—into a grid of thirty-six-mile-square townships. Each square was to be assigned a unique coordinate: the vertical index was the range; the horizontal index was the township. Because the area to be surveyed was so large—from Mexico to Canada to the Pacific Ocean—the country was divided into "principal meridians" and "baselines," zones in which the range and township indices would begin anew.

There was always a race between government surveyors and settlers. In fact, the settlers arrived in St. Paul almost a decade before the surveyors, and informal claims based on landmarks were made—all to be sorted out after the survey. To make their grid, the sturdy surveyors walked and measured each of the section lines: a mile north, a mile south, a mile west, a mile east, cutting their way through brush and trees, wading the creeks, and climbing the hills. They also made notes of the trees, soil, watercourses, and any other characteristics that might affect the sale price of the land. At each section corner, they marked "witness trees," or "bearing trees," so future subdivisions of the section might be accurately made.

St. Paul consists of parts of Township 28 North, Range 23 West; Township 28 North, Range 22 West; Township 29 North, Range 23 West; and Township 29 North, Range 22 West, all West of the Fourth Principal Meridian.

When the early settlers and speculators began to develop the city, they purchased land in squares: perhaps a one-half section of 320 acres, or more likely a sixteenth section of 40 acres. Developers mapped the streets around the border of their investment property and worked toward the center, adding lots and streets. Because the initial land purchase was usually square, streets ran at right angles to each other, and building lots were rectangular.

Downtown St. Paul was laid out in a square, but instead of aligning the square in a north-south direction, the initial square was aligned to the diagonal riverfront. Subsequent developments adopted a true north-south alignment, leaving the downtown streets askew with the rest of the city.

Today the grid pattern, though not obvious, can be readily discerned in the city, and most of us have a rectangular lot. The witness trees are long gone, and only contemporary surveyors, with their arcane instruments and knowledge, can distinguish the exact points of the original public land survey—the spot where it all began. But knowing which streets follow the original section lines can be very useful in determining distances and directions within the city. In the western part of the city, for example, the section lines follow Dale Street, Lexington Parkway, Snelling Avenue, and Cleveland Avenue, all of which are one mile apart. Accordingly the distance from Dale Street to Cleveland Avenue is four miles. In the other direction, the section lines—one mile apart—are Highland Parkway, St. Clair Avenue, Marshall Avenue, Minnehaha Avenue, Maryland Avenue, and Larpenteur Avenue. With these section lines as a reference, knowing they are exactly one mile apart, can you identify the section lines in the rest of the city?

ALDINE PARK This one-and-one-half-acre public park at Aldine Street and Iglehart Avenue was purchased for $35,000 in 1929. See also *Aldine Street*.

ALDINE STREET Platted as Wright Street for William Wright, one of the developers, the name of this Midway street was changed by the city council in 1886. The name may refer to the Aldine Press of sixteenth-century Venice, associated with the production of small, excellently edited pocket-size books printed in inexpensive editions. The name has a nice sound and pleasant associations, although unusual as a personal or place name. Between Summit and Carroll Avenues, Aldine is only thirty feet wide, giving it an appropriately European flavor. See also *Woodland Park*.

ALGONQUIN AVENUE One of several American Indian names in the 1917 addition of Beaver Lake Heights, this one refers to a group of Indian tribes. A number of small, somewhat original cottages from the 1920s and 1930s grace this winding, narrow street. See also *Beaver Lake Heights*.

ALGONQUIN TRIANGLE This small, flat grassy triangle of public land was platted at the intersection of Ruth Street and Nokomis and Algonquin Avenues.

ALICE PARK This one-half-acre public park at Ohio Street and Cherokee Avenue was dedicated in Dawson's Addition and named in 1879 for Alice, daughter of William and Mary Dawson. See also *Alice Street*.

ALICE STREET Both the street and park were named in 1879 for Alice, daughter of William Dawson (1825–1901), who developed the area. He was at one time the mayor of St. Paul, a banker, and a leading land speculator. Unfortunately his Bank of Minnesota failed in 1896, and Dawson died a poor man. See also *Alice Park*.

ALLSTON STREET Allston is an area within the city of Boston, on the right bank of the Charles River. This Highwood street was named in 1887 in Burlington Heights by the Union Land

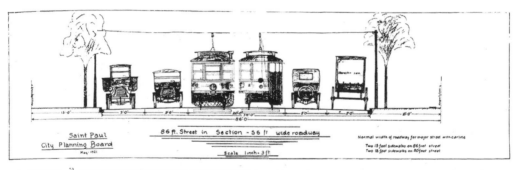

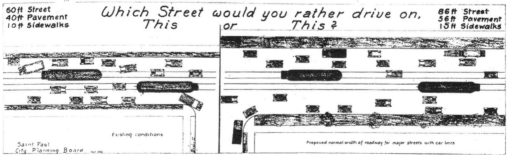

In the 1920s, streets were widened to accommodate an increasingly active mix of pedestrians, automobiles, horses, and streetcars. From *Plan of Saint Paul, The Capital City of Minnesota*, 1922.

Company, a syndicate of St. Paul and Boston investors. See also *Burlington Heights*, *Desnoyer Park*, *Highwood*.

ALMOND AVENUE Originally named Orange Street between Como Park and the Minnesota State Fairgrounds, the city council changed the name in 1886 to avoid duplication with the present Orange Avenue. Many St. Paul street names were switched at this time; very few of their nutty replacements had any particular significance.

ALTON STREET Alton is a city in Illinois best known locally as the home of Robert Smith who gave Smith Park (now Mears Park) to the city. This West End street was named in 1872 by another Illinois developer, Charles A. B. Weide. See also *Mears Park*, *Weide Street*, *West End*.

AMES AVENUE This street was named in 1886 in Hazel Park for William Leonard Ames (1846–1910) and his wife, Helen (1854–1940), the developers of Hazel Park. William, born in New Jersey, journeyed with his father of the same name to St. Paul in 1850. His father purchased land in and about the city, including a three-hundred-acre stock farm, where he raised nationally known shorthorn cattle in the area today bounded by Hazelwood Street and Arlington Avenue, by Case and White Bear Avenues. William Jr. attended the Naval Academy at Annapolis and later worked in the cattle business in the West, returning to St. Paul upon his father's death in 1873. By this time, the family owned 1,200 acres southeast of Lake Phalen, which he platted into Hazel Park and other real-estate subdivisions. William and Helen's home, built about 1890, still stands at 1667 Ames Avenue. The brick Italianate house at 1880 Ames Avenue is reputed to have been a boarding house for the workers at the nearby Harvester Plant. See also *Ames Island*, *Ames Lake*, *Hazel Park*, *Mechanic Avenue*.

AMES CREEK This creek, which is well depicted in the 1928 Hopkins atlas, drained Beaver Lake—through a second lake—flowing to Ames Lake and from there into Phalen Creek. Most of it is confined in the sewer today, but a brief remnant of the stream surfaces behind 1690 Ames Avenue with public access in the woods behind Sackett Recreational Center. The intrepid urban traipser might wish to follow the course of the liberated creek and reflect on how the landscape has changed in the past 150 years. See also *Ames Avenue*, *Howard Street*, *Stillwater Avenue*.

AMES ISLAND This approximately one-acre island appears on the 1857 plat of Lyman Dayton's Addition in the Mississippi River south of what is today Kellogg Boulevard as it approaches Dayton's Bluff. It was named for William L. Ames (1812–73), who had a mill on the riverbank close to this island (it was also called Mill Island). The island was undoubtedly swallowed up by the railroads as they extended the shoreline to build numerous tracks into downtown St. Paul. The legal description of the island is Government Lot 6, Section 32, T29N, R22W. See also *Ames Avenue*, *Islands*.

AMES LAKE Throughout the development of St. Paul, a great many small lakes and wetlands have been drained and filled, but this is the first and only example of a lake being resurrected. Ames Lake, named for William Leonard Ames (1846–1910) and his wife, Helen, appears on all the early maps of the Lake Phalen area. The lake disappeared from sight in 1960 when the Phalen Shopping Center at Johnson Parkway and Prosperity Avenue was built over it. However, the large shopping-center parking lot sunk and constantly needed repair.

Over time, the retail fortunes of the center dipped, and by the early 1990s, city officials planned to make a splash by restoring the area to a more natural state. In 1998, the parking lot was ripped up, the buildings demolished, and Ames Lake resuscitated, to the delight of many. On the occasion of its revival, Karen Swenson, executive director of the North East Neighborhoods Development Corporation, said:

> It wants to become a swamp again. There was a crack in the asphalt in the parking lot and a cattail was growing up in it. It will provide habitat, an amenity, . . .

In its natural state, Ames Lake, which drained into Phalen Creek, had been fed by springs to the northeast of the lake, and from a creek originating in Beaver Lake. Today the lake is filled only with groundwater, while native species are gradually being restored to its shores.

Not all the residents gushed over the new wetland, and one mother spoke of her fear that her young son might drown in the ten-foot-deep lake. Judging from the many children who drowned in the early days of St. Paul, the mother's fears have some justification, and it may explain why a number of small ponds and wetlands have been drained or filled through the years. See also *Ames Avenue, Ames Creek, Beaver Lake, Howard Street, Lakes/Ponds, Phalen Creek, Phalen Village, Stillwater Avenue*.

AMES LAKE (neighborhood) This newly coined neighborhood name, with its community center, is reckoned to be between Rose Avenue and Magnolia Avenue, between Barclay and Hazelwood Streets.

AMES PLACE Originally part of Stillwater Avenue, this segment was renamed by the city council in 1940. The imposing Ames School remains at 1760 Ames Place, along with a striking 1890s house at 1750 Ames Place. See also *Ames Avenue*.

AMHERST STREET Like the other streets within Macalester Park, this one was named in 1883 for a college, in this case, Amherst College in Amherst, Massachusetts. Other streets similarly named were Princeton, Cambridge, Oxford, Rutgers, Dartmouth, and Macalester. See also *Macalester Park*.

ANDREW STREET Platted as Jackson Street, this was renamed by the city council in 1876, possibly for the seventh president of the nation, Andrew Jackson. Many West Side street names were changed to avoid duplication when West St. Paul was annexed to St. Paul, which already had its own Jackson Street.

ANGST UND BANG According to a manuscript by Alexius Hoffman, who grew up in St. Paul in the 1870s, the hill where the State Capitol now stands was mockingly known as Angst und Bang. In 1862, the newly arrived German settlers on that hill, isolated from their downtown neighbors, feared American Indians. When any were seen out their way, the men would form night patrols while the rest of their families quaked in their shanties. "De wild es einen Angst und Bang" [the Indian is all fear and anxiety], someone said, and the phrase stuck. There are those who would claim, however, that Angst und Bang is still an appropriate description when the legislature is in session. See also *Bohnenviertel, Bunker Hill, Capitol Hill, Frogtown, Hog-back Hill*.

ANITA STREET The West Side Land and Cottage Company named this street in 1883 in the Prospect Plateau Addition. The use of feminine names was a common practice then, as now. See also *West Side*.

ANN ARBOR STREET This name in the Capitol Addition of 1890 near the Town and Country Club was most likely chosen both for its euphony and for the city of the same name in Michigan. See also *Federal City*.

ANN STREET James M. Winslow platted this West End street in 1851 in Winslow's Addition. Because an adjacent street was named Blair, perhaps Ann represents the wife of John Blair, a nationally known capitalist and political figure who was active in railroad promotion. See also *West End*.

ANNAPOLIS STREET Originally named in part Thirteenth Street, and in part Cottage Street, the city council designated the full length of the street Annapolis. With the annexation of the West Side in 1876 by St. Paul, this street became the southern boundary of St. Paul and the dividing line between Ramsey and Dakota counties. The name is most likely from the capital city of Maryland. On the land survey, this street marks a section line. See also *West Side*.

Looking east on Annapolis Street from Robert Street in the 1920s. The houses in the background remain, but the corner grocery store has been replaced. The streetcar made several trips in the neighborhood each day. Photograph by Kenneth Melvin Wright; courtesy of the Minnesota Historical Society.

The car on the lower right is heading north on Arcade Street from East Seventh Street about 1932. Photograph courtesy of the Minnesota Historical Society.

ANTONIO DRIVE The St. Paul City Council named this as one of the streets within Highland Park in 1967. Antonio was the father of Victor Tedesco, park commissioner and longtime city council member. See also *Aida Place, Tedesco Street.*

ARBOR STREET Platted as Third Street, the name of this West End street was changed by the city council in 1872 to avoid duplication with another Third Street (now Kellogg Boulevard). *Arbor* signifies trees or a shady garden spot. See also *West End.*

ARCADE STREET An arcade is an arched or covered passageway or avenue, specifically one between rows of shops. As an example of pioneering optimism, Bernard Sinnen bestowed this street name on his undeveloped property in 1872. The first surveyor's notes record that in 1847, an east-west road between St. Paul and Stillwater crossed the section line of Arcade Street about where Bush Avenue does today. See also *Sinnen Street, Stillwater Avenue, White Bear Avenue.*

ARCH STREET On the 1856 plat of Dewey, Bass and Rohrer's Addition, this street forms an arch on the top of the drawing that is discernible on the street map of today. By 1922, Arch Street was being considered as a link in an alternative truck route from Highway 12 (now Interstate 94), through the East Side, and onward to the Northern Route (now Pierce Butler Route). This improved routing would have taken the trucks directly into the industrial Midway area, by diverting them around the downtown area and congested University Avenue. See also *Pierce Butler Route; East Side, Midway.*

ARGYLE STREET Argyle is a county in Scotland that gives title to the Campbell family; in other words, members of the Campbell family are the dukes, earls, and marquesses of Argyle. Among the developers of this street near Como Park in 1885 were Henry and Minnesota Campbell.

ARKWRIGHT STREET Sir Richard Arkwright (1732–92) was the first manufacturer of cotton cloth and an important figure in the textile industry. The developer of Warren and Winslow's Addition in 1853, John E. Warren, was from New York State, near the village of Arkwright. See also *Mt. Ida Street*.

ARLINGTON AVENUE Previously the Lake Como–Phalen Road, the name was changed by the city council in 1940. It was originally a county road between Lakes Como and Phalen and also the northern boundary of the city in the 1880s. This name change was part of a city-wide reorganization and was inspired by the Arlington Hills Addition, platted some eighty years earlier near the eastern edge of this street. The original name, however, was more historic, descriptive, and exact. On the land survey this street marks a one-half section line. See also *Arlington Hills*.

ARLINGTON HEIGHTS A neighborhood roughly defined as between Maryland and Magnolia Avenues, between Clarence and Edgerton Streets.

ARLINGTON HILLS This is the name of an addition made in 1872 by a number of developers: Elias Drake, William Dawson, Robert Smith, Vincent Walsh, James Stinson, and Casper Schurmeier. It encompasses a large part of the East Side: between Edgerton and Arcade Streets, between Minnehaha and Magnolia Avenues. The original plat drawing is quite detailed. It illustrates a pond between Blocks 14 and 17 (Jenks Avenue between Payne Avenue and Greenbrier Street). Block 9 (between Cook and Lawson Avenues, between Weide and Walsh Streets) appears as a swamp. The east one-half of Blocks 26 and 35 (the east side of Edgerton Street between Wells Street and Sims Avenue) is also indicated as swampy. See also *Alice Street*, *Alton Street*, *Drake Street*, *James Avenue*, *Walsh Street*.

ARMSTRONG AVENUE Born in Ohio, George W. Armstrong (1827–1917) traveled to St. Paul by way of Keokuk, Iowa. He was state treasurer from 1857 to 1860; later he dealt in real estate, naming this street in 1873. Armstrong believed the easiest and best way to make money was to earn interest, "for interest goes on when you sleep, when you wake, when you weep, when you rejoice, when you die." The stout limestone building remaining at 626 Armstrong Avenue in the West End once housed the Henry Orme Brass and Iron Works. It served as a workplace for the Molders Union, one of the earliest organized labor unions in St. Paul. See also *Boyd Park*, *Energy Park Drive*, *Kilburn Street*, *Rice Park*, *Sherburne Avenue*, *West End*, *William Mahoney Street*.

ARONA STREET Arona is a town in northern Italy about thirty miles west of Como; the proximity to Lake Como evoked this street name in 1885 in the Lake Park Addition.

ARUNDEL STREET In 1855 Charles Mackubin named this Summit-University area street in Mackubin and Marshall's Addition for Anne Arundel County in Maryland, his native state. See also *Mackubin Street*.

ASBURY STREET Autocratic, domineering, and a man of resolute will, Bishop Francis Asbury (1745–1816) was a prime organizer and driving force in the Methodist Episcopal Church of America. It is estimated that during his ministry, Asbury traveled more than 270,000 miles, preached more than 16,000 sermons, ordained more than 4,000 ministers, and presided at 224 conferences. The street was named for him in 1881 because of nearby Hamline University, which was supported by the Methodist Episcopal church.

ASBURY TRIANGLE This small triangular public park at Asbury Street and Frankson Avenue was acquired by the city in 1913.

ASHLAND AVENUE Like the two adjacent streets, Laurel and Holly, this name was selected in 1870 for its pleasant connotations and general euphony. Ashland was also the name of the estate of the popular American statesman Henry Clay (1777–1852).

At the time of their accidental deaths, Democratic Senator Paul Wellstone (1944–2002) and his wife, Sheila (1944–2002), resided in a condominium at 455 Ashland Avenue. Wellstone was first elected as a U.S. senator in 1990, and his admirers revered him as an outspoken liberal with an unwavering passion for social justice. See also *Woodland Park*.

ATLANTIC STREET Platted as Collins, the name of this East Side street was changed by the city council in 1874. An adjacent street called Ocean most likely prompted the new designation. See also *East Side*.

ATTY STREET Named in 1885 as a very short street within St. Anthony Park, this rather puzzling appellation is either a personal name or the abbreviation for attorney. See also *St. Anthony Park*.

ATWATER CIRCLE This street, previously Maxson Steel Way, was renamed in 2002 at the request of the St. Paul Port Authority and Custom Drywall, the only two businesses on the street. See also *Great Northern Business Center*.

ATWATER STREET Originally Pleasant Street, the name of this North End street was changed by the city council in 1872, probably to honor Edward D. Atwater, secretary of the land department of the St. Paul and Pacific Railway. A civil engineer by profession, he was born in Vermont about 1834 and departed St. Paul in 1879. There is also a village in Kandiyohi County named for him. See also *Litchfield Street*, *Pacific Lake*, *Wayzata Street*.

AUDITORIUM STREET First named Franklin Street in 1849 for Benjamin Franklin, this name was changed by the city council in 1940 to avoid confusion with Franklin Avenue. Auditorium refers to the St. Paul Auditorium opened in April 1907. Promoted by Edmund W. Bazille, designed by Reed and Stem, built at a cost of $435,000, with a capacity of up to 10,500 people, this was the showplace of St. Paul. The newspapers lavishly praised the swinging

Ticket holders converged at the Fifth Street entrance to the new St. Paul
Auditorium about 1908. Photograph by Truman Ward Ingersoll; courtesy
of the Minnesota Historical Society.

balconies, the twenty-two boxes in the theater, the hanging lamps, the frescoed foyers, and
the fireproof construction. Today, both the auditorium and the street have disappeared as part
of the construction and design of the Civic Center and Xcel Energy Center.

AUGUSTUS GAUGER PARK Greenbrier, Seventh, and North Streets and Bates Avenue surround
this small park, owned by a nonprofit corporation. It is named for Augustus Gauger (1852–
1929), a well-known architect who began his local work as a draftsman in the office of Edward Bassford, one of St. Paul's most successful architects in the late nineteenth century.
Gauger designed hundreds of buildings in St. Paul in a long career; among them is the Stutz-
man Building at 725–733 East Seventh Street adjacent to the park. See also *Cass Gilbert Memorial
Park*.

AURORA AVENUE A popular noun of the nineteenth century, *Aurora* means literally "the rising light of the morning," "the dawn of the day." There are a number of cities in the United States with this name, and it was an appealing woman's name as well. It was applied to this street in the 1857 Ashton and Sherburne's Addition—at the foot of the hill where the Capitol would rise fifty years later.

AVON STREET Platted as Cayuga Street in 1871, the name was changed to Avon by order of the city council in 1872. Avon, chosen to fit in with the other English names of the area, signifies the historic river of England with Shakespearean associations.

AYD MILL ROAD In 1860, John Ayd, a German immigrant, built a house and gristmill on what is today Jefferson Avenue about halfway between Lexington Parkway and Victoria Street. It was the first and only gristmill in Reserve Township, as that area of the city was then known. The mill was water powered from a millpond supplied by Cascade Creek, which ran in the ravine now occupied by Ayd Mill Road. In 1879, the railroad purchased the rights to use the gradual grade of the stream bed for their tracks, cutting off the water supply from the millstream and draining the millpond. By 1886, the mill property had been divided into lots as the Ridgewood Park Addition. According to Mike Klassen of the public works department,

The Ayd family built this gristmill, from which the road takes its name. Today the road provides much grist for discussion. From the *St. Anthony Hill Graphic*, July 12, 1889, page 1; courtesy of the Minnesota Historical Society.

who has spent much of his career on this road, the city began acquiring property in 1960 to build a diagonal road linking Interstate 94 with the soon-to-be-completed Interstate 35E. By 1965 the road had been constructed between Lexington Parkway and Selby Avenue under the name Short Line Road, an allusion to the railroad that had first followed the course of the stream. By 1965, however, opposition to the road had crystallized in the Merriam Park neighborhood, which would be bisected if the road connected to Interstate 94. Moreover, the construction of Interstate 35E faced a serious court challenge to its route through the Pleasant Avenue corridor. In view of the circumstances, the city ceased work on the road, and—because of continued neighborhood opposition and a lack of funding—Ayd Mill Road remains a four-lane route without a destination.

In the course of researching the first edition of this book, the author discovered a plat subdividing the Ayd property, inspiring him to write a detailed history of the mill and property, published in *Ramsey County History*, Fall 1974. Members of the Ayd family who remained in St. Paul read the article with great interest and worked successfully to have the name changed to Ayd Mill Road in October 1987. See also *Cascade Creek*, *Reserve Township*, *Ridgewood Park*, *Short Line Road*.

B STREET See *A Street*.

BADLANDS An ethnic mix of poor Italians, Irish, Jewish, and blacks occupied this hilly neighborhood, subsisting roughly between Mississippi and Jackson Streets, between Pennsylvania Avenue and Thirteenth Street. The children attended Franklin Elementary School at Tenth and Sibley Streets, and Mechanic Arts High School at Robert and Columbus Streets. In a report about housing conditions in St. Paul in the 1930s, this area was characterized as

> comprised of housing closer approaching the eastern conception of slums than any other section of town. The homes are ramshackle, dating back 60 or more years in age, and are built on very narrow lots leaving barely room between each for access to the rear. The homes present impossible conditions as pertains to fire, health and moral hazards.

Most of the area was cleared for public housing and Interstates 35E and 94 in the 1950s and 1960s.

Before the Capitol was built in 1905 and the area graded extensively, this was a neighborhood of steep and jagged terrain. (A sense of the original topography can be found in the plat of Lambert & Co's Addition.) According to one resident, Angelo Vruno, the name Badlands for the neighborhood was in common usage when he was a boy in the 1920s. Whether this name referred to the topography of the area—similar to the Badlands of South Dakota—or the characteristics of its residents is left for us to ponder. See also *Barton-Omaha Colony, Bohemian Flats, Connemara Patch, Swede Hollow, Upper Levee, West Side Flats*.

BAILEY STREET John Vincent Bailey (1872–1943) operated a nursery in the area when this street was named in 1926. His grandchildren now manage the thriving business, but the short St. Paul segment of Bailey Street in the Highwood area was vacated in 1979. See also *Stinchfield Street*.

BAKER STREET Daniel A. J. Baker (1825–1909) was a developer of the West Side in 1857 when this street was named. He was born in Maine and arrived in St. Paul in 1849, where he taught in one of the first public schools in the Territory. He later practiced law and was among the founders of Superior, Wisconsin. Just after the Civil War, he acquired 160 acres in what was then Rose Township, and built a house near the intersection of Pelham Boulevard and Wabash Avenue. Baker School, now converted to office space, stands on land he donated near the northeast boundary of his farm.

This hilly topography may have given the Badlands its name. These stairs from Valley Street up to Mt. Airy Street are shown in about 1926. Photograph courtesy of the Minnesota Historical Society.

There is a humorous anecdote recorded about Baker, who, trying to save his barn from his creditors, had it moved off his property into the middle of a public street on a Sunday—the one day when legal papers preventing the move could not be served. He later argued that the men moving the barn were under the influence of liquor and could not be blamed for their actions, and further, if no one were responsible, the barn must have moved itself. See also *Rose Township, West Side.*

BALIAN STREET This is the only street between Interstate 35E, Jackson Street, and Maryland and Arlington Avenues. The name came into popular usage in 1996 when—despite the pleas of the owners—the St. Paul Port Authority replaced a ten-acre farm with the Arlington Jackson Industrial Center. Aram H. Balian, an Armenian immigrant carpenter, had purchased the property in 1916, and the family lived in the house he built at 236 East Arlington Avenue for over seventy years. According to his daughter, Harriet, Aram is reputed to have planted the first St. Paul Haralson apple tree in his orchard. On some maps, this street appears as a continuation of L'Orient Street.

BALSAM STREET This short industrial-blah street near downtown was named for the tree in 1946.

BANCROFT AVENUE Platted as Cambridge Street, the name of this West Side street was changed by the city council in 1886. Bancroft is a common name, but there may have been a passing thought for George Bancroft (1800–1891), American politician and historian. See also *West Side*.

BANCROFT STAIRS It is a daunting climb of 125 metal steps, built in 1952, along the line of Bancroft Avenue from Cesar Chavez Street up the bluff to Prescott Street. Even the intrepid urban traipser might pause before reaching the top. See also *Intrepid Urban Traipser*.

BANDANA BOULEVARD (private) A road in Energy Park named to commemorate the many engineers who chugged through this busy railroad corridor waving their bright red bandanas. See also *Energy Park*.

BANFIL STREET Considered "a man of sterling worth," a brick maker by trade, "Colonel" John Banfil (1812–87) was a native of Vermont and subsequently a resident of New Orleans. He moved to Prairie du Chien, Wisconsin, with his wife, Nancy, in 1840, then to St. Paul in 1846, where they named this West End street in Winslow's Addition in 1851. They moved to Manomin (now Fridley), where he built a sawmill on Rice Creek, and then on to Bayfield, Wisconsin, in 1866. Banfil is a narrow street in one of the oldest residential districts of the city. We know because we lived there for a number of years. See also *West End*.

BANHOLZER'S BREWERY CAVE William Banholzer's "North Mississippi Beer" facilities in the West End included a total of nine buildings and a one-half-mile-deep, multi-chambered cavern accessible from the bottom of the river bluff south of the brewery, and from the top of the cliff inside the plant's main stone building. Generations of curious youngsters have explored this underground attraction—known locally as Frankenstein's Cave—which still extends from the riverbank under Shepard Road to the vicinity of Butternut Avenue.

In 1885 Banholzer built a magnificent $10,000 stone house above the brewery at 689 Stewart Avenue, one of the more impressive nineteenth-century residences in St. Paul. The following year he established "Banholzer's Park" in the empty lots north of the brewery, a neighborhood recreation area with an outdoor beer garden, barbeques, bowling, German band music, and balloon rides to Lilydale. Banholzer died at the age of forty-eight in 1897, but his Stewart Avenue home remains. See also *Butternut Avenue, Carver's Cave, Fountain Cave, West End*.

BAPTIST HILL In 1904, local librarian Josiah Chaney wrote the best description of Baptist Hill:

> Occupying the space between Jackson street and Broadway, from Fourth to Seventh street, stood a high drift hill, called by various names, as Mount Pisgah, Baptist hill, and Burbank's hill. It was best known as Baptist hill, so called from the fact that a Baptist church once stood upon its summit. The northeast corner of this hill crossed Seventh street, and the southwest corner crossed Fourth street. A spur of it followed the line of Fifth street to Neill street, or a little below, and thence up Neill to Seventh street, connecting there with one running from Kittson street to Westminster avenue, which forms the left bluff of Trout brook for a long distance up the stream.

The Banholzer family and employees are celebrating 1889 outside the brewery. They used caves to warehouse the beer. Photograph courtesy of the Minnesota Historical Society.

Sibley street was graded through Baptist hill in 1876, making a cut of fifty-one feet. I think that was about the highest part of the hill, and the point from which cannon salutes were fired, during the Civil War, in honor of Union victories. Fifth street was graded through this hill in 1877; Sixth street was also graded through it in 1877; and Wacouta street in 1877 or 1878. When these four streets had been cut through the hill, they left the block bounded by them standing as a plateau about fifty feet high. The hill was composed of a heterogeneous mass of drift clay, gravel, boulders, broken limestone, and pretty nearly everything else in the way of hill building material. It was just what was needed in other places near by, but not there. . . . A large portion of the material was used on lower Fourth and Third streets, to fill the bogs and other bottomless mud holes. It was free dirt, and every one was at liberty to help himself. The hill gradually disappeared, and the area bounded by the four streets named is now Smith [Mears] Park.

See also *Mears Park, Trout Brook.*

BARCLAY STREET Previously Moore Street, the city council changed this East Side street name in 1886. Barclay is a common surname and place name, with the additional advantage of being easy to pronounce and spell. On the east side of Barclay Street, just north of Maryland Avenue, there are two small Jewish cemeteries that have been there nearly a century. See also *Cemeteries.*

BARGE CHANNEL ROAD The St. Paul Port Authority named this road in October 1983 as an access to the Southport Industrial Development with its river barge facilities. This is a street name that strikes fear and trembling in the heart of many a St. Paulite because it is the chilling address of one of the snow emergency impound lots where the reader will have to spend well over $125 to retrieve an automobile left parked in a snowplow's path. See also *Cathlin Street*.

BARNES ISLAND This island at the foot of Eagle Street is depicted on the first two maps of St. Paul in 1851 (Nichols) and 1857 (Goodrich and Somers). It might have been a part of Harriet Island but appeared as a separate island in high water. The identity of Barnes is unknown. See also *Islands*.

BARRETT STREET Frank and Carrie Crowell developed Crowell and Barrett Streets in 1907 in the Royal Oaks Addition near Lake Como. John W. Barrett was vice president of the Western Land Company, an investor in the addition.

BARTLETT COURT This was named in 1885 for John M. Bartlett (1830–1922) of the Minneapolis real-estate firm of Bartlett and Marsh. He had a financial interest in the St. Anthony Park Company. This street, east of Everett Court, was vacated in 1984 for industrial purposes. See also *St. Anthony Park*.

BARTON-OMAHA COLONY Barton and Omaha were two intersecting streets south of Randolph Avenue, east of the Omaha railroad shops. As early as 1884, squatters lived in more than a dozen houses along the river between the shops and the railroad bridge. The colony lacked any municipal services and, according to the author's recollection, had a distinctly rural flavor to it. The city lost a bit of colorful disorder when both streets and the houses were taken for the realignment of Shepard Road in the 1990s. In one of his books, Gareth Hiebert writes about a visit to the colony in the 1950s. See also *Badlands, Bohemian Flats, Connemara Patch, Swede Hollow, Upper Levee, West Side Flats*.

BATAVIA STREET Previously Beacon Street, this street in the Highwood neighborhood was renamed in 1940 by the city council to eliminate duplication. Batavia was the old name for Holland, the Batavi having been a tribe first recognized by the Romans. By extension, the name was used in the Dutch immigrant settlements in the United States. See also *Highwood*.

BATES AVENUE Maria Bates Dayton, the daughter of Master Bates, was a native of Providence, Rhode Island, where she was born about 1811. The wife of Lyman Dayton, a successful real-estate speculator, she moved to the village of Dayton in Hennepin County after his death in 1865. This street and Maria Avenue, both in the Dayton's Bluff neighborhood, were named for her in 1857. In the 1920s the suggestion was made to connect the Arlington Hills Addition and Dayton's Bluff with a bridge across Swede Hollow, joining Bates and Payne Avenues. See also *Arlington Hills, Dayton's Bluff, Lincoln Park, Swede Hollow*.

BATES TRIANGLE This small triangular public park at Bates Avenue and North Street was acquired in 1910. It was created when Lyman Dayton's Addition and Irvine's Second Addition intersected at a 45° angle. Within the past decade, this park has been enlarged with the vacation of Bates Avenue. See also *Bates Avenue*.

BATTLE CREEK This two-mile-long creek flows from Battle Creek Lake in Maplewood through Battle Creek Park into Pigs Eye Lake. The Battle Creek neighborhood might be roughly defined as between Interstate 94 and Upper Afton Road, between Point Douglas Road and McKnight Road. See *Battle Creek Park, Brooks/Creeks*.

BATTLE CREEK PARK Parts of Minnesota, including the area around the Twin Cities, were the location of territorial battles between the Dakotas and Ojibwes. In the summer of 1842, a band of Ojibwes, in retaliation for a raid by the Dakotas, prepared to attack the Dakota village of Kaposia, about where South St. Paul is now located. They advanced on the east side of the river and impetuously killed two Dakota women who were gardening on the flats below Pine Coulee. The Dakotas, alerted by the gunfire, followed the Ojibwes and defeated them in Pine Coulee. Because of this conflict, Pine Coulee became known as Battle Creek. (In his book *Past and Present of St. Paul, Minnesota*, W. B. Hennessy provides a graphic account of this bat-

Battle Creek Park, with its steep hills, was the enticing setting for this ski jump in the early 1940s. Photograph courtesy of the Minnesota Historical Society.

tle, which included live scalping, infanticide, and other gory details.) It was the last recorded battle in the area of St. Paul between these tribes.

This picturesque ravine has been a recreation and picnic area from the early days of the city. William McMurray acquired 25 acres in 1922 and donated it to the city. Between 1923 and 1925, the city was able to purchase another 40 acres, creating a city park that would function as a wilderness preserve rather than a controlled landscape. Through the years it has expanded to an 846-acre regional public park—preserving a large natural area in a developing city neighborhood. See also *McMurray Field*.

BATTLE CREEK ROAD Originally the south end of Hazel Street, this segment was renamed at the request of the residents in 1957 because the distance between this street and the remainder of Hazel Street had made it difficult to find. *Battle Creek Court* and *Battle Creek Place*, like the road, are named for their proximity to the park. See also *Battle Creek Park*.

BATTLE STREET See *Rev. Walter L. Battle Street* and *Rev. Dr. James W. Battle Street*.

BAY STREET This West End street was named in Stinson, Brown and Ramsey's Addition in 1854 for the bay tree, better known as a laurel tree. In the first half of the twentieth century, according to an article in the *St. Paul Dispatch*, October 14, 1959, the hill on Bay Street between Stewart Avenue and Butternut Avenue was called Spring Hill. See also *Butternut Avenue, West End*.

BAY TRIANGLE Acquired in 1907, this three-acre triangular public park at Bay Street and Tuscarora Avenue was created where the Asylum Addition #1 and Finch's Addition intersected at a 45° angle. See also *Cullen Street*.

BAYARD AVENUE Frederick L. Bayard was a local real-estate man just beginning his business when this street was named in Lexington Park in 1886. Born in New York, he settled in St. Paul about 1882; he died in 1927 at age seventy-five, having dealt in St. Paul real estate for close to forty-five years. The family pronounces the name Bye-erd. The well-known street of the same name in New York City is named for distant ancestors of this family. See also *Lexington Park*.

BAYFIELD STREET (private) Originally Fourth Street, this common place name was adopted by the city council in 1883. The street has since been incorporated into the St. Paul Downtown Airport. See also *St. Paul Downtown Airport*.

BAYLESS AVENUE Vincent W. Bayless, a Minneapolis resident, was president of the St. Anthony Park Company incorporated in 1885. Before moving to Dubuque, Iowa, in 1926, he also dealt in timberlands, investments, and fuel. A nicely restored Queen Anne–style home—one of several—was built in 1885 by the St. Anthony Park Company and remains at 923 Bayless Avenue. See also *St. Anthony Park*.

BEACON AVENUE Named in 1886, this is part of Howard Park in the Midway area. The namesake is uncertain; the best guess is that it commemorates the exclusive residential Beacon Street district in Boston. See also *Midway*.

BEAUMONT STREET Platted as Vine Street on Dayton's Bluff, the name was changed by the city council in 1872 in honor of Joseph I. Beaumont (1827–1905), who migrated to St. Paul in 1855, was a member of the city council and chief fire warden of the city, and served as Ramsey County assessor. He was generally liked and remembered as a quiet and pleasant gentleman. See also *Dayton's Bluff*.

BEAVER LAKE According to an 1881 history, the lake takes its name from "the industrious little animals that built dams on its shores and tributaries, and raised their young in its waters." The lake is seventy-two acres, four to ten feet deep, and supplied from a watershed to the east, including a natural creek flowing into the southeast corner of the lake. In its natural state, a creek once flowed out of Beaver Lake and, by way of Ames Lake, joined with Phalen Creek to flow to the Mississippi River. Today a sewer captures that outflow. An occasional beaver still shows up at the lakefront. See also *Ames Lake, Howard Street, Lakes/Ponds, Phalen Creek, Stillwater Avenue*.

This aerial view of Beaver Lake taken in June 1946 shows the northeast corner of St. Paul just as the postwar housing boom was beginning. Maplewood is in the background. Photograph from the *St. Paul Dispatch & Pioneer Press*, June 16, 1946; courtesy of the Minnesota Historical Society.

BEAVER LAKE HEIGHTS The intrepid urban traipser will be intrigued to discover this obscure and charming bungalow neighborhood of narrow, twisting streets with American Indian names platted in 1917 by the Schurmeier Land and Improvement Company. The boundaries are approximately between Case and Minnehaha Avenues, between Hazel Street and Mc-Knight Road. In reaction to an Amherst H. Wilder Charity study reporting the wretched low-income housing in St. Paul, this neighborhood was created as an early planned development designed to become the ideal workingman's residence. Thomas Holyoke, a prominent architect, submitted as part of the report a number of sketches and drawings of affordable $2,500 to $2,800 homes.

BEAVER LAKE PARK This is a fifty-five-acre public Ramsey County park within the City of St. Paul. As early as the 1920s, the city parks department had hoped to acquire parkland around Beaver Lake but could never unearth the funds. In 1954, the Lincoln Park Improvement Association, trying to prevent building on the shore that would limit their access to the lake, approached the county, which agreed to preserve the land. See also *Beaver Lake, Lincoln Park*.

BEAVER STREET Originally Douglas Street, this street below Cherokee Heights Park was vacated in 1981. See also *Cherokee Heights Park*.

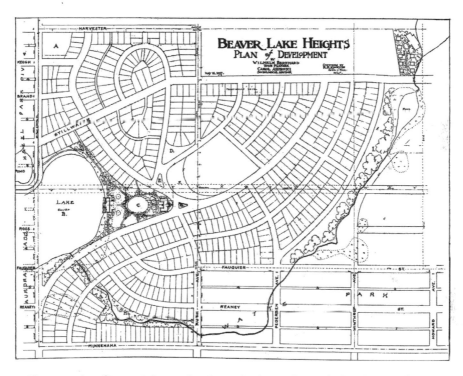

This 1917 plat of Beaver Lake Heights shows the design for an ideal workingman's community. From *Housing Conditions in the City of St. Paul*, 1917.

BEDFORD STREET Previously Main Street, this East Side name was switched by the city council in 1872. There are a number of places bearing this designation; probably all stem from the county and city in England. A handsome Victorian fire station, built in 1890, remains at 676 East Bedford Street. See also *East Side*.

BEECH STREET A reference to the tree, Beech Street on the East Side was platted in 1857 as Franklin Street. The street was renamed by the city council in 1872 to avoid confusion with Franklin Street downtown. See also *Auditorium Street*.

BEECHWOOD AVENUE Applied in 1925 in Lane's Highland Park, this is one of many, many streets within the city showing a beleaf in trees. The houses at 1829 and 1833 Beechwood Avenue, built in 1927, were the first two on this street. See also *Highland Park*.

BELLOWS STREET This was designated Bellows Street by the city council in 1876. Many of these West Side streets were renamed when West St. Paul was annexed to St. Paul in 1876. Bellows is probably a surname. See also *West Side*.

BELVIDERE STREET Originally Martha Street, the name of this West Side street was switched by the city council in 1883. *Belvidere* is Italian for "beautiful view." See also *West Side*.

BENA STREET *Bena*, said to be an Ojibwe word meaning "partridge," was given to this one-block-long street in Beaver Lake Heights in 1917. See also *Beaver Lake Heights*.

BENCH STREET This is one of the first fifteen street names of the city, originating in 1849 on the plat of St. Paul Proper, named because it was a shelf halfway up the bluff from the river. Today it is called Second Street.

BENHILL ROAD Platted as Ridgewood Avenue in Ridgewood Park, the name was changed in 1915; Benhill Road, a prominent London street, apparently had more charm. Nevertheless, the change of name inspired a caustic letter to the editor in the *St. Paul Dispatch*, August 10, 1915:

> As a taxpayer of this city, I take this means of notifying my fellow property owners that if they, for any reason whatsoever, should happen not to like the name of the street on which they live, they can now be granted a brand new name ... by just merely applying to our highly intelligent Mayor and city council (and very readily so if the name you choose is of English origin).
> (Signed) A Taxpayer on Ridgewood Avenue.

See also *Ayd Mill Road, Ridgewood Park*.

BENSON AVENUE George and Emma Benson of Wabasha County, Minnesota, were the developers of this West End street in the Palisade Addition of 1884. See also *West End*.

BERKELEY AVENUE Previously named Lydia Street, the street was renamed by the city council in 1913. This was done, no doubt, at the wish of the developer of the Macalester Villas Addition, who wanted his street names identified with the desirable residential enclave of Macalester Park. Berkeley refers to the University of California in Berkeley. For a time, part of Palace Avenue between Snelling Avenue and Lexington Parkway also bore that name. See also *Macalester Park*.

BERLAND PLACE In 1960, Isaac Berland, his son Morton, and their wives, Ethel and Shirley, developed Afton Heights in the Highwood neighborhood. As Cardinal Construction Company, they named their streets in an alphabetical sequence: Afton Road, Berland, Cardinal, Dellridge, Edgebrook, Falcon, Glenridge, Hillsdale, Kipling, Longfellow, and Morningside. According to Shirley Berland, the names are without further significance. See also *A Street, Highwood*.

BERRY STREET Either the fruit, or an individual, prompted this name in 1886 in Warner's Prospect Park on the border between St. Paul and Minneapolis.

BEULAH LANE Born in Kansas City, Missouri, a graduate of Villa Maria Academy in Frontenac, Minnesota, Beulah Bartlett (1890–1969), served as executive director of the St. Paul Humane Society from 1923 to 1963. When the organization's new headquarters was built at its present location in 1954, the street leading to it was named in her honor.

BEVERLY ROAD The Union Land Company named this Desnoyer Park street in 1887 for the city and summer resort on an inlet of the Atlantic Ocean, near Boston.

BIDWELL STREET Ira Bidwell (1804?–76?) was one of the investors in West Side land when this street was named about 1855. A native of Vermont, Bidwell, known for his cheerful greetings, came to St. Paul from Wisconsin around 1854, when he opened Bidwell's Exchange Bank, but later devoted himself exclusively to real estate. He had two sons, Albert and Henry, both of whom farmed on the West Side. The original Bidwell Street was one block west of its present location. See also *West Side*.

BIGELOW AVENUE This development was platted in 1918 as the Midway Industrial Division by Herbert H. Bigelow of Brown and Bigelow, Gebhard Bohn of the Bohn Refrigerator Company, and Eli S. Warner, of McGill-Warner Corporation. The area, known as Kittsondale, had been the horse stables and race track of Norman W. Kittson, reputedly the richest man in the Northwest. Herbert H. Bigelow (1870–1933) was born near Brookfield, Vermont. At age thirteen, he moved to Iowa with his family and, after graduating from Grinnell College, worked as a calendar salesman.

In 1896, he joined with Hiram D. Brown, a printer, to form Brown and Bigelow, a firm printing and selling advertising calendars. In 1907, Bigelow made his first purchase of Midway property and built an imposing office building at 1286 University Avenue completed in 1914. (Today the building has been replaced with new commercial development.) Under his management, the firm grew to be the largest of its kind in the world. Mr. Bigelow died under very questionable circumstances in September 1933. See also *Kittsondale Sewer*.

BIGLOW LANE This street was added to the city in 1950 in the McDonough public housing complex. Robert Biglow (1922–43) was a seaman second class who was missing in action after the sinking of the destroyer U.S.S. DeHaven off Guadalcanal during World War II. His name was suggested by a veteran organization. John J. McDonough (1895–1962), for whom the project was named, was mayor of St. Paul from 1940 to 1948. See also *Klainert Street, McDonough Park, Timberlake Road*.

BILANSKI POINT This idyllic site in the early city, a point of land formed by the confluence of Phalen Creek and Trout Brook, was the residence of Ann and Stanislaus Bilanski in 1859. Her husband was old and sick; her "nephew" was young and sprightly; and Ann, convicted of poisoning her husband, became the first and only woman ever hanged in Minnesota. You can read all the juicy details in *Legacy of Violence: Lynch Mobs and Executions in Minnesota* by John Bessler. See also *North Street, Phalen Creek, Trout Brook*.

BIRCH STREET Platted in 1926 in the Bachman Addition, this street in Highwood was most likely named for the tree. See also *Stinchfield Street*.

BIRCH VIEW COURT Overlooking a clump of birch, this Highwood street was named in 1965 in Highland Hills. See also *Highwood*.

BIRMINGHAM STREET Thomas F. Birmingham (1848–1932), his wife, Mary, and his brother William platted this East Side street in 1884 in Birmingham's Addition. Birmingham arrived in St. Paul in 1857 with his parents and worked at several occupations while dabbling in real estate. By 1884 he and his brother were proprietors of a grocery store. Birmingham's residence, built in 1892, survived at 1567 West Seventh Street until razed a few years ago.

BISON AVENUE Thomas Frankson named this street in 1913 in Frankson's Como Park plat for his herd of bison (American buffalo). He had purchased the animals in Iowa and displayed them in his zoo in Spring Valley, Minnesota, where he lived. He subsequently transported them to St. Paul, where he exhibited them in an enclosure between Bison Avenue and Midway Parkway, hoping for a stampede to his lots for sale. Unfortunately for Frankson, the obvious street name, Buffalo, was already in use. Could it be said he used bison to buffalo buyers? The Frankson house, built about 1913, remains at 1349 Midway Parkway. See also *Frankson Avenue*.

BLAIR AVENUE This street was named in 1872, quite possibly for Francis Preston Blair (1821–75) and his father of the same name (1791–1876). Both journalists and politicians, they ad-

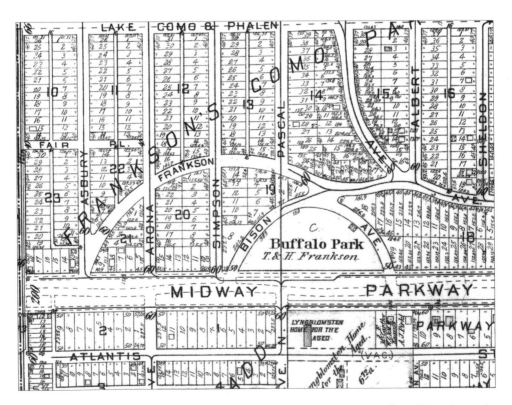

Originally a gimmick attracting potential buyers to view his lots, Frankson's Buffalo Park gave the adjacent Bison Avenue its name. From the *Plat Book of St. Paul, Minn. and Suburbs*, 1916, Plate 36.

vocated development of the West, cheap lands for settlers, and other policies, endearing themselves to the frontier Midwest. The younger Blair actively campaigned in Minnesota for Lincoln and the Republicans' antislavery platform.

St. Agnes Church is one of the most prominent and visible institutions in this Frogtown area. According to local historian Kevin Kittilson, there are two houses remaining on Blair Avenue that played a key role in the church's early history. In 1887, Father James Trobec, seeking a site for the new St. Agnes church, purchased the first house, a private residence located on three lots at the northeast corner of Kent Street and Lafond Avenue. This house served as the rectory and weekday chapel, and later as a two-room schoolhouse known as the "boys baby room." In 1901, Frank Lentsch purchased the house and moved it to 538 Blair Avenue. The house was too large to fit the single lot, so Lentsch relocated the front door and porch to face Blair Avenue. He severed the kitchen wing on the east side and, with German frugality, moved the dislocated kitchen to the back of the lot, where it remains today as one of St. Paul's few quaint "alley houses."

The story of the second house begins in 1890 when the new parochial school of the St. Agnes parish was filled, and several temporary frame buildings housed the overflow. One of these was erected both for classroom space and to serve as a parish hall. It was long and narrow, so the neighborhood wags immediately nicknamed it the "sheepstable." Like other early St. Agnes buildings, this "sheepstable" was later sold. After being sawed in two, one half now serves as a home at 534 Blair Avenue. The other half (now gone) was a home at 387 Edmund Avenue.

At one time, the eastern part of Blair Avenue between Western and Como Avenues was named Lake Street because it bisected a lake in the area, long since drained. See also *Frogtown, Lafond Avenue, Lafond Lake, Mt. Eudes.*

BLAKE AVENUE Anson Blake, his nephew, Charles H. Pratt, and also William R. Marshall were principal owners and agents of the south part of St. Anthony Park, platted in 1885. All three were incorporators of the St. Anthony Park Company, and Blake served for a time as secretary and treasurer. He died in 1906 at the age of eighty-seven. His prominent home, built in 1886, remains at 2205 Scudder Street. See also *Gordon Square, Marshall Avenue, Raymond Avenue, St. Anthony Park.*

BOAL ISLAND See *McBoal Island.*

BOHEMIAN FLATS Although this name is better known for its location along the Mississippi River in Minneapolis, a similar community of squatters took up residence in St. Paul below the High Bridge on the upriver side as early as the 1870s. Their community is described in a colorful account from the *St. Paul Pioneer Press*, November 11, 1888:

> Few persons care to set foot on the East side river flats excepting the members of the Slavonic community which has established itself there, and those whom business may call into that low-lying district. The locality has no attractions for the man out for a walk and carriage people would never think of driving down there. The shanties of

the settlers, which seem to be shared equally with them by the hens and the geese that they keep, lend a certain picturesqueness to the view, it is true, but this is offset by the odors that float across the flats from the garbage dock on the river bank and that arise from the door yards of the rough board dwellings. Hence visits to the flats, like angel's visits, are few and far between.

The squatters were evicted over the next couple of decades, and what remained of the community was displaced with the building of the electric generating plant (now owned by Xcel Energy) about 1905. See also *Kahout's Ponds; Badlands, Barton-Omaha Colony, Connemara Patch, Swede Hollow, Upper Levee, West Side Flats.*

BOHLAND AVENUE Adam Bohland (1834–1913) owned an eighty-acre farm between Cleveland and Fairview Avenues, between Montreal and Bohland Avenues. He was born in Sulzheim, Germany, and came to Minnesota in 1856, fought in the Civil War, served as Ramsey County commissioner, and was later county assessor. Adam's brother, Peter Bohland (1837–1910), owned the remaining quarter section: eighty-acres between Cleveland and Fairview Avenues, between Montreal and Magoffin Avenues. The brothers' homes faced each other across Montreal Avenue, approximately where Prior Avenue would cross. Peter represented the district for two terms in the state legislature. This street was named in 1887 in Otto's Addition. See also *Bohland Triangle, Quirnia Avenue, Xina Park.*

BOHLAND TRIANGLE Platted in 1927 by Peter Bohland in Bohland's Edgcumbe Hills, this large triangular public park with several trees is at the intersection of Hampshire Avenue and Edgcumbe Road. See also *Bohland Avenue.*

The wagons on the right are traveling on top of the levee along the Mississippi River, a course later followed by Shepard Road. On the left are the Bohemian Flats, a collection of squatters' shanties long since replaced with an electric generating plant. In the background is the first High Bridge. Photograph courtesy of the Minnesota Historical Society.

BOHNENVIERTEL This neighborhood was full of beans, according to a manuscript by Alexius Hoffman, who grew up in St. Paul in the 1870s. The area between Wabasha and Sixth Streets, between Summit Avenue and Kellogg Boulevard, was known among the German settlers as Bohnenviertel (Beanville) because the German women specialized in growing beans. Each little house had a little garden bristling with beanpoles. Today Beanville bristles with buildings and bustles with business. See also *Angst und Bang, Bunker Hill, Cleveland Circle, Frogtown.*

BONNIE LANE William E. Leonard and his wife, Bonnie L., were the developers of this Highwood area plat, Leonard Oak Hills, Number 5.

BOOM ISLAND While Minneapolis has a better-known island by this same name, this St. Paul island appears on the 1852 plat of Kittson's Addition at the foot of Pine Street. It was about one-and-one-half blocks long, and about three-quarters of a block wide. The name probably refers to a log boom used to gather and sort logs. See also *Islands.*

BORDNER PLACE Kenneth Bordner (1905–83), a real-estate broker, purchased this tax-forfeited Highland Park property from the city in 1946. He worked nationally for many years as a land-use consultant.

BOURNE AVENUE Walter B. Bourne, a clerk for the sale of lots, notarized this St. Anthony Park North plat in 1885. He lived in St. Paul until his death in 1916, at age fifty-seven. The Bourne Hill was a popular sliding and tobogganing spot around the turn of the century. See also *St. Anthony Park.*

BOWDOIN STREET The streets in this Hiawatha Park Addition in Highland Park were named in 1890 for colleges: Colgate, Cornell, Yale, and Colby. Henry Wadsworth Longfellow—who wrote the famous narrative poem *The Song of Hiawatha*—attended Bowdoin College in Maine. See also *Hiawatha Park.*

BOXMEYER BAY This name appears in Pigs Eye Lake only on official city maps created by Rudy Paczkowski, a whimsical cartographer in the public works department. The bay is just north of Rudy's Donut Plantation, which is in a nearby swamp. The appellation honors newspaper columnist Don Boxmeyer, a fervent fisherman and one of a handful of writers who have written with genuine fondness about St. Paul and its people. See also *Millett Outlet.*

BOXWOOD AVENUE Platted in 1889 in Riverside Park along the river, this street name has been extended north along the top of the bluff in Highwood. Other street names in Riverside Park were Blackwood, Redwood, Whitewood, Basswood, and so on, all of which remain unmarked and unimproved "ghost streets." Boxwood Avenue marks a section line on the land survey. See also *Ghost Streets, Riverside Park.*

BOYD PARK This public park at Selby Avenue and Virginia Street was dedicated—after much discussion—in 1987 to Frank Boyd (1881–1962), an outstanding leader of both the Brotherhood of Sleeping Car Porters Union and the St. Paul African American community. His was a life of courage, sacrifice, dedication, and service to the cause of labor. At the age of fifty-nine,

Boyd Park is named for noted labor activist Frank Boyd, pictured here in his home on Mackubin Street about 1951. Photograph by Buzz Brown Photographic Studios; courtesy of the Minnesota Historical Society.

he was a member of the electoral college in 1940, casting his vote for Franklin Roosevelt. This park and William Mahoney Street are the only public monuments to local labor leaders in St. Paul. See also *Armstrong Avenue, Energy Park Drive, Kilburn Street, Rice Park, Sherburne Avenue, William Mahoney Street.*

BRADFORD STREET William Bradford (1590–1657), one of the original Pilgrim immigrants, served as governor of the Plymouth Colony in Massachusetts. This street named in 1885 in St. Anthony Park honors him. See also *Brewster Street, St. Anthony Park.*

BRADLEY STREET Newton Bradley was a merchant who lived at Broadway and Sixth Street; Joshua Bradley was a Baptist clergyman who died in St. Paul in 1855. Either may have served as the namesake of this East Side street platted in Benjamin W. Brunson's Addition in 1852. See also *East Side.*

BRAINERD AVENUE In 1867, two years after the Civil War, a road meandered north out of St. Paul, following roughly the course of Interstate 35E today. At Maryland Avenue, the road swung northeast and climbed the hill through a natural ravine, establishing the current course of Brainerd Avenue to Edgerton Street. This New Canada Township road then swung north to Little Canada.

Horace J. Brainerd (1825–1902), a native of Cleveland, Ohio, moved to New Lisbon, Wisconsin, with his family at the age of sixteen. In 1849 he married, moved to Ramsey County in 1851, and purchased his twenty-three-acre farm (today bordered by Ivy, Payne, Clear, Greenbrier, Sherwood, and Edgerton streets) in 1854. He was very active in the affairs of the township, serving as a state legislator and Ramsey County commissioner. This street, which passed by his farm, officially took his name in 1886.

In the 1970s, Jim and Karen Sullivan lovingly restored the old Jacob Hinkel house at 531 Brainerd Avenue. It was one of the first complete house restorations in St. Paul. There are only two remaining homes in the city that have a cupola, an adornment very common in Brainerd's era.

BRANSTON STREET The English village in Lincolnshire provided this name on the St. Anthony Park plat in 1885. British names have always been a fertile source of inspiration and nostalgia. See also *St. Anthony Park.*

BREDA AVENUE Originally platted west of Fairview Avenue in 1885 in St. Anthony Park, the street was extended east, and the western part vacated. The present-day Breda Avenue was first named Lydia Street. Breda is a town in the Netherlands, where a peace pact between England and Holland was signed in 1667. See also *St. Anthony Park*.

BREEN AVENUE Frederick L. Breen was chief deputy register of deeds for Ramsey County from 1896 to 1934. This East Side street was named in 1928 in Edgar's Addition.

BREWERY TRIANGLE Created by the diagonal course of West Seventh Street, this public triangle across from the old Schmidt Brewery buildings at Jefferson Avenue and West Seventh Street is now the site of a sculpture evoking the nearby Mississippi River limestone caves.

BREWSTER STREET Previously Alden Street and Alden Place, this St. Anthony Park name was changed by the city council May 4, 1940. William Brewster (1567–1644) was an elder of the Pilgrim Church who came to America on the *Mayflower*. See also *Alden Square, Bradford Street*.

BRICKYARDS LAKE This lake first appears on the 1867 map of Mc-Lean Township; alongside it is the notation "brickyards." On today's map, the lake would be located northwest of the intersection of Hudson Road and Johnson Parkway. Until recently, the lake bed remained at least a wetland, but new construction has obliterated any sign of it. See also *Lakes / Ponds*.

BRIDAL VEIL CREEK Although this stream now exits the storm sewer next to the Franklin Avenue Bridge in Minneapolis, the romantic name refers to the natural waterfall that once spilled the creek over the bluff into the Mississippi River. The full extent of the creek and its watershed is presently under investigation, but the creek does surface briefly in the duck pond on

Bridal Veil Creek had not yet been confined to a sewer when this Civil War–era photograph by Whitney's Gallery was taken. Courtesy of the Minnesota Historical Society.

the north side of Kasota Avenue, about one-fourth of a mile west of Highway 280. This is just inside the Minneapolis city limits, although the creek originates in St. Paul. See also *Creeks/ Brooks; Kasota Ponds*.

BRIDGES While there are many bridges in St. Paul, relatively few have distinctive names. See *High Bridge, Merle Harris Bridge, Sri Chin Moy Bridge, Stone Arch Bridge, Wabasha Freedom Bridge, Westminster Junction*.

BRIDLEWOOD DRIVE (private) This street was named in 1981 in the Pathways Addition.

BRIGHTON PLACE In Victorian times, Brighton was the principal seaside resort of England, with many elegant streets, squares, terraces, and fine parks. The spirit of this most fashionable resort came to the shores of Lake Phalen within the Overbrook Addition in 1886.

BRIMHALL STREET William Brimhall (1825–97), born in Hardwick, Massachusetts, began working on a neighboring farm at the age of ten; eight years later he was apprenticed to the plow maker's trade. He subsequently worked as a carpenter, almost losing his life when a dam he helped construct across the Connecticut River gave way. He came to Minnesota in 1851, boarding with his uncle, Lot Moffett, a well-known pioneer. Later, taking a claim of eighty acres in an area today between St. Clair and Randolph Avenues, between Snelling Avenue and Pascal Street, Brimhall grew experimental varieties of fruits and vegetables, planting twenty-five acres of apple trees. He was also proprietor of the Reserve Nursery and a lifelong member of the State Horticultural Society. In 1886 "having outlived the climate," he platted his farm into building lots as Sylvan Park and moved to San Diego, California.

BROADWAY A common name most readily associated with New York City, this street was platted in the 1849 Whitney and Smith's Addition. It was never broader than any of the other downtown streets, none of which was originally more than sixty feet wide.

There are two remaining segments to the street. The southern part is in the 1890s warehouse district with attractive architectural detailing on some of the old brick buildings. The northern part of the street is a freeway frontage road that merges into Mississippi Street. The Broadway-Mississippi streetcar line was once a major route north from downtown St. Paul, in the same way Interstate 35E serves today.

BROMPTON STREET This street was named in 1885 in St. Anthony Park for Brompton, a district of London, England. See also *St. Anthony Park*.

BROOKLINE STREET Brookline was a village near Boston noted for its elegant villas, beautiful gardens, and parks. The name was given to this street in 1887 by the Union Land Company in their Burlington Heights addition. See also *Burlington Heights*.

BROOKS/CREEKS Several named creeks and brooks flowed through Saint Paul in its earlier days. Most of them have since been banished into the storm sewer system to make way for residential and commercial development. See *Ames Creek, Bridal Veil Creek, Cascade Creek, Fish Creek, Fountain Creek, McCloud Creek, McLeod Creek, Odell's Creek, Phalen Creek, Rice's Brook, Trout Brook*.

BROWN AVENUE Born near Urbana, Ohio, William Reynolds Brown (1816–74) moved to Wabash County, Illinois, in 1833, where he became a journeyman carpenter. In 1841, with the promise of a year's work and good wages, he accompanied a Methodist missionary via St. Louis to Red Rock (Newport), Minnesota. He and his wife, Martha, became the first white settlers on that prairie. He farmed there, moving to West St. Paul in 1852, where he purchased some property and named this street in 1857 in the West St. Paul plat. In 1857, he considered himself worth $50,000; the financial crash that same year reduced him to poverty. He lived for a time in St. Paul, served in the Civil War, and later returned to Newport, where he died. See also *West Side*.

BRUCE VENTO NATURE SANCTUARY Dedicated in 2005, this twenty-seven-acre public nature-cultural-history park at the foot of Dayton's Bluff includes Carver's Cave. It took two years for heavy earthmoving machines to transform the polluted railroad yards covered with scrub plants and litter into a landscaped area with graded paths, three ponds, and groves of oak and cottonwood trees. Volunteers have created a rock-lined stream using the seepage from the caves in the bluff.

Congressman Bruce Vento (1940–2000), a member, then chairman of the House sub-committee on public lands between 1985 and 1994, was in a position of authority to add millions of pristine acres to national parks, trails, scenic rivers, and wilderness areas. Throughout his political life, Vento was a champion of liberal causes; often unable to contain his enthusiasm, he found it difficult to put a period to his rambling sentences. Vento is remembered not as a born politician, nor as a polished speaker, but rather as a man on a serious mission. See also *Carver's Cave*.

BRUCE VENTO REGIONAL TRAIL Previously the Burlington Northern (Railroad) Trail, extending northeast from downtown St. Paul to the Maplewood Mall Shopping Center, the name was changed to the Bruce Vento Regional Trail by the St. Paul City Council in April 2000. See also *Bruce Vento Nature Sanctuary*.

BRUCE VENTO WILDLIFE VIEWING AREA Overlooking the Mississippi River, a guidepost to this site can be found at the intersection of Annapolis Street and Cherokee Heights Boulevard. See also *Bruce Vento Nature Sanctuary*.

BRUNSON STREET Originally a continuation of Burr Street, the name of this Railroad Island street was changed in 1885 to honor Benjamin W. Brunson (1823–98). Born in Detroit, he moved to St. Paul in 1847 with his wife, Martha, where he assisted in surveying the original plat of St. Paul. Brunson, a leading citizen of the city for fifty years, served in the Territorial Legislature. He was reputed to be a man "with decided opinions, of independent character, who thinks a good deal more than he talks." He built, in 1855, one of the early brick houses in the city on the corner of Patridge (now Kenny Road) and Brunson Streets, where he lived until his death in 1898. This restored home still stands at 485 Kenny Road, one of the oldest houses in the city, providing a direct link with the beginnings of St. Paul. See also *Railroad Island*.

One of the first homes in Railroad Island, Benjamin W. Brunson's residence, pictured here in November 1896, remains at the corner of Kenny Road and Brunson Street. Photograph courtesy of the Minnesota Historical Society.

BUFFALO STREET This North End street near Oakland Cemetery was named in 1870 in Edmund Rice's Second Addition. An adjacent street is called Elk. In the early days of the city, before there were water pipes, the fire department built and maintained cisterns collecting water for dousing fires in the neighborhood. One such cistern was on the southeast corner of Buffalo and Genesee Streets. As the water department expanded its lines, the cisterns were gradually replaced by fire hydrants. See also *North End, St. Peter Street*.

BUFORD AVENUE This street was named in 1885 in St. Anthony Park to commemorate Abraham Buford (1820–84). Member of a prominent Virginia family, Buford graduated from West Point and participated in the war with Mexico. At the outbreak of the Civil War he was appointed a brigadier-general in the Confederate Army. After the war he returned to his successful stock farm, but in later years, suffering the loss of his son, wife, and home, he took his own life. A syndicate of Virginia capitalists who provided financial backing for this addition selected his name for the street. See also *St. Anthony Park*.

BUNKER HILL According to Alexius Hoffman, who grew up in St. Paul in the 1870s, this was one of the early names of the hill where the State Capitol now stands. The current aptness of this early name is left up to the reader. See also *Angst und Bang, Bohnenviertel, Capitol Hill, Frogtown, Hog-back Hill*.

BURBANK'S HILL See *Baptist Hill*.

BURG STREET Leo J. Burg of Hennepin County was the mortgagee on this property in the extreme southeast corner of St. Paul when it was platted in 1926. It remained a "ghost street" (unmarked, unopened) until 2005, when houses were built on part of it. At the south end of Burg Street (still a "ghost street") lies Bolser Walk, a "ghost walk." One might speculate this is a haunted burg. See also *Ghost Streets*.

BURGESS STREET Platted without a name, this Como Park area street was named in 1874 by the city, most likely for Clarence Burgess, an engineer, and his sister Louise M. Burgess, a clerk, both of whom worked in the city engineer's office at that time. Louise subsequently worked with David L. Curtice for many years. See also *Curtice Street*.

BURLINGTON HEIGHTS In 1886, a syndicate of St. Paul and Boston businessmen purchased about 1,200 acres above Point Douglas Road, between what is today Lower Afton Road and Ogden Avenue, and platted it into streets and lots. It was to be a railroad commuter suburb similar to Merriam Park and St. Anthony Park. The two railroad stations, Highwood Station and Oakland Station, were less than a mile apart at the base of the bluff. By 1887, the trains ran six times a day from downtown St. Paul to Dayton's Bluff, Highwood, Oakland, and St. Paul Park.

The value of each house had to be at least $1,500:

> This judicious limitation [price of houses] insures buildings of exclusively desirable character, a condition the Land Company is zealously determined to exact from all builders, so far as may be possible.

Furthermore,

> Nature has so bounteously beautified this spot that no effort of man can improve upon its charms. No outlay is necessary for the improvement of grounds.

The steep terrain and the lack of city services inhibited the development of the area. Because the train station was named Highwood, as was one of its principal streets, gradually Burlington Heights became known as Highwood. An indication of when this happened can be found in the fact that the Burlington Heights Women's Club, organized in 1912, changed their name to the Highwood Park Women's Club in 1940. Today, only the historian knows it as Burlington Heights. See also *Highwood, Merriam Park, St. Anthony Park, Warrendale*.

BURLINGTON POND See *Great Northern Pond*.

BURLINGTON ROAD The nearby Chicago, Burlington, and Quincy Railroad gave the name to this Burlington Heights street in 1886. According to an early promotional brochure, the main street of this railroad suburb, Burlington Road, was described as follows:

> Chief among the improvements already undertaken by the Land Company has been the laying out of a grand boulevard [Burlington Road] connecting with the Afton

Highwood Station was one of two train depots serving Burlington Heights. Photograph courtesy of the Minnesota Historical Society.

road on the north, and passing centrally through the Company's property to a junction with the Newport road at the south. It follows the undulation of the hills, thus preserving and enveloping their most picturesque features.

See also *Burlington Heights, Highwood, Wiggins Pond.*

BURNQUIST STREET Joseph A. A. Burnquist (1879–1961) was governor of Minnesota when this street near Como Park was named in 1916 in the Lane-Hospes Addition. Born in Dayton, Iowa, he graduated from Carleton College in 1902 and later from the University of Minnesota Law School. He began his political career when blue-collar Swedes from St. Paul elected him to the state legislature in 1908. In 1912, he was nominated as lieutenant governor to provide his party with a progressive sheen.

He inherited the governor's office in 1915 and was elected in 1916 with working-class support. However, Burnquist owed his true allegiance to the Republican business interests and had little independent status of his own. One contemporary said of him: "Poor Burnquist, who I think is a good man at heart, is weak." While in office, he was associated with the Minnesota Public Safety Commission, a zealous organization that used the patriotic fervor of World War I to initiate "a policy of brutal intolerance" toward their many enemies, including all Germans, labor unions, opposing political parties, and anyone else who challenged the business interests in the state. After his term in office, Burnquist briefly took up the gentler profession of historian and wrote a mediocre four-volume history of Minnesota. See also *Clough Street, Gorman Avenue, Hubbard Avenue, Johnson Parkway, Marshall Avenue, Merriam Lane, Ramsey Street, Scudder Street, Sibley Street.*

BURNS AVENUE Benjamin Hoyt sold a $10,000 interest in his 1856 Suburban Hills plat to John Burns and his wife, Priscilla. It does not appear they were ever residents of St. Paul.

In marking this section line in 1847, the first surveyor made note of a road from St. Paul to Stillwater that crossed (today) Burns Avenue between Clarence Street and English Street. He also noted a road from the old settlement at Pigs Eye to the newer village at St. Paul that crossed (today) Burns Avenue east of Frank Street. According to an 1881 history, this Pigs Eye and St. Paul road was built about 1840 by local residents.

BURR STREET Benjamin W. Brunson named this East Side street in 1852 in Brunson's Addition to honor his mother, Eunice Burr. A native of Bridgeport, Connecticut, she came to Prairie du Chien, Wisconsin, with her missionary husband in 1836. Ten years later she died there from influenza. On the southeast corner of Burr Street and Geranium Avenue, the 1928 Hopkins atlas shows a pond that covered about a quarter of the block. See also *Brunson Street.*

Governor Joseph A. A. Burnquist, for whom the street is named, was chairman of the controversial Minnesota Commission of Public Safety in 1918. He is seated directly beneath the lamp. Photograph courtesy of the Minnesota Historical Society.

BUSH AVENUE Originally named Fauquier Street in 1857 (for the county in Virginia), the city council changed the name one hundred years later to honor Archibald G. Bush (1887–1966), a chief executive of the 3M Company, which for many years had its headquarters at 900 East Bush Avenue. Born and raised in Granite Falls, Minnesota, Bush joined 3M as assistant book-keeper in 1909, early in the company's history. He was rapidly promoted to sales manager in 1914, a director of the company in 1921, executive vice president in 1948, and chairman of the executive committee the following year. Bush, reputed to be one of the richest men in Minnesota, was an active philanthropist through the Bush Foundation. Most of the residents, tired of sly remarks about the original street name, welcomed the change.

BUTTERNUT AVENUE Part of the Protestant Orphan Asylum property, this street name was selected in 1882 for a grove of butternut trees nearby. In an article in the *St. Paul Dispatch*, October 14, 1959, there is a lament for the secluded colony of Butternut Avenue because all the houses on the south side of Butternut were to be cleared for the extension of Shepard Road. One of the residents who grew up on Butternut recounted youthful relationships with the Italians who lived on the Upper Levee and worked in the stone quarry below Butternut Avenue.

> We dug holes in the street and then covered them over expecting the Italians to step into them when they walked by on their way home from work. They fixed us by walking around them. They may not have understood English, but they knew about boys.

See also *Banholzer's Brewery Cave, Cullen Street, Upper Levee.*

C

C STREET See *A Street*.

CALIFORNIA AVENUE Following the pattern established in Washington, DC, this street was named for the state in 1886 in Merrill's Division. This part of the city near Lake Como includes other western state names. Hoyt Avenue was originally Kansas Avenue. *California Drive* (private) is an extension of the street.

CALVARY CEMETERY This is the only Roman Catholic cemetery in St. Paul, one of eight cemeteries remaining within the city. Calvary ("skull" in Latin) is the place where Jesus was crucified. Since its founding in 1856, more than one hundred thousand people have been buried here. For a listing of some famous people interred here, see the book *Six Feet Under: A Graveyard Guide to Minnesota* by Stew Thornley. See also *Cemeteries*.

CAMBRIDGE STREET Like the other streets within Macalester Park, this one was named in 1883 for a college, in this case, Cambridge University in England. Other streets were Princeton, Amherst, Oxford, Rutgers, Dartmouth, and Macalester. The noted architect Cass Gilbert built the nicely preserved house at 161 Cambridge Street in 1890 as a country estate. See also *Macalester Park*.

CAMBRIDGE TRIANGLE This small public park at the intersection of Cambridge Street and Princeton Avenue was acquired in 1915. It is named for the street and results from the irregular layout of Macalester Park. See also *Macalester Park*.

CAMELOT STREET Camelot, a place of idealized beauty, peace, and enlightenment, the seat of King Arthur's Court, was often used as a metaphor for the presidency of John F. Kennedy (1917–63). This street near Rice Street and Larpenteur Avenue was named by the city council in April 1973.

CANFIELD AVENUE; CANFIELD STREET (Fairgrounds) This street, which originates within the Minnesota State Fairgrounds and continues as an avenue outside the fairgrounds, honors Thomas H. Canfield (1875–1965), longtime secretary and general manager of the Minnesota Agricultural Society (State Fair). Born in Vermont, he came to Minnesota as a young man, where he operated a large stock farm near Detroit Lakes. From 1916 to 1930 he was with the fair, later moving to Glendale, California, where he died.

CANTON STREET This was a very popular place name, occurring in about twenty-five states, and having as its origin Canton, China. About the middle of the nineteenth century it was

Thomas H. Canfield, for whom the street is named, stands at the right hand of future President Warren Harding (*center front*) in 1919. The others are all members of the Minnesota Agricultural Society Board. Photograph courtesy of the Minnesota Historical Society.

common to give foreign and exotic names to towns and villages, such as Memphis, Cairo, Hannibal. These names were fashionable, stemming in part from a post office requirement that no city name be duplicated within a state, and no street name be duplicated within a city. The name was given to this West End street in 1874 in the Protestant Orphan Asylum Addition, Number 2. See also *Cullen Street, West End*.

CAPITOL BOULEVARD Originally Brewster Street, the name was changed by the city council in 1897, reflecting the proximity of the street to the State Capitol, then under construction. However, plans for making it part of a scenic boulevard between the capitol and Como Park never materialized. See also *Commonwealth Avenue, Grand Rounds*.

CAPITOL HEIGHTS This street was originally part of Jackson Street, but when the State Capitol was built in 1905, Jackson Street was rerouted to the east, and this segment of Jackson Street was renamed Capitol Heights.

This neighborhood name, whose boundaries are roughly between the State Capitol and Pennsylvania Avenue, between Rice and Jackson Streets, has been in use for over a century.

CAPITOL HILL Occupied by the Minnesota State Capitol building, this is the hill at Cedar Street and Constitution Avenue. See also *Angst und Bang, Bunker Hill, Hog-back Hill*.

CAPITOL TRIANGLE Acquired in 1887 at Robert Street and University Avenue, this small public park was subsumed by the intersection in 1960.

CAPP ROAD Martin Capp's 1957 Addition in the Midway industrial area reclaimed and improved railroad property previously used as a dump. A Twin Cities developer since 1946, Mr. Capp estimated at the time that his development increased tax income to the city by over $100,000. See also *Midway*.

CARDINAL PLACE See *Berland Place*.

CARLETON STREET Applied in 1881 in (Alice) Hewitts Outlots, this Midway name has no apparent significance. See also *Midway*.

CARLING DRIVE (private) The facts are thin, and the research trail cold, but Janet Johnson, who chose the name, recalled basing her selection on a newspaper clipping reporting that Captain Carling awarded a bid—possibly a government contract—to the firm of Amherst H. Wilder. The Amherst H. Wilder Foundation, established by a bequest of Amherst, played a large part in the development of Energy Park in which this street name occurs. See *Energy Park*, *Wilder Street*.

CARNES AVENUE (Fairgrounds) Previously Minnesota Avenue, this street was renamed to honor Norris K. Carnes (1895–1997), who served the Minnesota State Fair for more than fifty years. During his tenure as a board member of the State Agricultural Society from 1944 to 1981, Carnes supervised the cattle, horse, meats, and space rental departments of the fair. Upon being offered the fair's fifty-year award, Norris declined the honor saying, "All it means is that I hung around a long time." See also *Minnesota Avenue*.

CARPENTER PARK See *Summit Lookout Park*.

CARROLL AVENUE Charles Carroll (1737–1832) of Maryland was a Revolutionary War leader and patriot. He was the last surviving signer of the Declaration of Independence and the wealthiest citizen of the United States. (Who claimed Revolution doesn't pay?) The developer of this street in 1855, Harwood Iglehart, was a native of Maryland. See also *St. Albans Lake* (2).

CARTER AVENUE A syndicate of Virginia capitalists, including Hill Carter, James H. Dooley, and Manley B. Curry, all of Richmond, Virginia, financed this plat, St. Anthony Park North. Each had a street named for him. The site of the second Breck School remains a private home at 2102 Carter Avenue. See also *St. Anthony Park*.

CARTY PARK This three-and-one-half-acre public park occupying a whole block at Iglehart Avenue and St. Albans Street was named in 1975 to honor the Reverend Denzil Angus Carty (1904–75), the rector of St. Phillip's Episcopal Church. Carty was a voice of reason in the tumultuous black civil rights movement of the 1960s and helped mitigate the level of racial tensions that resulted in a 1968 riot at the St. Paul Auditorium.

The St. Paul Housing and Redevelopment Authority cleared the older homes from this

The Reverend Denzil Angus Carty, namesake of the park, is shown here (*standing center*) with a young Dr. Martin Luther King Jr. in St. Paul during the Montgomery, Alabama, bus boycott. Photograph courtesy of the *Minneapolis Spokesman-Recorder*.

park site as part of an urban renewal scheme. At the same time, the Authority also coined the name St. Albans Park for the surrounding community between Concordia and Marshall Avenues, between Victoria and St. Albans Streets. Thirty years later that name seems to have faded from common parlance.

CARVER AVENUE First mapped as North Avenue, subsequently changed to Polander Road (for the Polish farmers who lived along it), this Highwood street assumed its present name in 1923. Carver Lake, the destination of the street, takes its name from Thomas Carver (1819–83), whose farmland surrounded the lake. Born in Glasgow, Scotland, Thomas was a descendant of Jonathan Carver, the early Minnesota explorer for whom Carver's Cave is named. In 1852, Thomas came to McLean Township, as the area was then known. Family members have been active in the affairs of the community for over 150 years. The present Carver School in Maplewood is named for the family, and Carver was considered as a possible name for the new suburb now known as Maplewood. See also *Carver's Cave, Highwood, McLean Township*.

CARVER'S CAVE One of the oldest and best-known natural landmarks on the upper Mississippi River is located on Dayton's Bluff below Mounds Park. The name is that of Jonathan Carver, who first visited the cave in 1766 and is said to have received a deed to the cave and surrounding property. (There is a fascinating account of Carver's visit and his deed in *A History of the City of St. Paul to 1875* by J. Fletcher Williams.) The Dakotas called the cave Wakan-Teebe, "The Dwelling of the Great Spirit." In 1867, the Minnesota Historical Society held a Carver centennial celebration in the cave; at that time, its entrance measured 50 feet, and the depth was approximately 129 feet. There was a pool within the cavern, and the roof was 18 feet above the water level. Twenty years later, the railroad had cut back the face of the cliff and reduced the depth of the cave. One historian said of the landmark: "It is slowly dying of civilization." For the next century the history of the cave was a cycle of natural erosion of the sandstone cliffs burying the entrance, the cave forgotten for a decade or two, and then renewed interest in the cave. In 1977, the en-

Boy Scouts explore the lake inside Carver's Cave during one of its periodic reopenings. Photograph courtesy of the Minnesota Historical Society.

trance was once again found under the auspices of the city, and plans were formulated to work with the American Indians on a long-range plan for this singular place—now the centerpiece of the Bruce Vento Nature Sanctuary. See also *Bruce Vento Nature Sanctuary, Dayton's Cave, Fountain Cave.*

CASCADE CREEK This creek, which originated in a wetland near what is today Hamline and Randolph Avenues, drained down the streambed presently occupied by the Ayd Mill Road, flowed down the hill just north of Jefferson Avenue, where it served as the waterpower for the Ayd Mill, and then continued on to join the Mississippi River in a dramatic waterfall near the foot of Western Avenue. (*Cascade* was a nineteenth-century synonym for *waterfall*.) The course of this stream can be followed on several early plats in the West End area.

An intrepid urban traipser wanting to visit the site of the waterfall would go to the south end of Colborne Street and walk east toward downtown along the railroad tracks. Within a block or so a railroad trestle spans the ravine where the falls cascaded down to the river. For the full story of this creek, see the excellent article "Stairway to the Abyss" by Greg Brick. See also *Ayd Mill Road, Creeks/Brooks.*

CASE AVENUE Born in New York, James A. Case (1823–96) traveled to St. Paul in 1853, where he worked as a surveyor and civil engineer. He was active in many early St. Paul enterprises when this East Side street was named in the Arlington Hills Addition in 1872. Perhaps the

An advertisement for the services of James A. Case, namesake for Case Avenue, in the *Business Directory for the City of St. Paul, Minnesota Territory*, published in 1856 by Goodrich & Somers.

most handsome old school building in the city, the William L. Ames School, built in 1915, is on the northwest corner of Ames Place and Case Avenue. On the land survey, this street marks a one-half section line. See also *Arlington Hills*, *Ames Avenue*, *East Side*.

CASS GILBERT MEMORIAL PARK This five-acre public park at Sherburne Avenue and Cedar Street, previously known as Merriam's Overlook, offers a capital view. Zoned by the Capitol Area Architectural and Planning Board as permanent open space, this park on state land is planted and burned as a prairie. Its name commemorates Cass Gilbert (1859–1934), the architect of the State Capitol building. Conscientious and prosperous, but not particularly original, he was an acknowledged leader in the United States during a period dominated by monumental architecture. See also *Augustus Gauger Park*, *Merriam's Overlook*.

CASTILLO PARK (PARQUE CASTILLO) At the time of his death, Nicolas Castillo Sr. (1911–87) was honored with the name of this public park on the West Side at the intersection of Concord and State Streets. Castillo, pictured in the ornate park monument, was a talented musician and composer who wrote corridos—the ballads used by Chicano musicians to chronicle the activities of their communities. A social activist, Castillo was generous and always ready to help those in need. His funeral overflowed Our Lady of Guadalupe Church. An annual film and music festival is held at this gathering spot. See also *District del Sol*, *West Side*.

CATHEDRAL SQUARE The city acquired this one-acre public park, across from the Cathedral of St. Paul on Summit Avenue, in 1929. Covered with dilapidated tenements that were demolished, this new park provided an open space in a crowded part of the city. By agreeing to pay the assessments necessary to obtain the park property, the Archdiocese of St. Paul and Minneapolis was also able to open up an impressive view of the cathedral from downtown. The last wooden sidewalk in St. Paul was removed from this park in 1975. See also *Selby Avenue Tunnel*.

CATHLIN STREET Originally part of Prior Avenue, this street was redeeded to the city in 1963 by the adjacent Northern Pacific Railroad. Cathlin could not be identified. This is a street name that strikes fear and trembling in the heart of many a St. Paulite: it is the chilling address of one of the snow emergency impound lots where the reader will have to spend well over $125 to retrieve an automobile left parked in a snowplow's path. See also *Barge Channel Road*.

CATO PARK Samuel C. and Eleanor Tatum of Cincinnati named this small public park at Fairview and Englewood Avenues in 1885 in the Midway Heights addition. Cato was a Roman statesman, but whether this be the source of the name is lost to history. See also *Midway Heights*.

Nicolas Castillo Sr. is honored with this park, one of the many colorful spaces unique to the West Side. Photograph by Kathleen M. Vadnais.

CAYUGA PARK Originally the site of the Edmund Rice Public School and later a small recreation center, today this two-acre public park and playground are at the intersection of Cayuga and L'Orient Streets, across from the beginning of the Gateway Trail. See also *Edmund Avenue, Gateway Trail.*

CAYUGA STREET Cayuga County in New York State provided this street near Oakland Cemetery with its name in 1870. That county derived its designation from the Cayuga Indian tribe, one of the six nations of the Iroquois League. Developer Edmund Rice also named the adjacent streets Seneca and Genesee for New York counties. See also *Edmund Avenue.*

CECELIA PLACE This short, one-block street intersecting St. Clair Avenue was added to the city in 1886 in Haupt's Addition. Herman Haupt Jr. was a patent attorney, whose father was general manager of the Northern Pacific Railroad. Cecelia's biography is unwritten.

CEDAR STREET This is one of the original fifteen street names of the city, named in 1849 on the St. Paul Proper plat because of the red cedar trees on the Mississippi River bluff at the south end of the street. According to the Census Bureau, in 1993 Cedar Street was the thirteenth most common street name in the United States, with 5,644 streets having that name.

CEMETERIES There are presently eight cemeteries within the St. Paul city limits. See *Calvary, Chesed Shel Emes, Elmhurst, Oakland, Riverview, Sons of Abraham, Sons of Jacob (Moses), West Side Hebrew.* There have also been a number of cemeteries abandoned or moved. A few of them are described in a newspaper article in the *St. Paul Pioneer Press,* August 9, 1903, section 2, page 8.

The Edmund Rice School, pictured around 1900, occupied the site of what is today Cayuga Park. Photograph courtesy of the Minnesota Historical Society.

Given the aggregate number of burials in all the city cemeteries, it is almost certain there are more dead bodies within St. Paul than live ones—an observation that has been made over the years by various visitors to the city seeking a frolic.

CENTRAL AVENUE Named in the Central Park Addition in 1884, the street name was extended west into the Midway area. The first surveyor's notes in 1847 describe what must have been one of the first houses and its field in the Midway area as being in what today is the vicinity of 1118 Central Avenue. See also *Central Park, Midway.*

CENTRAL PARK This two-acre public park just north of the State Centennial Building on Cedar Street was dedicated in 1884 as a part of the Central Park Addition. Around the turn of the twentieth century it was one of St. Paul's most delightful and prestigious parks, serving an upper-class neighborhood. But the creeping decline and demolition of the homes around the park, the erection of new state office buildings, and the construction of Interstate 94 doomed Central Park. In 1974 the green space was replaced by a parking ramp whose design—as required by rules of the Capitol Area Architectural and Planning Board competition—incorporated landscaping on the top deck, and in the early 1990s, legislation required a plaque on the site acknowledging the space as Central Park. (As we were writing this book, the park was further reduced to provide additional parking. One state employee was quoted as saying, "They call it a park, but all it is is grass and weeds.") There continues to be pressure to convert more of the park space to additional parking. For further information, see the excellent article "Lost Neighborhood" by Paul Nelson. See also *Lafayette Park*.

CENTRAL PARK EAST & WEST The streets on the east and west side of Central Park (now atop a State of Minnesota parking ramp) were named by action of the St. Paul City Council, August 18, 1887. See also *Central Park*.

CENTRAL VILLAGE This suburban enclave in the center of the city, complete with cul-de-sacs and ranch-style homes, between Central and Aurora Avenues, between Western Avenue and Dale Street, was created in the late 1970s. The incongruous village design, part of a larger effort by the city termed the Western Redevelopment Project, was marketed to middle-class African Americans by offering suburban amenities, complete with ready access to downtown and the familiar Rondo Avenue neighborhood. The strip mall Uni-Dale at University Avenue and Dale Street was intended to complement Central Village. See also *Old Rondo Avenue*.

CENTRAL VILLAGE PARK is a four-acre public park within Central Village at Central Avenue and Mackubin Street. See also *Central Village*.

Chesed Shel Emes Cemetery. Half of the cemeteries in St. Paul are Jewish cemeteries. Photograph by Kathleen M. Vadnais.

CESAR CHAVEZ STREET Previously a part of Concord Street, this street was renamed in November 2003 to honor César Estrada Chávez (1927–93), an American farm labor leader. Although Chávez had no Minnesota connection, his name was chosen because the West Side has a vibrant Hispanic population, and this street is the focal point for cultural celebrations, including the annual Cinco de Mayo parade. Twenty-three businesses and 208 residents changed their street name; the cost of changing the street signs was estimated at $3,500. See also *District del Sol, West Side*.

CHAMBER STREET Previously Oxford Avenue, the name was changed to avoid duplication in 1940. Other original street names in the vicinity of Lake Phalen were Harvard, Yale, and Vassar. The significance of this new name, if any, is not apparent.

CHAMBERS STREET (Fairgrounds) There are two members of the Chambers family—father and son—who seem equally worthy of this street name within the fairgrounds. Alexander Chambers was born in New York and moved to Minnesota in 1859. Like many of the pioneers, he was very interested in agriculture and served as president of the Minnesota State Agricultural Society in 1868. His son, Clarke A. Chambers (1839–1919), helped run the society as a manager from 1882 until 1897. This street, first named Simpson for an early secretary of the society, was changed at the request of Clarke Chambers's widow.

CHANNEL STREET First mapped as Ninth Street, Channel Street on the West Side was named in 1883 as it followed the channel cut by Odell's Creek. Now unmarked and barely discernible, Channel Street ran west along the base of the cliffs—in front of Castle Royal, an extravagant nightclub hollowed into the cliff at Wabasha Street—for a couple of blocks, then turned north to intersect Plato Boulevard. All this can be clearly seen on the 1884 Hopkins atlas. This significant street was, alas, vacated in 1969. See also *Odell's Creek, West Side*.

CHARLES AVENUE A brother of the developer Edmund Rice, Charles Rodney Rice (1821–73) was a merchant here for a short time but later moved to Washington, DC. Other street names originating in this 1854 plat, Warren and Rice's Addition, were Edmund and Ellen. See also *Edmund Avenue, Lafond Avenue*.

CHARLOTTE STREET Charlotte Taylor, with her husband, William, purchased this property in 1873, platted it as College Place, Taylor's Division, in 1882, and sold it in 1887. They were not St. Paul residents.

CHARLTON STREET Charlton, Massachusetts, was the birthplace of Dwight Woodbury, one of the investors in West Side real estate. See also *West Side*.

CHATSWORTH STREET "Chatsworth House," the home of the Duke of Devonshire, was one of the most magnificent private residences in England when this street was named in 1871. The developer, John Wann (1829–1905), born in Belfast, Ireland, worked for the East India Company before arriving in St. Paul in 1865. He built his large mansion on the northwest corner of Victoria Street and Summit Avenue, which he sold to Archbishop John Ireland, who planned to erect a great St. Paul–Minneapolis cathedral on this site midway between the two cities. Instead, Our Lady of Peace, a Catholic girl's school, was built on the corner, which became William Mitchell College of Law. See also *Paulapolis; Lexington Parkway, Mt. Eudes.*

CHELMSFORD STREET Chelmsford was a municipal borough of England and capital of Essex County in 1885 when this St. Anthony Park street was named. See also *St. Anthony Park.*

CHELSEA HEIGHTS The 1916 Chelsea Heights Addition was the remainder of the Joshua Robertson (1822–1913) farm. Robertson married the sister of Auguste L. Larpenteur; after their marriage they moved to St. Paul in 1852. Two years later Robertson bought eighty acres between Snelling and Hamline Avenues, between Arlington and Larpenteur Avenues; he later expanded his farm to the northeast. The Robertson farmhouse once stood on what is today the northeast corner of Arlington and Hamline Avenues. Chelsea, a fashionable London suburb, is on the north bank of the Thames River. See also *Larpenteur Avenue.*

CHELSEA STREET This street was named in Chelsea Heights in 1916. See also *Chelsea Heights.*

CHELTON AVENUE This Midway Heights addition street name was derived in 1885 from Chelten Hills, a railroad station a few miles north of Philadelphia, where Hannah Tatum, one of the investors, lived. See also *Midway Heights, Tatum Street.*

CHEROKEE AVENUE The park and *Cherokee Heights Boulevard* borrow from one of a series of American Indian tribe names used in this 1855 West St. Paul plat. See also *West Side.*

CHEROKEE HEIGHTS This neighborhood is roughly between Cherokee Heights Park and Smith Avenue, between Morton and Annapolis Streets.

CHEROKEE HEIGHTS PARK In 1903 the city parks commission recognized the potential of this West Side land with its spectacular view from the bluffs above the Mississippi River. The public park was acquired in segments with donations by James J. Hill and others between 1903 and 1914. Originally used as a tourist campground, it took much of its present form in 1924, when the roads were paved, trees and shrubs were planted, and horseshoe courts and a ball field were added. The name comes from the adjacent street. See also *West Side.*

CHERRY STREET This street was named in Lyman Dayton's Addition for the fruit in 1857; an adjacent street is Plum. See also *Lincoln Park.*

CHESED SHEL EMES CEMETERY Its name translated from the Hebrew as "true kindness," this small Jewish cemetery—established in 1912 for nonpracticing Jews who wanted to be buried in the Jewish tradition—is located at Christie Place and Germain Street near Lake Phalen. See also *Cemeteries.*

CHESTER STREET Originally Perch Street, the name of this West Side street was changed in 1883. It could refer to Chester Arthur, U.S. president at this time, or to Chester Hitchcock, who platted an addition to West St. Paul in 1859, or both. See also *West Side.*

Prior to 1924, Cherokee Heights Park was a campground for tourists to the city. Photograph by the Northwestern Photographic Studio, Inc.; courtesy of the Minnesota Historical Society.

CHESTNUT STREET Following a pattern of tree names first used in Philadelphia, Chestnut Street, like the adjacent streets, was named in Rice and Irvine's Addition in 1849. Prior to the 1850s, Rice's Brook flowed down the course of Chestnut Street, eroding a ravine through the river bluffs that provided access for steamboats to land and unload. See also *Rice's Brook, Upper Landing; Irvine Park*.

CHILCOMBE AVENUE The village in Dorset County, England, provided this name in 1885 in St. Anthony Park North. See also *St. Anthony Park*.

CHILDS ROAD Born in Fergus Falls, James A. Childs (1886–1935) graduated from the University of Minnesota in 1909 as a civil engineer. He worked as a sanitary engineer with the State Board of Health until 1927, when he became chief engineer of the Metropolitan Drainage Commission, which laid the groundwork for the sewage disposal system. When the commission was dissolved in 1933 to make way for the Minneapolis–St. Paul Sanitary District, Childs refused the chief engineer's job in favor of a lesser position. A $16-million sewage disposal plant on the river, planned by Childs, was under construction when this access road was named by the city council in 1937.

CHIPPEWA AVENUE One of a series of American Indian names, this street refers to the Chippewa, or Ojibwe, tribe, which at one time extended from northern New York to Minnesota. This West Side street was named in the West St. Paul plat. See also *West Side*.

CHRISTIE PLACE Previously part of Prosperity Avenue near Lake Phalen, the street was re-named in 1940. Who Christie may have been is not recalled or recorded. A small Jewish cemetery has been at Christie Place and Germain Street for at least seventy-five years. See also *Cemeteries*.

CHURCHILL GARDENS See *Van Slyke Triangle*.

CHURCHILL STREET This street near Lake Como was named in 1885 in Warrendale, a develop-ment by Cary Warren of Louisville, Kentucky. John and Henry Churchill provided the land for the Churchill Downs racetrack—which has become the home of the Kentucky Derby—in Warren's hometown. See also *Warrendale*.

CLARENCE STREET Platted in 1886 as the Pease Brothers Addition, this street name near Lake Phalen is said to remember Clarence Bergman (1882–1933), whose father, Solomon, came to St. Paul in 1867, where he operated a hide and tallow company. *Clarence Court* (private) takes its name from the street.

At 1290 Clarence Street is one of the earlier houses built in this neighborhood, high on a hill—at the time—overlooking Lake Phalen. At 1344 Clarence is an early lake cabin with its extensive porches.

CLARK STREET This East Side street was named in 1855 in Edmund Rice's Addition, possibly for Martin D. Clark, a carpenter who built over two hundred houses in the early days of St. Paul. Born in Ohio in 1824, Clark moved to St. Paul in 1851. A second namesake possibility is Charles H. Clark, who came to St. Paul in 1854 and dealt in real estate. See also *East Side, Edmund Avenue*.

CLAY STREET Previously Olive and Prince Street, the name of this very short West End street was changed in 1872, perhaps in honor of Henry Clay, American statesman. See also *West End*.

CLAYLAND PARK Samuel C. and Eleanor Tatum of Cincinnati named this small public park in 1885 in their Midway Heights addition. They undoubtedly knew the source of this name, but we don't. See also *Chelton Avenue, Midway Heights, Tatum Street*.

CLAYLAND PLACE See *Clayland Street*.

CLAYLAND STREET First platted as Eleanor Street (for the wife of Samuel C. Tatum) in 1885, the name was changed the following year to eliminate duplication. The new name came from the original plat. See also *Clayland Park*.

CLEAR AVENUE Frederick and Louise Fogg along with Edward Holloway added the Denny Hill Addition near Lake Phalen to the city in 1889. The addition brought two new street names to the city: Denny Street and Clear Avenue. Denny Street has since become Sherwood Avenue. The Foggs' intention in naming Clear Avenue is hazy.

The houses at 1999, 2000, 2003 Clear Avenue, all of them once identical with a front shed roof and offset chimney, are representative of the first homes built during the early 1900s in Hayden Heights. There are several of these distinctive small cottages remaining in the area. See also *Hayden Heights*.

CLERMONT STREET Platted as Ravine Street near Mounds Park, the name was changed in 1872. Another street was renamed Fulton at this same time. The steamboat *Clermont*, designed and used by Robert Fulton on his first trip from New York to Albany in 1807, initiated steam-powered navigation. To a river city like St. Paul, these were significant street names. See also *Fulton Street*.

CLEVELAND AVENUE Grover Cleveland was president of the United States when this street was named in 1886 in Merriam Park. Horace W. S. Cleveland (1814–1900), a landscape architect who had a dramatic and positive impact on the development of the Twin Cities, may also have been the source of this name.

In 1924, Cleveland Avenue was extended through the state agricultural college land to connect the increasing traffic coming from the northern suburbs via Raymond to University Avenue, the main east-west thoroughfare between downtown Minneapolis and downtown St. Paul. Cleveland Avenue marks a section line on the land survey. See also *Grand Rounds*, *Merriam Park*, *University Avenue*.

CLEVELAND CIRCLE This is a new name for a four-acre parcel of public land strategically located at Seventh and Fifth Streets in downtown St. Paul opposite the Xcel Energy Center. This was the original location of the historic Armstrong-Quinlan house, which was moved near Irvine Park in 2001. In 2004, the Winter Carnival ice palace was built on this empty site.

A bus transit hub and large parking ramp are to be built on the northern part of this valuable piece of real estate; the use of the south half remains with the omniscient city planners. The name refers to Horace W. S. Cleveland, the noted landscape architect who shaped St. Paul in the nineteenth century. See also *Bohnenviertel*, *Cleveland Avenue*, *Grand Rounds*.

CLIFF STREET Although it is only a few blocks long, Cliff Street has been on the brink of the city's development. It began as a segment of the first road between Fort Snelling and downtown St. Paul, running along the edge of the bluff, and named Old Fort Road. In the early 1870s the name of Old Fort Road was changed to Stewart Avenue, continuing along the same bluff-top route. (The brick house at 338 St. Clair Avenue was built to face old Stewart Avenue and the river.) When Stewart Avenue was abbreviated to its present location, this piece became Bluff Street. As part of the city's vigilant effort to eliminate duplicate street names, the name was again changed in 1883, this time to Cliff Street.

As early as 1922, there was a plan to extend Cliff Street east along the bluff to Wilkin Street, creating an alternate route to West Seventh Street, thereby avoiding the traffic congestion at Seven Corners. This alternate route would have guided the motorist via the Kellogg Viaduct to Exchange Street to Wilkin Street to Cliff Street to St. Clair Avenue. But this route was never completed. In fact, it was not until 1961 that St. Clair Avenue was connected to Cliff Street, creating a slightly shorter and redundant route to the High Bridge. See also *Emma Street*, *Fort Road*, *Rabbit Hole*, *Stewart Avenue*.

CLIFFORD STREET Like the other streets in Desnoyer Park, this one was named in 1887 for a village in Massachusetts. See also *Desnoyer Park*.

CLIFTON PARK This small, one-half-acre public park that was east of Hiawatha Street, opposite Mound Street, has been incorporated into Indian Mounds Park. See also *Indian Mounds Park*.

CLIFTON STREET Originally John Street, the name of this West End street was changed in 1872 to avoid confusion with another John Street; it may have been named for a bluff at its northern end. See also *John Street, West End*.

CLINTON AVENUE This was a popular name of the nineteenth century, which could have been used in the 1855 West St. Paul plat for its familiarity. See also *West Side*.

CLOUGH STREET (Fairgrounds) David Marston Clough (1846–1924) was governor of Minnesota from 1895 to 1899, but it was for his participation in the management of the Minnesota State Agricultural Society that this street within the fairgrounds honors him. A Minneapolis resident active in the lumbering business, Clough served as president of the society in 1891. He opined that "it is not necessary to have six days of good weather to make the Fair a financial success. Four days, with a good management, will always pay our bills." See also *Burnquist Street, Gorman Avenue, Hubbard Avenue, Johnson Parkway, Marshall Avenue, Merriam Lane, Ramsey Street, Scudder Street, Sibley Street*.

COACH ROAD (private) This Energy Park road, in the locale of the earlier car repair and maintenance shops for the Northern Pacific Railroad, recalls the railroad passenger coaches. See also *Energy Park*.

COCHRANE PARK This one-half-acre public park at Summit and Western Avenues was Thomas Cochrane's boyhood playground, which he donated to the city in 1923. In 1926, his family commissioned noted art deco sculptor and St. Paul native Paul Manship to create a playful water fountain titled "Indian Hunter and His Dog." Because of vandalism, it was replicated and the original removed to Como Park in 1967. Thanks to a neighborhood initiative by Alma Joseph and the Ramsey Hill Association, the sculpture was returned to its original location in 1994. See also *Ramsey Hill Historic District*.

COHANSEY STREET This street northeast of Lake Como was platted in 1908 in the Cumberland Addition by Edward Morton Ware (1834–1918), for many years a real-estate and insurance broker in St. Paul. Cohansey is the name of a creek and settlement in Cumberland County, New Jersey. Chairs crafted by the Ware family in Cumberland County late in the eighteenth century are popular with collectors of old American furniture. See also *Cumberland Street*.

COLBORNE STREET This West End street name first appears in 1854 in Stinson, Brown and Ramsey's Addition. In 1872, Ontario Street and Canada Street were melded into Colborne Street. Because James Stinson came from Ontario, the most likely reference would be to the port city of Colborne, Ontario, or to Sir John Colborne, lieutenant governor of Upper Canada in 1828–36.

For almost one hundred years, St. Paul's city hospital, Ancker Hospital, was at the inter-

The original statue by Paul Manship had not yet been removed from Cochrane Park in 1950. Photograph courtesy of the Minnesota Historical Society.

section of Jefferson Avenue and Colborne Street. When it was replaced in the 1960s by what is now called Regions Hospital near the State Capitol, the old hospital buildings were demolished and replaced by headquarters of the St. Paul school system at 360 Colborne Street. In his book *The City Planning Process*, Alan Altschuler describes the tumultuous politics of relocating this public hospital. See also *James Avenue, Ramsey Street, Vance Street, West End.*

COLBY STREET The Highland Park streets in this Hiawatha Park Addition were originally named in 1890 for colleges: Colgate, Cornell, Yale, Colby, and Bowdoin. Colby College in Waterville, Maine, was founded in 1813 and is still operating. See also *Hiawatha Park.*

COLETTE PLACE Colette Bisanz (1908–96) was a sister to Leonard and Norbert Bisanz, who developed this Highland Park area in 1951 as the Bisanz Brothers Addition #2. See also *Dorothea Avenue, Matterhorn Lane, Susan Avenue.*

COLLEGE AVENUE This avenue was named in 1851 because it ran by the Episcopal mission and school established the previous year. Their building, the beginning of the Episcopal Church in Minnesota, stood approximately where the Minnesota Historical Society is today. Early St. Paul had several other College streets, none of which ever hosted a college.

COLLEGE PARK This ten-acre public park at Carter and Raymond Avenues in St. Anthony Park was acquired by the city in 1907 through assessments on the surrounding properties. Samuel Green, dean of the College of Forestry at the University of Minnesota, provided the impetus for its acquisition. Turning a glacial kettle hole, thirty feet deep, into a usable park required some deep thinking. See also *St. Anthony Park.*

COLLEGE PLACE See *Hamline Village.*

COLLINS STREET Loren C. Collins owned property in the Railroad Island area when this street was named in 1853. He is listed in the 1860 census as a merchant with $10,000 in real estate; the city directories list him as a dairyman. He was born about 1813 in Massachusetts; after the Civil War he moved to Chicago.

In July of 1980, at the request of the Payne-Minnehaha Community Council and District

5 Planning Council, the name of this street was changed to (Victor) Tedesco Street, honoring a longtime city councilman, community activist, and musician. The St. Paul City Council resolution authorizing this change notes that a nearby new housing development occupies property once owned by Tedesco's parents. See also *Aida Place, Antonio Drive, Tedesco Street.*

COLNE STREET Colne was a city in Lancaster County, England, when this street just south of Lake Como was named in 1885 in Maxfield's Subdivision. See also *Kilburn Street, Ryde Street.*

COLORADO STREET Originally John Street, the name was changed by the city council in 1883 as one of a series of state names on the West Side. See also *Alabama Street, Florida Street, Kentucky Street, West Side.*

COLUMBUS AVENUE Added to the city as part of the new Capitol Approach in 1953, the name was suggested and endorsed by the Knights of Columbus and the Columbus Memorial Association. There is also a statue of Columbus nearby, installed in 1931 by the Columbus Memorial Association.

COLVIN AVENUE Standing high on the hill, the Alexander and Sarah Colvin house, built about 1909 at 1175 Davern Street, served as a landmark for early automobile trips to the Highland Park area. Dr. Colvin (1867–1948), born in Ontario and a graduate of McGill University in Montreal, immigrated to St. Paul in 1897. By 1919 he had become chief of instruction and subsequently chief of surgery at Ancker Hospital. He is said to have owned and operated the first X-ray machine in St. Paul.

His wife, Sarah, was a militant suffragist. In February 1919, after spending five days on a hunger strike in a Washington, DC, jail for building a protest fire in front of the White House, she said:

> I believe, too, that it is an excellent thing that a group of women when they receive political power shall have had prison experience and shall know the injustice constantly done the poor; both in our courts and our prisons. They will be better able to remedy these conditions.

Upon Dr. Colvin's death in 1948, his estate was subdivided, and Colvin Avenue was included. See also *Colborne Street, Highland Park.*

COMMERCIAL STREET In a backwater of the city, even the intrepid urban traipser would be challenged to find this street along Phalen Creek below Dayton's Bluff named in 1857 by an optimistic developer. Adjacent streets were called Canal and Water. Today the new Bruce Vento Nature Sanctuary will bring more people to this old part of the city. See also *Bruce Vento Nature Sanctuary, Dayton's Bluff.*

Sarah Colvin, a suffragist, thought it might be educational for women to spend some time in prison. Photograph courtesy of the Minnesota Historical Society.

COMMONWEALTH AVENUE Originally Dooley Avenue for James H. Dooley of Richmond, Virginia, one of a group of capitalists who platted the area, the street name was changed in 1902. The new name, first suggested in the 1901 report of the Board of Park Commissioners, was to designate one link in the "great trunk line of parkways" stretching from the State Capitol through Como Park, the Minnesota State Fairgrounds, and the Agricultural College, and branching to the University of Minnesota on one side and the Mississippi River Boulevards on the other side. *Commonwealth* symbolized this noble arrangement connecting St. Paul and Minneapolis as well as the state institutions. See also *Grand Rounds*.

COMMONWEALTH PARK This one-acre public park on Commonwealth Avenue between Como and Gordon Avenues was donated in 1902.

COMO AVENUE Officially named in 1871, this avenue follows an early Rose Township road between St. Paul and Lake Como. The very first road to Lake Como was a private road graded by Henry McKenty in the 1850s to entice potential customers to his lots for sale. A remnant of that 150-year-old road remains as the alley behind the houses numbered 716–806 Como Avenue. In the 1928 Hopkins atlas, this alley is labeled as Como Lane. See also *Lake Como, Orchard Avenue, Rose Township*.

COMO BOULEVARD Much of the land used for this boulevard around the lake became available when the lake level fell precipitously in the 1890s. See also *Lake Como*.

COMO LAKE See *Lake Como*.

COMO PARK Como Park was the first of St. Paul's large public city parks. In 1872—after the resounding success of Central Park in New York City—the St. Paul City Council passed the following resolution:

> Resolved: That in order that this city may avoid the errors of other large cities, and begin in time to provide for parks, wide avenues, public squares, and other improvements, on a scale suitable to our future growth, commensurate with the wants of a crowded city, in a manner best calculated to utilize our natural advantages and promote the health and comfort of the citizens, on a basis which engineering skill and experience will approve, Mr. H. W. S. Cleveland, landscape architect of Chicago, be and is hereby invited to make a general outline plan for such improvements, and report to the Council, and that his proposition to perform this work is hereby accepted.

In that same year, the legislature passed a bill empowering St. Paul to issue bonds not to exceed $100,000 to purchase 257 acres around Lake Como. But, alas, the depression of 1873 halted any improvements in the park, and for years it lay neglected. In fact, its very acquisition was generally denounced as a useless extravagance. A petition was initiated on April 4, 1874, by the Chamber of Commerce to the city council, to wit:

> The indebtedness of St. Paul is increasing at an alarming extent, and we the undersigned taxpayers would ask of your honorable body to sell the park property, provided

Como Park had extraordinary landscaping and plants at the turn of the twentieth century, such as the lily pond pictured here. Photograph courtesy of the Minnesota Historical Society.

it can be sold at cost, and reduce our liabilities. What we most need is sewerage, elevators, free bridges and good roads. We ask you as taxpayers that you so regulate the burden of taxation for the purpose of promoting the future prosperity of St. Paul, and not of the advancement of private interests of wild real estate speculators.

The park was not improved until the explosive growth of the city and the economic boom of the 1880s. Despite its contentious beginnings, Como has become St. Paul's premiere public park. See also *Cleveland Avenue, Grand Rounds*.

CONCORD PARK This four-acre public park on the east side of Concord Street between Curtice and Annapolis Streets was acquired in 1929.

CONCORD STREET When West St. Paul was annexed to St. Paul in 1876, Cedar and Virginia Streets were combined under the name Concord Street. Concord is the name of historic towns in both Massachusetts and New Hampshire.

CONCORDIA AVENUE Reconstructed as the southern frontage road along Interstate Highway 94 and renamed in 1964, the street follows the historic route of parts of Roblyn, Rondo, and Carroll Avenues. Concordia University near Hamline Avenue was originally the site of the Minnesota State Reform School founded on a tract of land called "The Burt Farm" in 1868. Established "as a house of refuge" for wayward boys, at one time it had over a hundred children in its care. Since 1962, the four remaining reform school buildings on the campus have been foolishly razed. Do they teach history at that college?

CONGRESS STREET Renamed in 1886, parts of this street were previously named Grove and Susan. Congress is an old street name from Boston and symbolically suitable as a street name connecting people.

CONNEMARA PATCH This neighborhood was a collection of modest working-class houses and businesses constructed along Phalen Creek beneath the Third Street Bridge. The Irish immigrants brought to Minnesota by Archbishop John Ireland in the nineteenth century imported the name from a district of County Galway in Ireland. Their neighborhood was completely obliterated by urban renewal in the 1950s. See also *John Ireland Boulevard; Badlands, Barton-Omaha Colony, Bohemian Flats, Swede Hollow, Upper Levee, West Side Flats.*

CONSERVATORY COURT In response to a query by Linda Murphy of the public works department, the developer Forrest Harstad replied that he picked this street name in 2002 for its proximity to the Como Park conservatory.

CONSTITUTION AVENUE Previously part of Central Avenue and Park Street, this new name was bestowed in March 1987 during the celebration for the bicentennial year of the U.S. Constitution. The only address affected was that of the State Office Building, which became 100 Constitution Avenue. The lawmakers' commitment to Constitution was short-lived, and in 2002 most of Constitution Avenue was renamed again. See also *Rev. Dr. Martin Luther King Jr. Boulevard.*

CONWAY One of the East Side neighborhoods whose boundaries are roughly between Minnehaha Avenue and Old Hudson Road, between McKnight Road and White Bear Avenue. The name comes from Conway Street running through the area. See also *East Side.*

CONWAY STREET Replacing First Street and Levee Street in 1872, this new East Side street name referred to Charles R. Conway. Born in 1822 in Indiana, he drifted to Minnesota in 1849 by way of Michigan, Illinois, and Wisconsin. A journalist by profession, he managed the *Los Angeles News* during the Civil War, thus becoming one of the first Minnesotans to migrate to California. Conway owned much valuable real estate in early St. Paul, but it brought him no profit because, according to a contemporary, "He knows how to make money, but he can't get it, because he won't lie and steal." See also *East Side.*

COOK AVENUE John B. Cook (1818–1910) was president of the St. Paul Omnibus Company when this East Side street was named in the Arlington Hills Addition in 1872. A contemporary described him as a "quiet, undemonstrative, excellent citizen." See also *Arlington Hills.*

COOPER STREET (Fairgrounds) Born in Pennsylvania, John Francis Cooper (1836–1907) migrated to St. Cloud, Minnesota, in 1856, where he developed an extensive livestock breeding operation, including a famous herd of Cruikshanks Short Horn cattle. Known as "a very useful member," Cooper was elected to the Board of Managers for the Minnesota State Agricultural Society, the organization responsible for operation of the state fair. After his tenure as a manager from 1884 to 1891, Cooper was elected president of the society from 1898 to 1901.

CORNING AVENUE Charles T. and Frances Corning platted this unimproved "ghost street" near Lake Phalen in 1887. He was a brother of John W. L. Corning, with whom he was for a short time a partner in the building materials firm that operates today as Corning-Donohue. Charles came to St. Paul in the 1880s but died in 1888 at age forty-five. His obituary records the cause of death as pneumonia aggravated by a constitutional weakness produced by over-exertion at athletics. See also *Ghost Streets*.

CORNMEAL VALLEY According to a 1983 history written for Rondo Days, this was the area of Rondo Avenue east of Dale Street, a poor neighborhood where the black packinghouse workers and the unemployed lived. It was conjectured that this low area, where flooding occurred after each intense rainstorm, was an old creek bed. It is quite possible this is a reference to Rice's Brook. The social counterpart of Cornmeal Valley was Oatmeal Hill. See also *Oatmeal Hill, Old Rondo Avenue, Rice's Brook*.

CORTLAND PLACE Originally New Canada Road, the name was changed to Cortland in 1874. Most of the street running parallel to Oakland Cemetery has since been renamed as Jackson Street. Cortland is a city and county in New York State. See also *Oakland Cemetery*.

COSGROVE STREET (Fairgrounds) "Whenever a Minnesota farmer sees a Hereford, he thinks of Cosgrove." Upon that observation, Carson N. Cosgrove (1853–1936) was elected president of the Minnesota State Agricultural Society. Born in Westfield, New York, Cosgrove settled in Le Sueur, Minnesota, at the age of eighteen. Well-known as a breeder and exhibitor of Hereford cattle as well as a merchant in hardware and agricultural machinery, he served as president of the society from 1902 to 1907 and as secretary from 1907 to 1910.

COTTAGE AVENUE There were a number of Cottage streets in earlier St. Paul, the most memorable being in the Homes for the Homeless Addition. However, the present Cottage Avenue received its name in the 1855 Cottage Homes Addition east of Lake Como.

COZY LAKE This small lake in Como Park was just west of and connected to Lake Como. Cozy Lake even had an island: Cozy Island. But the potential of cozy was apparently not on par with the potential of golf, for in the 1920s the lake was drained to expand the golf course. See also *Lakes/Ponds*.

CRAIG PLACE Craig was the second son of Alexander G. Tankenoff, president of the Hillcrest Development Company, which platted this area in 1948.

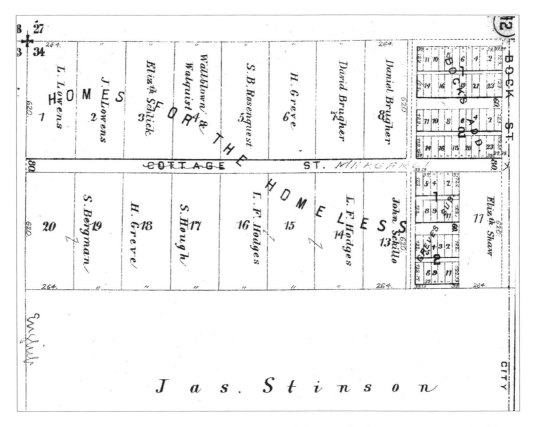

Cottage Street as it runs through a housing addition titled Homes for the Homeless. From *Atlas of the Environs of St. Paul,* 1886.

CREEKS/BROOKS Several named creeks and brooks flowed through Saint Paul in its earlier days. Most of them have since been banished into the storm sewer system to make way for residential and commercial development. See *Ames Creek, Bridal Veil Creek, Cascade Creek, Fish Creek, Fountain Creek, McCloud Creek, McLeod Creek, Odell's Creek, Phalen Creek, Rice's Brook, Trout Brook.*

CREEKSIDE WAY (private) This street was named in 1981 in the Pathways Addition near Battle Creek Park.

CRETIN AVENUE Running between the St. Paul Seminary and the University of St. Thomas, this street was named in 1890 for Joseph Cretin (1799–1857), first Roman Catholic bishop of St. Paul. Born, educated, and ordained in France, Cretin journeyed to America in 1838 with Bishop Loras of Dubuque, Iowa. The accounts of his early travels and his description of the first St. Paul Cathedral in *Acta et Dicta* give a vivid impression of the early city. At Bishop Cretin's funeral, twenty-four pallbearers took turns carrying his casket in a circuit of downtown before it was placed in a hearse and taken to Calvary Cemetery, followed by more than a thousand mourners. See also *Galtier Street.*

STREET NAMES
The Minneapolis Perspective

Over the years many writers have vehemently denounced the hodgepodge of St. Paul street names in comparison to the superior and more orderly Minneapolis system. As a poet able to discern those yearnings deep within all of us, Garrison Keillor wryly evokes the consolation of Minneapolis's streets in contrast to the consternation caused by St. Paul's. Is he right?

ODE TO THE STREET SYSTEM OF SOUTHWEST MINNEAPOLIS
Garrison Keillor

When you are beset by doubt,
Take Lyndale Avenue due south
Where you can put your mind at rest,
Knowing all streets run east and west
And all are perfectly numbered.
(There is, of course, no Twenty-third.
It was logically omitted to make
Thirtieth come out as Lake
Instead of an odd Thirty-first or -second.)
For years, successful men have reckoned
By this system, trained the self
To follow Lyndale and hang a ralph
At Fiftieth, into a neighborhood
Where homes are stable, children good,
Earnings are high and soundly invested
In products *Consumer Reports* has tested,
Where life is not paranoid, moody or radical,
But Republican, Lutheran and Alphabetical.
Aldrich, Bryant, Colfax, Dupont:
You can put your trust upon't
When hopes are few and times are hard—
Emerson, Fremont and Girard.
Humboldt, Irving, James and Knox:
This our foundation, these our bedrocks.
While Logan, Morgan, Newton, Oliver and Penn
Justify the ways of man to men.
There is order in the promise
Of Queen, Russell, Sheridan, Thomas.
O do not stop or make a turn
At Upton, Vincent or Washburn,
Knowing by then the system meaneth,
Past Xerxes, York, we'll reach our Zenith.

Be thankful this is not St. Paul.
There is no sense to it at all.
Where the Church, for all its spiritual and temporal powers,
Permits a jungle of streets named after trees and flowers.
Where a Minneapolis person can only look up to the heavens
As, driving on Eighth Street, he finds himself on Ninth and then on Seventh.

CROCUS HILL (street) Although always known as Crocus Hill, this short street was officially a part of Goodrich Avenue. In February 1984, at the request of the property owners, the city council changed the name to correspond with common usage. This street is unique in the city because the house numbers are not in sequence, or indeed in any discernable order whatsoever. The name comes from the plat Crocus Hill, a name said to be given by local journalist and attorney James Taylor because of the many crocus flowers that bloomed there in the early spring.

CROCUS HILL (neighborhood) In the 1880s, the Crocus Hill and West Crocus Hill additions established this small neighborhood at the east end of Fairmount Avenue: between Crocus Hill street, Crocus Place street, and St. Albans Street. However, because many people aspire to live in this locale, "realtor creep" has expanded the definition of the neighborhood to raise the price of houses in adjacent areas.

CROCUS HILL PARK See *Crocus Terrace Park*.

CROCUS PLACE This southern end of Dale Street and a second street named West Crocus Hill were combined and renamed in 1889.

CROCUS TERRACE PARK This obscure one-and-one-half-acre hillside public park on the south side of Crocus Place—opposite the houses numbered 18 to 54 Crocus Place—was dedicated to the public in 1889. *Terrace* is a nineteenth-century word for a hillside.

CROCUS TRIANGLE Also called Crocus Park Place, this small, .18-acre triangular public park at Goodrich Avenue and Dale Street was dedicated in 1871 in the Crocus Hill plat.

CROMWELL AVENUE Oliver Cromwell (1599–1658), lord protector of England, Scotland, and Ireland from 1653 to 1658, is honored by this St. Anthony Park street designated in 1885. The name has been extended south, identifying a frontage road along Interstate 94. See also *St. Anthony Park*.

CROMWELL SQUARE PARK This small public triangle in St. Anthony Park at Cromwell Avenue and Manvel Street was named on the original plat in 1885. See also *St. Anthony Park*.

CROSBY ISLAND This twenty-five-acre island, which appears in the 1884 Hopkins atlas as Government Lot 5, Section 14, T28, R23, was just off the shore of what is today Crosby Regional Park, the site of the old Thomas Crosby Farm. See also *Crosby Regional Park, Islands*.

CROSBY LAKE One of two lakes within Crosby Regional Park, it is moderately deep: ten to twenty feet. The lake level is maintained largely by spring flooding and ground water from the Mississippi River, as well as a trickle from the springs in the nearby bluffs. Fishermen enjoy catching bluegill, crappie, northern pike, perch, bowfin, carp, and bullheads. See also *Lakes/Ponds, Upper Lake*.

CROSBY REGIONAL PARK Thomas (1827–86) and Emma (1840–1902) Crosby purchased a 160-acre farm along the Mississippi River near the end of Montreal Avenue in 1858. As early

One hundred years ago, there was a working farm in what has since become Crosby Regional Park. Photograph courtesy of the Minnesota Historical Society.

as 1911, A. B. Stickney, noted local financier, recommended that St. Paul buy the Crosby Farm, along with 240 wild and wooded acres off West Seventh Street, for recreational use. Ten years later, the city planning board recommended the farm be purchased as a bird sanctuary. By the 1950s, a syndicate of nine public-spirited citizens held 254 acres of the Crosby Farm in trust, hopeful the city or county would buy it. But it was not until 1962 that the St. Paul Port Authority finally purchased the land and leased it to the city as a park. Additional land was acquired in 1978, bringing the riverside park acreage to 736 acres. In 1984, when developers proposed building housing in the middle of the park, a group of citizens united to defeat the scheme and formed the Friends of the Parks and Trails of St. Paul and Ramsey County.

Today this well-used scenic and natural retreat in the midst of the city offers everyone marsh ponds, lakes, wildflowers, migrating birds, and walks along the river.

CULLEN STREET In 1872, the Protestant Orphan Asylum of St. Paul purchased, for $29,000, the Cullen farm comprising thirty-six acres of land, a large stone house, and a stone barn. When the asylum failed to raise the money to pay off the three-year mortgage, part of the farm was platted into building lots in 1874, when this West End street was named. By 1885 the house was too small, and the asylum moved into a new building on the southeast corner of Marshall Avenue and St. Albans Street.

The Cullen farm was the property of Major William J. Cullen (1817–70), who came to St. Paul in 1857 as superintendent of Indian Affairs. His house, an elaborate French-style mansion built in 1861, remains, greatly remuddled, at 698 Stewart Avenue. Cullen was remembered as a "man of great force of character, self-reliant, original, positive, persuasive, ambitious, and he moved about more like a young elephant than an ordinary man."

Cullen Street, which had several houses along its length before the railroad was constructed, is now only a dirt track cutting across an area known as the Bay Triangle. See also *Bay Triangle, West End*.

CULVERT STREET A candidate for the most unimaginative name given any street in all of St. Paul, this one was bestowed in 1886 by John and Susan Wagener. The culvert's questionable claim to fame was that it carried Phalen Creek out of Swede Hollow and under East Seventh Street. Early residents of Swede Hollow, in cleaning up the creek at their doorstep, considered the task completed when the sewage had been flushed down the Hollow and into this culvert, where it was out of sight and on its way to the Mississippi River. This street was vacated in 1998. See also *Swede Hollow; Phalen Creek, Wagener Street*.

CUMBERLAND STREET This street northeast of Lake Como was platted in 1908 in the Cumberland Addition by Edward Morton Ware (1834–1918), for many years a real-estate and insurance broker in St. Paul. Chairs crafted by the Ware family of Cumberland County, New Jersey, late in the eighteenth century, are popular with collectors of old American furniture. See also *Cohansey Street*.

CURFEW STREET The south part of Curfew Street is a short street within Desnoyer Park added in 1888 in Hollinshead's Addition. People curb their activities on this street after dark. See also *Desnoyer Park*.

CURTICE STREET Born in New York, David L. Curtice (1828–1902) traveled to St. Paul in 1856, working with James A. Case, city engineer, when this street in the West St. Paul plat was named in 1858. Curtice, a surveyor, engineer, and mapmaker, served as city engineer from 1869 to 1874. It was upon his recommendation that Baptist Hill, a fifty-foot embankment in the vicinity of Mears Park, was leveled.

On Curtice Street, between Howard Street and Mt. Hope Avenue and Harvard Street, there are a number of houses curiously below the street level. Number 255 East Curtice Street will help you understand. This lopsided streetscape, resulting in homes you descend to enter, ensues when houses are built before the street has been graded, or, in this case, when the street is constructed into a hillside. It is not uncommon to see this in older areas of the city. See also *Baptist Hill, Case Avenue*.

CURVE STREET Because of its diagonal course following the St. Paul and White Bear Electric Railway, this street was named in 1913. There was a train station on the northeast corner of

Maryland Avenue and Hazel Street. At the instigation of the Furness Parkway Improvement Committee, Curve Street and Furness Street were combined into Furness Parkway in December 1979. See also *Furness Parkway*.

CUSHING CIRCLE (private) Energy Park occupies what had been the railroad car maintenance and repair shops of the Northern Pacific Railroad. George W. Cushing was a railroad superintendent. See also *Energy Park*.

CUSTER STREET Changed from Clay Street in October 1876, the new name reflected public opinion about General George A. Custer, U.S. Army officer, who, along with his 264 men, was killed in the battle of Little Bighorn on June 25, 1876. Custer's time was up when this street was vacated in 1973 as part of the Riverview Industrial Park.

CUTLER ACRE This piece of public property on Phalen Creek at North Street was given to the city in 1939 by Edward Cutler to be maintained for "forest purposes." It has been incorporated into Swede Hollow Park. See also *Swede Hollow Park*.

CUTLER STREET Shortly after the Civil War, William Jonathan Cutler invested in a one-hundred-acre farm near Battle Creek. Named "Fairoaks," this farm also served as a summer health resort for the Boston family. William's son, Edward, chose to live in St. Paul, becoming a partner in the wholesale firm of Noyes Brothers and Cutler. This street was named in 1959 by the city council.

CYPRESS STREET One of the many tree names, this East Side street, originally platted as Boston Street, was renamed in 1872. On the 1876 plat of McLean's Reservation, there is a lake depicted between Cypress and Earl Streets, between McLean Avenue and Hudson Road. See also *East Side, McLean Township*.

Dale Street looking north toward University Avenue around 1952. Photograph by Norton and Peel; courtesy of the Minnesota Historical Society.

D

DAHL AVENUE No guy or Dahl has come forward to accept responsibility for naming this short street in Highwood. See also *Highwood*.

DALE STREET This street name first appears in a number of additions in 1871, giving a name to the section line marking St. Paul's western boundary. Because the topography in the area was far more irregular then, the name probably indicated a valley or vale, as in the marching song: "Over hill, over dale." See also *Dayton Avenue Lake, St. Albans Lake* (1), *St. Albans Lake* (2).

DALY STREET Thomas Daly, the developer of this street in 1857, was a well-to-do young man from Canada. He did not remain in St. Paul long, and his daily activities were not recorded.

DAN ELMER WAY (Fairgrounds) This new street was named for Dan Elmer (1915–2002), the architect and manager of the fair's park-and-ride system. Through his commitment, dedication, legendary persuasive powers, and good humor, this blue-ribbon system has blossomed from a single parking lot to a twenty-seven-lot network with capacity of 18,000 cars.

DAN PATCH AVENUE (Fairgrounds) This is a newer street within the fairgrounds, combining what was Midway Parkway on the east and Commonwealth Avenue on the west. Dan Patch was a legendary Minnesota harness racehorse that established in 1905 a world pacing record of one mile in 1 minute, 55¼ seconds, which prevailed for thirty-three years. In 1906 at the Minnesota State Fairgrounds, he paced a mile in 1 minute, 55 seconds flat—but this feat was not officially recognized. He paced a mile in 2 minutes or less on thirty occasions, a world record unsurpassed until the 1960s. Until his retirement in 1909, he traveled around the United States in his own railroad car and raced against the clock in exhibitions that drew large crowds.

DANFORTH STREET Willis and Nancy Ann Danforth of Milwaukee, Wisconsin, platted this street near Lake Como in 1885 in Danforth Park.

DARLENE STREET This two-part street near the eastern boundary of the city was opened in 1954, but Darlene has escaped detection.

DAVERN STREET William Davern (1831–1913) emigrated in 1848 and arrived in St. Paul the following year. He purchased a 160-acre farm between today's Snelling, Fairview, Montreal, and St. Paul Avenues, where he built his house about the time of the Civil War. This house still stands, although greatly remodeled, at 1173 Davern Street. A farmer and dairyman, Davern at

The famous horse Dan Patch, for whom the street within the fairgrounds is named, traveled with his own private rail car and personal attendants. Photograph by Charles J. Hibbard; courtesy of the Minnesota Historical Society.

one time owned Pike Island. The original "Davern Road" ran from his house down to West Seventh Street; it was extended north and became a city street in 1887.

The first surveyor made a note in 1847 that the road leading from the Minnesota River to intersect the road between St. Paul and the Falls of St. Anthony ascended the hill roughly along the course of Davern Avenue. See also *Marshall Avenue, Pike Island*.

DAVID STREET Opened by the city in 1954, this street by Hillcrest Golf Course—and the address of former mayor Randy Kelly—was named for the grandson of Herbert S. West, a plat commissioner at the time.

DAWSON PARK This approximately two-acre "ghost park" between Lexington Parkway and Edgcumbe Road just west of Deer Park street was dedicated to the public as part of the West End Addition in 1884—long before there was development in this area. Today this undeveloped hillside appears on the city map as Old Dawson Park. At one time, access to the park was by means of a thirty-foot bridle path descending the hill from Edgcumbe Road, but today the intrepid urban traipser will find the only public access is an unmarked alley. Follow the uphill course of Deer Park street (on the north side of Lexington Parkway, across from Albion Avenue) and continue west across the grass to the fence gate. At one time, a St. Paul city attorney wished to buy the park and build his home on the site, but the parks department steadfastly refused.

William Dawson (1825–1901) was a mayor of St. Paul, a banker, and a prolific land speculator, but when his Bank of Minnesota failed in 1896, Dawson died a poor man. See also *Deer Park, Ghost Parks; Alice Street, Edmund Avenue, Kittson Street, Larry Ho Drive, McDonough Park, Nelson Street, Olmstead Street, Otis Avenue, Powers Avenue, Prince Street, Smith Avenue, Stewart Avenue, William Mahoney Street.*

DAYTON AVENUE In 1854, this street was named in part of Dayton and Irvine's Addition for Lyman Dayton (1810–65), one of the leading real-estate speculators of early St. Paul. See also *Dayton's Bluff, Dayton Avenue Lake, William Mahoney Street.*

DAYTON AVENUE LAKE This lake, the most southern of three area lakes, was at the intersection of what is today Dayton Avenue and Dale Street. In 1847, the first intrepid surveyor, traveling north on the line of the future Dale Street, documented a lake 166 feet south of Marshall Avenue. The lake also appears on the 1853 plat of Smith and Lott Subdivision. According to librarian Josiah Chaney, this lake drained through a log culvert under Marshall Avenue north into a second lake. See also *St. Albans Lake (1), St. Albans Lake (2); Dale Street, Lakes/Ponds.*

DAYTON PLACE In 1880 this small cul-de-sac off Maria Avenue on Dayton's Bluff was platted. This landscaped approach to Lyman Dayton's residence at 284 Mounds Street featured a fountain. See also *Dayton's Bluff.*

DAYTON'S BLUFF This early East Side neighborhood extends roughly between Payne Avenue and Johnson Parkway, between Minnehaha Avenue and Mounds Park.

Lyman Dayton (1810–65) was born in Connecticut and worked as a merchant in Providence, Rhode Island, before coming to Minnesota in 1849, where he became one of the leading real-estate speculators in early St. Paul. In a revealing sketch, written some fifty years after his death, Dayton is described as six feet tall and weighing 300 pounds, attired in an outfit consisting of a high hat with an immense brim, a long coat, a velvet vest with white embroidery, and a colossal watch chain. Usually in financial difficulty, Dayton often put his land in the name of a third party so his creditors could not confiscate it.

Notwithstanding these eccentricities, another source recalls him as a man "possessed of great energy, kindhearted, and public spirited." He was an important figure in the development of St. Paul, and had he lived into the real-estate boom of the 1870s, he would have been one of its richest men. The present-day department store family is not directly related. Dayton Avenue is named for him, as is the town of Dayton in Hennepin County. Maria and Bates Avenues are named for his wife.

A 1930s report on housing conditions in St. Paul described Dayton's Bluff as:

comprised of one of the first residential sections in town, originally settled by those of German extraction who built sound homes. In recent years the inhabitants have been of a transient nature who have permitted the homes to deteriorate rapidly, the original soundness of construction alone saving the structures from utter ruin.

Hon. LYMAN DAYTON
St. Paul

(left) Bank notes printed by Lyman Dayton in 1860. Issued because of a lack of currency in frontier St. Paul, they were based largely on Dayton's real-estate holdings and were generally known as "wildcat money." Photograph from *A Scrapbook Documenting Junior Pioneer Association Activities, St. Paul, 1896–1936*; courtesy of the Minnesota Historical Society. (right) Lyman Dayton, the namesake of Dayton's Bluff, was quite a dandy dresser. This portrait is from *An Illustrated Historical Atlas of the State of Minnesota, 1874*.

Dayton's Bluff residents have established a Historic District, enthusiastically restoring the old homes within this multifaceted community. See also *Indian Mounds Park, Im-in-i-ja Ska, Weld's Bluff*.

DAYTON'S CAVE According to geologist Greg Brick, Dayton's Cave, a smaller twin of nearby Carver's Cave, was often confused with the latter. Both contained pools of water and aboriginal pictographs sketched by the antiquarian T. H. Lewis. Located in Dayton's Bluff, this natural sandstone vault was walled up in pioneer days and used as a vegetable cellar and bottling room. The cave probably still exists but is buried by erosion. See also *Carver's Cave, Fountain Cave*.

DEAD HORSE LAKE See *Loeb Lake*.

DEALTON STREET Ivan J. and Catherine Kipp applied this West End street name in the Glen Terrace Addition in 1912. It is said to acknowledge Alton D. Smith, a family member who farmed in the area. See also *Kipp's Glen, West End*.

DE COURCY DRIVE Elizabeth De Courcy (d. 2004) was a St. Paul councilwoman from 1956 to 1962, and Ramsey County commissioner from 1967 to 1974. This street was named in 1956 but renamed Energy Park Drive in 1982. However, a remnant remains as *Decourcy Circle*. See also *Energy Park*.

DEER PARK The city council approved this name in May 2002. A new street was necessary because there was insufficient street frontage to provide a separate house number on Lexington Parkway for each of the planned twelve town houses. When asked about the naming of his hillside development, John Kratz explained there were deer in the adjacent Dawson and Walsh Parks. He also had memories of a Deer Park in central Illinois that he visited in his youth. See also *Dawson Park, Walsh Park*.

DELANO PLACE Platted as Calvin Street, the name was changed to avoid confusion with nearby Colvin Street. Renamed in 1950, it may be a passing reference to Franklin Delano Roosevelt.

DELAWARE AVENUE This is one of a series of American Indian names in the 1855 plat of West St. Paul. The first surveyor, who established this section line in 1853, noted that the road between St. Paul and Mendota passed close to what is today the location of the house at 769 Delaware Avenue. He also noted "Mr. Morrison's Field" (perhaps the first land cultivated by settlers on the West Side) as being near what is today the intersection of Delaware Avenue and Page Street. See also *West Side*.

DELLRIDGE AVENUE See *Berland Place*.

DELLWOOD PLACE This short diagonal street was originally a part of Eighth Street on the East Side. It is diagonal because the plat creating Eighth Street ran parallel to the river rather than on a north-south axis. See also *Eighth Street*.

DELOS STREET Delos A. Monfort (1835–99), a prominent banker of the city, first traveled through St. Paul in 1854, returning here in 1857. Beginning with Charles Mackubin and Erastus Edgerton in their banking house, he subsequently became cashier for the Second National Bank, with which he remained off and on for the remainder of his career. In his early years at People's Bank, Monfort won an extraordinary race to St. Peter, Minnesota, stopping a run on his bank. St. Paul historian Henry Castle lends color to the drama:

> It was known that the Nicollet County Bank had at St. Peter about $5,000 in gold, as a redemption fund. Every bank dispatched a swift messenger to St. Peter with all of the notes on the Nicollet County institution that could be readily obtained. The People's Bank secured the prize. Its messenger, D. A. Monfort, gathered up about $5,000 of the Nicollet bank notes and set out for St. Peter on horseback. Riding three horses to exhaustion and not drawing bridle save to make the relays, he passed every other carrier on the road and made the seventy-eight miles in eight hours. He secured the gold. He was greatly fatigued, but the following morning he set out and returned to St. Paul just in time. There was a "run" on the People 's Bank, and the last dollar was in sight when cashier Monfort staggered in with his heavy pair of saddle bags. The reinforcement was believed to consist of $25,000 instead of $5,000. The "run" subsided and was soon over.

Rumor had it the heroic banker ate standing up throughout the following week. Delos Street, named in the 1855 plat of West St. Paul, marks a section line on the land survey. See also *West Side.*

DENSLOW STREET This short street off Como Avenue was named in 1892, probably for LeGrand N. Denslow, the developer and a professor at the St. Paul Medical College. His brother was William W. Denslow, well-known illustrator of the 1900 first edition of the children's book *The Wonderful Wizard of Oz.*

DESNOYER AVENUE Although the area had been platted in 1887 as Desnoyer Park, there was no street by this name until 1919 when Maplewood Avenue was changed to Desnoyer Avenue. Stephen Desnoyer (1805–77) was born in St. Jean d'Iberville, Quebec. He was subsequently a farmer in New York State, a clothier in St. Louis, and a lumber merchant in Dubuque, Iowa, before settling in St. Paul in 1843. He bought the 320-acre claim of Donald McDonald between what is today Cleveland Avenue and the Mississippi River, between Marshall and St. Anthony Avenues, and thus became one of the first white settlers in the Midway area. For many years he ran "Halfway House" for stagecoach travelers between St. Paul and Minneapolis. He died of an "apoplectic attack" two weeks after being thrown from his carriage. Rumor had it he was wealthy and had money buried in his fields. See also *Glendale Street, Midway.*

According to the plat, Shields Enlargement of Roseville, Stephen Desnoyer's "Halfway House" for stagecoach travelers between St. Paul and Minneapolis stood near what is today Fairview Avenue and Interstate 94. Photograph by B. J. Sturtevant; courtesy of the Minnesota Historical Society.

DESNOYER PARK Located at Pelham Boulevard and Doane Avenue, this two-and-a-half-acre public park was originally the location of the Desnoyer Park Elementary School. The Department of Parks and Recreation purchased the park site in 1974, and the current recreation center was opened in 1978. There is a second Desnoyer Park, platted in 1887, a small triangle of public land at Desnoyer Avenue and Pelham Boulevard.

DESNOYER PARK (neighborhood) This neighborhood on the western end of the city takes its name from a railroad suburb platted in 1887 by the Union Land Company. It is bounded approximately by Marshall and Cretin Avenues, by the Mississippi River Boulevard and Interstate 94. The railroad station, on the Short Line, was near where Pelham Boulevard crosses the railroad tracks.

The Town and Country Club occupies one-half of the neighborhood. The only business located there is a radio station established in 1936. The remainder is quite a mixture of housing: everything from splendid mansions on Mississippi River Boulevard to 1920s Tudors to small post–World War II bungalows to 1980s split levels. See also *Burlington Heights, Desnoyer Avenue, Short Line Road, Warrendale*.

DESOTO PARK See *Hopkins Park*.

DESOTO STREET Hernando de Soto, the Spanish explorer, who "discovered" the Mississippi River, is the inspiration for this East Side street named in 1853 in Warren and Winslow's Addition. John E. Warren, an early mayor, was also one of St. Paul's most scholarly developers. Between Minnehaha Avenue and Tedesco Street, Desoto Street is only twenty-eight feet wide, giving it the air of a European lane. See also *Mt. Ida Street*.

DEUBENER PLACE Originally Roebe Street, the name of this short street near Linwood Park was changed in 1940 to avoid conflict with Robie Street. Walter H. and Lydia Deubener were longtime residents of the city who, about 1916 in a St. Paul grocery store, invented the square-bottom paper bag with handles. They subsequently established a factory in Indianapolis to manufacture the bags, prompting a prominent St. Paul banker to tell Walter that he and Lydia had done almost as much for the American economy as Henry Ford. The couple owned extensive real estate within the city, including an apartment building on this street.

DEVIL'S DITCH This ravine, located on the west side of Birmingham Street north of East Seventh Street, conjures chills among locals. For a spell, it was once a popular hangout for spirited teenagers; today it is officially the Birmingham York Pond, one of the city's East Side detention ponds used to capture the overflow when the underworld storm sewer floods. However, this particular ravine is only a segment of a larger valley—now intersected by streets—that runs north and south through the East Side west of Hazelwood Street. South of Minnehaha Avenue, the ravine was known as the "Van Kirk Dump" for the family who owned the property. West of Harding High School, the ravine was known as the Harding Woods. See also *Grotto, Hillcrest Knoll, Roger Puchreiter Pond, Stillwater Avenue, Valley, Willow Reserve*.

DEW DROP According to information supplied by Sister Margery Smith, CSJ, archivist of the College of St. Catherine, the spring-fed pond on the campus was originally called the "Canoe Lagoon." A short poem in the 1922 college yearbook elucidates its new name:

> To The Dew Drop:
> How come you there near the Indian Trail?
> Does the forest your birth inscribe?
> You are sprung from the tear some old chief shed
> In farewell to the haunts of his tribe.

An end-of-the-school-year party held at the pond became the annual Dew Drop Bop. Noise complaints about the doo-wop at the first party led the school to opt, in subsequent years as a sop, to lop the Bop from the Dew Drop, and the Dew Drop Bop has since been held within the enclosure of the campus buildings. See also *Lakes/Ponds*.

Two adventurous students from the College of St. Catherine test the ice on the Dew Drop despite the warning sign. Photograph courtesy of the Archives Collection, College of St. Catherine Library, St. Paul, Minnesota.

DEWEY STREET At one time Laura Avenue, the name was changed in 1898 to avoid confusion with Laurel Avenue. Admiral George Dewey (1837–1917), born in Vermont and educated at the U.S. Naval Academy, served in the Civil War and had risen to the rank of commander at the onset of the Spanish-American War in 1898. On May 1 of that year, Dewey slipped his American fleet into Manila Bay and destroyed the overwhelmed Spanish fleet without a single fatality among his own men, making him a national hero overnight.

DICKERMAN PARK In 1906, the area between Fairview Avenue and Aldine Street, between University and Thomas Avenues, was platted into building lots under the subdivision name Dickerman Park by the Dickerman family. The lots extended to the line of University Avenue. Six years later, the Dickerman Investment Company and Griggs, Cooper & Co. reconfigured the two blocks fronting University Avenue between Fairview Avenue and Aldine Street to establish a 160-foot strip of land facing

University Avenue that was left free of building lots. The 1929 Hopkins atlas notes the land is "dedicated for a parkway"—possibly an allusion to a future University Avenue greenway. Since then, this small parcel has become a public park, and the Dickerman family has contributed money toward its improvement. See also *Riverside Park*.

DIETER STREET William F. Dieter (1828–96) ran a shoe store in St. Paul for many years. Born in Germany, he immigrated to St. Paul in 1854 and was active in business circles here for the remainder of his life. This short street near Frost Lake was named in 1887. See also *Frost Lake*.

DISTRICT DEL SOL The West Side has created a vibrant multicultural thoroughfare on Cesar Chavez Street between Wabasha and Ada Streets and on Robert Street between Cesar Chavez and Wood Streets. Fashioned about 2000 to give an identity to the business district, the name combines an English word with the simple Spanish word *sol*, chosen because the sun is honored worldwide. This is a visually distinctive area of the city with its vivid palette of colors, oddly angled streets, wafts of food cooking, foreign languages, diverse architecture, and abundance of public art. See also *West Side*.

DOANE AVENUE In 1887, some Desnoyer Park streets were named for towns in Massachusetts, or surrounding states. Doane may be one of these towns, or it may be a personal name selected because of its euphony. Or it may not have any local significance. At the east end of Doane Avenue where it intersects with Raymond and St. Anthony Avenues, there is a triangular garden within which is a marker erected by the Ramsey County Historical Society commemorating the oxcart trail that generally followed the route of today's St. Anthony Avenue. See also *Desnoyer Park, St. Anthony Avenue*.

DODD ROAD The West Side portion of what is today Dodd Road was originally part Bridge Street and part Owatonna Road before being changed to Dodd Road in 1876. William B. Dodd (1811–62), born in New Jersey, educated as a machinist, later became a civil engineer. Moving to Minnesota in 1850 as a partner in a land company, he platted the city of St. Peter in 1854 and built the first house there. With the growth of his city in mind, he laid out a sixty-five-mile road between St. Peter and St. Paul, riding the ridge that separated the drainage basins of the Minnesota and Cannon rivers. This road was later adopted for use by the government, and Dodd was eventually reimbursed for part of his expenses. He was killed defending New Ulm against the Dakota attacks in 1862. Parts of his road in Rice and Le Sueur counties that have retained their original integrity are on the National Register of Historic Places.

DONOHUE AVENUE Originally Bohn Street, the name was changed in 1957 to honor John H. Donohue II (1883–1956). In 1916 he founded the building materials firm Corning-Donohue, Inc., located on this Midway street from 1955 to 1970. See also *Midway*.

DORA LANE Herbert and Dorothy Halverson platted Dora Lane in 1949. *Dora Court* takes its name from the same source.

DORIS SQUARE This small public square in St. Anthony Park at Hillside Avenue and Knapp Street was named on the original plat in 1885. Doris remains anonymous. See also St. Anthony Park.

DOROTHEA AVENUE Dorothea was the wife of Norbert Bisanz, one of the brothers who developed this Highland Park area as Bisanz Brothers Addition #2 in 1951. See also Colette Place, Matterhorn Lane, Susan Avenue.

DOSWELL AVENUE Brooke Doswell of Fredericksburg, Virginia, helped finance this St. Anthony Park North plat in 1885. See also St. Anthony Park.

DOUGLAS PARK Previously the site of the Douglas School, this one-and-one-half-acre West Side public park is on the east side of Orleans Street between Stevens and King Streets.

DOUGLAS STREET Stephen A. Douglas (1813–61) was U.S. senator from Illinois, who, as chairman of the Committee on Territories, advocated the formation of the Minnesota Territory in 1848. The West End street was named the following year within Leach's Addition. Douglas is perhaps best known as the candidate whom Abraham Lincoln defeated for president in 1860. See also West End.

DOUGLYNN LANE This Highwood street was named in 1959 for the two children of Jene and Gloria Sigvertsen, who had purchased a building lot at the end of the street. Before building on the property, however, Sigvertsen, an architect, sold the lot to live elsewhere. See also Highwood.

DOUSMAN PARK This small West End public park at Goodhue and Dousman Streets is not mentioned in the parks department records; it appears the land is only leased. See also West End.

DOUSMAN STREET Hercules L. Dousman (1800–1868) of Prairie du Chien, Wisconsin, an agent of the American Fur Company, had extensive property holdings throughout the state. This West End street was named in 1851 in Winslow's Addition, in which Dousman probably had a financial interest. He is credited as being the first to suggest the name Minnesota for the new territory. See also West End.

DR. JUSTUS OHAGE BOULEVARD Dr. Ohage, St. Paul commissioner of health from 1899–1907, had public baths built on Harriet Island, which he owned at the time. He later donated the island and the baths to the city. Dr. Ohage is perhaps best known in medical circles as performing the first successful cholecystectomy (gall bladder removal) in the United States. His house, built in 1889 and overlooking downtown St. Paul, remains at 59 Irvine Park. See also Harriet Island Park, Irvine Park.

DRAKE STREET Elias F. Drake (1813–92) was born in Ohio, where he practiced law and banking until 1852 when he began building railroads. In 1862, he brought the first train to Minnesota. He was later president of the St. Paul and Sioux City Railroad, whose track and shops were adjacent to this West End street named in 1880.

Drake was a shrewd, well-educated, and wealthy businessman who, after an eight-month trip to Europe in 1882, returned feeling that "our government is the only one in all the world where opportunities are open to all the people alike to attain the highest state of prosperity and happiness." See also *West End*.

DREWRY LANE Previously part of Payne Avenue, the street was renamed in 1933 when Payne Avenue was rerouted. Edward Drewry (1829–1926) was born in Reading, England; he journeyed to St. Paul in 1857, where he opened a porter ale bottling business in Dayton's Bluff. Ten years later he relocated to the present-day Drewry Lane. The company flourished until Prohibition, when the firm turned to producing soft drinks. Edward's son sold the family business in 1932, although it continued under the Drewry name until 1952. A second son went to Winnipeg in 1875 and founded a branch of the company there that grew to be the largest brewery in western Canada. Today the lane has survived with its original granite curbs but is truncated to less than one block long.

DUCHESS STREET At one time Greenwood Street on the East Side, the name was changed in 1887. Duchess, with an agreeable sound and a hint of royalty, is short and easy to pronounce. See also *East Side*.

An employee of the Drewry and Son Bottling Plant at 704 Drewry Lane mixes a potion that will induce customers to buy more beer. Photograph courtesy of the Minnesota Historical Society.

DUDLEY AVENUE This is a common family and place name in England. Though generally without local significance, English names were popular in St. Anthony Park in the 1880s. See also St. Anthony Park.

DUKE STREET Thomas Daly, a well-to-do young man from Canada, named three West End streets in 1856: Duke, Richmond, and Canada. The logical inference would be that they honored the Fourth Duke of Richmond, one-time governor general of Canada, who died from the bite of a pet fox. Daly was here for only a short time. See also West End.

DULUTH STREET Originally Phalen Street, the name was changed in 1885. The northern boundary of this street was the St. Paul and Duluth Railroad.

DUNEDIN TERRACE Previously Isabel Street, the name was changed around 1900. The name is Gaelic (Dun Eideann) for Edinburgh, Scotland, and means literally "Fort of Eidyn." Terrace is a nineteenth-century word for hillside, so the name means literally Eidyn's hillside fort. The Dunedin Terrace Apartments, a city public housing unit, take their name from this street although the address of the apartments is 469 Ada Street. It is doubtful the residents feel too besieged on this quiet West Side street. See also West Side.

DUNLAP STREET William Dunlap (1833–1901) was a builder and real-estate dealer in St. Paul when this street adjacent to Lexington Parkway was named in 1873. One of Dunlap's residences, a fine Civil War–era house, still stands at 531 Brainerd Avenue. After being denied a building variance, he committed suicide by drinking carbolic acid. See also Brainerd Avenue.

DUNNING FIELD This twenty-six-acre public playground at Marshall Avenue and Griggs Street, acquired in 1912, was one of the first in St. Paul. Following the movement to acquire public parks in the 1870s, there was another nationwide effort to create safe, supervised playgrounds in congested city areas for children and adults. This movement was reinforced by the fact that automobiles were killing children accustomed to playing in the streets. Dr. Arthur Dunning, a medical doctor and instructor at the University of Minnesota, born in Fond du Lac, Wisconsin, in 1860, became chairman of St. Paul's first committee on playgrounds. Dunning Field was named for him in 1916.

The first annual report of the St. Paul Playgrounds Committee in 1904 explains the rationale:

> "But," someone asks, "why the need of playgrounds? We had none when we were children." Consideration of such queries recalls the early life on the farm with hard work, its association with nature, fishing, hunting, "the ole swimmin' hole," the country school house with its acres of yard, its long recesses and vigorous games. Under such conditions the instincts of nature can develop unhampered. Life in the city is artificial; there are so many disturbing influences that the child needs a guiding hand in order that he may not stumble or stop at some of the lower stages of development. The city gang is simply a case of group loyalty gone wrong for want of proper training.

Tennis was a more popular sport back in 1915, when Dunning Field had twenty-eight tennis courts. Central High School is in the background. Photograph courtesy of the Minnesota Historical Society.

Moreover, the report continued:

> Another principle firmly grounded in the minds of all concerned was that a playground without competent supervision is bound to be a failure. The central idea of this movement is that educational play conduces to character building, and through that to good citizenship; while on the other hand, aggregations of children without the guiding and restraining influence of supervisor and instructors lead to perversion, quarrels, rioting and immorality.

The first playground in St. Paul was next to the Scheffer School at Lafond Avenue and Marion Street.

In the background at the end of Earl Street is the Burlington Hotel, which catered to railroad workers from the yards below. Photograph courtesy of the Minnesota Historical Society.

E

EAGLE PARKWAY The name of the short street changes from Eagle Street to Eagle Parkway at Exchange Street. Part of a realignment that took place when the new Science Museum of Minnesota was built, this segment became a "parkway" at the insistence of the parks department—but no one seems to know why.

EAGLE STREET The eagle was a popular symbol of the United States when this downtown street was named in 1849 in Rice and Irvine's Addition. See also *Eagle Parkway*.

EARL STREET Platted as East Street in 1857, the name was changed in 1872. It is a personal name of uncertain identity. At the foot of Earl Street, overlooking the railroad tracks along Warner Road, the Burlington Hotel, an ungainly and solitary building, survived for many years. It was the last of the old-time railroad hotels, accommodating the men working in the yards below.

EAST AVENUE The east boundary of St. Paul was defined by this street opened in 1892. Over the years, most of it was renamed McKnight Road; the remaining bit was vacated in 2003.

EAST CONSOLIDATED This East Side neighborhood took its identity from the former East Consolidated School, since renamed the Bruce Vento Elementary School. It is roughly between Edgerton Street and Interstate 35E, between Maryland Avenue and the Bruce Vento Regional Trail. Perhaps, in time, it will become the Bruce Vento neighborhood, but at the moment it seems to be known by a combination of the two names: Econ-Vento. See also *Bruce Vento Nature Sanctuary, East Side*.

EAST SHORE DRIVE Originally Overbrook Avenue, the name was changed in 1926 when the drive was extended farther along the east shore of Lake Phalen. At 1492 East Shore Drive is the clubhouse of the Weequah Canoe Club, built in 1924 by Swedish businessmen. A few years later, after establishing a golf course, it became the Weequah Country Club; today it is a private residence. South of Arlington Avenue on East Shore Drive is "the hole," a tunnel—which served as a passageway from the lake to the residential section—under what were once the tracks of the St. Paul and Duluth Railway.

EAST SIDE There are many definitions of the East Side. In delineating locations of the streets in this book, we have considered the East Side as that one-third of the city east of Interstate 35E and north of the Mississippi River.

The East Side suffers from an unfortunate reputation as a place where crime, drugs, and substandard housing flourish, but that is a thoughtless generalization. There are many distinct communities within the East Side, ranging from historic Dayton's Bluff to suburban Frost Lake. Residents range from newly arrived immigrants to fifth-generation families. And there are devoted and loyal "East-Siders" who seldom venture to—and would never live in—any other part of the city.

Within the vast and diverse East Side, there are many subneighborhoods. Some of these locales are apparent from the street intersections in their name, for example, the Payne-Arcade neighborhood; however, our interest is in acknowledging the time-honored neighborhood names that are not so obvious. See also *Arlington Hills, Battle Creek, Beaver Lake Heights, Bilanski Point, Burlington Heights, Connemara Patch, Conway, Dayton's Bluff, East Consolidated, Eastern Heights, Eastview, Frost Lake, Hayden Heights, Hazel Park, Highwood, Hillcrest, Hillcrest Knoll, Lincoln Park, Montville, Parkway, Pavilion Point, Payne-Phalen, Phalen Heights, Phalen Village, Post Side Track, Prosperity Heights, Railroad Island, Riverside Park, Swede Hollow, Upper Swede Hollow, Willow Reserve.*

EASTERN HEIGHTS Robert L. Ware's 1909 plat of Eastern Heights encompassed the area between White Bear and Minnehaha Avenues, between Conway Street and McKnight Road. The neighborhood referred to by this name seems to be somewhat larger.

EASTVIEW The boundaries of this neighborhood are roughly between Minnehaha Avenue and Birmingham Street, between White Bear Avenue and Old Hudson Road. The name comes from a series of plats named Eastview that subdivided the area in the mid-1950s.

EATON STREET Described as "a sort of general locomotive crushing down all obstacles in his way," Samuel S. Eaton (1825–99) was born in Vermont and traveled to California in 1849 by way of Canada. From there, he moved to Buffalo, New York, and came to St. Paul in 1855, where he engaged in the insurance business for the remainder of his life. The developer of this West Side street in 1857 is said to have written the first insurance policy in Minnesota. His Railroad Island home, at 468 Hopkins Street, was moved to Irvine Park in 1979, where in the course of its restoration, the 124-year-old building burned on January 5, 1982. See also *Railroad Island.*

EBERTZ COURT In 1972, Walter J. Ebertz of St. Paul named this street near Battle Creek for his father, William Ebertz (1884–1952), who was also a contractor.

ECHO AVENUE Who could ever guess why a street might be named for an echo? Were there reverberations resounding around this swampy site? Were the repetitious residents reeling? Were the bog beasts babbling? Were the hills alive? But no, none of these. It took repeated telephone calls to ascertain that—read on—Echo was the wife of Edwin Johnson, who was associated with the real-estate firm developing this locality in 1946. So now we know! For those who like to hear themselves talk, visit Ms. Echo's short street in the northeast corner of the city. See also *Kingsford Street.*

ECON-VENTO See *East Consolidated.*

EDGAR AVENUE In 1904, several investors from Stillwater named this short diagonal street in Ware and Hospes Addition near Lake Como. Who Edgar was remains a mystery.

EDGCUMBE ROAD This St. Paul parkway, without an "edge," was first named Summit Avenue South and was intended to be an extension to Summit Avenue. In the current city parkway scheme, Edgcumbe Road is a link between Lexington Parkway on the east and Mississippi River Boulevard on the west. The road was named in 1912 by Charles B. Dunn, Philadelphia banker and owner of the property, for his home in Chestnut Hill, Pennsylvania, which in turn had been named for Mount Edgcumbe in his native Cornwall, England.

In the 1920s there was a plan by the city to extend Edgcumbe Road to connect with Mississippi River Boulevard by way of Mt. Curve Boulevard. As a future objective, planners envisioned extending Edgcumbe Road north from its present terminus at Lexington Parkway, following the bluff through Linwood Park and reaching Summit Avenue near Western Avenue. This would have opened the bluff view to the public and linked up the parkway system with the Capitol Approach. Considering the valuable property and influential citizens residing in the path of this envisioned route, it is understandable why this connection has not been made. *Edgcumbe Place* takes its name from the parkway. See also *Grand Rounds*.

EDGEBROOK AVENUE Platted as Eastview Avenue in 1960 in Highwood, the name was changed two years later. Both names were picked to fit the local alphabetical sequence of the area. See also *A Street, Berland Place, Highwood*.

EDGEMONT STREET This fancy name, applied in 1887 to this street off Wheelock Parkway, gives the impression of height, view, and mountains.

EDGERTON STREET Born in New York State, where he worked for a time as a fearless deputy sheriff, Erastus S. Edgerton (1816–93) moved to St. Paul in 1853. He opened a bank here— Charles Mackubin was his first partner—with money inherited from his father's estate and spent the remainder of his life in banking. Upon his retirement, he returned to New York City, where he was often seen riding his Kentucky-bred horse in Central Park. This East Side street, originally called Miller Street, was renamed for Edgerton in 1872. The street marks a one-half section line on the land survey. See also *Mackubin Street*.

EDGEWATER BOULEVARD A popular name when it was added to the city in 1946, this street follows the west edge of Beaver Lake. See also *Beaver Lake*.

EDMUND AVENUE Remembered as a kind and generous man of placid disposition, Edmund Rice (1819–89) must be considered one of St. Paul's finest citizens. Born in Vermont, he came to Minnesota in 1849 from Michigan. A member of the legislature for several terms, he was also a county commissioner and twice mayor of St. Paul. His activities in various railroad companies earned him the nickname "father of Minnesota railroading." As a leading land speculator and developer, he named several streets for members of his family. Despite his many achievements, however, Rice lived his later years close to poverty. Streets named Edmund, Charles, and Ellen originated in 1854 in Warren and Rice's Addition. See also *Dawson Park, Kittson Street, Lafond Avenue, Larry Ho Drive, McDonough Park, Nelson Street, Olmstead Street, Otis Avenue, Powers Avenue, Prince Street, Smith Avenue, Stewart Avenue, William Mahoney Street.*

EICHENWALD STREET John M. Keller (1833–96) platted this street in 1877 and named it for his dramatic estate and house on what is today the north corner of Sixth and Eichenwald Streets in Dayton's Bluff. The name comes from Keller's German birthplace, a small village named Eichwald near Dresden. The name translates as "oak woods," befitting Keller, a master carpenter, who owned a lumberyard for many years. His son, Herbert P. Keller, was mayor of St. Paul from 1910 to 1914. See also *Dayton's Bluff.*

EIGHTH STREET One of the earlier St. Paul street names dating from Bazil and Guerin's Addition in 1850, this eighth street from the river was the location of many of the city brothels in the 1880s. Downtown the street is presently only three blocks long, the rest of it having been renamed Seventh Street. St. Mary's Church, established about 1865 on Eighth Street between

The name of the street was taken from the name of John Keller's lavish estate, Eichenwald. From *An Illustrated Historical Atlas of the State of Minnesota,* 1874.

Wacouta Street and Broadway, evokes the area's earlier residential days. The street continues northeast from downtown in about eight segments until it terminates in Dellwood Place. See also *Dellwood Place*.

EILEEN WEIDA PARK The one-and-one-half-acre public park, Lafayette Playground, at Burr and Tedesco Streets in the Railroad Island neighborhood of St. Paul, was renamed in 1988 for Eileen Weida. A community activist who died at age fifty-eight on January 26, 1988, Weida was esteemed for her energy and commitment to improving the community. See also *Railroad Island*.

ELEANOR AVENUE Horace and Mary Rugg named this street in Rugg's Addition in 1882. Their house remains at 251 Summit Avenue, but Eleanor's identity has been lost.

ELEVENTH STREET Named in Bazil and Guerin's Addition in 1850, this downtown street was eleven blocks from the river.

ELFELT STREET Abram S. Elfelt (1827–88) and Charles D. Elfelt (1828–99) opened the first dry goods store in St. Paul in 1849. Their second store, built in 1851, stood at the corner of Third and Exchange Streets, the largest downtown building at that time. The upper floor of this building became St. Paul's first theater. This North End street was named in 1855. See also *Lafond Lake, North End*.

ELIZABETH STREET What woman inspired this name in the 1855 West St. Paul plat is not evident. See also *West St. Paul Park*.

ELK STREET This North End street was named in Edmund Rice's Second Addition in 1870; an adjacent street is Buffalo.

ELLIOT PLACE Other than a nice British sound, the name, applied in Schafer's Addition in 1933, of this short Mounds Park street does not seem to have any obvious significance.

ELLIS AVENUE Without doubt, this is a personal name, perhaps that of an investor in St. Anthony Park when this street was named in 1885. See also *St. Anthony Park*.

ELM SQUARE No one would guess, but this small public triangle at Elm and Exchange Streets near Irvine Park was deeded to the city in 1871, making it one of the oldest public spaces in the city. As you drive west from Irvine Park on Exchange Street, the road curves to the right, becoming Forbes Avenue. If you were to stop at that curve, you would be smack in the middle of the original Elm Square. To your left is a grassy triangle that appears to be part of the Little Sisters of the Poor grounds but is actually part of Exchange Street. In other words, if Exchange Street did not curve but continued straight into Wilkin Street along the line of the sidewalk, the triangle formed on the right side of Exchange Street and east side of Wilkin Street would be the original Elm Square. In truth what has happened is that the public space has been shifted from the north side of Exchange Street to the south side. Clear as mud? Wonder why a square is a triangle? The 1928 Hopkins atlas plainly delineates the park; one picture is worth a thousand words. See also *Ghost Parks, Holcombe Park Circle*.

ELM STREET Named in Rice and Irvine's Addition near downtown in 1849, Elm is the fifteenth most common street name in America, with 5,233 occurrences. Moreover 80 percent of the towns in the Midwest have at least one street named for a tree. It is interesting to speculate that as our civilization progresses, one tree looks pretty much like any other to most people.

ELMHURST CEMETERY This is an old cemetery, established in 1865 northeast of Lake Como, as a German Lutheran cemetery. *Hurst* is an Anglo-Saxon suffix revived in the nineteenth century meaning "wooded hill," and it was often coupled with tree names, such as Oakhurst. This is one of eight cemeteries remaining in St. Paul. For a listing of some famous people buried in this cemetery, see *Six Feet Under* by Stew Thornley. See also *Cemeteries*.

ELMWOOD STREET Named in 1888, this Highwood street was part of Burlington Heights. See also *Highwood*.

ELSIE LANE Elsie was the wife of Den E. Lane, probably St. Paul's leading land developer in the 1920s and 1930s. He platted large areas of Highland Park and the area around Lake Phalen, including this street, which he named in 1950. He showed admirable restraint for not promoting his name by proliferating Lane's lanes throughout the city. See also *Upper St. Dennis Road*.

ELWAY STREET It is most likely that some individual prompted this street name in the West End Addition in 1881. See also *West End*.

EMERALD LANE This street is part of a development entitled Emerald Estates.

EMERALD STREET In 1886, this street was named in Warner's Prospect Park. With its associations of green, evoking growth and plants, the emerald stone was probably the inspiration for this street name. The south part of Emerald Street (formerly Regent Street), one block long, is within Desnoyer Park. The northern end of the street is part of the boundary between Minneapolis and St. Paul and marks a section line on the land survey.

EMMA STREET There were a number of developers in this 1879 Drake's Addition; none of them was named Emma. Several of the even-numbered houses now officially on Emma Street originally had addresses on Stewart Avenue. The intrepid urban traipser might like to stroll south from Western Avenue on this short quaint West End street. At the south end of the street, directly ahead, there is a wooded area along the top of the bluff, marking the course of old Stewart Avenue. A turn to the left leads into a discrete alley connecting to St. Clair Avenue. See also *Cliff Street*, *Stewart Avenue*, *West End*.

EMPIRE DRIVE This street within the Empire Builder Industrial Park was named at the request of the St. Paul Port Authority by the city council in November 1993. It refers to what were the Great Northern Railroad freight car shops in the vicinity, the Great Northern being the railroad of James J. Hill, the Empire Builder.

EMPSON ALLEY An obscure byway, this alley and its name honor the author of this volume—a kind, scholarly, well-endowed eponymous toponymist who wishes no more than to quietly pass through life patiently researching perplexing enigmas and orphic conundrums. After his death, he will settle in the Marine on St. Croix cemetery and attempt to unearth the meaning of life. See also *Way Round About*.

ENDICOTT STREET In the Midway industrial area, this one-block-long street named in 1885 in St. Anthony Park commemorates John Endicott (1588?–1665), several times governor and official of the Massachusetts Bay Colony. See also *St. Anthony Park*.

ENERGY LANE This street is part of the Energy Park development. See also *Energy Park*.

ENERGY PARK Funded by a number of sources, city, state, federal, as well as profit and non-profit corporations, Energy Park redeveloped and revitalized the area of the Northern Pacific Railway passenger car shops. Energy Park is between Jessamine Avenue and Pierce Butler Route, between Lexington Parkway and Snelling Avenue. Completed in the late 1970s, the name reflects a period when energy prices were very high and energy conservation was a rational response. Energy Park has a central power plant providing heating and cooling. Building design and orientation took advantage of solar energy, and the old railroad shops were recycled rather than demolished. At the time, these energy-saving measures were quite innovative, and a few farsighted individuals continue to expand techniques applied in this project.

Russell Erickson's solar sculpture was a fitting symbol for Energy Park, which included a number of energy-saving measures. Photograph by Kay Shaw; courtesy of the Minnesota Historical Society.

ENERGY PARK DRIVE What previously was De Courcy Drive and part of Kasota Avenue was renamed Energy Park Drive by action of the city council in 1982. Quality Tool Company, 2135 Energy Park Drive, was the site of the first strike by the recently immigrated workforce of Southeast Asians, members of the International Union of Electronic Workers (IUE) in 1989–90. See also *Armstrong Avenue, Boyd Park, Energy Park, Kilburn Street, Rice Park, Sherburne Avenue, William Mahoney Street.*

ENGLEWOOD AVENUE This street was previously Capitol Avenue. Englewood is a city in California. Many of the street names changed in 1940 were borrowed from more romantic places in that state. See also *Alameda Street.*

ENGLISH STREET In 1880 when this street was named, William H. English (1822–96) was the Democratic candidate for the vice presidency as the running mate of General Winfield Scott Hancock. Streets were named for both candidates by the developer Franz Sigel, a Civil War general with political connections, living in New York City.

English Street from Arlington Avenue north to County Road B follows the course of the Lake Phalen–White Bear road that had been laid out during the Civil War. This road went northeast from downtown St. Paul, around the south end of Lake Phalen, and north on the course of English Street, which marks a section line on the land survey. See also *Hancock Street.*

ERIE STREET This West End street was named in 1851 for Lake Erie. Adjacent streets were other Great Lakes: Michigan, Superior, Ontario, Huron, and St. Clair. Charles Willis (1819–98), the developer, grew up on Lake Erie. See also *West End.*

ESCANABA AVENUE *Escanaba* is said to be an Ojibwe word meaning "land of the red buck." In this instance, however, it was probably borrowed, in 1917, as part of Beaver Lake Heights, directly from the river and city in Michigan of the same name, without regard for its literal meaning. See also *Beaver Lake Heights.*

ESTABROOK DRIVE John D. Estabrook, a civil engineer by profession, was the first superintendent of parks in St. Paul, a position he held less than a year between 1888 and 1889. He moved to Westborough, Massachusetts, in 1901, but his house at 699 Lincoln Avenue remains. The city council honored him in 1967 by this street name within Como Park.

ETNA STREET Platted as John Street near Mounds Park, the name was changed to avoid duplication in 1872. Etna is a volcano in Sicily, and the name may have been chosen because of the street's position on the hill, or simply because it was short and easy to pronounce. Over the past century, however, the street seems to have erupted in fragments on its flow north to the city boundary. Etna Street between Hoyt and Idaho Avenues is one of the few remaining unpaved streets in the city. See also *Indian Mounds Park.*

EUCLID STREET Labeled by one historian as the "eccentric troubadour," Ossian Euclid Dodge (1820–76) was a nationally known vocalist, journalist, and composer of popular music.

When his music store on Euclid Street in Cleveland, Ohio, failed and his literary efforts brought him little profit, he moved to St. Paul in 1862. Here he built a house downtown called Alpine Cottage, sold pianos, and speculated in real estate, naming this East Side street in 1873. Dodge also acted as the correspondent for a local newspaper in reporting the 1865 Lake Vermilion gold rush in northern Minnesota and served as secretary of the St. Paul Chamber of Commerce. However, Dodge made enemies, and a scandalous divorce gave him reason to sail for England, where he died two years later.

"The eccentric troubadour," Ossian Euclid Dodge, who named Euclid Street. Photograph courtesy of the Minnesota Historical Society.

EUSTIS STREET Samuel S. Eustis (1815–84) and his wife, Emily Clark Eustis (1819–1909), had a farm directly west of this street named in 1885 as part of St. Anthony Park. Samuel was born in Maine, Emily in New Hampshire; together they came to Minnesota with their children in 1855, settling at "Groveland," as the Midway area was then called. In 1867 they bought 200 acres at fourteen dollars an acre in an area today roughly west of Highway 280 and north of University Avenue. Their farmhouse, built in 1872, still stands at 3107 Fourth Street SE, Minneapolis, but it is now converted to apartments. The farmland was gradually sold off in the 1880s and 1890s for railroad and commercial use at prices of $1,000 to $2,000 an acre. See also *Groveland, Midway, St. Anthony Park*.

EVA STREET Originally Goodhue Street, the name was changed in 1876 to avoid duplication when the West Side was annexed by St. Paul. Many of these new names were those of women who remain unidentified. See also *Ada Street*.

EVERETT COURT Everett P. Wheeler, a New York attorney, was a major investor in St. Anthony Park when this street was named in 1885. The building at 1048 Everett Court is the former St. Anthony Park Train Depot, which originally stood west of the Raymond Avenue bridge on the north side of the tracks. See also *St. Anthony Park*.

EVERGREEN PLACE Intended as part of a connection between Summit Avenue and Edgcumbe Road, this street had been given a separate name in 1917 because it was then entirely within the confines of Park Nursery. Although never improved, it remained a public street until vacated in 1978 when the Wilder apartments were built on the Park Nursery site.

EXCHANGE STREET This downtown street was named in Rice and Irvine's Addition in 1849, probably for the commercial implications of the name, as in stock exchange and grain exchange. It is one of two streets in St. Paul that run north, south, east, and west. The oldest school building in the city, Assumption Catholic School, a gray limestone structure built in 1864 during the Civil War, is at 68 Exchange Street.

EXETER PLACE Previously part of Marlboro Avenue, this street was renamed when its neighborhood, Shadow Falls Park, was slated for upscale development in 1922. Exeter is a common English name without significance in this city. See also *Shadow Falls Park*.

FAIR PLACE Proximity to the Minnesota State Fairgrounds prompted this fair and reasonable name in 1913.

FAIRMOUNT AVENUE Originating in Crocus Hill as part of the Highland Park Addition, this street was named in 1883 for its pleasing sound. *Fair* is a common prefix; *mount* suggests its height over the river valley. See also *Crocus Hill, Kellogg Boulevard*.

FAIRVIEW AVENUE There have been several streets within the city bearing this unremarkable name at one time or another. The present one was named in 1886 in Howard Park. In 1924, because of increasing residential development west of Fairview Avenue and south of Randolph Avenue, the street was widened from 60 feet to 86 feet between Randolph Avenue and Edgcumbe Boulevard. Because width encourages speeding, this stretch of road has been a profitable source of fines from speeding drivers. The city's most recent response to increasing traffic is a center turn lane. This street marks a one-half section line on the land survey.

FALCON AVENUE See *Berland Place*.

FARRINGTON STREET Considered reticent and undemonstrative but an excellent businessman, John Farrington (1827–1905) was born in Ireland. He journeyed to the United States about 1833 and to St. Paul in 1850. After constructing the first brick store in the city, he engaged in the fur trade business and subsequently sold real estate, naming this street—now in the Ramsey Hill Historic District—in 1854 in Dayton and Irvine's Addition. For several years he was also a member of the Board of Public Works. See also *Lafond Lake, Ramsey Hill Historic District*.

FAUQUIER PLACE Named in the 1857 Borup and Payne's Addition, Fauquier is a county in Virginia, the home of Rice W. Payne, for whom Payne Avenue is named. See also *Albemarle Street, Bush Avenue, Greenbrier Street, Payne Avenue*.

FAYE STREET Faye (Mrs. Ernest H.) Williams worked for a local nursing home; her husband worked for the police department. Both were friends of Grege Beckett, plat commissioner when this street near Battle Creek was named in 1965. See also *Kim Place*.

FEDERAL CITY The intrepid urban traipser will search in vain for this fantasy. Toward the end of the nineteenth century, there were several attempts to create a new city between Minneapolis and St. Paul that would ultimately merge the two large cities. Federal City, the site of the new State Capitol Building, was to be in Desnoyer Park near the Town and Country Club, on twenty acres of land donated by John L. Merriam. The Minnesota Historical Society

Library has a copy of a pamphlet written by an "Optimist" and published in 1891 that purports to look back from 1916 on all the advantages that have accrued since Minneapolis and St. Paul combined to create Federal City. In terms of area, it would have been the largest city in the world. See also *Iglehart Avenue, Interurban District, Midway, Mississippi City, Paulapolis.*

FELLOWS LANE The Housing and Redevelopment Authority named this street near Lake Phalen in 1951 for Lieutenant Reid F. Fellows of the Army Air Corps, who was killed in Italy in 1943. This Franklin D. Roosevelt Homes development was dedicated to those who died in World War II.

FERDINAND STREET Originally named Willius Street, the name was changed in 1886 to avoid duplication. Ferdinand Willius (1830–1916) was a banker and onetime member of the city council. See also *Willius Street.*

FERNWOOD STREET This very common place name in the United States was applied in 1916 in Chelsea Heights. *Fern* implies coolness, and *wood* is a popular suffix. See also *Chelsea Heights.*

FERONIA AVENUE Like the others in Union Park, this name was most likely chosen in 1884 for its pleasing, green, and somewhat exotic sound. *Feronia* evokes the whisper of a fern, with its hint of a shaded, quiet place. Other street names in Union Park were Lynnhurst, Oakley, Pomona (now Fairview), Albion (Dewey), Westwood (Prior), and Waltham (St. Anthony). See also *Lake Iris, Union Park.*

FIELD AVENUE Emil A. Field was the president, and J. H. Field, secretary, of the Northwestern Lumber and Wrecking Company of Minneapolis, who platted the Homecroft Addition in 1907. *Croft* is an Old English word meaning "enclosure," a popular suffix at the time. See also *Homecroft.*

FIFIELD STREET Fifield is a lumbering village in Price County, Wisconsin, named for Lieutenant Governor Samuel S. Fifield. Two of the St. Anthony Park investors were in the Wisconsin lumber business when this street was named in 1885. See also *St. Anthony Park.*

FIFTH STREET The fifth street from the river, this is one of the original fifteen street names of the city, named in 1849. The 1928 Hopkins atlas shows a large pond (500 feet by 200 feet) between Hazel and Ruth Streets, between Fifth and Margaret Streets, just south of Eastern Heights Elementary School. Homes have been built around the perimeter of the block, leaving the old lakebed in the center as undeveloped open space. This is typical of the East Side, where developers skirted natural barriers instead of removing them. See also *East Side.*

FILLMORE AVENUE McCarthy Street, the original name of this West Side street, was changed in 1883, to what is most likely a reference to Millard Fillmore (1800–1874), president of the United States from 1850 to 1853. There is also a Minnesota county named for him. See also *West Side.*

FINN STREET William Finn (1819–89), the first permanent white settler in this area, was born in Ireland, immigrated to the United States, and enlisted in the Mexican War. In 1848,

The streetcar tracks are removed from Fifth Street between Broadway and Jackson Street. The St. Paul Hotel is in the distance. The old wood-block pavement is exposed under the newer asphalt. Photograph courtesy of the St. Paul Department of Public Works.

as payment for his military service, he received a grant of land extending from today's Marshall Avenue to St. Clair Avenue, and Fairview Avenue to the river. He built his house where the University of St. Thomas now stands and farmed the adjacent property. Later he sold his farm to the Catholic Church for an industrial school, and it was Archbishop John Ireland who bestowed this street name in 1889 within the Groveland plat. See also *Groveland*.

FINN'S GLEN Adjacent to the St. Paul Seminary, south of Summit Avenue, this small, private ravine is on the east side of Mississippi River Boulevard. Presently used as a place of meditation, it was named for the first white settler in this area, William Finn. The glen contained a small stream draining a wetland between (today) Fairview and Snelling Avenues, between St. Clair and Randolph Avenues, a fact well illustrated on the 1867 map of Reserve Township. See also *Finn Street*, *Grotto*, *Reserve Township*.

FIR STREET Previously Bellevue, the name of this Highwood street was changed in 1940. See also *Highwood*.

FISH CREEK Fish Creek in the southeast corner of the city is one of the few streams left within the city limits. It takes its name from Fish Lake (now renamed Carver Lake), which in turn was probably named for David Fish, an early settler in McLean Township with a farm along Upper Afton Road. This name also embraces a 130-acre Ramsey County Open Space accessible off Highway 61. The intrepid urban traipser wishing to dip a toe in the creek would go south of Carver Avenue on Point Douglas Road about two blocks. Between 1388 and 1464 Point Douglas Road, you will find a bump-out on the north side of the road with a metal utility cabinet reading "Peller Lift Station, 1444 Pt. Douglas Road." Walk into the woods behind the utility cabinet, and you will discover the creek bubbling through the woods. A stroll up the path along the creek will reveal the WPA stonework from the 1930s as well as the scenic sandstone bluff eroded by the creek. See also *Creeks/Brooks*.

FISH HATCHERY ROAD The nation's first fish hatchery opened in New York State in 1864. In 1877 the Minnesota Legislature authorized the construction of a hatchery in St. Paul, below Dayton's Bluff. Within a year, the Willow Brook state fish hatchery opened under the auspices of the Minnesota State Fish Commission. Tourists descended a steep, zigzagging road to visit this early landmark with its small wildlife museum. The hatchery was the foundation for a grandiose plan by the fish commission to stock trout and Pacific salmon throughout Minnesota. Turn-of-the-century records indicate salmon were supplied to Lake Minnetonka, the Minnesota River, and other locations, where, as the early breeders learned, the fish could not survive.

Originally the hatchery contained seven spring-fed ponds, although by the 1940s, the springs had begun to dry up. Outdoor raceways and ponds were abandoned and the fish moved to indoor tanks. After the springs completely dried up in the 1960s, wells were dug to supply water. During the 1980s the Minnesota Department of Natural Resources raised Atlantic salmon for stocking in Lake Superior, a program discontinued in 1992 because of poor results. Before it closed in 1995, the hatchery was used to raise rainbow trout, lake trout, and splake, a cross between brook and lake trout.

FISK STREET Born in New York, James L. Fisk (1835–1902) came to Minnesota in the 1850s. He rose to the rank of captain in the Civil War and subsequently led expeditions to the gold fields of Montana. His Summit-University–area street was named in 1857. An adjacent street was originally named for Stephen Miller, also a Civil War commander. See also *Summit-University*.

FLANDRAU STREET Remembered as a "first-class lawyer and a first class man," Charles E. Flandrau (1825–1903) was a soldier and judge. Born in New York City, where he studied law in his father's office, he moved to St. Paul in 1853. He became an influential member of the Minnesota Constitutional Convention, after which he was appointed associate justice of the Minnesota Supreme Court. Flandrau was commander of the defense of New Ulm during the Dakota Conflict and later an unsuccessful candidate for governor. This street was named in his honor in 1886. *Flandrau Place* is a southern extension of this street near Battle Creek. See also *Battle Creek*.

A worker tending to the fingerlings in the fish hatchery around 1900. Photograph courtesy of the Minnesota Historical Society.

FLORENCE AVENUE William and Carrie Johnson of Ramsey County added this street to the city in 1910. Florence is most likely connected with that family, but it would be tricky to locate her among all the Johnsons. This street in the vicinity of Battle Creek Park was vacated in 1988. See also *Battle Creek Park*.

FLORIDA STREET Previously Eighth Street, the West Side name was changed in 1876 and, like the adjacent streets, named for a state. See also *Alabama Street, Colorado Street, Kentucky Street*.

FLYNN STREET Known as "the confidant of half of the Court House and City Hall," Hilary J. Flynn (1898–1954) was born in St. Paul. Educated at St. Thomas College and admitted to the bar in 1922, Flynn subsequently became prosecuting attorney for the city. In 1956, this street name recognized his career with the city as research bureau director, where he drafted ordinances, provided the city council with background material, and represented the city to the legislature. Alas, famous Flynn's fame was fleeting. This street was vacated in 1983 with the development of Energy Park. See also *Energy Park*.

FOLSOM STREET Considered "tenacious as an old hickory tree," Simeon Pearl Folsom (1819–1907) was city plat commissioner at the naming of this street, part of Como Heights, in 1887. A true pioneer of the city, Folsom was born in Canada, grew up in New Hampshire, and roamed the West before coming to St. Paul in 1847. Here he took up the real-estate business, becoming city surveyor in 1854. He founded the first abstract and title company in the city, served in various civic posts, fought in the Civil War, later worked extensively for the railroads, and served as attorney for the St. Paul water commissioners.

FORBES AVENUE William Henry Forbes (1815–75) was a clerk for the American Fur Company post at Mendota when this West End street was named in Leach's Addition in 1849. With his wife, Agnes, he became a resident of St. Paul in 1847, when the settlement had five stores, about twenty families, and thirty-six children, composed of French, English, Swiss, Dakota, Ojibwe, and African descent, making the total population no more than fifty. Forbes—impulsive, kind-hearted, generous, social—served in the Civil War and later served as Indian agent at Devil's Lake, North Dakota. See also *Leech Street*, *West End*.

FORD PARKWAY Originally platted in part as St. Catherine Avenue, the street was renamed Edsel Avenue and, in 1924, Ford Road. Both Edsel and Ford are references to the Ford Motor Company, which purchased 200 acres of land along the Mississippi River to build its $10,000,000 manufacturing plant in the 1920s. In a unique negotiation, this land purchase was contingent on obtaining the hydroelectric power from Lock and Dam Number 1 (Ford Dam), which had been recently constructed to accommodate navigation upriver to Minneapolis. After a contentious battle between Minneapolis and St. Paul over the use of the waterpower, the Ford Motor Company leased the electricity generated by the dam to operate its Highland Park assembly plant. The Ford Parkway bridge was located to provide Minneapolis workers easy access to employment at the Ford Plant. See also *Highland Park, St. Paul Avenue*.

FORBES & KITTSON,

Corner Third and Roberts Streets,

SAINT PAUL, - MINNESOTA.

WHOLESALE AND RETAIL DEALERS IN

Indian Goods, Furs and Pelts.

ALSO A LARGE ASSORTMENT OF

FANCY DRY GOODS.

THE HIGHEST MARKET PRICE PAID FOR FURS AND PELTS.

William H. Forbes, for whom the street is named, dealt in real estate as well as fancy dry goods. Advertisement in the *Business Directory for the City of St. Paul, Minnesota Territory*, 1856.

Cars manufactured at the Ford Motor Company are loaded onto river barges below the factory, circa 1925. Photograph courtesy of the Minnesota Historical Society.

FOREST HILL OVAL See *Woodlawn Oval*.

FOREST STREET Applied in 1857, this East Side street name evokes the image of a dense growth of trees and underbrush. Adjacent streets were Birch, Elm, and Hazel. All those names have disappeared, thus toppling the old adage, "You can't see the trees for the forest."

FOREST STREET TRIANGLE This tiny public park at East Seventh and Forest Streets, nicely land-scaped with trees and benches, was acquired in 1902. Today there are only two sides to the "triangle," the third side appropriated by a parking lot.

FORSTER STREET Previously unnamed, this West End street was designated by the city council in 1887. This was a fairly common surname; it is uncertain who, what, or where might be signified. See also *West End*.

FORT ROAD This is an alternate name for West Seventh Street, based on the fact it was an early road between downtown St. Paul and Fort Snelling. However, the original road between downtown St. Paul and Fort Snelling, called Old Fort Road, actually followed the river bluff. See also *Cliff Street, Stewart Avenue*.

FOUNDRY PARK A one-acre public park on the North End, dedicated in the Foundry Addition (St. Paul Foundry Company) in 1883, was on the east side of Arundel Street between Topping and Burgess Streets. The park, where factory workers could catch a glimpse of the sun while they ate lunch, was sold about 1937 and has since been swallowed up in an industrial complex. See also *Topping Street*.

FOUNTAIN CAVE Located in a West End triangle bounded by Randolph Avenue, Drake Street, and Shepard Road, this cave was first described by explorer Major Stephen H. Long in 1817, who named it for the spring water flowing from its opening. In 1838, whiskey entrepreneur Pierre "Pig's Eye" Parrant stashed his illicit wares in the cave and built a shack at the entrance, which legend has it was the first building in the city. Thus, Fountain Cave is sometimes called the birthplace of St. Paul; Native Americans called it the New Stone House.

By the 1850s, Fountain Cave had become a commercial attraction, hosting subterranean torchlight tours. According to Greg Brick, an authority on the underground Twin Cities, the glory days of Fountain Cave ended about 1880 when the overlying Omaha railroad shops drilled a shaft into the cave and began using it as a convenient sewer.

Physically it was far grander than Carver's Cave downriver. Fountain Cave, with a length of over 1,000 feet, was the longest natural sandstone cave in Minnesota. A surface stream, known as Fountain Creek, draining the Fort Road wetlands, entered a sinkhole at the upstream end of the cave and flowed through the cave and out into a winding, 400-foot ravine

A stereo view looking out from Fountain Cave. Photograph courtesy of the Minnesota Historical Society.

leading to the Mississippi River. The cave contained four rooms, one bestowed with the enticing name of Cascade Parlor because it had a waterfall.

The entrance was buried during the construction of Shepard Road in 1960, but the cavern remains, commemorated by a historical marker. For more information, see the excellent article "St. Paul Underground" by Greg Brick. See also *Carver's Cave, Dayton's Cave, Fort Road, Pigs Eye, West End*.

FOUNTAIN CREEK See *Fountain Cave*.

FOUNTAIN PARK A one-half-acre public triangle at Lexington Parkway and Watson Avenue (an unopened street at this point) dedicated to the public in the Lexington Park plat in 1886—well before there were homes in this part of the city. Today this "ghost park" is nothing more than an unmarked wooded vacant lot between 579 and 603 South Lexington Parkway. The name may have come from a hillside spring in the park. See also *Ghost Parks*.

FOUNTAIN PLACE Originally part of Preble Street, the name was changed in 1890. A century ago, on the sweeping hillside in front of the only home on the street, number 614, a series of waterfalls cascaded into a large stone pool in Swede Hollow. The whole arrangement was graced with stone fences, walkways, terraces, and to one side, a wrought-iron rose trellis. To follow this obscure street into the past, the intrepid urban traipser would turn north on Bates Avenue off East Seventh Street, go west on North Street, and turn right into the cul-de-sac of Fountain Place.

FOURTEENTH STREET Platted in 1856, this is the fourteenth street from the river.

FOURTH STREET The 1849 plat of St. Paul Proper established this among the original fifteen street names of the city. The intrepid urban traipser will want to experience one of the few time-warp passageways remaining from the pioneer days—it runs east from downtown John Street, across and under the railroad tracks to Commercial Street below Mounds Park. This is a remnant of the first road between St. Paul and Point Douglas, a trading center where the St. Croix and Mississippi rivers meet. It is along this street, beneath an early stone railroad bridge, that Trout Brook breaks out of the storm sewer and gurgles to the river. The brook, an important geographic feature in the development of St. Paul, flowed from McCarron's Lake, powering several early mills. Large, dramatic stone walls, imparting an old-world look to this forgotten bit of cityscape, embrace this historic fragment of Fourth Street now incorporated into the Bruce Vento Regional Trail. See also *Bruce Vento Nature Sanctuary, Bruce Vento Regional Trail, Trout Brook, Trout Brook Sewer*.

FOXRIDGE ROAD As the developer William D. Clapp put it, this 1970 name "just sounded nice."

FRANK STREET William Dawson, Robert Smith, and John Terry (1824–1902) platted this street in 1873. Terry's son, Frank, lived in Seattle at the time of his father's death. A pond, almost a block square, is illustrated in the 1928 Hopkins atlas at the end of Wakefield Avenue between Frank Street and Johnson Parkway. See also *Alice Street, Brickyards Lake, Mears Park*.

FRANKLIN AVENUE Previously Bayard Street, the name was changed in 1926 to continue the Minneapolis avenue into the Midway. The original Franklin Street in downtown St. Paul was changed to Auditorium Street, which has since been vacated. See also *Auditorium Street*.

FRANKENSTEIN'S CAVE See *Banholzer's Brewery Cave*.

FRANKSON AVENUE Thomas Frankson (1869–1939) was lieutenant governor of Minnesota from 1917–21. Born in Fillmore County, he graduated from the University of Minnesota Law School in 1900. Returning to his home in Spring Valley, Minnesota, he entered the real-estate business, where he had far-flung investments. Frankson, who later served in the state legislature, purchased and developed property around Como Park, naming this street in 1913. He lived in St. Paul in his later years; Frankson's house, built about 1915, remains at 1349 Midway Parkway. See also *Bison Avenue*.

FRED STREET This street was named in 1882 for Fred M. Turnbull, son of George and Amanda Turnbull, the developers. Only sixteen-and-one-half-feet-wide between Desoto and Burr Streets, it is the narrowest street in the city—so small, it was a good thing it wasn't named Frederick! See also *Petit Street*.

FREEDOM BRIDGE See *Wabasha Freedom Bridge*.

FREMONT AVENUE Originally Hazel Street, the name was changed in 1872 to honor John C. Fremont (1813–90), an American soldier, explorer ("the pathfinder"), and politician. In 1856 and 1864 he was a presidential candidate and later served as governor of Arizona Territory. Between White Bear Avenue and Hazel Street, between Third and Fifth Streets, there is a private wooded area the intrepid urban traipser would want to explore. Fremont's pathfinding prowess prevails, providing peripatetic public perusal of this place through a sun-dappled passageway along an unimproved portion of Fremont Avenue, west of Hazel Street.

FROGTOWN This neighborhood is roughly between University and Minnehaha Avenues, between Dale Street and Rice Street–Como Avenue. Of several explanations for this name, Alexius Hoffman, who grew up in St. Paul in the 1870s, offers the most convincing origin. He writes that the area south of University Av-

This lone tamarack tree across from St. Agnes Church is a remnant of the time when much of the area in eastern Frogtown was tamarack swampland. Photograph by Kathleen M. Vadnais.

enue, between Rice Street and Western Avenue, was known as Froschenburg, or Frogtown, because of the many vocal frogs in the local swamps. As this early neighborhood jumped north across University Avenue into an equally swampy area with its own frogs, the name became attached to the environs we describe as Frogtown today. See also *Angst und Bang, Bohnenviertel, Bunker Hill, Lafond Lake.*

FRONT AVENUE This was the first, or front, street on the 1856 plat map of Lake Como Villas. The other names were equally unimaginative, and thankfully none of them remains. However, around 1900, the city attempted to change the name of Front Avenue to Larpenteur, but the street's residents came forward to present a united front, standing behind the original name. In the earliest days of the city, Oakhill Cemetery was situated on the northeast corner of Front and Western Avenues. This street marks a one-half section line on the land survey. See also *Cemeteries, Larpenteur Avenue, Weber's Pond.*

FRONTENAC PLACE Previously Glenham Avenue, the name of this Desnoyer Park street was changed in 1940 to avoid duplication. Frontenac is a place name in several states; in Minnesota the village is on Lake Pepin. There is a striking pueblo-inspired house from the 1920s at 510 Frontenac Place. See also *Desnoyer Park.*

FROST LAKE This is both the name of a lake and the surrounding neighborhood. John W. S. Frost (1822–1903), a dairy farmer, and his wife, Elizabeth Ide Frost (1824–1905), made a claim in Section 22, south of the lake bearing their name, in 1852. He was born in Vermont, she in Quebec; both are buried in Oakland Cemetery. The propitiously named Pioneer Real Estate and Building Society invested in this property near Lake Phalen in 1882. The lake, once much larger, has become a storm-water pond. The neighborhood might be roughly defined as between Kennard and Clarence Streets, between Arlington and Larpenteur Avenues. See also *Lakes/Ponds, McAfee Street.*

FROST LAKE PARK This twelve-acre public park at Hoyt Avenue and Barclay Street takes its name from the adjacent Frost Lake.

FRY STREET William and Ann Fry were among the developers of this Midway street in 1875. Fry was born in Germany and came to St. Paul about 1872, where he worked as an insurance agent. He apparently left St. Paul in 1879. See also *Midway.*

Federal funds flowing into many St. Paul neighborhoods, like Frost Lake, have given them a new sense of identity and pride. Photograph by Kathleen M. Vadnais.

FULHAM STREET Fulham is a part of London; this is one of several English names used in St. Anthony Park in 1885. See also *St. Anthony Park*.

FULLER AVENUE Alpheus G. Fuller (1822–1900), born in Connecticut, arrived in St. Paul around 1850 and built a well-known downtown hotel called the Fuller House, now long gone. Remembered as a man of "spare and tall" build, he moved to Sioux Falls, the first white settlement in South Dakota. He named this street—near University Avenue—in 1856 in Fuller's Addition. See also *Hare's Lake*.

FULTON STREET Originally Fourth, the name of this West End street was changed in 1872 to honor Robert Fulton (1765–1815), inventor of the steamboat. Fulton also developed the submarine, torpedo, a type of cast iron bridge, and a device to hoist canal boats. Another street was renamed Clermont at this same time, for his first steamboat. See also *Clermont Street*.

FURNESS PARKWAY Furness Street was named in 1913 when the 160-acre farm of Governor Alexander Ramsey was subdivided into the Furness Garden Lots. Marion Furness, the daughter of Governor Ramsey, inherited this East Side property. The original farmhouse remains, although much altered, at 1488 Furness Parkway.

In December 1979, at the instigation of the Furness Parkway Improvement Committee, Curve Street and Furness Street became Furness Parkway, incorporating the abandoned right-of-way of a streetcar line to White Bear Lake. From Larpenteur Avenue the parkway extends southwest to Maryland Avenue, turning due south where it crosses the railroad tracks on a recycled pedestrian bridge brought here after years of service on Hamline Avenue. See also *Ramsey Street*.

Marion Ramsey Furness, the daughter of Governor Alexander Ramsey, with her children. She sold his estate and named a street for herself. Photograph courtesy of the Minnesota Historical Society.

G

GABRIEL ROAD Formerly the driveway to the ten-acre Highwood estate of Thomas and Gabriel McGuire, this street was added to the city in 1955 when the property was divided among the descendants. The original McGuire house, built in 1913, remains at 2100 Spring-side Drive. See also *Highwood*.

GALTIER STREET Originally Oak Street, the name of this street originating near the Capitol was changed in 1872 to honor Lucien Galtier (1811–66), a Roman Catholic priest. Born in France, he was ordained in Dubuque, Iowa, and moved to Mendota (then called St. Peter's) in 1840. As part of his missionary work, he built a log chapel near what is today Minnesota Street and Kellogg Boulevard, dedicated to St. Paul—and thus our city derived its permanent name. In 1941, a granite block with two bronze tablets commemorating the Chapel of St. Paul was dedicated on the Kellogg Mall close to Robert Street, where it remains today. Edwin Lundie, a well-known St. Paul architect, designed this monument. See also *Cretin Avenue, John Ireland Boulevard, Lafond Lake, Pacific Lake, Ravoux Street, St. Paul*.

GANNON ROAD In a reconfiguration of Shepard Road and West Seventh Street, West Seventh Boulevard was changed to Gannon Road by the city council in 1979. Tom Gannon was the first owner of the once-popular Gannon's Restaurant at 2728 West Seventh Street.

GARDEN WAY This private street on the west side of Hazel Street between Wilson Avenue and Old Hudson Road was authorized by the city council in August 2005.

GARFIELD STREET Previously Green Street in the West End, it was renamed in October 1881 for James A. Garfield, president of the United States, who had been assassinated the previous month. See also *West End*.

GARY PLACE Alexander G. Tankenoff, president of the Hillcrest Development Company, who platted this area as Hillcrest Center, named this street in 1948 for his eldest son, Gary.

GATEWAY DRIVE This is the gateway to Como Park.

GATEWAY PARK Opened in 1993, this park at Energy Park Drive and Raymond Avenue is not owned by the city.

GATEWAY TRAIL This is the local connection to the multiple-use Willard Munger State Trail system between St. Paul and Duluth. This popular twenty-mile segment provides biking, hiking, in-line skating, horseback riding, and cross-country skiing along an abandoned railroad right-of-way.

GATEWAY VILLAGE A new $93-million housing development for about six hundred residents is on the south side of West Seventh Street, between Norfolk Avenue, Davern Street, and Munster Avenue. The name heralds a key entrance from the west into St. Paul. See also *West End*.

GAUGER PARK See *Augustus Gauger Park*.

GENESEE STREET Edmund Rice named this North End street in 1870 for the county of the same name in western New York State, originating from an Iroquois word meaning "valley beautiful." In the early days of the city, before there were water pipes, the fire department built and maintained cisterns collecting water for dousing fires in the neighborhood. One such cistern was on the southeast corner of Buffalo and Genesee Streets. As the water department expanded its lines, the cisterns were gradually replaced by fire hydrants. See also *North End, St. Peter Street*.

GEORGE STREET George W. H. Bell (1812–1900) was the first white settler across the river in what is now the West Side of St. Paul. Arriving in Minnesota, he claimed 160 acres in 1851, including property between Bancroft Avenue and State Street, and the present-day Riverview Industrial Park. This street, one of the first on the West Side, was named in 1855 in what was then West St. Paul. As the city grew, he gradually divided his claim into building lots and sold them. In 1929, South Robert Street (then the Capitol Highway) was cut down between Concord and Sidney Streets, and an automobile bridge constructed at George Street, along with a pedestrian bridge at Stevens Street. See also *West Side*.

GERANIUM AVENUE Harwood Iglehart, William Hall, and Charles Mackubin, natives of Maryland, may have had that state's more temperate climate in mind when naming this East Side street in 1857. See also *East Side, Iglehart Avenue, Mackubin Street*.

GERMAIN STREET The first Germain Street near Lake Phalen was named in 1886. Two years later, the name relocated two blocks west to its present position. The germane facts are that the street name on the plat appears to be Germania, the Latin word for Germany, while Germain is the French word for Germany. Germania was a popular term at the time; Germain most likely borrows from it. *Germain Court* takes its name from the same source.

GHOST PARKS The author has coined this term denoting parks that have been dedicated to the public but for one reason or another are unmarked. See *Dawson Park, Elm Square, Fountain Park, Hamline/Ashland Park, Howell Park, Leroy Triangle, McDonough Park, Oakland Terrace Park, Point of View Park, Putnam Park, Skidmore Park, Sunshine Place, Walsh Park*.

GHOST STREETS The author has coined this term to denote invisible streets that have been platted and officially exist as public right-of-way but for one reason or another have never been graded, paved, or signed. There are a number of these streets within St. Paul, representing a valuable cache of public land that could be useful in the future. Locating these "ghost streets" requires considerable time and research; there is no compilation. After one of them does come to public attention, it is often vacated: a process in which the street becomes the private property of the adjacent owners. There are also "ghost walks." See *Boxwood Avenue, Burg Street, Corning Avenue, Greenland Avenue, Mystic Street, Neill Street, Nettleton Avenue, Piedmont Street, Randall Street, Scherers Lane, Wheeler Walk, Wilmot Avenue, Wolsey Street*.

GIBBS AVENUE Previously Rich Street, the name was changed in 1888. Heman R. Gibbs (1815–91), an early pioneer in the area—who was not rich—claimed 160 acres in an area today between Cleveland Avenue and Fulham Street, between Larpenteur and Roselawn Avenues. He built a frame house in 1854 and greatly enlarged it in 1867. His house remains at 2097 West Larpenteur Avenue, maintained as a museum by the Ramsey County Historical Society.

GILBERT AVENUE This Midway street was platted in 1887 by Celestia and Newington Gilbert of Washington County, Minnesota. See also *Midway*.

GLEN TERRACE Part of the Glen Terrace Addition, this West End street was named in 1912. *Terrace* was a nineteenth-century word for hillside. See *Kipp's Glen, West End*.

GLENDALE STREET *Glen* is a popular prefix, *dale* a popular suffix; both mean "valley." This Midway street name was applied in 1887. It has been written that Stephen Desnoyer's Halfway House was located at the corner of Glendale Street and St. Anthony Avenue; however, the plat of Shield's Enlargement of Roseville, drawn in 1873, depicts the Halfway House near what would be today the intersection of Fairview Avenue and Interstate 94. See also *Desnoyer Avenue*.

GLENRIDGE AVENUE See *Berland Place*.

GOODHUE STREET Originally platted as Grove Street in 1849, this West End street name was changed in 1872 to honor James M. Goodhue (1810–52). He was born in New Hampshire, admitted to the bar in New York, and practiced law in Illinois and Wisconsin before migrating to St. Paul in 1849, where he established the first newspaper in the state. Goodhue was a man of what used to be called "warm temperament," meaning he had a quick temper and strong opinions that made him many enemies and friends. Although the masthead of his newspaper read, "Sound Principles, Safe Men, And Moderate Measures," he was once attacked and stabbed as the result of his fervent editorializing. An ardent booster of St. Paul and Minnesota, he exploited every opportunity to promote their increase. A Minnesota county is also named in his honor. See also *West End*.

GOODRICH AVENUE "A walking encyclopedia of ancient and biblical history; an arsenal of fun and fact; a magazine full of argumentative missiles; a volcanic explosion in the midst of the religious element, and a generally accepted electric battery, from which a thousand positive forces penetrate the citadels of bigotry and ignorance." Thus reads one description of Aaron Goodrich (1807–87), for whom this street was named in Leach's Addition in 1849. Chief justice of Minnesota Territory, active in the legal organization of the state, he was also a founder of the Republican Party in Minnesota.

The intrepid urban traipser might want to visit the very eastern end of Goodrich Avenue at Leech Street to discover at 178 Goodrich Avenue a handsome Civil War–era limestone house. During a period of expansion in the 1980s, United Hospitals sought to purchase and demolish this residence along with many others. A true heroine of history, Joan Lisi safeguarded her unique home. Impoverished and barely able to pay her utilities, she endured with a hole in an exterior wall, and a kitchen ceiling that had fallen in. After the surrounding houses had been demolished, her mission became even more fervent. United Hospitals and a number of speculators were knocking at Joan's door with increasing enticements to buy her house for demolition. But, uncomfortable as she was in her decrepit dwelling, often without heat, Joan withstood all requests to buy, knowing this rare historic stone house would disappear the moment she moved out. At last, after years of negotiation, United Hospitals agreed to move the house from 314 North Smith Avenue to its present site, and bring it into compliance with the building code as a condition of the purchase from Joan. See also *Iglehart Avenue, Mt. Curve Boulevard*.

GORDON AVENUE This street name, applied in 1885 in St. Anthony Park, is probably that of some investor, but his identity has not been saved. *Gordon Place* is an extension of Gordon Avenue. See also *St. Anthony Park*.

GORDON SQUARE This small public square in St. Anthony Park at Gordon and Blake Streets was named on the original plat in 1885. See also *St. Anthony Park*.

GORMAN AVENUE Called an "ill-bred, second-rate, barroom politician," Willis A. Gorman (1816–76) was governor of Minnesota Territory when this West Side street was named in

---

NAVIGATING WITHOUT NUMBERS OR ALPHABET

The Great St. Paul Street Name Debate

There have been sporadic attempts to change the street naming system in St. Paul, but only one sustained effort has been made. In August 1907 Postmaster Edward Yanish proposed to the Commercial Club that St. Paul adopt the Philadelphia plan of naming and numbering streets. According to Yanish, Rice Street, Wabasha Street, Summit Avenue, and Hudson Avenue would divide the city into quadrants, each of which would have its own numbered sequence of streets. The West Side, with just twenty-six streets, would be arranged alphabetically.

By the following March the city council had appointed a committee to investigate changing the street name system. The local representative of the R. L. Polk Company, publisher of the city directory, proclaimed that St. Paul was as chaotic as Boston, and the sooner a new plan was adopted, the better off the city would be.

A month later, reinforcement for a new system came from an editorial in the *St. Paul Pioneer Press* venturing the opinion that

> in view of the fact that streets are named not for the purpose of embalming the memory of departed real estate dealers and their children, or of demonstrating their

poetic fancy, but to serve as indices of the location of homes and business houses, and in view of the further fact that under any plan suggested there is room for the presentation of all important names of local flavor and significance, the Pioneer Press is at present inclined to think that the practical advantages to be gained by any reasonably simple and systematic plan far outweigh the sentimental and practical objections that have been raised.

By now, the opposition had mustered.

A letter to the editor signed by "A conservative" queried "Who wants to be located by a vulgar fraction?" and reminded the readers of Henry Wadsworth Longfellow, who said, "We cannot buy with gold the old associations." In July, an article appeared in the St. Paul Dispatch proclaiming the women of the city against any change. In ending, the article declared:

> No, the women are dead against it; they think St. Paul would lose its distinctiveness, and they believe that it would be to dishonor the men who struggled to make it what it is, to obliterate the old names and give us numbers as if we were in a penitentiary. So there, Mr. Postmaster, you know how we feel about it.

In December 1908 the women circulated a petition containing hundreds of signatures protesting any change in the system of street names. Besides the sentiment involved, they also claimed that the peculiar topography of certain parts of the city prevented any regular arrangement of the street names.

In March 1909, a year and a half after the new system was first proposed, the committee appointed by the city council was still meeting, but by this date they found it expedient to invite the women to meet with them. By September the committee was prepared to submit its recommendations to the city council for action. Miffed by the continuing opposition from so many prominent women in the city, the committee members, with male arrogance, ventured their opinion that if the women only thoroughly understood the new system, they would certainly favor it.

In December the committee was still refining a master plan that by then included a number of personal names that would also serve as numerical streets, in the way that Lake Street in Minneapolis also serves as Thirtieth Street.

In the summer of 1911, the proposed street name system finally came before the city council, where it was promptly referred to the Committee on Streets, who waited to act until "all voices had been heard." In October of that same year, while the proposed ordinance was still in council committee, several of the aldermen expressed their feelings that popular sentiment was opposed to any change. The aldermen further asserted that while one of the objects in adopting the ordinance would be to facilitate the delivery of mail in St. Paul, the post office had recently cut back its service and consequently districts of the city formerly having two or three deliveries a day were now receiving only one delivery. Thus, the aldermen concluded, because the post office had retrenched on their service, the city would not gain by changing the names of the streets to expedite delivery of the mail.

There the matter ended.

Aren't you relieved?

1855. Born in Kentucky, he moved to Indiana with his parents, graduated from law school, was elected to the legislature for several terms, and served in the Mexican War. In 1853, President Franklin Pierce appointed him governor of our territory, largely because Gorman favored slavery. He was an astute, ruthless, and blustery officeholder who felt the end justified the means. As governor, he and several legislators owning large chunks of land near St. Peter, Minnesota, conspired to hijack the capital from St. Paul to St. Peter. They were defeated only when a craftier legislator stole the enabling bill and disappeared. Shaking his head, a disappointed Gorman was heard to snarl that he would "live long enough to see grass grow in the streets of St. Paul." (Actually there is grass growing in the streets of St. Paul. See *Osceola Avenue*.) See also *Burnquist Street*, *Clough Street*, *Hubbard Avenue*, *Johnson Parkway*, *Marshall Avenue*, *Merriam Lane*, *Ramsey Street*, *Scudder Street*, *Sibley Street*, *West St. Paul Park*.

Governor Willis A. Gorman was called an "ill-bred, second-rate, barroom politician." Photograph by Whitney's Gallery; courtesy of the Minnesota Historical Society.

GOTZIAN STREET Adam and Josephine Gotzian were the developers of this East Side street in 1883. Born in Germany, Adam came to St. Paul in 1860, working with his brother, Conrad, in the boot and shoe trade. Not wishing to cobble together a living in this fashion, he later dabbled in real estate. See also *East Side*.

GOVE PLACE Emma B. Gove was secretary of the St. Paul Mutual Insurance Company, one of the two companies deeding this land to the city in 1937 for a St. Anthony Park street. See also *St. Anthony Park*.

GRACE LANE Theron and Grace B. Anderson lived on Upper Afton Road for many years and named this nearby street in 1953.

GRACE STREET Originally platted as College Street in 1856, the name was changed in 1872 for Thomas L. Grace (1814–97), a Roman Catholic archbishop whose name appears on several additions to St. Paul. Like Archbishop John Ireland, it appears Bishop Grace was a land speculator. This new name was probably heartily endorsed by Thomas Grace (1826–1905), a building contractor and mason, who was a member of the City Council Committee on Streets at the time of the change. The western part of Grace Street is now Stanford Avenue. See also *John Ireland Boulevard, West End*.

GRAHAM AVENUE John A. Graham owned fifty-five acres in the southwest corner of the city near this short street in 1891. He is listed as a resident of the city for only one year.

GRAND AVENUE *Grand* has two meanings: the English sense of magnificent and sublime, common in the eastern United States; and the Spanish sense of large, more common in the western states. An Englishman, John Wann, named this street in 1871. Wann, an official of the St. Paul Railway Company, operated the first horse-drawn car line on tracks along Grand Avenue in 1872, where the cars, distinguished by a red flag, ran hourly. In 1890, an electric streetcar line replaced the horses. Today Grand Avenue is a bustling retail street in the city, attracting thousands to an annual festival. See also *Chatsworth Street, Hare's Lake*.

GRAND HILL When Oakland Avenue was changed to Grand Avenue in 1970, this portion of Grand Avenue was changed to Grand Hill. The change was at the insistence of the Grand Avenue Business Association, which wished to extend Grand Avenue to West Seventh Street and thus have it become a signed exit on Interstate 35E to attract customers to Grand Avenue. However, it did not quite work out because the southbound exit for the expected influx was nixed. See also *Grand Avenue, Oakland Avenue*.

GRAND MARAIS See *Pigs Eye*.

GRAND ROUNDS In the 1870s as the St. Paul parks system was being fashioned, the progressive landscape architects, including Horace W. S. Cleveland, thought of the park system as more than a few municipal parks. They conceived of a park as a continuous element, a green ribbon embellished with flowers pervading the city. In their scheme, the large open parks, or "public reservations," were connected by parkways or boulevards, which in themselves served as a linear park. With this in mind, they devised a citywide plan that resembles the figure eight. Over the years, the details have changed, but in general, one "round," or loop, begins at Como Park and continues west on Midway Parkway, Commonwealth Avenue through the Minnesota State Fairgrounds, Raymond Avenue to Pelham Boulevard, Mississippi River Boulevard to Edgcumbe Road, Lexington Parkway, and back to Como Park to complete one loop of the figure eight.

The second round would grace Summit Avenue to Kellogg Boulevard, the Third Street bridge to Mounds Parkway and Boulevard, Johnson Parkway to Lake Phalen, and Wheelock Parkway back to Como Park.

The figure eight was intersected by Como Avenue, which connected, by way of Capitol Boulevard, Central Park near the Capitol, and Como Park.

This whole system, sometimes called the "Grand Rounds," linked with a comparable parkway system in Minneapolis by way of Mississippi River Boulevard at both its north and south ends. For many years, these St. Paul parkways were patrolled by a separate law enforcement unit called the St. Paul Park Police, and since almost the beginning, large trucks and commercial vehicles have been banned on the parkways. Today there is an attempt to incorporate some of the new city trails into this scheme, although there seems to be some misunderstanding of the original Grand Rounds. See also *Central Park, Cleveland Avenue, Como Park, Edgcumbe Road, Mississippi River Boulevard, Nusbaumer Drive, Summit Lookout Park, Warrendale.*

GRANITE STREET A rock inspired this North End street named in Edmund Rice's Second Addition in 1870, suggesting permanence, steadfastness, and beauty. The intersection of Agate and Granite Streets is a hard place to find. See also *Edmund Avenue.*

GRANTHAM STREET A village in England, near London, inspired this St. Anthony Park street name in 1885. See also *St. Anthony Park.*

GREAT NORTHERN BUSINESS CENTER Twenty-two acres are embraced by this Port Authority project on the southeast corner of Topping and Dale Streets. Although acquiring and cleaning up the land cost the Port Authority $13.5 million, businesses in the center receive free land in exchange for an agreement to create new jobs and hire mostly St. Paul residents to fill them. A second phase of the center will be created on an adjacent thirteen acres. The name comes from the Great Northern Railroad tracks nearby. See also *Atwater Circle.*

GREAT NORTHERN POND This is a wetlands and pond just north of Pierce Butler Route at Prior Avenue on the east side of the composting site at that location. Part of the Bridal Veil watershed before the construction of Highway 280, the pond now drains to the Mississippi River through the sewer system. The first surveyor's notes in 1847 record the pond as being about 400 yards in length. The name comes from the railroad tracks that run nearby. See also *Bridal Veil Creek, Lakes/Ponds.*

GREEN STAIRS Officially known as the Wabasha South–Channel Street steps, this dramatic West Side landmark ascends 191 steps from Wabasha Street to Hall Avenue. The green steel and wood public stairway dates back to at least 1916. An earlier wood stairway was the subject of a bad poem in the 1886 *Northwest Magazine.* The intrepid urban traipser will want to climb to the lookout tower for the gee-whiz view from what was known as Prescott's Point. See also *Channel Street, Prescott Street, Stairways.*

GREEN STREET Joseph C. Green and his real-estate partner Edwin Sargent platted this short street near Lake Como in 1885. Green died in St. Paul on October 10, 1890, at the age of seventy-three.

GREENBRIER STREET Greenbrier County in West Virginia was the basis of this 1857 East Side street name originating in Borup and Payne's Addition. The West Virginia county takes its name from the Greenbrier River, named for the prickly, woody plant that made travel along its shores so difficult. See also *Albemarle Street, Fauquier Place, Payne Avenue.*

GREENLAND AVENUE Originally Wentworth Avenue, this Highwood "ghost street" was renamed in 1927. Fish Creek, one of the few streams left within the city limits, flows under Greenland Avenue. See also *Ghost Streets.*

The Green Stairs were built in 1916. Photograph courtesy of the Minnesota Historical Society.

GREENWOOD AVENUE This short West Side street name was lengthened from B Street in 1883. See also *A Street*.

GRIFFITH STREET This street was developed by Benjamin Hoyt and John Burns in 1856 in the Suburban Hills plat; Griffith was most likely a personal name. See also *Burns Avenue, Hoyt Avenue*.

GRIGGS STREET Described by a contemporary as "exceedingly social and pleasant in his nature, yet back of all this he is shrewd and scheming," Chauncey W. Griggs (1832–1910) was a merchant and lumberman who moved to St. Paul in 1856. After serving in the Civil War, he was a state senator and representative, invested heavily in real estate, and named this Midway street in 1873. In 1888, he abandoned his spacious mansion at 476 Summit Avenue—having the dubious distinction as the most haunted house in St. Paul—and moved to Tacoma, Washington, where he died. See also *Midway*.

GROTTO On the riverbank along Mississippi River Boulevard between Summit Avenue and Ford Parkway, there are a number of sites young people gather at night. The traditional attraction of an isolated riverbank party has been that the authorities were not keen on descending the steep bank in the dark; that if they did descend the bank, they would inadvertently give ample warning of their coming; and that, if worse came to worse, compromising evidence could readily be tossed into the river. The Grotto has been one of these gathering places, taking its name from a small ravine adjacent to the St. Paul Seminary on the east side of the boulevard. See also *Devil's Ditch, Finn's Glen, Valley*.

The home of Chauncey W. Griggs (for whom the street was named) has been called the most haunted house in all of St. Paul. Photograph courtesy of the Minnesota Historical Society.

GROTTO STEPS Fifty-six steps descending from Linwood Avenue to St. Clair Avenue along the line of Grotto Street were constructed in 1911. See also *Stairways*.

GROTTO STREET *Grotto* was a nineteenth-century synonym for *cave*. This street in the Summit-University area was named in 1857 in Holcombe's Addition, because, it is said, if the street were extended south, it would reach the Mississippi River bank very near Fountain Cave, an early city landmark. See also *Fountain Cave, Holcombe Park Circle, St. Albans Lake (1), St. Albans Lake (2), Summit-University, Weber's Pond.*

GROVE See *University Grove*.

GROVE STREET Originated in 1851 in Patterson's Addition near Mississippi Street, this popular name suggests a cool, leafy canopy. Today, however, this new business area is short on tall trees.

GROVELAND This is a 150-year-old name in the Midway area. Prior to the Civil War, the Groveland Nursery operated in what is Merriam Park today. In her 1857 book *Floral Homes*, Harriet Bishop wrote that Groveland is an "appropriate" name for the area midway between St. Paul and Minneapolis. Archbishop John Ireland gave the name to his Groveland Addition in 1890, part of his attempt to finance church buildings with land speculation. The Groveland Addition is between Summit and St. Clair Avenues, between Cleveland Avenue and Finn

Street; however, references to the Groveland neighborhood typically encompass much more than the specific addition. Groveland School and playground are on the northeast corner of Cleveland and St. Clair Avenues. See also *Eustis Street, John Ireland Boulevard, Harriet Island Park, Macalester-Groveland, Merriam Park, Midway*.

GURNEY STREET Henry B. and Adeline Gurney named this short street midway between Lakes Como and Phalen in 1886. Henry, a real-estate dealer, died in 1890; Adeline in 1912.

HADLEY STREET Like many street names in Burlington Heights that were platted by the Union Land Company in 1888, this one comes from a village in Massachusetts. See also *Burlington Heights*.

HAGUE AVENUE William Holcombe and his son, Edwin, platted this street in 1857 in honor of The Hague, the seat of government of the Netherlands. Holcombe had prominent Dutch ancestors on his maternal side. According to the first surveyor's notes, a large area west of the intersection of Hague Avenue and Dale Street was "high rolling prairie." See also *Holcombe Park Circle*.

HAGUE PARK This small, one-half-acre public playground at Hague and Hamline Avenues was acquired in 1978.

HALDEMAN PARK Although it served as a dump until 1929 when it was transformed into a playground, this small, one-and-a-half-acre public park on the west side of Victoria Street and the south side of St. Clair Avenue was dedicated in R. J. Haldeman's Addition in 1883. Today it is considered part of Linwood Park. See also *Linwood Park, Ridgewood Park*.

HALL AVENUE Amos W. Hall (b. 1824) was one of the developers of this West Side street in 1855. Born in Massachusetts, he lived in the city as a real-estate dealer until 1860. This street marks a section line on the land survey.

In 1853, the first surveyor marking this section line noted two streams crossing the line of the street: the first stream, about one-and-one-half feet wide, heading north, crossed about where 547 Hall Street is today. The second stream, approximately three-and-one-half feet wide, also heading north, crossed the line about where 497 Hall Street is today.

HALL LANE Originally a twenty-foot alley, this street takes its name from the adjacent avenue. It is said there are no alleys in the West Side, only lanes. See also *West Side*.

HAMLINE AVENUE Leonidas L. Hamline (1797–1865) began his career as an Ohio lawyer. Converted to Methodism in 1829, he spent several years as a circuit rider before his election to bishop in 1844. Shortly before his death in Iowa, he donated $25,000 to help establish what is now Hamline University. In 1874, the street, which follows a one-half section line on the land survey, was named within an addition near the university.

HAMLINE LAKE See *Lake Hamline*.

HAMLINE PARK The Hamline Playground Building at 1564 West Lafond Avenue, an understated Art Deco WPA project in 1940, is the centerpiece of this three-acre public park at Snelling and Lafond Avenues. Weather permitting, this park is noted for its seemingly continuous basketball games.

HAMLINE VILLAGE This railroad suburb encompassed the area around Hamline University in the 1870s and 1880s. Served by a railroad station on the Short Line between (today) Holton and Albert Streets just north of Pierce Butler Route, the village was known variously as Hamline, Minnesota; Hamline Village; or College Place for a plat surrounding the university. Between 1880 and 1891, there was a separate post office for the suburb. Before 1873, the area was known as Johanna Crossing, according to Warren Upham in his book *Minnesota Place Names*. In 1890, C. C. Andrews wrote in his *History of St. Paul, Minn.* that the settlement is "located on an elevated plat, formerly open prairie, and surrounded by neat and tasteful residences, forming what was properly and is still occasionally called the village of Hamline." See also *Short Line Road*; see also "St. Paul's Railroad Suburbs."

HAMLINE/ASHLAND PARK This unimproved piece of public land on the northeast corner of Hamline and Ashland Avenues was acquired in 1962 for the Ayd Mill Road project. See also *Ghost Parks*.

HAMM MEMORIAL PARK See *Landmark Plaza Park*.

HAMM PARK This small, triangular one-quarter-acre landscaped public park with benches at East Seventh and Maple Streets was created when Lyman Dayton's Addition and Irvine's Second Addition intersected at a 45° angle. Hamm Park was given to the city in 1910 by William Hamm, a member of the park board, and named in honor of his father, Theodore Hamm (1825–1903). A recent Maple Street vacation increased the size of the park. See also *Stroh Drive*.

HAMMER AVENUE George and Frederick Hammer were in the real-estate business when this one-block-long street southeast of Lake Phalen was named in 1886. George left St. Paul, but Frederick became prominent as Mayor Andrew Kiefer's secretary and was later nailed to serve as president of the Board of Public Works in 1900–1902.

HAMPDEN AVENUE John Hampden (1594–1643), an English political leader, is commemorated in this 1885 St. Anthony Park street name. At 926 Hampden Avenue is the historic Fire Station Number 13 built by the city in 1894. It is now an attractive private residence retaining much of its original appearance. See also *St. Anthony Park*.

HAMPDEN PARK Located at Raymond and Bayless Avenues, this three-acre public park was named in 1885 in the original St. Anthony Park. See also *Hampden Avenue, St. Anthony Park*.

HAMPSHIRE AVENUE This street was named in 1946 in Hampshire Park. English names are always fashionable. *Hampshire Court* would have the same meaning.

Engine House Number 13 remains today as a private residence on Hampden Avenue. Photograph courtesy of the Minnesota Historical Society.

HANCOCK STREET General Winfield Scott Hancock (1824–86) was a presidential candidate when this street was named in 1880 by his friend Franz Sigel (1824–1902), a fellow general in the Civil War. Sigel, who lived in New York, visited New Ulm and St. Paul in 1873 and invested in property here. A street with his name in this same area has since been changed. See also *English Street*.

HARDENBERGH PLACE Platted in 1886 by Joseph Lockey, a cashier at the National German American Bank, this North End street name is probably that of Peter R. Hardenbergh, who developed another addition to the city in 1887. This one-block-long street near Oakland Cemetery is one of the more obscure addresses in the city.

HARE'S LAKE Occupying a ravine along the course of Oxford Street between approximately Lincoln and Sherburne Avenues, this lake was said to be spring fed. Early city street grading records indicate the lake was about fifteen feet deep where Fuller Avenue now crosses the old ravine lake, and about thirty feet deep where Grand Avenue crosses. Writing in 1904, librarian Josiah Chaney attributes the name to the Hare family, one of the early families near the lake, and records a neighborhood boy who drowned in sixteen feet of water.

By 1900, most of the lakebed had been filled to street level, but a small portion remained. In an article for the *Grand Gazette*, local historian James Taylor Dunn reminisced about the Oxford Club, describing a hollow on the south side of Grand Avenue between Lexington Parkway and Oxford Street. Not realizing this hollow was a remnant of an old lake, Dunn wrote:

> Almost the entire south side of that block was a steep hollow, some thirty or forty feet down.... From the earliest days this deep ravine was used informally as a favorite winter sledding hill. Run off water from heavy rains sometimes formed a small pond at the bottom and when frozen it was used for ice-skating. If there were enough water there during the summer months, local kids would build a raft and play at Tom Sawyer.

The last vestige of Hare's Lake disappeared about 1930 when the hollow was filled. Today the venerable Lexington Restaurant occupies part of the old lakebed. See also *Lakes/Ponds*.

HARRIET ISLAND PARK Before the channel on the south side was filled in during the 1950s, Harriet Island was actually an island. Its Dakota name had been Waukon or Wakan Island, which translates as Spirit or Devil Island. It was named for Harriet Bishop, an early schoolteacher—not the first—who, like most everyone in the boom years of the 1850s, speculated in real estate. By 1856, the island, which was accessible by ferry, had been subdivided into building lots with six streets.

By 1900, Dr. Justus Ohage, owner of the island and the health commissioner of St. Paul, had donated the island to the health department to establish public baths, an important amenity for a city in which most houses did not have running water. However, as the river became more polluted and the number of residents hooked up to the city water department increased, the island became an expensive liability for the health department. Not only was it difficult to keep the grass mowed on the island and to deter "a group of people down there who continually dig up the sod in search of mushrooms," there was also the expense of a night watchman.

According to 1929 correspondence in the parks department, Dr. Ohage "is greatly disappointed in that this park was not properly maintained [by the Health Department] and he is getting rather old and is worried a great deal about this situation." Mayor Hodgson and Councilman Wenzel had a meeting with Dr. Ohage to encourage him to redeem the island to the parks department. The city officials decided they could best convince Dr. Ohage of their good intentions by sending a crew to Irvine Park, where Dr. Ohage lived, to blacktop the paths, plant shrubbery, and establish flower beds and particularly to maintain the park lawn. Thus, city officials reasoned, Dr. Ohage would only have to look out his front window at 59 Irvine Park to see the exemplary maintenance given to properties owned by the parks department. Apparently, Dr. Ohage was indeed impressed—he redeeded the island to the parks department. Today it is part of the Harriet Island Regional Park. See also *Dr. Justus Ohage Boulevard, Islands, Irvine Park*.

In the early 1900s, Harriet Island was the location of public baths for city residents without running water. Photograph by Charles P. Gibson; courtesy of the Minnesota Historical Society.

HARRISON AVENUE Originally Prairie Street, this West End street name was changed in 1889 to avoid duplication. Benjamin Harrison (1833–1901) was president of the United States at that time.

HARTFORD AVENUE The city in Connecticut most likely prompted this Highland Park street name in Lexington Park in 1886.

HARVARD STREET Previously Hancock Street, the name of this West Side street was changed in 1883. College names were popular in the nineteenth century. See also *West Side*.

HASTINGS POND This pond, probably named for an early resident of the area, was between Ivy and Cottage Avenues, between Greenbrier and Arcade Streets. In the 1928 Hopkins atlas, it is pictured as approximately one block in length, and about one-half block in width. According to Tom Raschke, who grew up beside the pond, it was deep enough to prevent wading through it, and home to a few small fish. Massive amounts of dirt were removed during the construction of Interstate 94 and used to fill in depressions and ponds on the East Side, including this one. Johnson High School was subsequently built on the site about 1960. See also *East Side, Lakes/Ponds*.

HATCH AVENUE Edwin A. C. Hatch (1825–82) was commemorated by this street near Como Park named in the year of his death. Born in New York State, he migrated to Minnesota in 1843 as an Indian trader and subsequently became Indian agent to the Blackfoot tribe. Like many of the traders, he later turned against the Indians, becoming the major of a cavalry battalion during the Dakota Conflict. It was Hatch who violated international law by kidnapping two Dakota chiefs from their refuge in Canada and returning them to the United States, where they were hanged for their part in the conflict. See also *Weber's Pond*.

HATHAWAY STREET This 1883 West End street name might have indicated William Hathaway, a clerk for the nearby railroad. In 2005, Hathaway Street magically disappeared in the process of realignment. See also *Thurston Street*.

HAWLEY STREET Jesse B. Hawley was the surveyor of this North End subdivision in 1885. See also *North End*.

HAWTHORNE AVENUE Harwood Iglehart, William Hall, and Charles Mackubin, natives of Maryland, may have had that state's more temperate climate in mind when naming the street in 1857 for this shrub. See also *Iglehart Avenue, Mackubin Street*.

HAYDEN HEIGHTS Hayden Heights Addition was platted in 1913 by George Benz and Sons, Inc. The plat—from which the neighborhood takes its name—was approximately between Hoyt and Ivy Avenues, between White Bear Avenue and Ruth Street. The Hazel Park, Wildwood, White Bear, and Stillwater Electric Line served the suburb. According to John Larson, a reference librarian at the public library, a 1955 Souvenir Edition published for the dedication of the Hayden Heights Branch Library ascribes the name to American geologist Ferdinand Vandiveer Hayden (1829–87), noted for his geological and natural-history surveys in the West, mainly in Colorado, Idaho, Montana, Wyoming, and Utah. See also *Clear Avenue*.

HAZEL PARK William Leonard Ames (1846–1910) and his wife, Helen (1854–1940), were the developers of Hazel Park in 1886. Served by the Chicago, St. Paul, Minneapolis, and Omaha Line, it was one of a number of railroad suburbs at this time. William, born in New Jersey, journeyed with his father of the same name to St. Paul in 1850. His father purchased land in and about the city, including a three-hundred-acre East Side stock farm, where he raised nationally known shorthorn cattle in the area today between Hazelwood Street and Arlington Avenue, between Case and White Bear Avenues. William Jr. attended the Naval Academy at Annapolis and later worked at the cattle business in the West, returning to St. Paul upon his father's death in 1873. By this time, the family owned 1,200 acres southeast of Lake Phalen, which William platted into Hazel Park and other real-estate additions. The Ames School is named for him. William's home, built about 1890, still stands at 1667 Ames Avenue. It is said Hazel Park was chosen when Helen Ames espied a group of happy children in bright clothing gathering hazel nuts in nearby pastures. See also *Ames Avenue, Ames Place, Warrendale*.

HAZEL PLACE This tiny East Side public park at the junction of Ames Avenue and Ames Place was platted and dedicated in 1886. The frame railroad depot for Hazel Park was on the southeast side of the intersection with the railroad tracks. See also *Ames Avenue, Hazel Park*.

HAZEL STREET Hazel was a common shrub in the area when this East Side street was named in 1890 in Hazel Park. The 1928 Hopkins atlas shows a large pond (500 feet by 200 feet) between Hazel and Ruth Streets, between Fifth and Margaret Streets, just south of Eastern Heights Elementary School. Homes have been built around the perimeter of the block, leaving the old lakebed in the center as undeveloped open space. This is typical of the East Side, where developers skirted natural barriers instead of removing them. See also *East Side*.

HAZELWOOD STREET Platted as Bock Avenue, the name was changed in 1915, perhaps because Hazelwood seems more in keeping with Hazel Park. This East Side street marks on the land survey a one-half section line. Between Hazelwood and Germain Streets, between Conway and Fourth Streets, where Harding High School is today, there was once a good-sized lake that is best illustrated on the plat of Lee's Suburban Homes made in 1878. According to Art Boeltl, who grew up on Kennard and Fourth Streets, it was known as Snake Lake. He remembers seining minnows through a hole in the ice on the lake. See also *Lakes/Ponds*.

HEATHER DRIVE Originally Floral Street, where the home of noted local architect Cass Gilbert was located, the name was changed at the request of its residents in 1959. The change was to emphasize its connection with Heather Place, just adjacent. See also *Cass Gilbert Memorial Park*.

HEATHER PLACE James W. and Alma N. Heather platted this street in 1889. They were not residents of St. Paul, although they may have lived within the county.

HENDON AVENUE This street was named in St. Anthony Park in 1885 for a suburb of London. At 2247 Hendon Avenue there is a striking Prairie School–influenced house designed by Morell and Nichols and built in 1914. See also *St. Anthony Park*.

HENDON TRIANGLE MONKEY ISLAND PARK Actually two triangles, less than one acre total, raised well above the adjacent streets, this piece of public parkland in St. Anthony Park at Branston Street and Hendon Avenue was acquired in 1922. Known locally as "monkey island," the name apparently refers to the many children who played in the park on a piece of playground equipment called "monkey bars." See also *St. Anthony Park*.

HENRY PARK Consisting of approximately twelve acres along the bluff off Skyway Drive in the Highwood area, this seems destined to become St. Paul's newest park. The land is informally known as Henry Park for the late sculptor and environmentalist Henry Valilukas, who lived on part of the site for many years. The proposed park is within the Mississippi National River and Recreation Area, a unit of the National Park System, and is part of the state-designated Mississippi River Critical area.

HERBERT STREET William Hamm named this street in 1887 in Hazel Park, probably for Herbert Ames, one in the family of developers. See also *Ames Avenue, Hamm Park, Hazel Park*.

HERSCHEL STREET Originally Franklin Avenue, the name was changed in 1886 to avoid duplication. Herschel is possibly a first name, but his identity is hidden in the stars. Between Dayton and Ashland Avenues, Herschel Street is only thirty feet wide, giving it a European flavor.

HERSEY STREET Platted in 1882, east of Hamline Avenue, this Midway street was extended west to its present location, while the name of the eastern portion was changed to Taylor Avenue. The developers were Roscoe (1841–1906) and Eva Hersey, and Edward L. (1856–1908) and Mary Hersey. These two Hersey brothers were born in Maine but moved to Minnesota to manage a lumber business established at Stillwater by their father. The sons inherited the business, originally known as Hersey, Staples and Company, and three houses occupied by the Hersey family remain in Stillwater. Edward Hersey later lived at 475 Summit Avenue in St. Paul, where F. Scott Fitzgerald often visited his daughter, Marie. See also *Midway*.

HEWITT AVENUE Girart Hewitt (1825–79) was born in Pennsylvania and opened a St. Paul real-estate office in 1856. He conceived the idea of an annual steamboat ride on the Mississippi River in December and made sure it was widely reported in the newspapers, serving to allay the "back East" opinion of our harsh winters. The street, near Newell Park, was named in 1875.

HIAWATHA PARK The 1887 St. Paul Board of Park Commissioners attempted to acquire a forty-nine-acre park along the Mississippi River bluff at the south end of Cleveland Avenue. It was to be named Hiawatha Park, pairing it with Minnehaha Falls— a premiere Minneapolis tourist attraction in the nineteenth century —relating to the poem *The Song of Hiawatha* by Henry Wadsworth Longfellow. Boosters envisioned a pedestrian bridge over the river to lure hordes of tourists from the falls. The park commissioners ordered the public works department to acquire the property, but inter-agency strife as well as legal and eminent domain issues halted the acquisition. Some of the area is now within Hidden Falls Park. See also *Hidden Falls Park, Lincoln Park, Mohawk Park, West St. Paul Park*.

In 1890, several investors, anticipating the new public park, platted an addition under the same name in the area roughly between Mississippi River Boulevard and Cleveland Avenue, between Hampshire and Itasca Avenues.

Girart Hewitt, for whom the street was named, promoted the mild climate of St. Paul with a December steamboat ride. Poster courtesy of the Minnesota Historical Society.

HIDDEN FALLS PARK The falls is not hidden, just a little obscured. However, this area does have a hidden story, revealing greed, speculation, double-dealings, lost fortunes, and the future of St. Paul, all worthy of a condensed version here. The complete story is in the biography of Joseph R. Brown by Nancy and Robert Goodman.

In the 1830s and 1840s, it was obvious to the few shrewd soldiers and fur traders in this region that settlers would soon be arriving in throngs, and the real money lay in future town sites that could be bought by the acre and sold by the foot. Fur trader Joseph R. Brown had his eye on a potential bonanza where Hidden Falls Park is today. Perfectly situated at the natural head of navigation on the Mississippi River at the time, it offered a fine steamboat landing, a spacious levee, and easy access to the gently rolling prairies atop the cliffs. Brown named his town Sintomonee ("known all over") and set about to secure his claim. However, the officers at Fort Snelling, land speculators themselves, were keenly aware of the potential of Brown's site and determined to wrest it from him. To stop Brown and others like him, the officers commandeered that riverbank as part of the Fort Snelling Reservation, making it off limits to civilians. In 1839, all the settlers' homes in the newly expanded reservation were burned—ostensibly because of illegal liquor trafficking with soldiers at the fort.

But Brown was not to be deterred, and the following year he, along with others, successfully politicked the creation of St. Croix County, Wisconsin Territory, encompassing all the land on the east side of the Mississippi River, thereby (he hoped) bringing his ideal town site back under civilian control. Suffice it to say, Brown's efforts were ultimately futile, and instead he established the village of Dacotah on the St. Croix River, known today as Stillwater.

In the absence of development at the site of Hidden Falls, the two less-than-ideal steamboat landings in what is now downtown St. Paul did attract the throngs of settlers. But had Brown been successful in obtaining his town site at Hidden Falls, St. Paul could be called Sintomonee, the downtown would be in what is now Highland Park—and there might be only one city instead of two.

The land for the park was acquired between 1900 and 1905 as part of Mississippi River Boulevard, but it was not developed until 1931. See also *Hiawatha Park, Old Rum Town.*

HIGH BRIDGE Properly known as the Smith Avenue Bridge, this West End/West Side connection spans the Mississippi River at Smith Avenue. The first bridge built at this site was in 1889, with a replacement opened in 1988. This landmark has a certain infamy because a jump from the High Bridge almost always ends in death. On a more cheerful note, the bridge is a popular vantage point for folksy fraternizing, fawning over fall foliage, fearsome floods, formidable flotillas, and flamboyant fireworks. See also *Bridges, West End, West Side.*

HIGH BRIDGE PARK The lookout parks at either end of the High Bridge are on the Minnesota Department of Transportation right-of-way.

HIGHLAND PARK (neighborhood) Highland was a popular term in St. Paul. The first Highland Park neighborhood is the twisty area roughly between St. Clair and Goodrich Avenues, between St. Albans Street, Dale Street, and Pleasant Avenue. However, the present-day neighborhood called Highland Park takes its name from a 1925 plat by Den E. Lane, "Lane's Highland

A bird's-eye view of the construction of the second High Bridge in 1986. Photograph by
Charles W. Burback; courtesy of the Minnesota Historical Society.

Park," which divided most of the area between Highland Parkway and Montreal Avenue, between Snelling and Prior Avenues into building lots. Anticipating the development spurred
by the new Ford Plant on Mississippi River Boulevard, this name is almost certainly taken
from the city in Wayne County, Michigan, surrounded by Detroit. Henry Ford opened his
first Model T plant there in 1910, introducing the assembly-line method of automobile production. When Lane's Addition in St. Paul was platted in 1925, the prediction was that hundreds, if not thousands, of jobs would be created, not only by the Ford Plant itself but also by
the many auxiliary parts suppliers who would build near the Ford Plant. See also *Ford Parkway*,
St. Paul Avenue.

HIGHLAND PARK As part of a city plan to buy parkland before the area became densely populated, this 264-acre public park at Hamline Avenue and Edgcumbe Road was acquired in
1924. One of the most potent premises used for purchasing parks was that it would add
value to the surrounding area, and it could be argued the improvement of a large, open public space like this park, which had been swampy, contributes to the desirability of this neighborhood. Before Highland Park was purchased, there was talk of acquiring the hillside between Edgcumbe Road and Lexington Parkway, extending south from Watson Avenue to
Montreal Avenue that would have included Fountain Park, Walsh Park, and Dawson Park. The
observation was made that "the area is well wooded and affords fine distant views." See also
Dawson Park, *Fountain Park*, *Walsh Park*.

A forlorn Highland Park swimming pool in 1935, before its improvement as a WPA project. Photograph courtesy of the Minnesota Historical Society.

HIGHLAND PARKWAY Platted as Otto Street, the name of this portion was changed in 1934. According to his son, Charles Claude, who lived at 1808 Otto Street, initiated a petition that resulted in the name change. Highland Parkway marks a section line on the land survey.

HIGHLAND SPRING In 1900, John Wardell purchased property with a spring on the southwest corner of Lexington Parkway and Randolph Avenue and set up his Consolidated Bottling Company. For sixty-five years, the Wardell family delivered ice and drinking water to businesses and private homes throughout the city. The spring that provided the livelihood to the family delivered a constant flow, summer and winter, of twenty-seven gallons per minute. The temperature of the water was a constant forty-two degrees. The water had twenty-five grains of hardness (13 calcium, 12 magnesia) and was said to flow from a drainage basin between Syndicate and Saratoga Streets, between Summit and Montreal Avenues, where it percolated down about twenty feet before flowing southeast. Today the spring is routed into the sewer system, but the intrepid urban traipser can trek behind Montcalm Estates and, by peering down the manhole grating, go with the flow of the spring from the hillside above, still running at its dependable twenty-seven gallons a minute. For further information, see "William Nettleton and the Highland Park Spring Water Company" by the author of this volume.

HIGHWOOD This is a charming and isolated neighborhood of challenging topography and winding, narrow country roads mapped out over a century ago. Platted as Burlington Heights in 1887, it takes its present name from the principal street and an old train station. This neighborhood defines its boundaries as between McKnight Road and Lower Afton Road, between the Mississippi River and the southeast city limits. In promoting the original 1887 railroad suburb, the Union Land Company promised in its brochure: "A cooler temperature in summer and a greater immunity from the cold winds of winter than any locality in the city." In his 1958 book, *St. Paul Is My Beat*, Gareth Hiebert wrote a short essay about the area. See also *Burlington Heights*.

HIGHWOOD AVENUE Giving the impression of height and trees, this 1887 name in the Burlington Heights plat is pleasant but trite. It was also the name of one train station in Burlington Heights. See also *Burlington Heights*, *Highwood*.

HILDING AVENUE Hilding Johnson (1898–1974) was the father-in-law of Warren Forsberg, the surveyor of this Battle Creek area plat in 1959.

Ice was cut from the Highland Spring pond in winter and packed away to cool drinking water in summer. Photograph courtesy of the Minnesota Historical Society.

HILL STREET Named in 1849 in Rice and Irvine's Addition for the hill it ascended between Eagle Street and Kellogg Boulevard, this old and infamous street was vacated in 2002 for the building of the Science Museum of Minnesota. See also *Larry Ho Drive*.

HILLCREST A reference to Hillcrest can be confusing because the two highest parts of the city are the northeast corner around Hillcrest Golf Course, and miles away in Highland Park around the Hillcrest Recreation Center. Generally, when the location of the Hillcrest neighborhood is mentioned, the allusion is to the East Side district around the Hillcrest Shopping Center and the Hillcrest Golf Course, roughly defined as the area between McKnight Road and Hazelwood Street, between Arlington and Larpenteur Avenues.

HILLCREST AVENUE Part of St. Catherine Park, this very common street name near the Highland Golf Course was platted in 1919.

HILLCREST KNOLL Hillcrest Knoll Park fills the block between Montana and Hoyt Avenues, between Flandrau and Kennard Streets. Once a swamp, this area developed during the post–World War II housing frenzy. After years of minor flooding, a flash flood in 1997 inundated nearly sixty homes. "I looked out my back window and saw the moon reflecting off a lake that wasn't there before," recalled one resident. Eventually, thirty-one homes were bought and razed or moved, and to prevent future flooding of this East Side neighborhood, the city dredged a seven-and-one-half-foot-deep basin to detain up to nine million gallons of storm water. It was suggested this detention pond be used—between floods—for informal soccer fields, but the neighbors quickly rejected the idea, saying they did not want a park that would attract people. A limestone marker on Montana Avenue, indicating the 1997 flood level, is engraved with a line three feet above the sidewalk. Applied to this low site, the puzzling name Hillcrest Knoll fulfills the definition of a hill in a hole. See also *Devil's Ditch*, *East Side*, *Hillcrest*, *Roger Puchreiter Pond*, *Stillwater Avenue*, *Willow Reserve*.

HILLSDALE AVENUE See *Berland Place*.

HILLSIDE AVENUE Previously Langford Avenue, the name of this St. Anthony Park street was changed in 1940. The prominent Twin Cities architect Clarence H. Johnston Jr. designed the house at 2266 Hillside Avenue in 1916. *Hillside Court* borrows its name from the avenue.

HILLSIDE TRIANGLE This public triangle with one tree and a few shrubs is at the intersection of Hillside Avenue and Knapp Street.

HILLTOP LANE The location prompted this Highland Park street name in 1948 in Magoffin's Hilltop Addition. See also *Magoffin Avenue*.

HILLWOOD COURT Euphonious.

HOFFMAN AVENUE Originally Dayton Avenue, the name was changed in 1872 to honor James K. Hoffman (1831–1905). Born in Pennsylvania, he came to St. Paul in 1851, where he operated three different sawmills, one of which stood at the bottom of Dayton's Bluff. Hoffman

This startling flood marker on the Montana Avenue sidewalk at Hillcrest Knoll Park testifies to a washed-out neighborhood. Photograph by Kathleen M. Vadnais.

later became a merchant and a state official; at the time of the name change, he was a member of the city council. This street was absorbed when Interstate Highway 94 was built east of downtown St. Paul.

HOG-BACK HILL According to librarian Josiah Chaney, this was a colloquial reference to the hill on which the State Capitol now stands. The name is probably a portrayal of the hill before it was extensively modified. See also *Angst und Bang, Bunker Hill, Capitol Hill*.

HOLCOMBE PARK CIRCLE This small park, an enlargement of the intersection at St. Albans Street and Laurel Avenue, was dedicated in 1857 in Holcombe's Addition. On the plat it was designated a "market square," indicating a public space available for commerce. The idea of a park, as we know it today, did not originate until two decades later. William Holcombe (1804–70) was a pioneer of the St. Croix valley, a resident of Stillwater, the first lieutenant governor of Minnesota, and a prolific speculator in town lots. See also *Elm Square*.

HOLLOW Evelyn Fairbanks writes of the Hollow, a private playground—acquired by the city in 1945—between Kent and Mackubin Streets, between St. Anthony and Central Avenues. An old lakebed, it is now under Interstate 94.

HOLLY AVENUE A number of prominent developers in the Woodland Park Addition named this street in 1870 for the Holly tree, which, because of its sound and Christmas associations, conveys an agreeable impression. See also *Woodland Park*.

HOLMAN FIELD See *St. Paul Downtown Airport*.

HOLTON STREET Named in 1880 in the Hamline plat, this is undoubtedly a personal name, but whose is not apparent. See also *Hamline Avenue*.

HOMECROFT This neighborhood takes its name from the 1907 Homecroft Addition, which subdivided the property between Field and Stewart Avenues, between Edgcumbe Road and Davern Street. However, the general sense of the name has been extended beyond the boundaries of the addition. See also *Field Avenue*.

HOMER STREET Previously Purnell Avenue, the name of this West End street was changed in 1940. See also *West End*.

HOPE STREET In 1872, the name of this East Side street was changed from Hill to Hope.

HOPKINS PARK About one-third of an acre at Desoto and Hopkins Streets, this park was purchased for $400 in 1939, with some tax-forfeit land added in 1949. In the mid-1990s, neighbors, fearing the park with its sandlot baseball field would become a battleground between the immigrant Hmong children and the local children, agreed to vacate the park for construction of a Habitat for Humanity house. See also *Xees Phaus*.

HOPKINS STREET Benjamin W. Brunson named this street in 1852 in Brunson's Addition for Daniel Hopkins, a native of New Hampshire who lived at Prairie du Chien, Wisconsin, along with the Brunson family from 1838 to 1844. Both Brunson and Hopkins moved to St. Paul in 1847, but Hopkins died June 13, 1852, a month before this street was platted.

Hopkins Street, like Railroad Island as a whole, has seen generations of new arrivals to St. Paul. The Minnesota Historical Society did in-depth research on the house at 470 Hopkins Street to bring to life that story of change. The home was built by German immigrants in 1888 and, over the years, occupied by Italian, African American, Native American, and Hmong families. An exhibit at the Minnesota History Center exploring the lives of these families will be on display from 2006 to 2011. See also *Railroad Island*.

HORSE TROUGH In earlier days the city maintained drinking troughs for horses at strategic points. With great foresight, most of these vessels were placed by saloons so horse and driver could imbibe simultaneously. The only remaining horse trough now serves as a flower planter in front of the city garage at 891 North Dale Street, where it was dedicated by the Junior Pioneer Association as a historical site on October 25, 1939.

HORSESHOE BEND The intrepid urban traipser will lean on the old walking stick, mesmerized by such an unexpected view near the northern boundary of the city. Between (roughly) Elmhurst Cemetery and Rice Street, between Nebraska and Larpenteur Avenues, this neighborhood takes its name from the horseshoe curve in Wheelock Parkway as it follows the bluff line between Matilda and Virginia Streets.

A bunch of Railroad Island teenagers mugged for the camera on Hopkins Street about 1937. Photograph courtesy of the Minnesota Historical Society.

HORTON AVENUE Hiler H. Horton (1857–1906), born in Wisconsin, graduated from Washington University in St. Louis and moved to St. Paul in 1878 as a clerk in the law office of Cushman K. Davis. He served on the Board of Park Commissioners and was later a state senator. The proximity of the street to the Como Park Zoo (and maybe the spirit of Horton the elephant) prompted the use of this name in 1885.

HORTON PARK Acquired in 1907, this three-and-a-half-acre park at Minnehaha and Hamline Avenues has become a mini-arboretum. In the mid-1970s, St. Paul lost thousands of elm trees to disease. As part of a citywide reforestation program beginning in 1977, the arboretum was donated by the St. Paul Companies on its 125th anniversary in 1978. In the park are selected varieties of trees intended to help residents decide which of these trees would best restore the traditional green canopy of the city. The name commemorates the death of Hiler H. Horton. See also *Horton Avenue*.

HOWARD STREET The Union Land Company named this street in 1887 in Burlington Heights. Since then, the street has been extended north in disconnected bits and pieces. It is unlikely it has any special meaning. *Howard Court* has the same unspecified meaning.

The intrepid urban traipser will be immersed in the hydrology exhibit between Howard Street and Waukon Avenue, between Stillwater Avenue and East Seventh Street. Between the two alleys is a swampy ditch, the remainder of Ames Creek, which once carried water from Beaver Lake southwest to eventually join up with Phalen Creek by way of Ames Lake. The first

This mini-arboretum in Horton Park suggests trees you might want to plant on your boulevard. Photograph by Kathleen M. Vadnais.

grading profile of Stillwater Avenue confirms the natural four-foot-deep channel through which the water flowed from Beaver Lake into this creek. See also *Ames Creek, Ames Lake, Beaver Lake, Phalen Creek, Stillwater Avenue.*

HOWELL PARK To find Howell Park, follow the intrepid urban traipser south on Fairview Avenue, continue onto Edgcumbe Road, turn right on Howell Avenue, and on your left you will see this two-thirds-acre park with a large rock near its east end. It was dedicated in the 1927 plat of Boland's Edgcumbe Hills. See also *Ghost Parks.*

HOWELL STREET Platted in Merriam Park in 1882, the name might be a reference to Samuel L. Howell, a Philadelphia real-estate dealer. See also *Merriam Park.*

HOYT AVENUE Lorenzo and Sarah Hoyt platted this street in 1872 and named it after his father, Benjamin F. Hoyt (1800–1875), pioneer preacher, who came to St. Paul in 1848, where he dealt largely in real estate. The story goes that when Lorenzo was breaking the sod at his farm near today's Hamline and Larpenteur Avenues, then worth five dollars an acre, and feeling his prospects were poor, his father reassured him: "Do not be discouraged; you will live to see this land sell for $50 an acre." On Hoyt Avenue, just east of Edgerton Street, the 1928 Hopkins atlas indicates a marsh, about 230 feet by 360 feet.

HUBBARD AVENUE Lucius F. Hubbard (1836–1913) was governor of Minnesota when this street near Hamline University was named in 1882. Born in New York, he came to Red Wing in 1857, where he established a newspaper and operated a grain and flour milling business. Hubbard County is named in his honor. He is best known for his naive declaration that corporations should be "the servants and not the masters of the public." See also *Burnquist Street, Clough Street, Gorman Avenue, Johnson Parkway, Marshall Avenue, Merriam Lane, Ramsey Street, Scudder Street, Sibley Street.*

HUDSON ROAD Previously Hastings Avenue, the name of this East Side street was changed in 1940, for Hudson, Wisconsin, the destination of the road. Today, remaining segments of it parallel Interstate 94.

HUMBOLDT AVENUE Originally Goff Avenue, the name, changed in 1916, is taken from Humboldt High School, built on this West Side street in 1910. The present school, second of that name, commemorates Alexander von Humboldt (1769–1859), a German naturalist and explorer, one of the earliest and most influential scientists. See also *West Side.*

HUNT PLACE This street was named in 1885 in St. Anthony Park, for Daniel H. Hunt (1833–91) and his wife, Annie (1846–1932), who owned a farm in the area today roughly east of Highway 280, between Ellis Avenue and Pearl Street. Hunt moved here from Maine in 1857, married Annie Lockwood, and purchased the Lockwood farm in 1870. As a truck farmer, he sold produce in the Twin Cities. The Hunt farmhouse at 2478 Territorial Road was built in 1874 and demolished in 1973 by the Stockwell Equipment Company. See also *St. Anthony Park.*

HUNTING VALLEY ROAD The city council named this street in 1960 at the request of the Quality Park Envelope Company, 2520 Como Avenue. At the time, the business wished to add a second mailing address to their same building as part of a promotion to boost sales. Could bestowing the pastoral image, Hunting Valley Road, on the freeway frontage road alongside their building be considered pushing the envelopes? See also *Wall Street.*

HURON STREET Part of Chelsea Heights, this street was named in 1916 presumably for the American Indian tribe in the eastern United States. See also *Chelsea Heights.*

HYACINTH AVENUE Harwood Iglehart, William Hall, and Charles Mackubin, natives of Maryland, may have had that state's more temperate climate in mind when naming this East Side street in 1857. Hyacinth Avenue, curving between Frank and Duluth Streets, is part of Phalen Heights Park, a development platted in 1910. On Hyacinth Avenue, between Clark and Desoto Streets, the 1928 Hopkins atlas shows a marsh, about 300 feet in diameter. See also *Iglehart Avenue, Mackubin Street.*

HYTHE STREET Hythe is a village in Kent County, England, near Dover. This street was named in St. Anthony Park in 1885. See also *St. Anthony Park.*

The ladies in this postcard are enjoying Indian Mounds Park about 1905. Photograph by Sweet; courtesy of the Minnesota Historical Society.

IDAHO AVENUE Like the potato, this street near the northern boundary of the city was named in 1886 for the western state. Hoyt Avenue nearby was once named Kansas Street.

IGLEHART AVENUE Remembered as "gentlemanly and courteous in his bearing, kind and considerate," Harwood Iglehart (1829–93) was born in Maryland and received his law degree from Harvard University. After practicing law in Annapolis for a short time, he moved to St. Paul in 1854. While continuing his profession here, he dealt heavily in real estate, developing several additions to the city, including this one, Mackubin and Marshall's Addition, in 1855. Iglehart served as president of the Mercantile Library Association, on the first board of trustees for St. Luke's Hospital, and in numerous other civic posts. It was Iglehart's optimistic conviction that St. Paul and Minneapolis would soon merge into one large metropolis.

The George Luckert house, at 480 Iglehart Avenue, was among the first houses in the Summit-University area. Built about 1858, it is one of the few limestone houses remaining in St. Paul. See also *Goodrich Avenue, Mt. Curve Boulevard, St. Anthony Hill, Summit-University*.

IM-IN-I-JA SKA According to J. Fletcher Williams's *History of the City of Saint Paul to 1875*, this was the Dakota name for the location of St. Paul. Meaning "White Rock," it referred to the white sandstone cliffs of Dayton's Bluff. See also *Dayton's Bluff*.

INDIAN MOUNDS PARK Covering seventy-nine acres, this park on Dayton's Bluff at the south end of Earl Street contains six of the original sixteen American Indian burial mounds dating from the prehistoric era of the Hopewell mound builders. At the urging of local residents, the city—despite the rapacious real-estate speculators—was able to purchase much of the parkland in the 1890s. Over the years, this has been the site of a toboggan slide, tennis courts, a warming house for ice skaters, horseshoe courts, a comfort station, a World War I German artillery piece, and a 110-foot navigation beacon built in 1929 to help pilots find their way at night as they delivered airmail. See also *Dayton's Bluff*.

INNER DRIVE (private) See *Village Lane*.

INTERSTATE HIGHWAY 35E The Interstate Highway System generally follows a couple of simple rules. North-south highways have two-digit odd numbers beginning on the West Coast with I-05 and increasing in number until you reach I-97 on the East Coast. East-west roads have two-digit even numbers beginning with I-04 in Florida and increasing to I-96 across Michigan.

Interstate highways with numbers ending in zero run from coast to coast, and interstates with numbers ending in five run from border to border. Interstate mileposts run from state line to state line, either from south to north or from west to east, and interstate interchange numbers are assigned based on the nearest milepost. Where more than one interchange is located within a mile, letters are assigned to designate the individual interchanges.

Interstate highways with three-digit numbers branch off or loop with the primary routes. The loop takes the number of its parent and adds a multiple of 100, as in I-494 and I-694. The E indicates the east branch of I-35 as it passes through the Twin Cities.

There will be a quiz later.

INTERSTATE HIGHWAY 94 See below.

A FOLDING THRONE FOR QUEEN VICTORIA
How Interstate 94 Ran over the St. Anthony Avenue Parkway

Construction of Interstate 94 near Fairview Avenue in September 1967. Photograph by the *St. Paul Dispatch and Pioneer Press*; courtesy of the Minnesota Historical Society.

George Herrold was just beginning his long career as St. Paul's first planning engineer in 1920 when he selected St. Anthony Avenue as the future route of an automobile thorough-fare. This major new road would divert traffic from University and Marshall Avenues, two of the busiest streets in the city. Railroads and industrial sites made it impractical to put the road north of University Avenue, and the many residential districts precluded a roadway south of Marshall Avenue. St. Anthony Avenue, between University and Marshall Avenues, also conveniently accessed the four major traffic-generating sites: downtown Minneapolis, downtown St. Paul, the Midway industrial area, and the University of Minnesota. Herrold designed a four-lane divided parkway, landscaped and tree-lined, with a 200-foot right-of-way, like Summit Avenue west of Lexington Parkway. But before the parkway could be built, the Depression intervened, followed by World War II.

In 1944 Congress authorized the Bureau of Public Roads to supervise the planning of a national 40,000-mile federally funded interstate highway system. The selection of routes and design in Minnesota fell to the engineers of the Minnesota Highway Department, who had spent the vast majority of their careers building rural roads. According to interviews by Alan Altschuler, the goal of the highway department was to solve traffic congestion. They openly declared they had neither the time nor expertise to deal with the social and economic impacts in locating a new highway through the city.

In 1955, after a number of studies, the highway department arrived at the same conclusion that Herrold had reached thirty-five years earlier: the best route for a major road west of downtown St. Paul would be along the course of St. Anthony Avenue. However, the highway engineers did not envision a parkway. They proposed a roadway that cut a blockwide swath through the city where automobiles would travel at high speed. Entrances and exits would be limited.

Herrold, who had spent most of his career accommodating the city to the automobile, was outraged with their proposal. A graduate in civil engineering, class of 1896, Herrold was a product of the "reform" and "nonpartisan" school of municipal government. He was dismissed by politicians who considered him impractical and idealistic, and he worked with almost no resources, staff, or political support. Herrold, who received strong support from the citizens of St. Paul, was not, however, intimidated by the highway department's coercive arsenal of statistics and studies.

Herrold believed the automobile was a handy gadget, but it should not dominate the city. Parkways with intersections, he declared, lined and divided by well-kept grass and majestic trees, with truck traffic excluded, would enhance a neighborhood. Herrold argued the freeway would be a gigantic, unshaded, unsightly, noisy ditch that concentrated pollution.

Facing overwhelming odds, Herrold took the offensive against the proposed freeway. He argued that running a freeway through the Rondo neighborhood would displace African Americans who, because of rigid segregation in St. Paul, would have no other place to buy or rent homes. He said it was better to have drivers slightly inconvenienced than to destroy a neighborhood and exacerbate racial tensions. He foresaw the freeway would separate people from their neighborhoods, churches from their congregations, students from their schools. He proposed an alternative: the Northern Route—now Pierce Butler Route. Using the Northern Route, the freeway could follow the railroad lines and create less disruption to the city; moreover, he argued, right-of-way would be cheaper and less controversial to obtain.

In an article in the 1956 *Northwest Architect*, Herrold pointed out that the German autobahns, upon which the new interstate freeways were modeled, had been routed around cities. He wrote,

> We do know that their construction [through the city] . . . will bring about many . . . disturbances to gracious living. After all, a city is for people. Their standards and values and way of life should be a first consideration.

But Herrold was just warming up:

In St. Paul, west of the Capitol Plaza, and between University Avenue and Summit Avenue, there are more than sixty institutions that have been built with tax money or private contributions by people living in that area. . . . I refer to hospitals, orphanages, academies, churches, public, parochial, and private schools. . . . This limited access, depressed highway will divide this district into two parts and alienate one from the other.

If these limited access routes must be run through the city as a military necessity, then they should, as far as possible, follow railroad rights-of way. The railroads were here first. Their 22 lines determined the pattern of the cities. The cities have been built up to conform to this pattern. The railroad lines have divided the cities up into islands. Why subdivide these islands into smaller ones by these depressed highways with all the disturbances that necessarily follow?

As to the pretzel type interchange design [Spaghetti Junction] in front of the new Capitol Plaza and Veterans Service Building. . . . This is a mistake. . . . I am reminded of the Yankee who years ago tried to sell Queen Victoria a patented folding bed and throne.

The controversy raged for several years. The black community rallied against the freeway. The residents of Prospect Park in Minneapolis—who ultimately lost a third of their homes to the freeway—protested. The St. Paul downtown businessmen finally came to realize the freeway would siphon business from them. But these disparate groups were never able to coordinate.

The highway department dismissed all protestors as simply special-interest, self-serving groups, maintaining that they, the engineers, were working for the vast driving and tax-paying public who had no spokesperson, that indeed it was the job of the engineers to "build the best damn highways possible."

In the end, Herrold, a bitter and frustrated old man of ninety, lost. City leaders, publicly disavowing knowledge of the highway department plans, approved the designs as far from public view as possible. George Shepard, a popular city engineer, sided with the highway department and advised city leaders that freeways were worthwhile.

The highway department followed a strategy that has served them well over the years. They never provided firm plans at meetings with city officials; all their plans were proposed as tentative, and the meetings were intended to elicit ideas for further study. The engineers were always agreeable, seldom saying no; yet as time went on, decisions were quietly made, and their plans prevailed. One city staff member at the time pronounced it "creeping fait accompli-ism."

The St. Anthony Avenue route has now been a freeway for more than forty years. Do you think this was the best solution for city residents?

INTERURBAN DISTRICT Another name, used from the 1880s to the 1920s, for the Midway area. See also *Federal City, Midway.*

INTREPID URBAN TRAIPSER The IUT is a character we have conjured to entice you, the gentle reader, to discover some of the offbeat St. Paul landscapes we chronicle. We believe those of you inclined to curiosity about your surroundings and interested in the city where you live may recognize parts of yourself in this somewhat tongue-in-cheek recitation: The intrepid urban traipser is entranced by maps, picks up litter, rides a bicycle, possesses good moral character, eschews buckthorn, often gazes into the distance for no apparent reason, carries three pens in the pocket, has both a Swiss Army knife and a Leatherman, is selectively eclectic, has an unerring sense of direction, and traipses in all seasons.

IOWA AVENUE Running between Lakes Como and Phalen, this street was named in 1886 for the state, following the precedent set in Washington, DC. This part of the city includes only the western states.

IRIS PARK This one-acre urban oasis at University and Lynnhurst Avenues within Union Park was acquired in 1884 by assessing the adjacent lots. See also *Lake Iris, Union Park*.

IRIS PLACE Lake Iris, a small artificial pond, prompted this street name in 1888. See also *Lake Iris, Union Park*.

IROQUOIS AVENUE Part of Beaver Lake Heights, this narrow, winding street was named in 1917 for the Iroquois, a confederation of several eastern American Indian tribes founded in the sixteenth century. See also *Beaver Lake Heights*.

IRVINE AVENUE Characterized as "a man of the people; a man of no ostentation; a laborer, always working; never idle; quiet in manners; strictly temperate, and very even in his everyday toil," John R. Irvine (1812–78) was born in Dansville, New York. He and his wife, Nancy, traveled to St. Paul in the winter of 1843 and purchased about 300 acres, at a dollar an acre, east and north of Wabasha Street—now some of the most desirable property in the city. Irvine Avenue, named in 1854 in Dayton and Irvine's Addition, is a delightful local byway hidden below the Summit Avenue bluff. The intrepid urban traipser, however, will have no difficulty finding it.

IRVINE PARK The two-acre park was included in the 1849 plat of Rice and Irvine's Addition as a nameless public square by the developer John R. Irvine. An elaborate fountain is the centerpiece of this park, which has been restored to much of its original grandeur and was rededicated in 1978.

The neighborhood of the same name is just west of downtown, clustered around Irvine Park. Some of the earliest houses in the city remain from this nineteenth-century enclave of the upper-middle class, although the area suffered a considerable decline in the beginning of the twentieth century because of the increased pollution from the nearby railroads. A report on housing in St. Paul in the 1930s characterized the neighborhood as

> near the center of town and takes in the less desirable rooming-house district; old homes, that at one time were mansions, but, over a period of years have been outmoded. Each successive tenant has been a little less able to pay adequate rent until the present occupants have commercialized the homes in one form or another.

By 1970, 96 percent of the area's housing was classified as substandard, and the city wanted to clear the area and build high-rise apartments. A vigorous battle ensued, but the logic of preservation prevailed, and since 1973 Irvine Park has been a National Register Historic District. See also *Ramsey Hill Historic District.*

IRVINE PARK AVENUE In 1876, the St. Paul City Council designated the street around Irvine Park as Irvine Park Avenue. The name is that of John R. Irvine (1812–78), who platted the public square in 1849. See also *Irvine Avenue.*

ISABEL STREET This street was named as part of the West Side about 1855; Isabel is unidentifiable. See also *West Side.*

ISLANDS As a river town, St. Paul has included a number of islands, many of which have disappeared as a result of railroad construction and the various river management strategies of the U.S. Army Corps of Engineers. See: *Ames Island, Barnes Island, Boom Island, Crosby Island, Harriet Island, Long Island, Marion Island, McBoal Island, Mill Island, Pigs Eye Island No. 1, Pigs Eye Island No. 2, Pike Island, Raspberry (Navy) Island,* and *Ross Island.* In addition, there was another seven-acre unnamed island across from the airport, described as Government Lot 6 in Section 4 and Government Lot 3 in Section 9, both in T28, R22. In the 1884 Hopkins atlas, it was an island; by the publication of the 1928 Hopkins atlas, it had been incorporated into the mainland, probably by the railroad.

In addition to the above, when the Ford Dam (Lock and Dam #1) was built in 1917 and raised the water level upriver from the dam about thirty-five feet, six unnamed islands in this upper gorge of the river were flooded over. According to original government survey information supplied by local historian and chief public works surveyor Mike Murphy, they were: (1) 14.92 acres, Government Lot 7, Section 17, T28, R23; (2) 16.08 acres, Government Lot 5, Section 8, T28, R23; (3) 2.36 acres, Government Lot 6, Section 8, T28, R23; (4) 4.8 acres, Government Lot 7, Section 8, T28, R23; (5) 6.8 acres, Government Lot 5, Section 5, T28, R23; (6) .62 acres, Government Lot 6, Section 5, T28, R23.

ITASCA AVENUE Originally Coburn Avenue, the name of this Highland Park street was changed in 1940. See also *Highland Park.*

IVAN WAY Ivan J. and Catherine Kipp were the developers of this addition in 1912; they moved to Los Angeles in 1925. See also *Kipp's Glen.*

IVY AVENUE Harwood Iglehart, William Hall, and Charles Mackubin, natives of Maryland, may have had that state's more temperate climate in mind when naming this East Side street in 1857. At 982 East Ivy Avenue are the brick Ivy Park Apartments that were once the ladies dormitory of St. Paul Luther College, the only building remaining of several that were on that campus. Across the street at 985 East Ivy is the only remaining building—beautifully restored inside and out—of the Gillette Children's Hospital, now the home of the Minnesota Humanities Commission. See also *East Side, Iglehart Avenue, Mackubin Street.*

J

JACKSON STREET As a developer of the 1849 plat, St. Paul Proper, Henry Jackson ascribed his name to this street, one of the original fifteen street names of the city. "A short, thick-set man, slow in speech, quiet in his movements, with a florid complexion, and a mouth full of tobacco"—such is the description of Jackson (1811–57), one of the first St. Paul pioneers. Born in Virginia, Jackson drifted through Texas, New York, Wisconsin, and Illinois before he and his wife, Angelina, settled in St. Paul in 1842, where he established a general store and served as the first postmaster. Originating at one of the city's steamboat landings, Jackson Street, then only thirty-nine feet wide, became a commercial thoroughfare of the city. In the early days, the northern part of Jackson Street was known as the "old cemetery road" for its route to Oakland Cemetery.

Writing in 1958 in *St. Paul Is My Beat*, Gareth Hiebert characterized three periods of downtown Jackson Street:

> It has been a gay street of commerce, hotels and cafes [1870–1915]. And Jackson has been a misery street of lost week-ends, poverty, and wobbly gaited men whose blank stares were as bare as the empty show cases behind plate glass windows into which they looked [1915–60]. And now, the wheels of commerce hum on Jackson again and, like Jericho, some of the old walls are tumbling down to make way for parking lot after parking lot and quite a few people think it is a mighty good thing for Jackson to be so accommodating [1960+].

See also *Chestnut Street, Lower Landing Park, Lowertown, Oakland Cemetery*.

JACKSON'S WOODS In the earliest days of the city, this name referred to an oak-covered bluff that would today be in the vicinity of Jackson Street and University Avenue. The hill was used for a time as an informal burying ground.

JAMES AVENUE James Stinson (1828–1917), one of the developers, named this West End street in 1854 in Stinson, Brown, and Ramsey's Addition. Born in Hamilton, Ontario, later a resident of Chicago, Stinson invested in at least twenty-four additions to the city of St. Paul, was one of the founders of Superior, Wisconsin, and invested heavily in Chicago canal lands. A quiet, reserved man of immense wealth, he was the largest landowner in Ramsey County during the nineteenth century. Stinson Boulevard in Minneapolis bears his name. For more information, see "Glimpses at a Hamilton Family" in the magazine *Ontario History*, June 1972. See also *Arlington Hills, Stinson Park, Stinson Street, Thomas Avenue, Woodland Park*.

JAMESON STREET Frank and Carrie Crowell named this street near Lake Como in 1907; the significance of the name is uncertain.

JAYNE STREET This short street near Battle Creek was named in 1951 for the daughter of Herbert West, city plat commissioner at the time.

JEFFERSON AVENUE Thomas Jefferson, third president of the United States, is commemorated in this 1854 street name, which first appears in Stinson, Brown, and Ramsey's Addition. He was related to the prominent Randolph family of Virginia. An intersecting street was named Madison. See also *Randolph Avenue*.

JENKS AVENUE Recalled as "a quiet, retiring man in his disposition, a gentleman of uniform habits and a good citizen," Jonathan R. Jenks (1832?–90) was born in Pennsylvania. He moved to St. Paul in 1855 to be with his brother-in-law, Governor Alexander Ramsey, and entered the drug business with Dr. David Day. A subsequent pharmacy went bankrupt, and the jinxed Jenks spent the remainder of his life as a clerk with the War Department at Fort Snelling.

The original plat drawing of this 1872 Arlington Hills Addition illustrates a sizable pond across what is now Jenks Avenue between Payne Avenue and Greenbrier Street (between Blocks 14 and 17). See also *Arlington Hills, Ramsey Street*.

JESSAMINE AVENUE Harwood Iglehart, William Hall, and Charles Mackubin, natives of Maryland, may have had that state's more temperate climate in mind when naming this East Side street in 1857. *Jessamine Court* derives its name from the same source. See also *East Side, Iglehart Avenue, Mackubin Street*.

JESSIE STREET Jessie Rice (1851–74) was the second daughter of Edmund Rice, the developer of this East Side street in 1855. Jessie married Frank H. Clark of Philadelphia, who had visited St. Paul as president of the Lake Superior and Mississippi Railroad Company. See also *East Side, Edmund Avenue*.

JIMMY LEE RECREATION CENTER Previously known as Oxford Playground, the center took its present name in 1980. Jimmy Lee is honored as the first black athletic official in the state, officiating at baseball, football, and basketball games in a variety of different leagues. Born in Vicksburg, Mississippi, he came to St. Paul at the age of twenty-three, later working as the director of the Hallie Q. Brown Center in 1936. He is remembered as a "pioneer, an enthusiastic fan, an outstanding sports official, and beyond all that, a truly great person."

JOHANNA CROSSING See *Hamline Village*.

JOHN STREET When created in 1852 in Kittson's Addition, this Lowertown street was assigned the most common of all male names. John Baptiste Coty, one of the original developers of St. Paul, was a man of some standing and property in the early city, but it is recorded that the infidelity of his wife with a prominent citizen so unnerved him he returned to his native Canada, where he died.

Jenks Drug Store at Kellogg Boulevard and Cedar Street, circa 1875.
Photograph by William Henry Illingworth; courtesy of the Minnesota
Historical Society.

JOHN IRELAND BOULEVARD This new boulevard was named in 1961 at the instigation of the Ancient Order of Hibernians, a Catholic Irish-American fraternal organization. John Ireland (1838–1918) was Roman Catholic archbishop of St. Paul from 1884 until his death. Born in Ireland, he immigrated to St. Paul in 1853 with his parents. An appealing and intellectual boy, he was sent to France by Bishop Cretin, where he was educated as a priest—always mindful of his inferior status as an Irish "charity case." After the Civil War, he actively entered the civic life of the city, exhorting his Irish-American congregation against political corruption and the liquor interests. He initiated the resettlement of Irish immigrants from the crowded cities of the East to western Minnesota.

He shrewdly used his influence as a churchman with the devoutly Catholic wife, Mary Mehegan, of James J. Hill, the wealthiest and most influential man in the state. In the real-estate boom years of the 1880s and 1890s, he risked the church's money, gambling that the creation of the University of St. Thomas and the St. Paul Seminary would increase the value of the surrounding lots he had purchased. As part of the speculation, he paid Thomas Lowry,

Father John Ireland, "the fighting chaplain."
Photograph courtesy of the Minnesota
Historical Society.

the streetcar mogul, a $250,000 "incentive bonus" to extend the streetcar routes to his lots, making them more salable. With the financial depression of 1893, Ireland's real estate lost most of its value, and it was a reluctant James J. Hill who came to his rescue.

Notwithstanding his failures, Ireland is generally regarded as an important figure in the building of Catholic St. Paul. Unfortunately he burned all his papers before his death, making it difficult for the historian to fully comprehend Ireland's contributions. For more information on Ireland and the role of Irish Catholics in St. Paul, see *Claiming the City* by Mary Wingerd. See also *Chatsworth Street, Connemara Patch, Finn Street, Grace Street, Groveland, Mother Teresa of Calcutta Boulevard, Paulapolis, Shadow Falls Park.*

JOHNSON PARKWAY The original East Side street in this location, named Johnson Street in 1856 in the Suburban Hills plat, was probably in honor of Gates A. Johnson (1826–1918), a surveyor and civil engineer. Born in New York, Gates moved to St. Paul in 1855, where he became chief engineer for one of the railroads. In 1930 the street was expanded into Johnson Parkway. Stretching between Indian Mounds Park and Phalen Park, this more recent name commemorated John A. Johnson (1861–1909), governor of Minnesota from 1905–9. See also *Burnquist Street, Clough Street, Gorman Avenue, Hubbard Avenue, Marshall Avenue, Merriam Lane, Ramsey Street, Scudder Street, Sibley Street.*

JONES STREET Edwin F. Jones (1896–1961) was city utilities engineer when this street was named by the city council in 1956. Born in St. Paul, he grew up in North Dakota, returning to graduate from the University of Minnesota in 1916. In his later years he was considered an expert on public utility rates. Alas, fame can be fleeting—at least for city employees—because this street was vacated in 1983 with the development of Energy Park. See also *Energy Park.*

JORDAN AVENUE This street was named in 1917 in Beaver Lake Heights for James W. Jordan, chief clerk of the department of public works. He was born July 4, 1863, in St. Paul of Irish parents and died August 12, 1934. See also *Beaver Lake Heights.*

JOSEPHINE PLACE Platted in 1886 as part of the Henry Herrn farm in Reserve Township, this short street was later extended south. Josephine's identity is unrecorded. See also *Reserve Township.*

Looking north on Johnson Parkway from Bush Avenue. Two of the houses in the background remain, at 852 and 862 Johnson Parkway. Photograph courtesy of the Minnesota Historical Society.

JOY AVENUE Charles and Jane Joy of St. Paul named this most obscure West Side street in 1884. He was a successful architect, who moved to St. Paul from New Hampshire in 1884 and remained here for at least a decade. Only reachable via Water Street, this unpaved avenue (today a sort-of parking lot) will bring joy to the heart of the intrepid urban traipser. The walk continues down a barricaded path to the long-abandoned Twin City Brickyards. A sign at its entrance proclaims a permit is necessary to continue further, and not being a scofflaw, the traipser will quickly discover other natural enticements nearby. See also *Water Street*.

JUDICIARY PLAZA A two-acre linear park with stone art and an amphitheater, the plaza is north of (behind) the Judicial Building on Cedar Street across from the State Capitol.

JUDSON AVENUE (Fairgrounds) Familiarly known as "Carl," Roswell Carlton Judson (1844–1905) was born in Chenango County, New York. After the Civil War, he moved to Farmington in Dakota County, his home when he was elected secretary of the Minnesota State Agricultural Society, the organization responsible for the state fair and the naming of this street within the fairgrounds. It was during his term as secretary, in 1885, that the state fair, having been held in Rochester, Owatonna, and other cities around the state, purchased their permanent home in the suburb of Hamline, a location deliberately chosen to avoid the appearance of prejudice toward either St. Paul or Minneapolis.

JULIET AVENUE William and Nell Nettleton and their son, George, owned a 130-acre dairy farm in the vicinity of Randolph Avenue and Lexington Parkway. William and Nell had a daughter, Julia; the diminutive of her name is Juliet, a street name given by the family in 1886 when Julia was seventeen years old. See also *Nettleton Avenue*.

JUNIPER LANE Designated by the city council in 1967, this Highland Park street name is derived from some juniper bushes planted along its route.

JUNO AVENUE In 1880 a new source of gold was discovered in Alaska; the following year the miners attracted to the site organized a town and called it Juneau for one of the mine workers. This West End street exploiting the gold rush was named in 1881, but because there was already a Juneau Street in the city, this alternative spelling was used. See also *Alaska Avenue*.

KAHOUT'S PONDS These three ponds of the same name were located on the levee just upriver from the High Bridge. The largest pond, used as a dump for the waste from McMillan's slaughterhouse, defied the term "fresh water." The third pond was more of a large puddle. The middle pond, separated from the others by a road, was where the neighborhood boys used to do their skinny dipping, occasionally trying to attract the attention of the girls walking along Cliff Street. The girls, of course, steadfastly refused to raise their eyes from the roadway. There were also small sunfish in the pond, which could be caught in a net of cheesecloth with breadcrumbs as bait and used to catch northern pike and other larger fish in the Mississippi River. Discarded railroad ties became rafts, and in the winter local kids skated on the pond. The Kahout family lived nearby. See also *Bohemian Flats, Lakes/Ponds.*

KANSAS AVENUE Originally Hoyt Avenue, the present name is that of the state.

KASOTA AVENUE Previously Wheeler Street, the name was changed in 1940 to avoid duplication. One source of this new name might be a reference to the famous gold-hued building stone quarried in the community of Kasota, north of Mankato.

KASOTA PONDS These three (or more) wetland ponds on Kasota Avenue, just west of the intersection with Highway 280, belong to the Bridal Veil Creek watershed. The first surveyor's notes in 1847 record these ponds. See also *Bridal Veil Creek.*

KATHLEEN'S PATH One of the well-worn trails offering a peaceful reverie along the timeless river, passing springs, old mill sites, and ancient mounds. Bask in dappled sunlight, soaring eagles, hypnotic hummingbirds, the occasional washout, and the awe of vibrant rainbows.

KAUFMAN DRIVE Named by the city council in 1967, this is one of the streets within Como Park. N. LaMont Kaufman (1894–1971) was superintendent of parks in St. Paul from 1932 to 1965. Born in Belmond, Iowa, he was a landscape architect when he moved to St. Paul in 1919. In 2005, this street was co-named Max Metzger Way. See also *Max Metzger Way.*

KELLOGG BOULEVARD Probably no other street naming in the history of the city commanded as much attention and publicity as that of Kellogg Boulevard. Originally platted as Third Street, it was the main business thoroughfare up into the 1880s, when it began to deteriorate, and its buildings, occupants, and customers became progressively more shabby and neglected. In 1927, the city began a massive renewal project, which included demolishing most of the buildings on the river side of the street, displaying a sweeping view that had been ignored since the earliest days of the city. To dispel the image of old Third Street, the *St. Paul Pioneer Press-Dispatch* newspaper and the St. Paul Real Estate Board sponsored a contest seeking a name reflecting the street's reincarnation. Albert Slawik, a theater organist in St. Paul, won the hundred-dollar prize. On December 20, 1932, accompanied by fireworks, a parade, and thousands in attendance, the city council met in special session on the stage of the Auditorium for the sole purpose of bestowing this new name.

Minnesota had a number of players on the national political scene, but at this time, few of them from St. Paul. Frank B. Kellogg (1856–1937) built his home at 633 Fairmount Avenue in 1889 and lived there intermittently until his death. Kellogg served as U.S. senator, 1917–23; secretary of state, 1925–29; U.S. ambassador to Great Britain, 1923–25. His most important achievement, for which he was awarded the Nobel Prize for Peace in 1929, was the Kellogg-Briand Pact of 1928, a multination agreement designed to prohibit war as an instrument of national policy. This remains a laudable goal.

KELLOGG MALL The park on the river side of Kellogg Boulevard.

KELLOGG VIADUCT See *Rabbit Hole*.

Construction during the dramatic transition from Third Street to Kellogg Boulevard, circa 1937. Photograph courtesy of the St. Paul Department of Public Works.

KENNARD STREET Kennard Buxton, not a local resident, was the attorney for the East Side developer Joseph Lee in 1878. *Kennard Court* takes its name from the same source. Between Fremont Avenue and Third, Kennard, and Flandrau Streets, there was originally a cranberry marsh depicted on the plat of Lee's Suburban Homes made in 1878. See also *East Side, Hillcrest Knoll*.

KENNETH STREET Eugene Underwood (1818–93) and his wife, Fredericka, of Louisville, Kentucky, platted this street in Underwood's Third Addition in 1887. They owned considerable property in the Groveland area, and at one time Wheeler Street was Fredericka Street, and Davern Street was Underwood Street. Eugene, who came from a prominent Kentucky family, was a distinguished attorney who lived in St. Paul between 1865 and 1875. His son, Oscar W. Underwood, was a candidate for the Democratic nomination for president in 1912. However, it does not appear any member of the family was named Kenneth. See also *Groveland, Magoffin Avenue*.

KENNY ROAD Originally Patridge Street in the 1850s, this Railroad Island street name was changed in 1960 because the Kenny Boiler and Manufacturing Company moved to a new site here. John and Terence Kenny founded this local company in 1869, soon after the first railroad came to Minnesota. John's sons, Louis T. (1887–1970) and Phillip J. (1894–1973), managed the company from the early 1900s until it passed out of the family in 1965. See also *Brunson Street*.

KENT STREET Charles Mackubin named this street in 1855 in Mackubin and Marshall's Addition in the Summit-University area. Mackubin was from Maryland, and Kent County is in that state. See also *Blair Avenue, Hollow, Mackubin Street, Summit-University*.

KENTUCKY STREET Previously Fourth Street, the name was changed in 1876 to commemorate the state. This street was vacated in 1975 as part of the Riverview Industrial Park. See also *Alabama Street, Colorado Street, Florida Street, West Side Flats*.

KENWOOD PARK This one-fifth-acre park dedicated in 1912 is a circle surrounded by Kenwood Parkway.

KENWOOD PARKWAY Originally Kenwood Terrace, the name was changed in 1888. The surrounding area is known as Kenwood Park, a popular name that originated with Kenwood, Illinois, a Chicago suburb. The area is unusual in that the streets remain paved with brick. See also *Maiden Lane, Virginia Street*.

KESTON STREET The village in England prompted this St. Anthony Park street name in 1885.

KIDD, THEODOSIA, PARK See *Theodosia Kidd Park*.

KILBURN STREET This street near Como Park was named in 1885 when English names were especially popular. Kilburn is a part of London, England, northwest of St. Paul's Cathedral.

Number 985 Kilburn was the home of Fred Ferguson, a machinist with the nearby Northern Pacific Railroad shops. In 1894, he became president of a local of the American

Railway Union led by Eugene V. Debs, who organized rail workers across the country. This national union won a historic victory over local railroad magnate James J. Hill in the Great Northern strike of 1894, but it was crushed later that year by federal troops sent in to break the Pullman strike. Ferguson continued his union activism as longtime president of Machinists Lodge 112. See also *Armstrong Avenue, Boyd Park, Colne Street, Empire Drive, Energy Park Drive, Minnesota Transfer Yards, Rice Park, Ryde Street, Sherburne Avenue, William Mahoney Street.*

KIM PLACE Kim was the daughter of Ernest and Faye Williams, who were friends of Grege Beckett, plat commissioner when this street was named in 1965. See also *Faye Street.*

KING STREET Platted in 1857, this West Side street was named by David H. King (b. 1829?) and others. Born in Connecticut, he traveled to St. Paul in 1857 with his family and brother, Henry J. King. Both are recorded as lumber merchants, and both had left the state by 1860. There is a representative showcase of compact, ornate, nineteenth-century brick workingman's homes on King Street between Gorman Avenue and Robert Street. See also *West Side.*

KING'S MAPLE WOOD This 1913 addition platted the area between St. Clair and Goodrich Avenues, between Cretin Avenue and Mississippi River Boulevard. William King along with John and Elizabeth Norton were the developers. See also *Macalester-Groveland.*

KINGSFORD STREET Once Balsam Street, the name was changed in 1947. Walter J. Kingsford (1874–1946) was manager of Twin City Hamline Realty, the company developing the property. Born in Rushford, Minnesota, Kingsford taught in the rural schools for five years before moving to St. Paul in 1908, where he entered the real-estate business, later becoming president of the Minnesota Realty Association. His widow remembered this East Side plat bearing his name as a large swamp that had to be filled in. See also *Echo Avenue.*

KIPLING STREET See *Berland Place.*

KIPP'S GLEN This hidden and delightful neighborhood above Crosby Lake is the result of the plat Kipp's Glen Terrace made in 1912 by Ivan J. and Catherine Kipp. The intrepid urban traipser will find it between West Seventh Street and Montreal Avenue, between Elway Street and Glen Terrace. In a column by "Oliver Towne" in the *St. Paul Dispatch*, April 30, 1959, there is a description of this "family valley" neighborhood. This isolated enclave did not get city sewers until the 1980s. See also *Glen Terrace, Ivan Way.*

KITTSON STREET Considered unassuming and undemonstrative in his manners, quiet and unobtrusive, and very reticent in business matters, Norman W. Kittson (1814–88) was ranked as one of the richest men in the Northwest. Born in Canada, he came to Minnesota as a sutler at Fort Snelling in 1834. He next worked as an independent fur trader, established steamboat transportation on the Red River, and invested heavily in railroads with James J. Hill. He was elected to the state legislature and served a term as mayor of St. Paul. In his later years, "Commodore" Kittson and his wife, Louise, spent much of their time in New York City. When asked why, he replied that in St. Paul, people constantly pestered him trying to get at his moneybags. This street was named in 1854 in Kittson's Addition. Today this street is no more than a stoplight on East Seventh Street, but in the early days of the city, it was part of the affluent Lowertown residential area. Kittson's home on today's site of the Cathedral of St. Paul was one of the most splendid mansions in nineteenth-century St. Paul. See also *Kittsondale Sewer, Lowertown; Dawson Park, Edmund Avenue, Larry Ho Drive, McDonough Park, Nelson Street, Olmstead Street, Otis Avenue, Powers Avenue, Prince Street, Smith Avenue, Stewart Avenue, William Mahoney Street.*

KITTSONDALE SEWER This is an extensive storm sewer system draining the Midway area of St. Paul. It is remarkable for its two spiral staircases (one brick, one metal) that descend over three hundred stairs through the limestone strata into the softer sandstone below. The stairs are used to break the waterfall that would otherwise quickly erode the sandstone.

Kittsondale was Norman W. Kittson's personal playground. Located between what is today University Avenue and Interstate 94, between Pascal and Dunlap Streets, Kittsondale had an enormous sixty-four-stall horse barn, a horse racing track with bleachers, and many other amenities. Among his noted steppers were the bay stallion Von Arnim and the bay mare Lady Ross, each valued at $10,000. The property was converted to industrial uses around 1900, and the name Kittsondale passed from common parlance over a century ago. For more information on this sewer, including photographs of the stairs, see the excellent article by Greg Brick on Cascade Creek, "Stairway to the Abyss." See also *Kittson Street, Midway.*

The Kittsondale horse-racing track near what is today University and Snelling Avenues. Photograph courtesy of the Minnesota Historical Society.

KLAINERT STREET This street was added to the city in 1950 in the McDonough public housing development. The name of Robert John Klainert (1924–45), a serviceman killed in World War II, was suggested by the Nels Wold (#5) Chapter of the Military Order of the Purple Heart because both Robert and his father, Joseph, were recipients of the Purple Heart award. John J. McDonough (1895–1962), for whom the project was named, was mayor of St. Paul from 1940 to 1948. See also *Biglow Lane, McDonough Park, Timberlake Road*.

KNAPP STREET John H. (1825–88) and Nellie Knapp were two of the developers of this street in 1885. The Knapps invested in St. Anthony Park but never lived in Minnesota. He was born in Elmira, New York, traveled to Iowa about the age of eight, and in 1846 moved to Menomonie, Wisconsin, where he invested in a sawmill. Business increased into the 1880s, when the Knapp, Stout Lumber Company was considered the largest lumbering concern in the world. *Knapp Place* takes its name from the same source. See also *St. Anthony Park*.

L

LACROSSE AVENUE William Leonard Ames (1846–1910) and his wife, Helen, the developers of Hazel Park, named this street in 1886. There is a Mississippi River city in Wisconsin by that name. See also *Ames Avenue, Hazel Park.*

LAFAYETTE PARK The neighborhood—largely commercial—is within a few blocks of Lafayette Square. See also *Eileen Weida Park, Lafayette Square.*

LAFAYETTE ROAD In 1872 the city council combined the three streets of Jefferson, Chestnut, and Herkimer under the name Lafayette, in honor of the Marquis de Lafayette (1757–1834), French statesman and soldier. Thomas Jefferson once described Lafayette as having "a canine appetite for popularity and fame." By the late 1940s, the St. Paul Planning Board was already recommending "widening Mississippi Street and Broadway, and a new bridge in the vicinity of Broadway or Pine to bridge the Mississippi River to the West Side, the Airport and South St. Paul." See also *Lafayette Square.*

LAFAYETTE SQUARE On property purchased by the city in 1884–85, this was once an elegant public park and fountain at Lafayette Road and Grove Street that graced a prestigious 1880s residential neighborhood. The park, sold in 1948, is now a parking lot in a business area. For more information, see the detailed article "Lafayette Park and the Vanished Houses of St. Paul's Elite" by Marshall Hatfield.

LAFOND AVENUE In 1857, when Benjamin LaFond (1819–1904) platted LaFond's Addition, he originated only three new east-west streets: Lafond, Lake Street (now Blair), and Bluff Street (now Van Buren). LaFond, born in St. Boniface, Canada, moved to St. Paul in 1851, where he dealt in real estate with Auguste Larpenteur and Alexander Ramsey. His numerous descendants continue to erroneously insist the parallel streets to the south of Lafond Avenue were named for members of the LaFond family. Let it be forever known that definitive research in the plat documents clearly proves the four street names—Thomas, Edmund, Charles, and Ellen (now Sherburne)—had all been named in other plats prior to LaFond's Addition. See also *Edmund Avenue, Lafond Lake, Mt. Eudes, Thomas Avenue.*

LAFOND LAKE On the plat of LaFond's Addition, what is today Blair Avenue between Farrington and Marion Streets was named Lake Street because it crossed a shallow lake in the area. The dimensions of this lake are well illustrated on the original plat of Lafond's Addition and in the 1884 Hopkins atlas. It covered the area between Minnehaha Avenue and Marion Street, between Farrington Street and Thomas Avenue. Judging from the first grading records of Elfelt Street, the lake was more of a large shallow basin than a well-defined deep lake. See also *Elfelt Street, Frogtown, Lakes/Ponds.*

LAKE COMO A popular nineteenth-century tourist attraction, Lake Como in northern Italy near the Swiss border is surrounded by mountains, and villas border its shores. The name was borrowed by Henry "Broad Acres" McKenty in the St. Paul real-estate boom years of the 1850s to enhance the sale of his lots around the shores of what had been known as Sandy Lake. As an example of how the lake has changed, here is a notice we would not see today: A farmer on Lake Como placed an ad in the *Pioneer-Democrat* newspaper in June 1857, "The undersigned will pay $3 for every loon and 50¢ for every king-fisher shot on lake Como and brought to his house—Wm. B. Aldrich."

In 1891, while planning a boulevard around the perimeter, the park board discovered the lake was dwindling at an alarming rate, and sunk artesian wells to maintain the depth. Today, however, the water level is sustained by the runoff from twenty-three storm sewers, and from time to time the lake must be treated to preserve the water quality. No swimming is allowed. See also *Como Avenue, Como Boulevard, Orchard Avenue.*

The Aldrich Hotel on Lake Como was built in the 1860s and burned in 1883. The hotel stood on what is today Como Boulevard, just north of Horton Avenue. Photograph by Charles Alfred Zimmerman; courtesy of the Minnesota Historical Society.

LAKE ELIZABETH See *Stonebridge Boulevard*.

LAKE HAMLINE Glacial Lake Hamline was a geological construct by Warren Upham, an amateur geologist, secretary of the Minnesota Historical Society, and fellow toponymist. His article delineating the ancient lakebed covering prehistoric St. Paul appeared in the 1897 *Bulletin of the Geological Society of America*. See also *Lakes/Ponds*.

LAKE IRIS Within Iris Park, this lake was originally a natural pond, but depletion of the groundwater precipitated a leaky lake, so it was first waterproofed in 1921. Today the lake has an asphalt bottom and, when filled with water, is about twelve inches deep. The intrepid urban traipser might conclude that encasing what had been a natural pond in asphalt and concrete tends to distract from its contemplative appeal. See also *Iris Park, Lakes/Ponds, Union Park*.

LAKE MENNITH According to information supplied by Ann Kenne, archivist of the University of St. Thomas, Lake Mennith was a man-made lake on the St. Paul campus of what is today the University of St. Thomas. It was created in 1887 on the east side of the campus by damming a stream running to the river. One source speculates this stream followed the course of today's Snelling Avenue, and then down Summit Avenue to the lake; another speculation is that the lake source was the same stream flowing into Finn's Glen. In any case, the lake drained away in 1902 with the installation of the city sewers. Archbishop Thomas L. Grace was appointed titular bishop of Mennith, a long-defunct see in Palestine, upon his retirement as archbishop of St. Paul. Grace lived on the St. Thomas campus until his death in 1897, and one of his principal recreations was a walk around the shore of Lake Mennith. See also *Finn's Glen, Grace Street, Lakes/Ponds*.

LAKE PHALEN The St. Paul Water Company, a private corporation, constructed its first supply plant at Lake Phalen (which took its name from the creek) in 1869, and water flowed in underground pipes by gravity to downtown St. Paul. Purchasing the company in 1882, the city tapped the lake as the primary source of its water until 1913. The impetus for a water utility in the early days of the city came not so much from a desire for drinking water as the necessity of having a water supply to fight fires.

There was originally a series of wetlands and ponds extending more than a mile off the southeast end of Lake Phalen, some of which is undergoing restoration. By contrast, parts of this same wetland have been filled to build developments like McAfee Circle. St. Paul continues to struggle between accommodating more houses and preserving what little natural space remains. See also *Lakes/Ponds, Linke's Landing, Phalen Creek*.

LAKE SARITA See *Sarita Wetland*.

LAKE STREET This East Side street was named in 1946 for its proximity to Beaver Lake. There are 4,901 other Lake Streets in the United States.

LAKES/PONDS There were a number of lakes and ponds in earlier St. Paul, many of which have since been drained, routed into the sewer system, or filled. See *Ames Lake, Beaver Lake, Boxmeyer Bay, Brickyards Lake, Cozy Lake, Crosby Lake, Dayton Avenue Lake, Dead Horse Lake, Dew Drop, Frost*

Much of the campus of the University of St. Thomas was built after Lake Mennith was drained into the sewer system. This photograph was taken in 1886. Courtesy of the Department of Special Collections, University of St. Thomas, St. Paul, Minnesota.

Lake, Great Northern Pond, Hare's Lake, Hastings Pond, Kahout's Ponds, Lafond Lake, Lake Como, Lake Elizabeth, Lake Hamline, Lake Iris, Lake Mennith, Lake Phalen, Lake Sarita, Lamprey Lake, Langford Lake, Larpenteur Lake, Loeb Lake, Mackubin Lake, Millett Outlet, Nigger Lake, Pacific Lake, Pigs Eye Lake, Rifle Park Lake, Roger Puchreiter Pond, St. Albans Lake (1), St. Albans Lake (2), Snake Lake, Suburban Pond, Upper Lake, Weber's Pond, Wiggins Pond, Willow Reserve.

LAKEVIEW AVENUE The street's location near Lake Como prompted this name in 1915.

LAMBERT LANDING Occupying the site of the first steamboat landing in St. Paul, the one-third-acre Lambert Landing at Warner Road and Jackson Street, the city's municipal dock, was constructed in the 1930s. It was named in 1937 for Colonel George C. Lambert (1867–1934), a prominent St. Paul attorney, businessman, and leader in the campaign for a nine-foot navigation channel in the Mississippi River. Born in Belgium, Lambert immigrated to St. Paul in 1887 by way of Ghent, Minnesota. Here he practiced law, served as adjutant general for a time, grew mushrooms, and was active in the organization of the Farmers Union Terminal Association.

On the north side of Warner Road between Jackson and Sibley Streets, across from Lambert's Landing, is the Lambert Landing Mural, created in 1986 by local artist Seito Jones. Planks from the old High Bridge boardwalk and stairway were memorably configured by Jones to represent the Mississippi River from Fort Snelling to Navy (Raspberry) Island. See also *High Bridge, Lower Landing Park*.

LAMB'S ISLAND This island is mentioned several times in an 1888 court case dealing with the St. Paul waterfront levee: *City of St. Paul vs. the Chicago, Milwaukee & St. Paul Railway Company*. The legal description was Government Lot 3, Section 5, T28, R22; and Government Lot 5, Section 32, T29, R22.

LAMPREY AVENUE Uri Locke Lamprey (1842–1906), a prominent attorney, named this street in 1887. He was appropriately active in the establishment of the Minnesota Game and Fish Commission, diving in as its president for many years. His wife was a daughter of Louis Robert, for whom Robert Street was named. This street has been vacated as part of the St. Paul Downtown Airport. See also *Lamprey Lake, Robert Street*.

LAMPREY LAKE This was a large, shallow lake now sucked up by the St. Paul Downtown Airport. An early surveyor noted the lake had a dense growth of tall rushes that, in decomposing, had gradually filled the lake so that it was reduced to a small shallow pond at its center,

Lambert Landing, St. Paul's municipal boat dock, hosted this riverboat circa 1936. Photograph courtesy of the Minnesota Historical Society.

some three or four feet higher than the adjacent Mississippi River. In 1885 the lake was platted into building lots with their own park. The 1884 Hopkins atlas illustrates its dimensions. See *Lakes/Ponds, Lamprey Avenue*.

LAMPREY PARK This four-acre park—in Lamprey Lake—was dedicated to the public in Lamprey's Addition in 1885. It is shown on the 1928 Hopkins atlas at the corner of Colorado and Trent Streets. Although the park was turned over to the Saint Paul Downtown Airport in 1929, it appears the city still owns it. See also *Lamprey Avenue, St. Paul Downtown Airport*.

LANDMARK PLAZA PARK This was formerly the Hamm Memorial Park, complete with its own waterfall and pond. The present name refers to the Landmark Center across the street. Opened in 2003, this new park, once the site of the city's bus depot, is at the downtown junction of St. Peter and Market Streets.

LANE PARK Den E. Lane, the developer, named this small East Side park at Jessamine Avenue and Lane Place in 1916. See also *Upper St. Dennis Road*.

To expand the St. Paul Downtown Airport, it was necessary to fill in most of Lamprey Lake. In the 1930s, this WPA project gave work to many who were unemployed. Photograph courtesy of the St. Paul Department of Public Works.

LANE PLACE Both this East Side street and the park nearby were named in 1916 for Den E. Lane, prominent real-estate developer. See also *Upper St. Dennis Road*.

LANGFORD LAKE See *Langford Park*.

LANGFORD PARK (street) This street was named in 1885 for Nathaniel P. Langford (1832–1911) and his second wife, Clara. Born in upstate New York, Langford came to St. Paul in 1854, where he worked in banking. In the 1860s, during the rampant gold rush days, he was often panned as the collector of internal revenue in Montana. Organizer of an expedition that discovered the Yellowstone geysers, he became the first superintendent of Yellowstone Park and wrote two books about his experiences in the West. In St. Paul he became a key organizer of investors for St. Anthony Park; much of today's Como Avenue as it passes through St. Anthony Park was originally Langford Avenue. Langford died one of St. Paul's most colorful and respected citizens. See also *St. Anthony Park*.

LANGFORD PARK The seven-acre park was also named on the original St. Anthony Park plat of 1885. Before the creation of the parks board in 1888, Langford Lake, occupying most of the park, was drained and filled by the public works department. See also *Lakes/Ponds*.

LARCH STREET The larch is a common North American tree better known as tamarack, which was a common species in this area. All the adjacent streets, most of which have been renamed, also bore tree names. This North End street was platted in Fuller's Addition in 1856. See also *North End*.

LARPENTEUR AVENUE Originally Minneapolis Avenue, the name was changed by the city council in 1904. Auguste L. Larpenteur (1823–1919) was born in Baltimore, grandson of a French émigré. As a young man, he moved to St. Louis and subsequently to St. Paul in 1843—one of its first twelve settlers. He helped lay out the original city and claimed 160 acres in the Midway, near Lexington Parkway and University Avenue, which he sold to his Uncle Eugene to farm. Engaged in the fur trading and merchandising business, in 1860 Larpenteur and his wife, Mary, built a family home, the "Anchorage," near what is today Dale Street and Interstate 94. He spoke French, English, and several Indian languages; he had a nervous, sanguine temperament, all life and animation, with black piercing eyes. Because he was the oldest surviving pioneer in St. Paul, the street was renamed in his honor. This street marks a section line on the land survey. See also *Front Avenue*, *Larpenteur Lake*.

Auguste L. Larpenteur, "Grandfather of the City." Photograph by William J. Hoseth; courtesy of the Minnesota Historical Society.

LARPENTEUR LAKE According to librarian Josiah Chaney, writing in 1904,

> Larpenteur Lake was a fine body of clear water. The east end was at a little distance west of Dale street, between Carroll and Marshall streets, and it extended to and a little beyond St. Alban's street. It was directly opposite the Protestant Orphan Asylum [southeast corner of Marshall Avenue and St. Albans Street]. A good many years ago a land owner, whose south line was in the water at the east end of this lake, filled in to his line, but did not improve the property. Iglehart Street was graded through it, and St. Albans Street across it; the remaining part was filled in, terminating its existence.

According to the first grading records of St. Albans Street, the lake, graphically shown on the plat of Smith and Lott Subdivision drawn in 1853, was about thirty feet deep. Auguste Larpenteur's home was in the vicinity. See also *Larpenteur Avenue, Lakes/Ponds*.

LARRY HO DRIVE Larry Ho was the pen name of Laurence Curran Hodgson (1874–1937), mayor of St. Paul from 1918 to 1922 and 1926 to 1930. Born in Hastings, he began work at age fourteen as a printer's devil on the *Hastings Democrat*, working his way up to the staff of the *Minneapolis Tribune* by 1897. In subsequent years, he held several posts within city government and wrote for St. Paul newspapers. A prolific writer and an entertaining speaker, he had a great facility for relating to people. He wrote a playful obituary of himself in 1935: "He was a sort of foolish fellow, but he never failed when we needed him. His brain may have been wabbly, but his heart was staunch. He was our friend." Upon his death, Hodgson's body lay in state at the foot of the giant statue of an Indian god of peace in the concourse of the city hall. This street near Battle Creek was named by the city council in 1959.

Today Hodgson is forgotten; the only living memory of his accomplishments is the ribald poem he is said to have written when the brothel of Nina Clifford on Washington Street was demolished to make way for the city morgue in 1937—which says something about what history comes down to us. For the sake of our bawdy readers and future historians, the poem is reproduced below:

THE LAY OF NINA CLIFFORD

The windows are grimy and covered with dust
In that old house under the hill
The door hinges rusty, the lock is bust
The spider webs cover it still
No longer do gay lights their welcome convey
Inviting the wayfarer in
To choose from the bevy, his favorite lay
To dally a while and sin.
    Gone are the sofas and plush covered chairs
From the parlor once happy and bright
No longer do douche pans in bedrooms upstairs
Clank busily all thru the night

No more do fat burghers play and carouse
And jounce pretty blonds on their backs
For Nina is dead and her once famous house
Is sold to pay up the back tax.
    They're widening the street so they're tearing it down
They're tearing its timbers apart
The whorehouse that once was the pride of the town
Soon won't be worth more than a fart
Its stone they are taking the morgue to repair
A purpose appropriate—true
For many a stiff has been lain in them both
Even as me and you.

See also *Dawson Park, Edmund Avenue, Kittson Street, McDonough Park, Nelson Street, Olmstead Street, Otis Avenue, Powers Avenue, Prince Street, Smith Avenue, Stewart Avenue, William Mahoney Street.*

LASALLE STREET This Midway street was named in 1881 for Sieur de La Salle (1643–87), French explorer. This name was selected, no doubt, for its classy cachet. See also *Midway.*

LAUREL AVENUE Like Ashland and Holly Avenues, this street was named for the tree in 1870 in the Woodland Park Addition. The classical use of the leaves as a crown of victory makes this an attractive name.

    The first mass transit system in St. Paul was the St. Paul City Railway Company in which horses hauled cars on rails. There were four barns; one was at the southeast corner of Dale Street and Laurel Avenue. Six different routes served the city, each indicated by a specific color because many residents were illiterate or foreign born and unable to read English. The St. Anthony Hill line (Green Light) originated at the Union Depot, came up Rice Street to Summit Avenue to Western Avenue to Laurel Avenue to Dale Street. The cars ran every seven minutes, and the fare was five cents. Overall, the system had twenty-six miles of street tracks, 455 horses, two hundred employees, and seventy-seven cars seating two thousand persons. See also *St. Anthony Hill, Woodland Park.*

LAWSON AVENUE Part of the Arlington Hills Addition in 1872, this street was most likely named in honor of an unknown individual. See also *Arlington Hills.*

LAWTON STEPS These seventy-seven steps, constructed in 1911 and rebuilt in 1992, ascend the hill from Grand Avenue to Lawton Street, where the intrepid urban traipser will meander through an exclusive enclave on the way toward Summit Avenue. See also *Stairways.*

LAWTON STREET Dr. George O. Lawton (1848–1909), a dentist, owned considerable property in St. Paul and named this street in 1871. His house stood on the corner of Grand Hill and Lawton Street.

LEE AVENUE (Fairgrounds) A father-son combination is honored in the naming of this street within the state fairgrounds. William Edwin Lee (1852–1920) of Long Prairie was a member

The St. Paul City Railway ran on Laurel Avenue between Western Avenue and Dale Street in the 1880s. Photograph courtesy of the Minnesota Historical Society.

of the Board of Managers of the Minnesota State Agricultural Society from 1903 to 1909. His son, Raymond A. Lee (1880–1956), was secretary of the society from 1930 to 1950. Raymond's dual occupations of banker and dealer in farm equipment kept him in touch with the vicissitudes of rural living, and his knowledge of finance and economics greatly benefited the fair during this period of extensive expansion.

LEECH STREET Samuel Leech, the developer, was appointed receiver of the U.S. Land Office at St. Croix Falls, Wisconsin, in 1848. He invested heavily in Minnesota land and named this street in Leach's Addition in 1849, complete with alleys (sixteen feet wide), a rarity at the time. Subsequently land officer at Quincy, Illinois, he served there until his death in 1861.

Although now in private hands, there is a remarkable old fire station at 1 Leech Street at Grand Avenue. Built around 1880 of brick, the Steam Fire Engine House No. 3 is a well-preserved example of utilitarian Victorian architecture.

LEIF ERICKSON PARK This three-acre, triangular state park on the south side of University Avenue between Rice and Park Streets houses a large statue of Leif Erickson incongruously in a grove of evergreens. Leif "The Lucky" was a Norse explorer, a favorite with the Scandinavian population of Minnesota, widely held to have been the first European to reach the shores of North America. The sidewalk cutting diagonally from southeast to northwest replaces what was once the course of Wabasha Street.

LELAND STREET Previously Parmer Street, the name was changed in 1940.

LENOX AVENUE Lenox is a town in Massachusetts and one of the most fashionable of the New England resorts. Although the name was assigned in 1887 by the Union Land Company, this short, narrow street in the Highwood area was only recently opened. See also *Highwood*.

LEONARD COURT Leonard Court in the Highwood area was platted by William E. and Bonnie L. Leonard in 1975. See also *Highwood*.

LEONE AVENUE Leone was the wife of Grege Beckett, plat commissioner when this street near Indian Mounds Park was named in 1960. Leone Beckett taught in the city schools for many years.

LEROY TRIANGLE This tiny park near Lake Como at Van Slyke Avenue and Argyle Street was dedicated to the public in 1885 in the Warrendale addition. Today it is a "ghost park": there but not marked. Its chief attribute seems to be a bus bench. The identity of Leroy is unknown. See also *Ghost Parks, Warrendale*.

LEVEE ROAD Named by the city council in 1964, this is the road running along the top of the dike from Wabasha Street to Water Street, and from Water Street to Raspberry Island. *Levee* is a synonym for *dike*.

LEWIS PARK This park is named for the "dean of St. Paul real estate men," Robert P. Lewis (1835–1934), who came to St. Paul from Pennsylvania in 1859 as a law school graduate. After the Civil War, he went into real estate, dedicating this one-acre North End park at Marion and Milford Streets in 1883 in Lewis' Second Addition. Since then the park has been expanded and enhanced. See also *North End*.

LEXINGTON PARK This neighborhood is a series of eleven plats made in the 1880s subdividing the area between Lexington Parkway and Hamline Avenue, between Randolph and Eleanor Avenues.

In 1948, sculptor John K. Daniels works on the statue of Leif Erickson that now towers over the park of the same name. Photograph courtesy of the Minnesota Historical Society.

LEXINGTON PARK BASEBALL STADIUM According to information from baseball historian Stew Thornley, this stadium formerly on the southwest corner of Lexington Parkway and University Avenue was opened in 1897 with about six hundred square feet of playing space. It was the home of the St. Paul Saints minor league team, the center of baseball in St. Paul, until 1956 when they struck out. In 1958, a plaque marking home plate was embedded in the floor of the Red Owl grocery supermarket on the site. The Halsey Hall Chapter of the Society for American Baseball Research has a new plaque they intend to put up when the site's current building project is completed. See also *Midway Stadium, Toni Stone Field*.

LEXINGTON PARKWAY John Wann, an Englishman, named this street in 1871 at the instigation of his American wife. Feeling some redress was needed for the many British street names (Avon, Oxford, Milton), his wife suggested this name to honor the Battle of Lexington in 1775, the first battle of the American Revolution in which the British were defeated. In 1907, an attempt was made to change the name to Wheelock Parkway, but it was blocked by patriotic organizations such as the Daughters of the American Revolution.

According to an article in the *St. Paul Globe*, May 12, 1901 (page 24), by William Hoyt, an early settler in the area, a Dakota trail connected Little Crow's village at Kaposia near South St. Paul to Lakes Josephine and Johanna. The path followed the course of Lexington Parkway north, turned west through the area that is today Energy Park, and north between Como Park and the state fairgrounds. In the 1850s, Hoyt wrote, hundreds of American Indians traveled this route on their annual rice-gathering expeditions. This parkway marks a section line on the land survey. See also *Hare's Lake*.

LIGGETT STREET (Fairgrounds) Dean of the Agricultural School and director of the State Experiment Station from 1888 to 1909, "Colonel" William M. Liggett (1846–1909) was involved in the management of the Minnesota State Agricultural Society from 1890 until his death. A resident of Benson, Minnesota, Liggett brought his expertise in cattle breeding to the State Fair. It was during his term as manager, in 1899, that seminal night entertainment was first introduced, including a fireworks exhibition titled "The Burning of Manila." See also *Dewey Street*.

LIGHTNER PLACE Elias and Caroline Drake named this street in 1882 for their friend and, later, son-in-law William H. Lightner (1856–1936). He was born in Pennsylvania, graduated from the University of Michigan, traveled to St. Paul in 1878, and became an attorney in 1880; in 1885 he married Carrie Drake. Lightner later served as a city councilman and was generally active in civic affairs. The cozy street, near Oakland Cemetery, is just one block long. See also *Drake Street*.

LINCOLN AVENUE This street was named in 1871 for Abraham Lincoln: other streets in the Summit Park Addition were Washington and Madison. Between 1890 and 1900, over a thousand abandoned infants were cared for at the St. Paul Babies Home, 846 Lincoln Avenue.

LINCOLN PARK (neighborhood) This neighborhood around Beaver Lake comprises two subdivisions: Norton's Lincoln Park (1946) and Tilsen's Lincoln Park (1955). The boundaries are roughly between the railroad tracks and Case Avenue, between Ruth Street and McKnight Road. See also *Beaver Lake Park, Tilsen Avenue.*

LINCOLN PARK This was to be a public park on Dayton's Bluff between Maria and Bates Avenues, between Cherry Street and the junction of Maria and Bates Avenues. The potential park was surveyed for the city parks department in 1889, but, alas, the land was not purchased. See also *Hiawatha Park, Mohawk Park, West St. Paul Park.*

LINDEN STREET This Mt. Airy street was named in Dewey, Bass and Rohrer's Addition in 1856 for the tree, also known as basswood. In earlier times, when most people walked to their destination, there were dozens of stairways in St. Paul. One of these climbed from Valley Street to near the south end of Linden Street, but most of the stairways, including this one, have been removed over the years. See also *Stairways.*

LINDER COURT Willard G. Linder was the trustee of an estate involved in financing this development in 1956.

LINKE'S LANDING In the early 1900s, Carl Linke owned ten acres of farmland on the east side of Lake Phalen near Larpenteur Avenue and rented boats for hunting and fishing on the lake. In 1924, a ski jump was built on this site, and the St. Paul Ski Club held weekly competitions. See also *Lake Phalen.*

LINWOOD AVENUE Originally Evergreen Avenue, the name was changed in 1895. Linwood takes its name from the basswood tree, the American linden.

LINWOOD PARK This park at Victoria Street and St. Clair Avenue, originally twenty-two acres, was acquired in 1909 with a $32,000 assessment against the nearby properties. It takes its name from the adjacent street. See also *Haldeman Park, Ridgewood Park.*

LITCHFIELD STREET The Litchfield family was active in developing the St. Paul and Pacific Railroad, which provided two North End street names in 1872. William B. Litchfield was general manager of the railroad, and a city councilman. Both Wayzata and Litchfield, Minnesota, were stops along the train's route. See also *Atwater Street, Wayzata Street.*

LITTLE BAVARIA A smaller neighborhood within the North End, between Western Avenue and Jackson Street, between Hatch and Maryland Avenues, is so named for its colorful population of Germans and Austrians. See also *North End.*

LITTLE CANADA ROAD There were several Little Canada Roads. The current one is the remnant of a Civil War road leading north out of St. Paul, along the course of Brainerd Avenue and Edgerton Street, where it swung diagonally northwest to Little Canada, passing close to Wheelock School. This street was vacated in 1981, but a small portion remains as a fragment of Desoto Street.

LITTLE ITALY See *Upper Levee.*

LIVINGSTON AVENUE This street was named about 1855; Livingston was, I presume, the middle name of John L. Stryker, a New York state investor in the plat of West St. Paul. See also *West Side*.

LOCKWOOD PARK: This two-and-one-half-acre park at Cook Avenue and Mendota Street was dedicated to the public in 1883 in Lockwood's Addition. Thomas Cochran, a Twin Cities land speculator, was the attorney-in-fact for H. H. and Anna Lockwood, out-of-town investors, when this park was dedicated.

LOEB LAKE: This popular North End lake takes its name from the Louis S. and Samuel Loeb real-estate company of Duluth, which platted the area in 1907. In earlier times, however, the lake was known variously as Dead Horse Lake and Nigger Lake, descriptive names that defy precise explanation. Writing in 1908, librarian Josiah Chaney described the lake:

> The first to which I will direct attention is called "Nigger lake" or "Dead horse lake." This fine body of water lies in a deep basin, extending from the east side of Dale street and the south side of the Northern Pacific railway tracks east nearly to Mackubin street. It formerly extended to Farrington avenue. It has several bays, and at least one island. It crossed Maryland street and the Northern pacific roadbed, only a few years ago. It is quite deep near the upper end, and, being fed by springs, is one of the sources of Trout Brook. It contains several varieties of fish.

See also *Lakes/Ponds, Loeb Street, North End*.

LOEB STREET: The Louis S. and Samuel Loeb real-estate company of Duluth platted this street in 1907. See also *Loeb Lake*.

LOMBARD AVENUE Lombard is the principal street in London of financial institutions, and by extension, it connotes money and capitalism. "The objects which you see in Lombard Street, and in that money world which is grouped about it, are the Bank of England, the Private Banks, the Joint Stock Banks, and the bill brokers." It was named in 1887 in the Ridgewood Park Addition. See *Ridgewood Park*.

LONDIN LANE Previously part of Lower Afton Road, this Highwood street was renamed in 1963 for Robert Londin, a local developer. *Londin Circle* and *Londin Place* take their names from the same source. See also *Highwood*.

LONG AVENUE Originally named Sidney Street in St. Anthony Park South, the name was changed in 1886. Long is most likely the personal name of some unidentified person. This Long Avenue is a pretty short street. See also *St. Anthony Park*.

LONG HILL This short-speak is iterated hundreds of times a day by St. Paul taxicab dispatchers. The "Long Hill-1" identifies a pickup in the part of the city north of Summit Avenue and west of Lexington Parkway to the city limits. The "Long Hill-2" identifies a pickup in the part of the city south of Summit Avenue and west of Lexington Parkway to the city limits. See also *Short Hill*.

LONG ISLAND This island appears on the 1852 plat of Kittson's Addition at the foot of John Street. It was about eight blocks long and about one-half block wide. It is most likely Government Lot 5, Section 32, T29N R22W. See also *Islands*.

LONGFELLOW AVENUE See *Berland Place*.

L'ORIENT STREET This is the French word for "east," applied in 1857 in Ashton and Sherburne's Addition signifying the eastern boundary of that plat. There were many French Canadians in the city at this time.

LOUIS STREET Joseph Rondo named this street in Rondo's Addition in 1857 for his oldest son, Louis (1835–1913). Joseph Rondo (or Rondeau) was born in Canada, worked as a voyageur, and later took up farming near Fort Snelling. When he had to abandon the military reservation, he occupied a small farm near Seven Corners; in 1862 he purchased a large tract of land northeast of the Cathedral of St. Paul, much of which was swamp at the time. His son, Louis, later killed in a train accident, lived at Centerville until 1893 when he moved to Mounds View. See also *Hidden Falls Park*, *Old Rondo Avenue*, *Seven Corners*.

LOUISE AVENUE Louise was the youngest daughter of Hyman J. Goldberg, office engineer in the Department of Public Works when this street near Indian Mounds Park was named in 1953. See *Indian Mounds Park*.

LOWER AFTON ROAD After climbing the hill from the St. Paul–Point Douglas Road (now Highway 61), this early road, built before the Civil War, ran east into Woodbury Township, where it intersected a second road from St. Paul; both continued into Afton. This street marks a section line on the land survey. See also *Upper Afton Road*.

LOWER LANDING PARK This twenty-two-acre park, opened in 1995 with its long concrete esplanade along the Mississippi River, is on the river side of Warner Road east of Jackson Street. See also *Lambert Landing*.

LOWER ST. DENNIS ROAD Den E. Lane (1881–1952) was one of the most active St. Paul real-estate men in the 1920s and 1930s. Born in Ireland, he came to St. Paul as a child and began his real-estate ventures while a student at St. Thomas College. Known as the "Own Your Home Man," Lane estimated that in the 1920s he had designed, laid out, and named 50 percent of the St. Paul streets platted in the preceding decade. By 1925, he had handled more than ten thousand property transactions. This Highland Park street was named in 1945 for his patron saint, Dennis. See also *Upper St. Dennis Road*.

LOWERTOWN In early St. Paul, there were two steamboat landings: one at the foot of Jackson Street in a swampy area known as the Lower Landing; the other at the foot of Chestnut Street, known as the Upper Landing. By extension, the adjacent communities became Lowertown and Uppertown.

To be precise, however, Lowertown has referred to two separate locations. The first Lowertown encompassed a district east of downtown St. Paul (Kittson's Addition) with bound-

Den E. Lane, "The Own Your Home Man." Drawing from *We Present: A Collection of Seventy-five Sketches of St. Paul Citizens*, 1925.

aries roughly between Grove and Fifth Streets, between Kittson Street and Broadway. From approximately 1860 to 1900, this thrived as an affluent residential area with schools, churches, and many elegant homes. However, with the expansion of the railroads, a corollary warehouse district encroached upon and finally replaced this entire neighborhood. The term *Lowertown* faded from the vocabulary until resurrected by the historic preservation movement of the 1970s. With renewed interest in historic St. Paul, the name Lowertown was revived to market lofts and condominiums in the old warehouse buildings on Sibley, Broadway, Wacouta, and Wall Streets.

There was also a Town of Lower St. Paul platted in 1853 by L. C. Kinney. It consisted of two squares of land, each embracing twenty blocks. Today the lots would be found east of the fish hatchery, south of Point Douglas Road, largely occupied by the railroad. There is no evidence any houses were ever built there. See also *Uppertown*.

LUDLOW AVENUE Previously Nourse Street, the name of this St. Anthony Park street was changed in 1940.

LUELLA STREET Angier and Luella B. Ames of Minneapolis were relatives of William L. Ames Jr., who platted Hazel Park. Luella Ames (1861–1915) was born at Union, Maine, and came to Minneapolis after the Civil War. Upon graduation from Central High and St. Cloud Normal School, she began a thirty-three-year teaching career in the Minneapolis Public Schools, including terms as principal of Kenwood, Humboldt, and Harrison schools. She was well liked and respected; her death was reported on the front page of the *Minneapolis Journal* newspaper. This East Side street was named in 1890. Their daughter was also named Luella. See also *Hazel Park*.

LUTHER PLACE Previously Grantham Street, the name was changed in 1938 for the street's proximity to Luther Seminary.

LYNNHURST AVENUE Chosen in 1884, this Midway street name, like the others in Union Park, was almost surely selected for its pleasing and somewhat exotic sound. *Lynn* comes from the linden tree; *hurst* is an Old English suffix, revived in the nineteenth century, meaning "wooded hill." See also *Union Park*.

LYON STREET Herbert Lyon was director of Civil Service when this street near Indian Mounds Park was opened by the city in 1960.

LYTON PARK This small, one-third-acre park at Lyton Place and Park Street was dedicated to the public in 1883 in Lyton's Addition. A century later, the city enhanced this tired North End commons with landscaping, a handsome wrought-iron fence, and three enchanting bronze sculptures termed "The Dreams of Children" by sculptor Nick Legeros. This $100,000 reincarnation and twenty-nine new homes invigorate this compact neighborhood. The intrepid urban traipser will be enthralled coming upon such playful art in this old, out-of-the-way part of the city.

In 1909, however, the parks board had not been optimistic about the future of the park. In their annual report, they wrote:

> This park . . . is another piece of property almost useless as a park. It is too small and would prove too expensive to police it, and adjoining property holders show a careless indifference for the preserving of any improvement. Trees and shrubs are regularly destroyed by boys, as soon as planted and cattle are allowed to run at large.

See also *Lyton Place, North End.*

LYTON PLACE Irish-born Catherine and Michael Lyton ran a small truck farm on this property purchased in 1856. In 1883, the land was platted, and Lyton's name was given to this North End street. He is listed as a resident of the city, under the spelling Lyden and Lydon until 1891, and descendants of the family still live in the area. See *Lyton Park.*

Deep in the heart of the old North End's modest homes, the intrepid urban traipser can find a reverie among the "Dreams of Children" in Lyton Park. Photograph by Kathleen M. Vadnais.

Macalester Park, "Tangle Town." From *Atlas of the Environs of St. Paul*, 1886.

M

MACALESTER-GROVELAND Taking its name from Groveland School and Macalester College, this midway neighborhood could be defined as being roughly between Mississippi River Boulevard and Lexington Parkway, between Randolph and Summit Avenues. See also *Finn's Glen, Groveland, Kings Maple Wood, Lexington Park, Macalester Park, Randolph Heights, Ridgewood Park, Rosedale Park, Shadow Falls Park*

MACALESTER PARK In 1881, the trustees of Macalester College formed an investment syndicate that purchased the Thomas Holyoke farm, a quarter section of land (160 acres) bounded by Snelling, Fairview, St. Clair, and Summit Avenues. They paid $150 an acre, giving 40 acres as a gift to Macalester College—an inducement to add value to the residential lots. Indeed, the college accepted the property fronting on Snelling Avenue, and the remaining 120 acres was platted in 1883 as Macalester Park. By 1885 the Short Line railroad ran through the Midway area, and Macalester Park became a railroad suburb.

MACALESTER PARK

With the opening of the short lines and the multiplication of trains between the cities, a new and delightful locality for homes has been opened up. . . . Of these residence parks none promise more beauty and attractiveness, and of none can a more rapid growth be noted than Macalester park. About four years ago one hundred and sixty acres were secured, and of these forty acres were set aside to be used for the site of a Presbyterian college, one wing of which has been built. The college was opened for students last fall and about the same time a new depot called "Macalester" was built on the line of the C.M. & St. P. R.R. The one hundred and twenty acres not devoted to college uses were held by a syndicate, who platted it in landscape style, suiting the streets and avenues to the topography of the ground and leaving the natural beauty of the locality undisturbed. A rapid sale of these lots then commenced, and prices doubled in a short time, and indications point to a still further and more rapid advance. Arrangements have been made for the erection of many fine residences, and before another year, with these completed and a large addition to the college built, as is contemplated, Macalester Park will take front rank among the many beautiful suburbs of St. Paul. (*Northwest Magazine*, April 1886)

See also *Macalester Street, Short Line Road, Tangle Town*.

MACALESTER STREET Platted in 1883, the street took its name from the college, which is named after Charles Macalester (1798–1873), a Philadelphia financier. Edward D. Neill, a fellow Philadelphian, wrote and requested financial aid for the college, which Macalester later provided through his will. In consideration of this bequest, the name was changed from Baldwin College to Macalester College. See also *Macalester Park*.

MACALESTER WALK This is an eleven-and-a-half-foot right-of-way on a line with Macalester Street, between Montreal and Beechwood Avenues. Of several such walks remaining in the city, this is the only one that is paved and marked. In the 1920s, these public walks were popular with developers because a walkway, instead of a cross street, allowed for very long blocks, which left more footage for salable lots. See also *Burg Street*, *Wheeler Walk*.

MACKUBIN LAKE This lake (named by the author) is indicated on the 1847 surveyor's notes as he walked the section line—Minnehaha Avenue today—east from what is now Dale Street. At the intersection with today's Mackubin Street, he noted a "small lake" that extended 330 feet east. See also *Lakes/Ponds*.

MACKUBIN STREET Remembered as having "a fine face, indicating good blood," Charles N. Mackubin (d. 1863) was the developer of this Summit-University street in 1855. A well-to-do gentleman from Maryland who wore gold spectacles, Mackubin moved to St. Paul in 1854, where he invested heavily in real estate and banking. The 1860 census lists his property holdings at $300,000, and a household with three servants and a coachman. See also *Summit-University*.

MADISON STREET Charles A. B. Weide, the developer, lived in Madison, Indiana, before he platted this West End street in 1872. See also *Weide Street*, *West End*.

MAGNOLIA AVENUE Harwood Iglehart, William Hall, and Charles Mackubin, natives of Maryland, may have had that state's more temperate climate in mind when naming this street in 1857. *Magnolia Lane* is an extension of the avenue. See also *Iglehart Avenue*, *Mackubin Street*.

MAGOFFIN AVENUE This street was named in 1890 in the Hiawatha Park Addition for Samuel and Beriah Magoffin. Born in Kentucky, sons of the Civil War governor of that state, they came to St. Paul in the 1880s where they, like the other Kentuckians Rhodes B. Rankin and Eugene Underwood, invested heavily in Highland Park real estate. Beriah (b. 1843) farmed for a time, was a state legislator for one term, and later left the city. Samuel (1859–1934) was an attorney in St. Paul throughout most of his life. One of Samuel's daughters became the Princess Ibain-Khan Kaplanoff. See also *Kenneth Street*, *Rankin Street*.

MAHONEY, WILLIAM See *William Mahoney Street*.

MAIDEN LANE A tiny, sixteen-foot-wide brick-paved street behind Summit Avenue, really an alley, was made necessary by the topography of the land. Platted in 1854, it most likely takes its name from a narrow street in London, famous as the home of Voltaire. See also *Kenwood Parkway*, *Virginia Street*.

MAILAND ROAD Opened by the city in 1917, this Highwood road passed through the farm of Julius C. Mailand. See also *Highwood*.

MAIN STREET Originally part of Fort Street, this downtown street name was changed by the city council in 1906. According to the Census Bureau, Main Street is the seventh most popular street name—with 7,644 other occurrences in the United States.

MANCINI STREET Named by city council resolution in 2003 as part of the new Upper Landing urban village, this name honors the Mancini family who came to the Upper Levee in the early part of the twentieth century. One of the sons, Nick Mancini, opened a bar and restaurant on West Seventh Street after the Second World War. The steak house has become a landmark where the rich and powerful mingle with blue-collar folks. See also *Upper Levee*.

MANITOBA AVENUE The "dean of St. Paul real estate men," Robert P. Lewis (1835–1934), came to St. Paul from Pennsylvania in 1859 as a law school graduate. After the Civil War, he went into real estate, naming this North End street in 1882. An adjacent street is named Winnipeg, the capital city of the Canadian province Manitoba. Both were stations on the St. Paul and Manitoba Railroad. See also *North End*.

MANITOU AVENUE Said to be the Algonquin word referring to the mysterious and unknown powers of life and of the universe, this name was given to a narrow street in Beaver Lake Heights in 1917. See also *Beaver Lake Heights, Waukon Avenue*.

MANOMIN AVENUE This West Side street was named in 1855 for the Ojibwe word for wild rice, a diet staple. There is also a county by this name in Minnesota. See also *Mohawk Park, West Side*.

MANTON STREET In 1891, Stendal and Maria Manton named this one-block-long street near Lake Phalen in Manton Park. A resident of the city from 1891 to 1910, Stendal was a music teacher on the East Side.

MANVEL STREET Allen Manvel of St. Paul was general manager of the St. Paul, Minneapolis and Manitoba Railway, whose tracks ran through St. Anthony Park close to this street. After naming this street in 1885, Manvel moved to Chicago in 1891. See also *St. Anthony Park*.

Nick Mancini stands under the marquee of his restaurant, a St. Paul institution, in 1981. Photograph by John Doman; courtesy of the *St. Paul Pioneer Press*.

MAPLE STREET This East Side street was named in 1857 for Mr. Leif Maple, who according to the seeds of legend, was an upright and sturdy citizen of colorful and towering reputation. See also *About Round Way.*

MARGARET STREET Originally Pearl Street, the name was changed in 1872. *Margaret* is derived from the Latin for "pearl." The 1928 Hopkins atlas shows a large pond (500 feet by 200 feet) between Hazel and Ruth Streets, between Fifth and Margaret Streets, just south of Eastern Heights Elementary School. Homes have been built around the perimeter of this previous pool—from which no pearls have been plucked—with large lots extending back into the dry pond bed. See also *Lakes/Ponds.*

MARIA AVENUE Lyman Dayton named this street in 1857 for his wife, Maria Bates, a native of Rhode Island born about 1811. After her husband's death in 1865, she moved to Dayton in Hennepin County. This busy Dayton's Bluff street is pronounced "Mah-rye-ah" by the locals. See also *Bates Avenue, Dayton's Bluff, Lincoln Park.*

Maria Bates Dayton, "her barque, lighted by the love and charity she has given others here on earth, will guide her safely to the dim unknown." Portrait from *History of the City of Minneapolis, Minnesota, 1893.*

MARIA AVENUE TRIANGLE The parks department acquired this small public triangle at Maria and McLean Avenues in 1911. It is adorned with a streetlight, one tree, and some bushes. See also *Maria Avenue.*

MARILLAC LANE St. Louise DeMarillac (1591–1660) is the inspiration for this 1954 Highwood street name. Born in Paris, she was a young widow who, with the aid of St. Vincent de Paul, established an order taking the name Sisters of Charity of St. Vincent de Paul. St. Louise was canonized in 1934 and declared the patron saint of social workers in 1960. The developer of this street, a widow herself, had a relative in the Sisters of Charity. See also *Highwood.*

MARION ISLAND This island appears on the 1852 plat of Kittson's Addition downriver from the foot of Neill Street. It was about two-and-one-half blocks long and about three-quarters of a block wide. See also *Islands, Kittson Street, Lowertown.*

MARION STREET Designated in 1855 in Robertson and Van Etten's Addition, the exact significance of this North End name is obscure. It may be a personal name, or more likely it may honor Francis Marion (1732–95), "the swamp fox," a general in the Revolutionary War and an epic figure in the nineteenth century. When it was named, this street traversed a tamarack swamp. See also *Lafond Lake, Rice Street.*

Looking south on Marion Street toward Thomas Avenue, about 1925. Scheffer School, since demolished, is on the left. Photograph courtesy of the Minnesota Historical Society.

MARKET STREET Because it ran by "Market Square," now known as Rice Park, this street name was applied in 1849. Rice and Irvine Parks were platted as public squares, a piece of undeveloped land; the concept of them as miniature parks, which we have today, did not develop until the 1870s. See also *Holcombe Park Circle*.

MARSH COURT Charles Marsh, of the Minneapolis real-estate and insurance firm of Marsh and Bartlett, was probably a stockholder in the St. Anthony Park Company when this street was named in 1885. Vacated in 1974, this street was within an encroaching industrial area. See also *St. Anthony Park*.

MARSHALL AVENUE A man whose life was described as "swinging on the see-saw board of fate—a good many times up and a good many times down," William R. Marshall (1825–96) was one of the developers of this street in 1855. Born in Missouri, he moved to Minnesota in 1849 and settled in St. Paul two years later as the first hardware merchant. Within a decade, he founded the newspaper *St. Paul Press* and was elected governor of Minnesota from 1866 to 1870. A tall, slender man with sandy whiskers, small features, and a bald head, Marshall was an inveterate real-estate speculator. There is a county in Minnesota named for him.

In marking this section line in 1847, James Marsh, the first surveyor, noted that a road crossed (today's) Marshall Avenue at Arundel Street—the first road from St. Paul heading northwest to the Falls of St. Anthony. Between Dale and Griggs Streets, the surveyor recorded high rolling prairie, while farther west the land was filled with brush and oak barrens. See also *Burnquist Street, Clough Street, Dayton Avenue Lake, Gorman Avenue, Hubbard Avenue, Johnson Parkway, Merriam Lane, Ramsey Street, St. Albans Lake (1), Scudder Street, Sibley Street.*

MARTIN LUTHER KING BOULEVARD See *Rev. Dr. Martin Luther King Jr. Boulevard.*

MARY LANE Platted in 1940 by John and Frances Moravec, this short street near Lake Como was named for their daughter.

MARYDALE PARK This twenty-five-acre park at the intersection of Maryland Avenue and Dale Street, encompassing Loeb Lake, was dedicated in 1974. See also *Loeb Lake.*

MARYLAND AVENUE Harwood Iglehart, William Hall, and Charles Mackubin, natives of Maryland, named this East Side street in 1857. This street marks a section line on the land survey. See also *Iglehart Avenue, Mackubin Street.*

MARZITELLI STREET This new street, part of the Upper Landing urban village, was named by city council resolution in 2002. The name commemorates the Marzitelli family who, like many of their fellow residents, came from a small, fortified medieval village in the wild mountains of Molise Province, Italy, to the Upper Levee in 1913 to work on the railroad. Mike and Mary (Detomaso) Marzitelli raised four children on the levee in their house at 387 Mill Street: Josephine, Frank, Cecelia, and Peter. Frank Marzitelli grew up to hold a number of high positions in city and state government, and, in an ironic twist, the Upper Levee village was condemned and demolished by the city under his jurisdiction. See also *Upper Levee.*

MATILDA STREET Remembered for her "bright, beautiful countenance with black hair and black eyes," this North End street commemorates Matilda (Whitall) Rice (1827–1906), the wife of Henry M. Rice, for whom Rice Street is named. Born in Rome, New York, she moved to Richmond, Virginia, when she was seven. Matilda met Henry Rice in Washington, DC, where she was attending school, and married him in 1849. Whitall Street is also named for her. See also *Rice Street, Whitall Street.*

MATRON'S GROVE See *Municipal Forest.*

MATTERHORN LANE In 1972, Leonard Bisanz, whose mother was born near Berne, Switzerland, named this street in the Swiss Meadows Addition. See also *Colette Place, Dorothea Avenue, Susan Avenue.*

MATTOCKS PARK The three-and-one-half-acre park at Palace Avenue and Macalester Street is named for the Mattocks School building on this site from 1928 to the 1980s. That school name was taken from an earlier Mattocks School built in 1871, which stood at Randolph and Snelling Avenues until moved to the campus of Highland Park Senior High School at Snelling and Montreal Avenues in the 1960s. The inspiration for these names was John Mattocks (1814–75), a Presbyterian clergyman who served as the superintendent of the St. Paul schools for ten years.

MAURY STREET A reserved, modest man with a worldwide reputation, Matthew Fontaine Maury (1806–73) was a naval officer and oceanographer. He wrote several treatises on navigation, the most significant being a basic clarification on winds and currents of the ocean that made possible a drastic reduction in sailing times. Other East Side streets named in this 1857 plat were for Stephen Decatur (1752–1808), James Lawrence (1781–1813), Thomas Truxtun (1755–1822), and Edward Preble (1761–1807), all famous naval officers of the early nineteenth century. See also *Preble Street, Truxton Street.*

MAX METZGER WAY In September 2005, the city council co-named Kaufman Drive in Como Park for Max Metzger, "the Maestro of Como Park." Over eighty years old at the time of this dedication, he had conducted a pops orchestra at the Como Pavilion since 1950. His ongoing involvement with the Como community theater group began even earlier, when his mother founded it about 1945 as the St. Paul Opera Workshop. See also *Kaufman Drive.*

MAY PARK Samuel C. and Eleanor Tatum of Cincinnati named this small park at Clayland Place and Chelton Avenue in 1885 in the Midway Heights addition. Who or what May signifies is unknown. See also *Midway Heights.*

MAY STREET Named in 1881, this West End street name is most likely a personal name, but the identity is uncertain. See also *West End.*

MAYALL ALLEY Real-estate dealer James H. Mayall had a residence on the alley when it was opened in 1879. His brother, Samuel, was a prominent attorney and real-estate dealer in the city for many years. This venerable right-of-way was vacated to the St. Paul Companies when they built their new headquarters building in 1991 at 385 Washington Street. Writing about the alley, Gareth Hiebert called it "a pleasant, well-traveled idiosyncrasy of the city's Loop."

MAYNARD DRIVE In 1951, Maynard Clough of Minnetonka Mills was one of the six investors who purchased forty acres in what had been a stone quarry, and constructed the Sibley Manor apartments and the Sibley Plaza shopping center. The developers were thought foolish to build an apartment complex in what was then a sparsely settled area; however, with its proximity to the airport, the project was quite successful, and soon there was a waiting list for the 550 apartment units.

MAYWOOD STREET Previously Coleman Street, the name of this street near Lake Como was changed in 1940. *Maywood Place* is an extension of the street.

MCAFEE STREET This area near Lake Phalen was platted in 1885 by the Pioneer Real Estate and Building Society, and the streets were named for the officers, who were Keller, Johnston, Fisher, Flint, and McAfee. The only street name remaining is for Hugh J. McAfee (1848–95), the treasurer of the building society at the time and the owner of a large foundry and machine shop on Sibley Street.

There is a remarkable brick and limestone house built by an Italian stonemason, which has been moved to 1317 McAfee Street. See also *Frost Lake, Lake Phalen.*

McBOAL ISLAND In 1950, fourteen men, four women, and three children, a volatile mixture of whites, blacks, Mexicans, and American Indians, were squatting without utilities or taxes within shouting distance of downtown St. Paul. Less than two acres in size, this small island was on the south side of the Mississippi River opposite Broadway street. In the 1950s, the island was condemned by the city and subsequently disappeared, although there is evidence that some of the island might now be part of the West Side riverbank. The name, which appears on the first map of St. Paul in 1851 as Boal Island, is for James McClellan Boal (1805?–62.) The legal description was Government Lot 10, Section 5, T29, R22. See also *Islands, McBoal Street*.

McBOAL STREET Described by an early resident as "one of the best and laziest mortals that ever lived," James McClellan Boal (1805?–62) came to Fort Snelling as a drummer boy under Colonel Leavenworth. He settled in St. Paul in 1846, where he worked as an artist and sign and house painter, was subsequently appointed adjutant general of Minnesota, and served in the state legislature. This West End name, originating in Leach's Addition in 1849, was Boal's nickname. See also *McBoal Island, West End*.

McCLOUD CREEK This name is misspelled on the 1851 Nichols Map of St. Paul. See *McLeod Creek*.

McDONOUGH PARK A seven-acre strip of unimproved "ghost park" land along the north side of St. Paul Avenue between Snelling Avenue and Davern Street, the park was dedicated on the 1945 plat of Lane's Edgcumbe Hills and named for John J. McDonough (1895–1962), mayor of St. Paul from 1940 to 1948. In the 1980s, the city wished to sell the park for housing but was prevented by the Friends of the Parks. See also *Crosby Regional Park, Ghost Parks, Dawson Park; Edmund Avenue, Kittson Street, Larry Ho Drive, Nelson Street, Olmstead Street, Otis Avenue, Powers Avenue, Prince Street, Smith Avenue, Stewart Avenue, William Mahoney Street*.

McGUIRE LANE This Highwood street was named in 1926 for Thomas and his wife Gabriel McGuire, who had a farm and twelve children in the immediate vicinity. The original Mc-Guire house, built in 1913, remains at 2100 Springside Drive. This street was vacated in 1979. See also *Stinchfield Street*.

McKENTY'S LAKE See Lake Como.

McKINLEY STREET William McKinley was president of the United States from 1896 until his assassination in 1901, and this short street near Lake Como was named in his honor in 1913.

McKNIGHT ROAD Originally called East Avenue, the name was changed by the city council in 1957 to honor William L. McKnight (1888–1978), a chief executive of the 3M Company, which has its main offices near this street. Born on a South Dakota farm, McKnight, disliking farm work, went to business school in Duluth. After graduation, he went to work for the Minnesota Mining and Manufacturing Company (3M) as assistant bookkeeper. Having considerable enthusiasm for the company, he was rapidly promoted to general manager. By 1929, he was president of the company; in 1949, he became chairman of the board. This street, the eastern border of the city, marks a section line on the land survey.

Sun Ray Shopping Center and 3M complex at Interstate 94 and McKnight Road in the mid-1960s. Photograph by Buz; courtesy of the Minnesota Historical Society.

MCLEAN AVENUE At the age of sixty, Nathaniel McLean (1787–1871) abandoned his newspaper business in Ohio and moved to St. Paul. Shortly after his arrival here, he was appointed Dakota Indian agent at Fort Snelling. In 1855, he was elected a Ramsey County commissioner, and three years later the Dayton's Bluff area was organized into a township and named in his honor. In 1856, the Suburban Hills plat added McLean Avenue to the map. See also *McLean Township*.

MCLEAN TOWNSHIP Organized in 1858, the boundaries of this early township were (what is today) between Minnehaha Avenue, the Mississippi River, and the boundary with Washington County, between Highway 120 and the nascent city of St. Paul on the west. By 1887, the entire township had been annexed into the city. The township took its name from Nathaniel McLean, who settled here in 1853. See also *McLean Avenue*.

MCLEOD CREEK In 1846, Alexander McLeod purchased 160 acres

> in what is called Faylin's Creek, and what is more generally known as Faylins falls . . . together with all and singular the Mill or Mill buildings, improvements, ways, watercourses. . . .

This name for Phalen Creek was used in the early years of the city. See also *Phalen Creek*.

McMURRAY FIELD This thirty-two-acre athletic field within Como Park was initiated in 1927 and named in 1929 for William McMurray. Born in Ireland in 1863, he came to St. Paul in 1894, where he became an exceedingly prosperous tea merchant. In 1922 he donated twenty-five acres on Battle Creek to the city as the impetus for Battle Creek Park. An exceedingly generous man, he gave away more than $120,000 to various good causes between 1913 and 1923 and "wrote off" another $117,000 owed his firm. In 1930, his firm declared bankruptcy, and McMurray put his personal fortune into paying off the firm's debts. By 1944, he was living in a downtown hotel at $15 a week when he was quoted as saying, "Where is the money? I haven't the slightest idea, but I hope it did some people some good. I guess I was just in business for the fun of it anyway." For the past two decades, thousands of Hmong have attended Hmong New Year sporting competitions and celebrations at McMurray Field. See also *Battle Creek Park, Xees Phaus.*

McQUILLAN PARK This approximately one-half-acre park at Laurel Avenue and Mackubin Street, once the site of "old" Webster School, was acquired from the Board of Education in 1955. The name honors Arthur Joseph McQuillan (1895–1954), known as the "Mayor of Selby Avenue." Well-connected politically, he was DFL Chair for Ramsey County and a reliable source of patronage jobs for neighborhood residents in the Depression years. He is also remembered as the first white master plumber in St. Paul to hire a black plumber. The McQuillan family has tended to business in St. Paul since 1857.

According to librarian Josiah Chaney, the area of this park had been, prior to the building of the school, a large marsh and a shallow lake that was later drained through the sewer. See also *Lakes/Ponds, Merle Harris Bridge.*

Norman Mears, namesake for the downtown park, was an early proponent for the preservation of Lowertown. File photograph courtesy of the St. Paul *Pioneer Press.*

MEARS PARK On the original 1849 plat, this two-acre, undivided square between Fifth and Sixth Streets, between Sibley and Wacouta Streets, contained only the word "rock." The fact there was no indication it was intended as a public square is not surprising, because in those early days, the park was the location of a rocky hill fifty feet high. In the 1870s, it became known as Smith Park, for Robert Smith of Alton, Illinois, one of the developers. Fifty years later, the park board made tentative efforts toward selling the park, claiming it had no use within this warehouse district. With the decline of railroad commerce in the 1950s and 1960s, the area around the park languished, but in the early 1970s, Norman Mears (1904–74), an industrialist whose family had owned a business in the area for years, proposed a plan to renovate the buildings in this area, now rechristened as Lowertown. Upon Mears's death in 1974, the park was renamed in honor of his efforts to revitalize Lowertown. See also *Baptist Hill, Elm Square, Irvine Park, Lowertown, Rice Park.*

MECHANIC AVENUE *Mechanic* has a general meaning of "skilled worker," a fitting name for this street platted in 1874 adjacent to the St. Paul Harvester Works.

In the last quarter of the nineteenth century, St. Paul was the railroad and riverboat gateway to thousands and thousands of acres of newly opened agricultural lands in the Dakotas, Montana, and western Minnesota. In this period of mechanical innovation in farming methods, St. Paul, Minneapolis, and Stillwater developed large farm implement manufacturing industries. In St. Paul, there were two Harvester manufacturing plants, both of them isolated on the northern boundary of the city.

One, the St. Paul Harvester Works Company, was located at the south end of Lake Phalen, just west of Mechanic Avenue. It was organized in 1872 to manufacture the Elward Harvester, Pioneer Corn Binder, and Eureka Mower. Besides the fifty acres needed for the manufacturing facilities, the company also had eighty acres laid out in lots for the workers, resulting in a small village with a chapel, schoolhouse, store, and post office. Employing close to five hundred men, the company manufactured over five thousand machines a year. Before 1975, Parkway Elementary School was named Deane School for Erasmus M. Deane, president of the St. Paul Harvester Company.

The second plant, the Walter A. Wood Harvester Company, was located between Maryland and Case Avenues, between Ruth and Hazel Streets. Consisting of a number of buildings, it opened in 1892 on the Chicago, St. Paul, Minneapolis, and Omaha Railroad as the largest factory west of Chicago. The buildings—most of which remain today as the 3M Distribution Center—were one-story brick, constructed to be "slow burning," and protected by a sprinkler system with water from artesian wells. The factory had its own electrical power plant used to light the factory buildings and supply power for the electric switch engines within the grounds. In 1904, the Minnie Harvester Company, as the manufacturing works was by then known, was purchased by the International Harvester Company, which set to work making twine from flax straw at the manufacturing works. The twine was used to tie up shocks of wheat and bales of hay to dry in the fields. It was a great technical success until the company realized the twine was a delicacy for grasshoppers, which devoured it without hesitation.

MENDOTA CIRCLE This new street on the north side of Phalen Boulevard was named by the city council in November 2005.

MENDOTA STREET Originally Oak Street, the name of this East Side street was changed by the city council in 1872. The name *Mendota* is a Dakota word meaning "mouth of a river." See also *East Side*.

MERCER STREET At one time Clinton Street, the name of this short West End street was changed by the city council in 1883. *Mercer* is a common place name, with a touch of elegance gained from the French *mer*, meaning "sea." See also *West End*.

MERLE HARRIS BRIDGE In 2004, a bronze plaque bearing the likeness of Merle Harris (1927–98) was unveiled at the opening of this handsome Selby Avenue bridge over Ayd Mill Road.

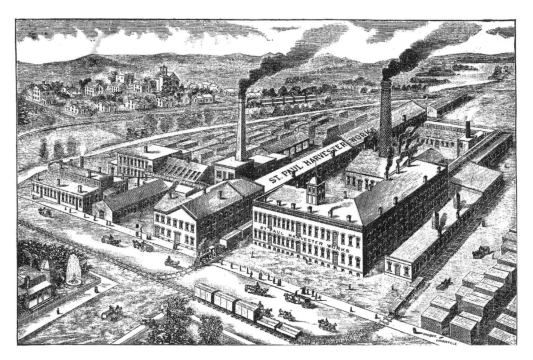

The St. Paul Harvester Works was near Mechanic Avenue at the south end of Lake Phalen. Notice in the upper left corner the little village with a church that grew up next to the factory. Lake Phalen is in the upper right. Today, all the buildings depicted here are gone. Drawing from a pamphlet on the St. Paul Harvester and Cord Binder published in 1882; courtesy of the Minnesota Historical Society.

A St. Paul businessman instrumental in obtaining the signature bridge, Harris helped organize the Selby Area Commercial Club and promoted development along the avenue. He became known as the "Mayor of Selby Avenue." The east and west concrete piers are encircled with the etched names of St. Paul railroads. See also *Bridges, McQuillan Park, Summit Lookout Park.*

MERRIAM LANE Previously Terrace Park Avenue, the name was changed in 1940. John L. Merriam (1825–95) and his son, William R. Merriam (1849–1931), were the developers of Merriam Park. John was one of the founders of the First National Bank and a state legislator; William was active in politics, governor of Minnesota from 1889 to 1893, and later director of the U.S. Census. Their residences faced each other across Cedar Street above the Capitol Building. One house was used for many years as the Science Museum until torn down; the other house burned seventy years ago, but the broad steps that led up to it remain at the end of Sherburne Avenue. See also *Burnquist Street, Clough Street, Gorman Avenue, Hubbard Avenue, Johnson Parkway, Marshall Avenue, Ramsey Street, Scudder Street, Sibley Street.*

MERRIAM PARK In 1882, John L. Merriam subdivided a 140-acre tract between the Short Line railroad and Marshall Avenue, between Dewey Street and Cleveland Avenue. He built a depot where the railroad intersected with Prior Avenue, and built the first Longfellow School. To prevent speculation in this railroad suburb, he stipulated a house worth at least $1,500 had to be completed within a year of the lot purchase. It was a successful venture, and within two years four more additions extended the boundaries of the original community. Within the addition, Merriam included an eight-acre park named Merriam Terrace. See also *Warrendale*.

MERRIAM'S OVERLOOK According to local author Larry Millett, "wealthy residents living near what is now the State Capitol area helped finance a magnificent overlook that became one of the city's most visited places." Known as Merriam's Overlook (John L. Merriam and his son, William, both owned mansions nearby), this beautiful spot on Sherburne Avenue included a small fountain, exceptionally handsome iron railings, and a winding stone staircase (part of which remains) down to Robert Street. The intrepid urban traipser will find a city panorama at this public park, but all the embellishments are long gone. See also *Cass Gilbert Memorial Park*.

MERRILL STREET William C. Merrill Jr. was sales manager for Thomas Frankson, one of the developers of Chelsea Heights in 1916. Merrill moved from St. Paul soon after. See also *Chelsea Heights, Frankson Avenue*.

METCALF LANE When the southern part of Hazel Street was changed to Battle Creek Road in 1957, it became necessary to change Battle Creek Lane to Metcalf Lane to avoid confusion. The name comes from the addition platted in 1948 by Allen A. and Elna Metcalf. This street was vacated in August 1966.

MICHAEL STREET James C. Michael (1863–1946), a district court judge in Ramsey County for thirty-one years, is honored by this 1959 street name near Battle Creek. Raised on a Virginia farm and educated in country schools, he moved to Red Wing at age twenty-one, where he worked as a law office clerk and was admitted to the bar in 1885. Four years later, he came to St. Paul, where he eventually served as corporation counsel for the city. Appointed a district judge in 1915, Michael, an avid reader and enthusiastic baseball fan, was known for his patience and tolerance.

MICHIGAN STREET Charles Willis (1819–98), the developer, who grew up on the banks of Lake Erie, named this street in 1851 for Lake Michigan. Adjacent streets were St. Clair, Superior, Ontario, Erie, and Huron. The CSPS (Czechoslavak Protective Society) Hall at 383 Michigan Street is a reminder of the many Czechs who settled in the West End. The Czech composer Anton Dvorak visited the hall in 1893. See also *Huron Street, St. Clair Avenue, Superior Street*.

MIDDLETON AVENUE James Middleton (1833–1902) was reckoned as one of the oldest and best-informed real-estate men in the city at the time of his death. Born in Northern Ireland, he came to Cottage Grove in Washington County about 1841. He lived on the family farm there until 1881, when he moved to St. Paul and entered the real-estate business, naming this West End street in 1887. A state legislator in 1876, Middleton was running for county commissioner the year of his death.

MIDWAY In giving locations of the streets in this book, we have used the term *Midway* to define a section of the city roughly between Lexington Parkway and the boundary with Minneapolis, between Pierce Butler Route and Interstate 94. Prior to the formation of the neighborhood district councils in the 1970s, the term *Midway* described a much larger area.

The Midway area, midway between downtown St. Paul and downtown Minneapolis, held great promise for several decades around the turn of the twentieth century. A 1922 St. Paul planning report summed it up: "The linking up of Saint Paul with Minneapolis will be of increasing importance with the expansion of each city. They will inevitably tend to become one great metropolis." Almost a century later, the hope that Minneapolis and Saint Paul would unite has not been realized, although all parts of the Midway area between the two cities have long since been developed. See also *Federal City, Paulapolis; Desnoyer Park, Energy Park, Kittsondale, Long Hill, Merriam Park, Midway Heights, Minnesota Transfer Yards, Peterson Point, Roseville, Union Park.*

MIDWAY HEIGHTS Samuel C. and Eleanor Tatum of Cincinnati named this addition in 1885. It includes the area between Pierce Butler Route and Minnehaha Avenue, between Fairview and Prior Avenues. See also *Tatum Street.*

MIDWAY PARKWAY When the streetcar company installed tracks and overhead wires on Como Avenue, spoiling that aesthetic approach to the popular Como Park and the Minnesota State Fairgrounds, this half-mile-long connection between Como Park and the fairgrounds was developed as an alternative approach. To atone for their philistine activity, the streetcar company paid the park board $2,500 to grade and landscape Midway Parkway.

In the 1890s, the park commissioners were anxious to connect the large parks to complement one another. Named in 1897, Midway Parkway was to be a link in the "trunk line of parkways" beginning at Central Park, extending up the hill past the State Capitol, north on Capitol Boulevard, west on Como Avenue to Como Park, from Como Park to the Minnesota State Fairgrounds, through the fairgrounds to St. Anthony Park, and from there in one direction to the University of Minnesota, and in another direction to Mississippi River Boulevard. See also *Grand Rounds.*

MIDWAY STADIUM According to baseball historian Stew Thornley, this stadium was opened in 1956 (after voters approved a $2,000,000 bond issue) in a gravel pit east of Snelling Avenue between two sets of railroad tracks. The St. Paul Saints played there for four years before the Twins began playing major league ball at Metropolitan Stadium in Bloomington. Midway Stadium lasted another twenty years hosting various athletic events, but it became a "white elephant," and in 1981 it was demolished to make way for the Energy Park development. Today there is another, smaller Midway Stadium (originally named Municipal Stadium) on the north side of Energy Park Drive west of Snelling Avenue, which hosts a new professional St. Paul Saints team with its tailgating fans and hokey antics for enthusiastic crowds. See also *Energy Park, Lexington Park Baseball Stadium, Toni Stone Field.*

MILFORD STREET Originally platted as Spruce Street, the name of this North End street was changed in 1872. This designation, although nondescript, does have the advantage of being short and easy to pronounce.

St. Paul Saints playing the opening game at Midway Stadium, April 1957. Photograph by the *St. Paul Dispatch and Pioneer Press*; courtesy of the Minnesota Historical Society.

MILL ISLAND This small island is nearly opposite the foot of John Street. About 0.86 acres, it is designated as Government Lot 6 in Section 32, T29, R22. It was the site of John S. Prince's rotary steam sawmill, according to Josiah Chaney. See also *Islands, Prince Street*.

MILL STREET No evidence exists of a mill in the area of this street, platted in the Upper Levee Addition in 1906. Abandoned after the floods of 1952, it has been revived with the development of the Upper Landing urban village. See also *Upper Levee*.

MILLER CREST LANE Carl S. and Agnes Miller platted this street near Battle Creek in 1954. The name is a compromise between the Millers, who wished the street called Miller Road, and the city engineers, who wished it called Crest Lane.

MILLETT OUTLET This imaginary outlet in Pigs Eye Lake appears only on city maps created by Rudy Paczkowski, a whimsical cartographer in the Public Works Department. The outlet is just south of Rudy's Donut Plantation—astonishingly located in a nearby swamp. The name is a tribute to Larry Millett, whose books on Twin Cities buildings have enlightened a whole generation to the fact that, at least in matters of architecture, the present is not necessarily an improvement over the past. See also *Boxmeyer Bay, Lakes/Ponds*.

MILTON STREET John Wann, the proprietor and an Englishman, named this Summit-University street in 1871 for the poet John Milton (1608–74). See also *Chatsworth Street, Lexington Parkway, Mt. Eudes*.

MINNEHAHA AVENUE This street marks a section line on the land survey. It was named in 1857 in DeBow, Risque and Williams' Addition for Minnehaha Falls, which had been immortalized two years earlier in Henry Wadsworth Longfellow's poem *Song of Hiawatha*. *Minne* means "water," and *haha* means "waterfall." Prior to 1849, the falls were called Brown's Falls by Europeans, and Little Falls by American Indians.

Beginning as early as 1918, it had been the intention of the city to link Minnehaha Avenue over the railroad tracks, creating a road traversing the city from west to east. While Interstate 35E precluded the connection of Minnehaha Avenue, the new Phalen Boulevard serves as an indirect link. See also *Lafond Lake, Mackubin Lake, Mt. Eudes, Pacific Lake*.

MINNESOTA AVENUE (Fairgrounds) Originally Main Street, the Works Progress Administration (WPA) officials decided there were already too many "Main Streets," and the principal thoroughfare within the state fairgrounds deserved a more pertinent title. In 2003, the name was changed to Carnes Avenue. See also *Carnes Avenue*.

MINNESOTA STREET This is one of the original fifteen street names of the city, named on the 1849 St. Paul Proper plat. For over two centuries the river we know as the Minnesota had been called St. Peter's River, a name bestowed by the early French explorers. When the pioneers here were casting about for an American Indian name befitting the new territory—following the pattern of the other Midwest states—they resurrected the Indian name for the river. Soon after, a law was passed officially changing the name of the river from the white man's name (St. Peter's) to the Indian name (Minnesota). A missionary to the Dakotas wrote that at various times the Dakota women explained the meaning of the word by dropping a little milk into water and calling the whitishly clouded water "Minnesota."

MINNESOTA TRANSFER YARDS The large number of rail lines intersecting in the Twin Cities by the early 1880s required transferring freight from one railroad company to another. James J. Hill is credited with the idea of a transfer facility where east- and westbound lines shuttled cargo between them. Hill purchased land near University and Prior Avenues approximately five miles from both downtown Minneapolis and St. Paul, and in 1883 the Minnesota Transfer Railway Company began operation. By 1890, the company owned 200 acres of land with 30 miles of track, and by 1912 the Transfer Railway was the second largest freight interchange in the nation with 160 miles of track. This bustling railroad access was largely responsible for the industrial and commercial development in the Midway area. See also *Empire Drive, Midway*.

MISSISSIPPI CITY See *Federal City, Paulapolis*.

MISSISSIPPI RIVER BOULEVARD In 1887, Horace W. S. Cleveland, Chicago landscape architect and consultant to the newly formed St. Paul Board of Park Commissioners, urged the natural grandeur of the river gorge between the two cities be preserved by purchasing the property along the top of the bluff. Hindered at the outset by unreasonable sale prices, then by a

The Minnesota Transfer Yards, shown here about 1916, was a major influence on the development of the Midway. Photograph courtesy of the Minnesota Historical Society.

depression and the construction of a dam, the whole route was not totally acquired until 1907, through gifts, condemnation, purchase, and platting. The boulevard was in use two years later with a watchman to protect against vandalism. Another segment, named Reserve Boulevard, to extend from the Smith Avenue High Bridge to the Fort Snelling bridge, was never built. See also *Cleveland Avenue, Como Park, Grand Rounds, Reserve Boulevard*.

MISSISSIPPI STREET This important North End street in early St. Paul was named in DeBow, Risque and Williams' Addition in 1857 for the river. For decades, this main thoroughfare exited downtown and funneled traffic north, as Interstate 35E does today. The Broadway-Mississippi streetcar line served as an important route well into the twentieth century. See also *Broadway*.

MITCHELL AVENUE Located on what was the eleven-acre farm of Simon Mitchell, an early pioneer in McLean Township, this Battle Creek street was named in 1959. He was a clerk of the town board intermittently from 1859 to 1878. The name may also refer to William Mitchell (1874–1955), for many years a St. Paul attorney and attorney general of the United States under President Hoover. See also *McLean Township*.

MOHAWK AVENUE This is one of several American Indian names used within Beaver Lake Heights in 1917. These narrow streets have what are called "mountable curbs," twelve-inch curbs that slant at a 45° angle away from the pavement. According to Larry Lueth of the public works department, these are often used on very narrow streets because they allow a parking car to pull up on the curb, so in effect the curb adds an additional twelve inches of width to the street. This type of curb is also used in new developments, making it unnecessary to remove a curb to accommodate future driveways. See also *Beaver Lake Heights*.

A Sunday drive on Mississippi River Boulevard just south of Marshall Avenue, about 1910.
The policeman on the bridge was stationed there to enforce the eight-miles-per-hour speed limit.
Photograph by Charles P. Gibson; courtesy of the Minnesota Historical Society.

MOHAWK PARK In 1889, the city surveyed a potential West Side public park between Smith and Manomin Avenues, between Page and Morton Streets. In the end, however, the land was not purchased. Smith Avenue was named Mohawk Street at this time. See also *Hiawatha Park, Lincoln Park, West St. Paul Park*.

MONKEY ISLAND PARK See *Hendon Triangle Monkey Island Park*.

MONKEY RUDDER BEND A monkey beam is a transverse post at the stern of a paddlewheel steamboat. A rudder hung from the monkey beam behind the paddlewheel is called the monkey rudder. In earlier days when the S curve in the Mississippi River near Hidden Falls Park was even sharper, the back of a steamboat maneuvering through the curve might brush against one of the banks, damaging or destroying the monkey rudder. This curve in the river is known to riverboat pilots as Monkey Rudder Bend.

MONROE COURT Once Palace Place, the name of this West End street was changed in 1942 to avoid confusion with Palace Avenue, which is parallel one block over. The name is that of the nearby school. See also *West End*.

MONTANA AVENUE Running between Lakes Como and Phalen, this street was named in 1886 for the state, following the precedent set in Washington, DC. This section of the city includes only the western states.

MONTCALM PLACE Part of Lexington Park, this street was named in 1886 probably with reference to Marquis Louis Joseph de Montcalm De Saint-Veran (1712–59), a French general killed when the British captured Quebec in 1759. The name was no doubt selected for its elegant sound rather than any local significance. *Montcalm Court, Montcalm Hill,* and *Montcalm Estate Road* all take their names from the same source. See also *Lexington Park.*

MONTGOMERY STREET Originally Havana Street, the name of this Midway industrial street was changed in 1886. The reason for this change or who Montgomery might be is not recorded.

MONTREAL AVENUE This Highland Park street, on a one-half section line, was first surveyed as a county road in 1861. It was apparently graded and opened along at least part of its length by 1878 and had its present name by 1892. However, it was not until the 1920s, with the development of Highland Park, that it assumed the dimensions of the main street it is today.

In 1861, a $2,000 Reserve Township schoolhouse (#8), one-story, 28 feet by 48 feet, with a forty-foot bell tower, was built on the northwest corner of Montreal and Snelling Avenues. It was replaced with a brick structure known as the Quincy School (now demolished) on the site of 1621 Montreal Avenue.

A third schoolhouse (#9) within Reserve Township, originally built on the southwest corner of Randolph and Snelling Avenues, has been preserved on the Highland Park Senior High School grounds on the southwest corner of Montreal and Snelling Avenues. *Montreal Circle* and *Montreal Way* are extensions of Montreal Avenue. See also *Highland Park, Mattocks Park, Reserve Township.*

MONTROSE LANE Introduced in the writings of Sir Walter Scott, a popular nineteenth-century novelist, Montrose is a common name combining the elements of height and flowers. The Desnoyer Park street name was applied here in 1887 by the Union Land Company. *Montrose Place* is on a line with the lane. See also *Desnoyer Park.*

MONTVILLE This village was platted in the Battle Creek area in 1856 as Dayton and Warren's Prospect Addition to St. Paul. The original sequence of streets ran from A through K, but only A Street to C Street remain. See also *A Street.*

MOORE STREET James P. Moore, a land agent, sold lots in Merriam Park when this street was named in 1882. He worked closely with John L. Merriam, serving as his private secretary. Moore came to St. Paul about 1880, moved to Minneapolis in 1890, and left the area shortly thereafter. See also *Merriam Park.*

MORGAN AVENUE A clerk in the city surveyor's office, George H. Morgan, may have been the source of this 1912 Highland Park street name. He later ran a grocery store with his father on the East Side. This street marks a section line on the land survey.

MORGAN TRAIL See *Samuel H. Morgan Regional Trail.*

MORNINGSIDE CIRCLE, MORNINGSIDE DRIVE See *Berland Place.*

MORTON STREET The namesake of this West Side street named in 1857 is uncertain. There is a unique geodesic dome home at Winslow Avenue, Morton Street, and Dodd Road. See also *Mohawk Park*, *West Side*, *West Side Park*.

MOTHER TERESA OF CALCUTTA BOULEVARD This is a co-name for Old Kellogg Boulevard, a two-block-long street running down the hill from the Cathedral of St. Paul. The Ancient Order of Hibernians, a Roman Catholic Irish-American fraternal organization, lobbied for this new name, dedicating it on St. Patrick's Day 2004. While we would all agree Mother Teresa was a laudable woman, the local significance of the name escapes us. See also *John Ireland Boulevard*.

MOUND STREET American Indian burial mounds, a few of which still remain in Indian Mounds Park, prompted this street name in the Suburban Hills plat in 1856. There were originally eighteen mounds in the area, and nineteen more along Dayton's Bluff. Today six remain. See also *Dayton's Bluff*, *Indian Mounds Park*.

MOUNDS BOULEVARD Developed as part of Indian Mounds Park, the boulevard was designed to connect with Phalen Park by way of Johnson Parkway. At one time Mounds Boulevard was projected to extend in the other direction, winding across Swede Hollow, along the crest of Mt. Ida, down to Mississippi Street, up to Mt. Airy, and west to the State Capitol. See also *Mt. Airy*, *Mt. Ida Street*, *Swede Hollow*.

MOUNDS PARK See *Indian Mounds Park*.

MOUNT PISGAH See *Baptist Hill*.

MT. AIRY This hill was one of the seven hills of St. Paul, and at one time part of an area known as the Badlands. Today it is the name of a neighborhood with boundaries roughly between Jackson Street and Interstate 35E, between Pennsylvania and University Avenues. Mount Airy, NC, was the model for the fictitious Mayberry on *The Andy Griffith Show*. See also *Badlands*, *Mt. Airy Street*, *Seven Hills of St. Paul*.

MT. AIRY STREET This street near the State Capitol was named in 1856 with an adjective used quite frequently in the nineteenth century. There is a suburb of Philadelphia titled Mt. Airy because it is in a "high and airy position." The hill took its name from the street. The public housing presently occupying the hill was first planned in 1934 as an effort to clear it of small one- and two-room shacks and squalid apartments that occupied the area at that time, and replace them with comfortable, low-cost housing. This plan, however, was not fulfilled until 1959 when 446 dwelling units were completed. The intrepid urban traipser, ever in search of new vistas, will want to rise to this opportunity. See also *Badlands*, *Mt. Airy*.

MT. CURVE BOULEVARD: This common street name was bestowed in 1915 by developer Den E. Lane in this area south of the University of St. Thomas.

One of the most notable historic homes in the city is the Frederick Spangenberg farmhouse, built 1864–67, at 375 South Mt. Curve Boulevard. Buff limestone from the nearby banks of the Mississippi River was hauled by sled over the snow to the building site. Spangenberg was a dairy farmer, and in 1867, his home stood well outside the city limits of St. Paul. See also *Goodrich Avenue, Iglehart Avenue.*

MT. EUDES This is a twenty-seven-and-one-half-acre plot of undivided property encompassing a large hill between Minnehaha and Lafond Avenues, between Chatsworth and Victoria Streets. It was purchased in 1883 by Sisters of Our Lady of Charity of the Good Shepherd, a Roman Catholic order devoted particularly to the care, rehabilitation, and education of girls and young women who have demonstrated delinquent behavior. The congregation traces its history to an order founded by St. John Eudes in 1641 at Caen, France. On this St. Paul hill, the sisters built an imposing brick building that struck fear into the heart of any teenage girl contemplating mischief. Today the Amherst H. Wilder Foundation owns the site. See also *Watermelon Hill.*

MT. HOPE AVENUE Designating this West Side street in 1874, this is a fairly common place name, including in Massachusetts, the native state of the developers. Mt. *Hope Circle* has the same derivation. See also *West Side.*

MT. IDA STREET It is written of John E. Warren, the developer of this East Side street: "He had traveled extensively and acquired a varied knowledge; being a man of large means, he took the world quite easily, following the bent of his inclinations." Warren's erudition and journeys are reflected in this 1853 street named in Warren and Winslow's Addition for the mountain in central Crete where, according to Greek mythology, Zeus was hidden in a cave to save him from his father. While there, Zeus was nurtured on goat milk and honey and tended by the nymphs Ida and Adrastea. Mt. Ida is one of the most evocative street names in the city. See also *East Side.*

MULBERRY STREET The mulberry tree provided this street name near the Cathedral of St. Paul in 1854 in Dayton and Irvine's Addition.

MUNICIPAL FOREST The major portion, some twenty acres, was a gift to the city from the state in 1915. It had been a part of the fish hatchery property, unusable because of its height. "Forest preserves" were fashionable in 1916 when the Order of the Eastern Star seeded the idea of planting memorial trees for its past matrons in this public park. The forest has since been merged into Indian Mounds Park, but the intrepid urban traipser will find it at the intersection of Point Douglas Road, Clarence Street, and Burns Avenue. Following a path to the top of the hill leads to a panoramic view stretching to South St. Paul, and the ever-observant traipser will be able to discern the star pattern of the trees planted in "Matron's Grove." See also *Fish Hatchery Road.*

MUNSTER AVENUE Possessing a statewide reputation, Andrew W. Munster (1853–1929) was born in Norway and immigrated to St. Paul in 1884, where he became chief bridge engineer. He designed several bridges, among them the 1889 Smith Avenue High Bridge. He is also

Andrew W. Munster, chief bridge engineer of St. Paul, is credited with building the Aberdeen Hotel at 350 Dayton Avenue. Photograph courtesy of the Minnesota Historical Society.

credited with building the Aberdeen Hotel, one of the finest hotels in the city. Although an esteemed city employee, Munster moved to Seattle, where he served as a consulting engineer to the railroads. This West End street was named in 1891. See also *High Bridge, West End*.

MURPHY AVENUE (Fairgrounds) Franklin N. Murphy (1869–1940) was a board member of the Minnesota State Agricultural Society (which named this street within the state fairgrounds) from 1910 to 1918, and president of that society from 1919 to 1920. Born in Wisconsin, he came to Minneapolis in 1891, moving to Wheaton, Minnesota, in 1893. An attorney by profession, Murphy also owned a large farm near Wheaton used as a demonstration station under the supervision of the State Agricultural School.

MURRAY STREET Charles Murray (1868–1964) surveyed this Highland Park street in 1924. He was born in Ireland and moved to St. Paul in 1898, where he worked as a civil engineer and surveyor until 1947, both for the county and privately. This street was platted on the Samuel and Elizabeth Magoffin property. See also *Magoffin Avenue*.

MYRTLE AVENUE This popular feminine and tree name was given to this Midway street in 1881. By the 1920s, the area west of Raymond Avenue and south of University Avenue was primarily dwellings. Today the area is industrial, surrounding a residential rental remnant on one block of Myrtle Avenue between Pelham Boulevard and Glendale Street. See also *Midway*.

MYSTIC STREET Mystic is a village in Connecticut, near New London. Its name was borrowed by the Union Land Company and assigned to this Highwood street in 1888. Before the automobile, one route to Burlington Road from the train station ascended the bluff by way of Piedmont and Mystic Streets. This route remains a public right-of-way—"ghost street"—but it is no longer marked or used. See also *Burlington Heights, Ghost Streets*.

Myrtle Avenue, between Raymond Avenue and LaSalle Street, suddenly becomes a private street for one block —a testament to community support and political connections. Photograph by Kathleen M. Vadnais.

N

NAGASAKI ROAD It took the city three tries to place this name where they wanted it, but it was finally bestowed on the correct street by the city council in 1965. The name was a tribute to Nagasaki, Japan, sister city of St. Paul, and Nagasaki's moral and economic merits were extolled in the council resolution initiating the name. After all the effort to get the name in the right place, the street was vacated in 1994 when the flood levee around Harriet Island Regional Park was refashioned. However, the spirit of the sister-city relationship prevails, most recently exhibited in a Global Harmony Labyrinth off Kaufman Drive in Como Park. Created by local artist Cynthia McKeen, this unique design represents a fresh gesture of abiding friendship and a blend of East-West sensibilities.

NASON PLACE George L. Nason (1886–1949) was superintendent of parks in St. Paul from 1924 to 1932. Born in St. Paul, he graduated from the University of Minnesota engineering school. From 1932 to 1936, he was chief inspector of Texas state parks, afterwards serving as district engineer for the National Park Service in Omaha. In later years, he served as consulting engineer and architect for the St. Paul Capitol Approach project. Remembered as one of the finest park superintendents, he is honored by this 1967 street name within Como Park.

NATHAN HALE PARK This small, one-half-acre park at Portland and Western Avenues, originally known as Portland Park, was dedicated to the public in 1882. In 1906, the Daughters of the American Revolution collected money to add a bronze statue of American patriot Nathan Hale, designed by William Ordway Partridge. In 1914, another $15,000 was donated to enlarge the park. The hedge around the perimeter evokes the colonial period.

NAVY ISLAND See *Raspberry Island*.

NEBRASKA AVENUE Running between Lakes Como and Phalen, this street was named in 1886 for the state, following the precedent set in Washington, DC. The adjacent street names include other western states.

NEID LANE The city council named this access road between Phalen Boulevard and Arcade Street in October 2004 for Karl Neid, a public employee and city councilman who died in 1992 at age forty-three, four months into his term. He grew up in a politically active East Side family, chaired the state Democratic-Farmer-Labor Party in 1985, and was the city's DFL chairman during the 1989 mayoral race. In addition to the street, the footbridge over Island Canal near Lake Phalen was named for Neid. See also *East Side*.

NEIDERHOFFER STREET The city council designated this West End street in 1886. Jacob Neiderhoffer, who had a saloon in the immediate area, later built a house on the street. He died at age sixty-five on November 21, 1891. Once part of a residential area behind the former Ancker Hospital, the street has been engulfed by the campus of the St. Paul school district headquarters at 360 Colborne Street and was vacated in 1976. See also *Colborne Street*, *West End*.

NEILL STREET Almost a "ghost street" now (try and find it!), this street was platted and named in 1852 in Kittson's Addition near downtown for Edward D. Neill (1823–93), clergyman, educator, and the first historian of Minnesota. Born in Philadelphia, he graduated from Amherst College and moved to St. Paul in 1849. He was subsequently a Presbyterian minister, state superintendent of Public Instruction, secretary to President Abraham Lincoln, secretary of the Minnesota Historical Society, and president of Macalester College. Neill was considered independent, self-reliant, progressive, benevolent, a man of research and thought. See also *Ghost Streets*, *Macalester Park*.

Edward Duffield Neill, "a man of letters, a man of literature, a man of research, a man of thought." Photograph by Frederick H. Mares; courtesy of the Minnesota Historical Society.

NELSON STREET (Fairgrounds) A soldier in the Confederate Army, Benjamin Franklin Nelson (1843–1928) came north to Minneapolis after the Civil War. From 1901 to 1907 he was vice president of the Minnesota State Agricultural Society, the organization responsible for the state fair and the naming of this street within the fairgrounds. During his term as president of the society from 1907 to 1909, Nelson observed, "The Fair may well be added to the list of the State's colleges and the visitor that will 'do' the Fair carefully, beginning with Division A, and going on leisurely and thoughtfully down the line to the end, will acquire a surprising amount of valuable information—more than he could in the same time in any other way."

NELSON STREET Arthur E. Nelson (1892–1955) was mayor of St. Paul from 1922 to 1926. Born in Brown's Valley, Minnesota, he graduated from Macalester College, attended law school, and was admitted to the bar in 1915. Five years later, he was appointed corporation counsel for St. Paul, parlaying his popularity for maintaining low streetcar rates into his election as mayor. He later ran for U.S. senator but was defeated. This street near Battle Creek was named for him in 1959. See also *Dawson Park*, *Edmund Avenue*, *Kittson Street*, *Larry Ho Drive*, *McDonough Park*, *Olmstead Street*, *Otis Avenue*, *Powers Avenue*, *Prince Street*, *Smith Avenue*, *Stewart Avenue*, *William Mahoney Street*.

NETTLETON AVENUE William Nettleton (1822–1905) was born in Ohio but moved to Minnesota in 1850, where he taught farming to the Ojibwes near Crow Wing. In 1853, he joined a land company that platted the town of Superior, Wisconsin. Three years later, with his brother, he founded the city of Duluth. In 1871, he purchased 130 acres near today's intersection of Randolph Avenue and Lexington Parkway, where he ran a dairy farm for several years. He subdivided his farm here, platting this street in 1886, and moved to Spokane, Washington, where he died. This "ghost street," unmarked and unopened, is a one-block, east-west street south of Randolph Avenue and east of Lexington Parkway. Noted in the bibliography is a detailed article by the author, "William Nettleton and the Highland Park Spring Water Company." See also *Ghost Streets, Juliet Avenue.*

A family frolicking in Newell Park, circa 1900. Photograph courtesy of the Minnesota Historical Society.

NEVADA AVENUE Running between Lakes Como and Phalen, this street was named in 1886 for the state, following the precedent set in Washington, DC. The adjacent street names include other western states.

NEW CANADA TOWNSHIP Organized in 1858, this township encompassed an area (in today's terms) between Minnehaha Avenue and County Road D, between Rice Street and Century Avenue. Within thirty years, the City of St. Paul had annexed the entire township north to Larpenteur Avenue. The township received its name from the fact that many of its settlers were French Canadians. See also *McLean Township, Reserve Township, Rose Township.*

NEWCOMB STREET Charles B. Newcomb was president of the St. Paul Harvester Works when this short East Side street was platted in 1881. Their factory was close by. See also *Mechanic Avenue.*

NEWELL PARK This ten-and-one-half-acre park at Fairview and Hewitt Avenues, acquired in 1907, is named for Stanford Newell, a member of St. Paul's first park board. This park is a living example of the oak savannas, or "oak openings," that covered much of the city before white settlement.

NEWELL POND See *Great Northern Pond.*

NIGGER LAKE See *Loeb Lake.*

NILES AVENUE Rudolph and Wilhelmina Knappheide, early pioneers of the area who home-steaded at Randolph and Cleveland Avenues, named two streets in 1886: Niles and Detroit. Both are cities in Michigan.

NINA STREET Platted in 1854 in Dayton and Irvine's Addition by a group of developers, it is most likely a personal name. It was not named for Nina Clifford, who arrived in the city some years later.

NINTH STREET In the early days of the city, a large reservoir was planned on Ninth Street to catch the abundant springs that flowed from the hillside there. It was anticipated that such a waterworks could supply twenty feet of pressure at Jackson and Third Streets. This street, the ninth from the river, was named in Bazil and Guerin's Addition in 1850.

NOKOMIS AVENUE Nokomis is the grandmother of Hiawatha in *The Song of Hiawatha* (1855), a popular narrative poem by Henry Wadsworth Longfellow. *Nokomis* is the Ojibwe term for "grandmother." This designation was one of the Indian names used in Beaver Lake Heights in 1917. See also *Beaver Lake Heights.*

NOKOMIS TRIANGLE A large undeveloped triangle of public land platted at the intersection of Bush and Nokomis Avenues and Hazel Street. One local resident observed that in other parts of the city this East Side triangle would be landscaped, or a garden, or used for public sculpture.

NORBERT LANE Norbert Bisanz (1914–94) was one of the brothers who developed this High-land Park area in 1951. Both brothers, Leonard and Norbert, had been in real estate most of their lives. *Norbert Place* takes its name from the same source. See also *Collette Place, Matterhorn Lane, Susan Avenue.*

NORFOLK AVENUE Previously part of Stewart Avenue, this section of the West End street was renamed in 1940. Norfolk is a common English name. *Norfolk Lane* is an extension of the avenue. See also *Stewart Avenue.*

NORPAC ROAD The Northern Pacific—now Burlington Northern—railroad tracks that parallel this Midway industrial street prompted this name in 1965.

NORRIS CIRCLE This street, part of Energy Park, was named for William Norris (b. 1911). He, along with others, founded Engineering Research Associates in St. Paul, generally credited with creating the first practical computer. In 1957, Norris formed Control Data Corporation (CDC), which went on to build some of the most successful supercomputers of its time. CDC was an occupant and partner in the Energy Park development. See also *Energy Park.*

NORTH END There are many definitions of the North End. In delineating locations of the streets in this book, we have considered the North End as the community north of downtown, roughly between the Burlington Railroad tracks and Larpenteur Avenue, between Western Avenue and Oakland Cemetery/Jackson Street. A report on housing conditions in St. Paul in the 1930s had this to say about the neighborhood:

> District "C" [as they called it] is in the main composed of those of Hungarian extraction or birth who as a group seem to be of low civic consciousness. For the most part they are a laboring class, and this would seem to indicate small well kept homes which is more or less true. The houses are however for the most part poorly built and no amount of attention will entirely remedy the initial inadequateness.

See also *Horseshoe Bend, Little Bavaria, Lyton Park, Tri Area, Trillium Park.*

NORTH PARK DRIVE Named by the city in 1961, this street follows the north side of Battle Creek Park.

NORTH STREET This street was the north border of the Brunson Addition plat filed in 1852. North Street, west of Payne Avenue, is in one of the most historic areas of the city. On a spit of land between Phalen Creek and Trout Brook, the area was first known as Bilanski Point for Stanislaus Bilanski, an early settler who was murdered by his wife. In later years, encircled by tracks, it has become known as Railroad Island. See also *Bilanski Point, Railroad Island.*

NORTHERN ROUTE See *Pierce Butler Route.*

NORTON STREET Opened in 1925, this short street near Maryland Avenue and Dale Street is probably a namesake of either John or Edward Norton, real-estate men. See also *King's Maple Wood.*

NORTONIA STREET This name, designated in 1917 in Beaver Lake Heights, is attributed as a compliment to John W. and William W. Norton, real-estate dealers of St. Paul. William left for San Diego in 1918; John (1872–1956) remained in St. Paul to become one of the most prominent and long-lived real-estate dealers. However, this attribution must be questioned because John's son and business partner could not remember his father ever mentioning that street name. See also *Beaver Lake Heights, Norton Street.*

NUGENT STREET This 1882 West End street name is possibly that of John Nugent, an employee of the nearby railroad. See also *West End.*

NUSBAUMER DRIVE Frederick Nusbaumer (1850–1935) was called the "father of the St. Paul park system" for his work as superintendent of parks from 1889 to 1922. Born in Baden, Germany, he attended the polytechnic school in Freiburg. Upon graduation at seventeen, he went to London to work in the famous Kew Gardens, after which he traveled to France, where he worked in its largest nursery. In France, Horace W. S. Cleveland, then recognized as one of the world's leading landscape gardeners, urged him to come to the United States. Nusbaumer immigrated to St. Paul in 1878 and did contract landscaping for twelve years until becoming superintendent. His skill earned Como Park a national reputation. This street within the park was named in his honor in 1967. See also *Como Park.*

O

OAK BLUFF CIRCLE (yawn)

OAK GROVE PLACE John L. and Helen Merriam named this tiny street near St. Clair Avenue and Ayd Mill Road in 1886. See also *Merriam Park*.

OAK VIEW COURT This Highwood street was named in 1965 because it overlooked a cluster of oaks. (Why do you never see an Elm View Court?) See also *Highwood*.

OAKDALE AVENUE Applied to this West Side street in 1874, it is a very common place name. See also *West Side*.

OAKLAND This was the name of a former train station in Burlington Heights. See also *Burlington Heights, Highwood*.

OAKLAND AVENUE This very common name was applied here in 1871 in the Terrace Park Addition. The original Oakland Avenue continued south and east from Grand Avenue down the hill to Ramsey Street; today this stretch of road is an extension of Grand Avenue. The close observer will notice, however, the old name Oakland etched on apartment buildings. A major public works project, this street was carved out of the hillside in 1885 at great expense to provide the gradual incline necessary for streetcars to ascend to Grand Avenue and what was then called the south side of St. Anthony Hill. The name was changed in the 1970s from Oakland to Grand Avenue in response to the Grand Avenue Business Association, which wished to have a Grand Avenue exit from Interstate 35E. See also *Grand Avenue, Grand Hill, St. Anthony Hill*.

OAKLAND CEMETERY This one-hundred-acre cemetery on Jackson Street near downtown was incorporated in 1853 as a municipal cemetery. The name is a very common one and has relevance here because much of St. Paul before white settlement was covered with oak trees. Enhanced by Horace W. S. Cleveland with its own artificial lake (since filled), this oldest cemetery in the city is the burial site of many of the newest immigrants to St. Paul, the Hmong people. During 2005 a doe lived in the cemetery, much to the delight of most visitors. (Not everyone is delighted; the staff has so far found four barbed hunting arrows.) For a listing of some well-known people among the fifty thousand buried here, see *Six Feet Under* by Stew Thornley. See also *Cemeteries, Cleveland Avenue*.

OAKLAND HILL See *Oakland Avenue*.

OAKLAND OVAL This small public park at the intersection of Grand and Oakland Avenues was acquired in 1929.

OAKLAND TERRACE PARK This one-acre hillside public "ghost park" on the south side of Grand Avenue about where it intersects the Lawton Steps was dedicated to the public in 1884 in the Terrace Park Addition. *Terrace* was a nineteenth-century synonym for "hillside," and this stretch of Grand Avenue was previously named Oakland Avenue. For many years, this park was the site of an apple orchard accessible from Pleasant Avenue below. See also *Ghost Parks, Lawton Steps, Pleasant Avenue*.

OAKLEY AVENUE Given in 1884, this Midway street name, like the others in Union Park, was almost surely chosen for its pleasing and somewhat exotic sound. Oakley contains the sound of oak, a tree noted for its strength and permanence. See also *Midway, Union Park*.

OAKLEY SQUARE This tiny island at Oakley and Lynnhurst Avenues was dedicated in 1884 in Union Park. See also *Union Park*.

OAKRIDGE STREET Part of Burlington Heights, this street was named in 1888. See also *Burlington Heights, Highwood*.

OATMEAL HILL According to *The Days of Rondo* by Evelyn Fairbanks, this was a section of Rondo Avenue west of Dale Street. It was a neighborhood where the black railroad porters, waiters, and postal workers lived: those with good jobs. Its social counterpart was Cornmeal Valley. See also *Cornmeal Valley, Old Rondo Avenue*.

OCEAN STREET Most likely prompted by the adjacent street, Atlantic, this East Side street name was given in 1882 by contractor Charles Leonard.

ODELL'S CREEK This prominent West Side creek—now captured in a sewer—began above the St. Paul Downtown Airport in what is now West St. Paul. It flowed through Lamprey Lake, next to the railroad tracks, and along the course of Channel Street to Water Street. After meandering west beside Water Street for a half mile or so, the stream dropped into the river. The course of the creek is graphically illustrated in the 1884 Hopkins atlas, and the name appears on Hitchcock's Addition to West St. Paul.

Thomas S. Odell (d. 1879) came to Fort Snelling after the Mexican War, helped survey the first town plat of St. Paul, and was the first settler on the West Side, building a log cabin there in 1850 when it was still American Indian territory. He subsequently worked as a river pilot and served as the first coroner of Dakota County. His wife, Elizabeth Williams, was the daughter of a Dakota woman and an army lieutenant. There was once an O'Dell Street on the West Side. See also *Brooks/Creeks, Channel Street, Lamprey Lake*.

OGDEN AVENUE Previously Chester Avenue, the name of this Highwood street was changed in 1940. *Ogden Court* is an extension of the avenue. See also *Highwood*.

OHIO STREET Once Randall Street, the name of this West Side street was changed—to the state—in 1880. As it rises from the floodplain to the bluff, it twists and turns, engendering its local appellation "Snake Hill." See also *West Side*.

OLD DAWSON PARK See *Dawson Park*.

Odell's Creek on the West Side, circa 1874, is in the foreground; off to the right is the Wabasha Street bridge. A circus sets up in the vicinity of today's Plato Boulevard. Photograph courtesy of the Minnesota Historical Society.

OLD HUDSON ROAD When Hastings Avenue was changed to Hudson Road in 1940, the previous Hudson Road became Old Hudson Road.

OLD KELLOGG BOULEVARD This short street descends the hill in front of the Cathedral of St. Paul to College Avenue. Before Interstate 94, it was one descent from Summit Avenue into downtown. It is co-named Mother Theresa of Calcutta Boulevard. See also *Mother Theresa of Calcutta Boulevard*.

OLD RONDO AVENUE In the 1950s, 85 percent of the black population of St. Paul was segregated into a densely populated area two miles long and one-half mile wide with St. Anthony and Rondo Avenues running through its center. When the national interstate highway network received funding in 1956, St. Anthony Avenue was selected to become the route of Interstate 94. By the time this project was completed a decade later, over six hundred black families had been relocated, and the black community was severed. In 1989, to commemorate the pre–Interstate 94 black neighborhood—and recognize the annual "Rondo Days" celebration—the St. Paul City Council authorized street name signs reading: "*Old Rondo Avenue, 1865–1966.*" See also *Central Village, Oatmeal Hill, Cornmeal Valley*; see also "A Folding Throne for Queen Victoria."

OLD RUM TOWN On the 1839 map of the Fort Snelling Military Reservation, the first detailed drawing of what is now the Highland Park area, the name Old Rum Town is applied to a group of four houses on the river bluff near what is today Elsie Lane. This is the first recorded reference to cocktails in the locale. See also *Hidden Falls*.

OLD SIXTH STREET While the original grid of numbered streets made perfect sense, at least a dozen reshufflings of the downtown streets have made the present configuration incomprehensible. This street, along with St. Joseph's Lane, was named by the city council in January 1977 at the request of St. Joseph's Hospital.

OLD WALSH PARK See *Walsh Park*.

OLIVE SQUARE This small square at Olive and Williams Streets, acquired in 1872, disappeared when Williams Hill became depressed. See also *Williams Hill*.

OLIVE STREET In the early years there were several Olive streets within the city. This one was named for the tree in 1852 in Kittson's Addition in the original Lowertown, a prominent residential area of the nineteenth century. The northern end of the street is enjoying resurgence with the new St. Paul police station on the corner of Olive and Grove Streets. There is, moreover, a completely new segment of Olive Street, wide and flat, entering the Williams Hill Business Center. See also *Lowertown*, *Williams Hill*.

OLMSTEAD STREET Characterized as "a well-built man; pleasant in his address; quiet in his manners; sensible in his speech; naturally polite, and a real gentleman," David Olmsted (1822–61) was the first mayor of St. Paul in 1854–55. Among other occupations, Olmsted was a miner, farmer, Indian trader, legislator, and newspaper editor. Olmsted County is said to be named for him. It was perhaps symbolic of the stature of history in St. Paul that even the most diligent would have been hard pressed to find this opened, but unmarked street, signifying its first mayor. Originally named Spring Street, this street was renamed (and misspelled) in 1872, and vacated in 1997 as part of the Williams Hill Business Center. See also *Williams Hill, Dawson Park; Edmund Avenue, Kittson Street, Larry Ho Drive, McDonough Park, Nelson Street, Otis Avenue, Powers Avenue, Prince Street, Smith Avenue, Stewart Avenue, William Mahoney Street*.

David Olmsted, the first mayor of St. Paul. From an oil painting in the collections of the Minnesota Historical Society.

OMABAN STREET Named in 1892, this short street near Lake Phalen is one of the most perplexing of all the street names. It is a probably a coined word, perhaps a combination of two personal names. See also *Roblyn Avenue*.

OMAHA-BARTON COLONY See *Barton-Omaha Colony*.

OMAHA STREET Originally platted as Ontario Street, the name was changed in 1872, indicating Omaha, Nebraska, the ultimate destination of the railroad whose tracks and shops were adjacent to this West End street, which was vacated for the reconstruction of Shepard Road in the 1990s. See also *Barton-Omaha Colony*, *West End*.

ONEGA STREET Originally Mendota Street, the name was changed in 1876. *Onega* appears to be an American Indian word of uncertain meaning. This tiny street off Concord Street was vacated in 1992.

ONEIDA STREET Oneida is a small village in Madison County, New York, famous for its communist experiment and the silverware that bears its name. That village was named for the Oneida tribe, one of the six tribes of the Iroquois League. This West End street was named in 1854 in Stinson Brown and Ramsey's Addition with an adjacent street named Madison. See also *West End*.

ONTARIO STREET Because of the many Canadian developers in the earliest days of St. Paul, there were several Ontario streets. Today all of those are gone, except for this remnant below the downtown bluff.

ORANGE AVENUE Harwood Iglehart, William Hall, and Charles Mackubin, natives of Maryland, may have had that state's more temperate climate in mind when naming this East Side street in 1857. See also *East Side*.

ORCHARD AVENUE Previously Locust Street, the name was changed in 1874. The property in this area around Lake Como was first developed by Henry McKenty (1821–69), who moved to St. Paul in 1851. A bustling little man, McKenty named Lake Como (which had previously been known as Sandy Lake or McKenty's Lake) as well as Lake Josephine (for his daughter) and Lake Johanna (for his wife). McKenty lost his money and property in the depression of 1857 and later ended his life. Both his wife and daughter also committed suicide. See also *Como Avenue*, *Lake Como*.

ORLEANS STREET This West Side street was named by the city council in 1883. See also *West Side*.

ORME COURT James E. Orme (1865–1941) for whom this Highland Park street was named in 1927, married Aurora Bohland, daughter of local pioneer farmers. He was a prominent Mason, and treasurer of the Washington Foundry in St. Paul. *Orme Lane* takes its name from the same source. See also *Bohland Avenue*.

ORRIN STREET In 1866, Orrin Curtis, an insurance agent, had a lease on the Cullen house at 698 Stewart Avenue; he was acknowledged when this West End street was named in 1874. See also *Cullen Street*, *West End*.

OSAGE STREET Originally Oak Street, this street name near Lake Como was changed in 1874 for the Osage, a tribe of North American Plains Indians of Missouri, Kansas, and Oklahoma.

OSCEOLA AVENUE Osceola (1800?–1838) was a revered Seminole warrior who fought against white encroachment in the Florida Everglades. He had become a popular and romantic figure when this street was named in 1871.

When walking on Osceola Avenue, the intrepid urban traipser can be headed in all four directions. When traipsers reach that section of Osceola Avenue one-half block east of Milton Street, and also between Grotto Street and Pleasant Avenue, they will be stepping back in history, treading on the old sandstone pavers (cobblestones) once used extensively throughout the city. East of Milton, the original granite curbs also remain; east of Grotto, the curbs are the original sandstone block. Governor Willis A. Gorman was prescient—there is grass growing in the middle of Osceola Avenue east of Milton Street. See also *Gorman Avenue, Summit Avenue*.

THE BEDRAGGLED HARLOT
Paving the Streets of St. Paul

If city streets were oiled often enough, their surfaces were similar to asphalt paving. This photograph was taken about 1920. Photograph by Brown's Photo Studios; courtesy of the Minnesota Historical Society.

Of all the things we take for granted, paved streets have to be near the top of the list. Yet, during the first century of St. Paul, street paving—or lack thereof—was a major issue. The earliest streets were a terrible mess. After the city surveyor staked them out, two furrows were plowed as rudimentary gutters to mark the edges of the street. The roadways were roughly graded to fill in the worst of the holes and remove the highest spots. The local soil type remained as the roadbed.

The streets were filthy with manure from horses that pulled the wagons. Cows, sheep, pigs, dogs, and geese, feeding on the slops and garbage in the street—before the days of garbage collection—added more manure. The occasional dead animal rotted in the street for days before the official city scavenger collected it to dump in the river.

In summer when the streets were dry, the traffic of hooves and iron wheel rims pulverized the ground into a constant dust. A fine mixture of manure, garbage, and grit drifted into crevices of the home, burning the occupants' eyes, and collecting in every fold of their clothing. Because there were no window screens, flies, fresh from the street effluvia, were a constant plague.

In spring and fall the streets became mucky, a mixture of dirt, water, manure, and garbage. Wagons would sink axle-deep, coating the wagon, horse, and occupants with a slimy coat of mud. Crossing such a street in a long dress and petticoats was a perilous undertaking for a woman, inspiring one fervent writer in an 1882 issue of the *Pioneer Press* to compare the muddy streets to

> the bedraggled harlot who sits beside the roadway gloating in her rags and filth and contagion and causing the passers by to lift high their garments lest the squalor of the unseemly figure shall cling to and besmear them. . . .

In winter, streets went unplowed, leaving it up to the horses with their sleighs to pick their way through the drifts.

As the nineteenth century wore on, a few measures were taken to make the streets less onerous. Sprinkling wagons were hired to wet down the dusty summer streets, and brick crosswalks were installed at many intersections to allow pedestrians to cross the street without sinking into the mud. (In London there was an army of young boys known as "crossing sweepers" who, for a penny or so, would sweep clean the brick crosswalks for the ladies in their long skirts.)

By the 1890s St. Paul had become a major city of the Midwest, and the municipal coffers were able to finance some street paving. Spurred on by thousands of bicyclists in the midst of a bicycle craze, the city sought to pave. But what was the best surface?

There were several options, each with its advantages and disadvantages.

One of the first trials was busy University Avenue, which in 1889 was paved with tree trunks about six to eight inches in diameter, cut to half-foot lengths, and set in the street on a cement base. Space between the trunks was filled with asphalt and cement grout.

The first choice for ordinary residential and retail commercial streets was wood blocks, four inches in depth and width, five to ten inches in length, impregnated with creosote. It appealed as the quietest of the pavements with little echo from horses' hooves; however, because of variations in texture among the blocks, the roadway would develop depressions and ruts. Norway pine, tamarack, cedar, and eastern hemlock were the most popular choices. On a grade, the wood was slippery and had to be sprinkled with grit.

According to a map published in the 1916 Hopkins atlas, University, Summit, and Snelling Avenues were among the streets paved with wood block. The cost of this pavement was about forty-two-and-one-half cents per foot. What may be the last wooden-block pavement exposed in the city today is in the alley between Summit and Portland Avenues, between Lexington Parkway and Dunlap Street.

On steep hills, sandstone block was the preferred option because, being soft, it gave horses the best traction. Although sandstone would wear out more rapidly, it was reckoned economical because the load pulled by the horse could be doubled. Among other main streets, it was used on West Seventh and Robert Streets, but the only remaining sample is Osceola Avenue east of Milton Street.

Where there was very heavy traffic and little retail trade, a granite-block pavement was preferred. It wore very well, but the horses' clopping hooves and grinding iron wagon wheels made it extremely noisy. In retail areas with granite pavements, clerks could not hear their customers. In St. Paul, granite was used only around the downtown Union Depot to accommodate heavy freight loads. The cost was an extravagant fifty cents a foot.

By 1916, asphalt was used to pave the city streets east of Dale between Summit and Selby Avenues, but the asphalt tended to crack and deteriorate quickly if the ingredients and the process were not perfect. It was also noisy under the horses' hooves. The cost was about thirty-two cents a foot.

Brick pavement was layered in the following manner: A six-inch concrete foundation with gravel on top was covered with one-and-one-half inches of sand. The bricks were pressed into the sand with a heavy roller. Then fine sand was heated until it became a liquid and swept into the cracks and crevasses, binding the bricks together. Brick was louder than wood but less durable than granite. It could also be slippery when wet or icy. Brick was used, among other streets, on East Seventh, Arcade, and Mississippi Streets. One of the old, exposed brick streets is Kenwood Parkway.

Macadam, a pavement of crushed rocks, was used in the more remote parts of the city like Mississippi River Boulevard. The secret of a good macadam road was that the rocks be less than two inches in diameter.

All these pavement types were used on business thoroughfares, but the vast majority of the residential streets remained unpaved well into the twentieth century. In the 1920s, the city began "oiling" the streets. The older residents of the city remember this practice well: large tank trucks would come down the street, spewing a film of pungent oil on the dirt, followed by another truck throwing out sand. After decades of biennial oiling, these "oiled" streets could not be distinguished from those paved with asphalt.

In the days of the horse—after the streets were paved—a legion of street cleaners was employed throughout the city to keep every type of pavement clear of manure and garbage. The advent of the automobile brought a collective sigh of relief. The automobile, the progressives effused, was so clean! Would you agree?

OTIS AVENUE Frank Newell, a civil engineer with the firm Hawley and Newell, named this Desnoyer Park street in 1887. Mary C. Otis, his wife, was the daughter of George L. Otis, mayor of St. Paul in the 1860s. *Otis Lane* takes its name from the same source. There is a baronial stone mansion at 71 Otis Lane built by lumberman Archibald C. Jefferson (1885–1961) in 1925. See also *Dawson Park, Edmund Avenue, Kittson Street, Larry Ho Drive, McDonough Park, Nelson Street, Olmstead Street, Powers Avenue, Prince Street, Smith Avenue, Stewart Avenue, William Mahoney Street.*

OTSEGO STREET This East Side street was named in 1853 in Warren and Winslow's Addition for a county and lake in New York State made famous by James Fenimore Cooper's "Leatherstocking" novels. Otsego Hall in Cooperstown was the name of the author's boyhood home; for a long time it was the most notable private residence in that part of the state. See also *East Side*.

OTTAWA AVENUE Applied to this West Side street in 1855, this was one of a series of American Indian names, in this case, that of the Ottawa tribe, which occupied much of Michigan. See also *West Side*.

OTTO AVENUE Leberich (1812–84) and Carolina Otto immigrated from Prussia around 1860. They purchased a forty-acre farm in what is today the area between Cleveland and Prior Avenues, between Highland Parkway and Bohland Avenue, including the area now occupied by the shopping center. Otto was a skilled musician and bandleader who played at many early dances and celebrations throughout the city. The street was first named in 1881, but in 1934 the western part was renamed Highland Parkway because it ran between Highland Park and Mississippi River Boulevard. See also *Highland Parkway*.

OTTO HUMMER DRIVE Previously unnamed, this street within Highland Park was named by the city council in 1978 at the request of the Highland Business Association. According to the resolution, Hummer, who died that year, had donated his services to many Highland park organizations and activities and supported the development of the Highland outdoor swimming pool. See also *Highland Park*.

OVERLOOK PARK See *Summit Lookout Park*.

OXFORD STREET Platted as Linden Street in 1871, the name of this long north-south street adjacent to Lexington Parkway was changed a year later. This is an English name chosen to fit with the others in the area. See *Hare's Lake, Lexington Parkway*.

PACIFIC LAKE According to librarian Josiah Chaney, this shallow lake (named by the author) covered most of the Pacific Addition, the area between Atwater Street and Minnehaha Avenue, between Western Avenue and Galtier Street. The first surveyor's notes in 1847 describe the area as a tamarack swamp. See also *Lakes/Ponds*.

PACIFIC STREET Originally Central and Centennial Avenues, the name of this East Side street was changed in 1883. This name was transferred from another street. The oldest public school building in the city remaining on its original site is the Mounds Park School built in 1891 at 998 East Pacific Street. See also *East Side*.

PAGE STREET In 1857 this West Side street was named for an individual whose identity is not documented on any page. See also *Mohawk Park*, *West Side*.

PALACE AVENUE While there have been many Cottage Streets, there is only one Palace Avenue. This West End name originated in 1854 on Stinson, Brown and Ramsey's Addition, most likely for its appeal to the future "starter castle" builder. See also *West End*.

PALMER PLACE Edward G. Rogers and his wife, Mary, platted this West End street in 1883. Palmer is probably a personal name—one guess might be Edward Palmer, a fellow attorney and general counsel for the nearby railroad. See also *West End*.

PARK PLACE Taken for the building of Interstate 94, this small landmark park was essentially a courtyard surrounded by buildings between Summit and College Avenues, between Rice and St. Peter Streets. Gareth Hiebert visited Park Place and called it "a neighborhood within a neighborhood in the backyard of the city." It was dedicated as a park in 1878 in Rice and Irvine's Addition.

PARK RIDGE COURT Near Battle Creek, this street was platted in the Park Ridge Addition in 1988.

PARK STREET The word evokes natural unspoiled beauty and green space, which made it an appealing street name in 1854 in Brewster's Addition near the Capitol. The street now extends beyond the northern border of the city. Park is the fifth most popular street name in the United States, with 8,926 other occurrences of the name.

PARKLAND COURT This street near Battle Creek was so designated in 1970 because, as the developer explained, "It just sounded nice."

PARKSIDE DRIVE (private) Near Battle Creek, this street was named in 1981 in the Pathways Addition.

PARKVIEW AVENUE Named in 1928, the street leads to a view overlooking Como Park.

PARKWAY Taking its name from Johnson Parkway and Parkway School, this East Side neighborhood is roughly between Case Avenue and East Seventh Street, between Johnson Parkway and Kennard Street.

PARKWAY DRIVE This early diagonal township road led to the New Canada Town Hall on the northeast corner of Lake Phalen. (The efficient diagonal route predated rectangular farmsteads.) The name was changed to Parkway Drive in 1927, referring to nearby Wheelock Parkway. On the east side of Parkway Drive, just north of Idaho Street, there is a Jewish cemetery established in 1878 by the Congregation of the Sons of Jacob. See also *Cemeteries, New Canada Township*.

PARNELL STREET Previously without a name, the street was so designated in 1886, possibly as a reference to Charles S. Parnell (1846–91), Irish political leader. Supported by the Irish in the United States, Parnell was the force winning home rule for Ireland. This one-block-long street on the West Side was vacated in 1973. See also *West Side*.

PARQUE CASTILLO See *Castillo Park*.

PASCAL STREET Blaise Pascal (1623–62) was a French geometrician, philosopher, and writer. A man of astonishing brilliance, Pascal was such a zealous student that as a child he was temporarily denied books; nonetheless, he reinvented geometry at the age of twelve. After making many contributions to mathematics and physics, he renounced the world at age thirty-one and joined a monastery, where he wrote on theology and philosophy. The street was named in 1881 because of its proximity to Hamline University.

PATHWAYS DRIVE (private) This street near Battle Creek was named in 1981 in the Pathways Addition.

PAULAPOLIS Archbishop John Ireland devised this name for what he envisioned as a merged Minneapolis and St. Paul in the Midway area, where he planned to build one cathedral serving the entire metropolitan area. See also *Chatsworth Street, Federal City, Groveland, John Ireland Boulevard, Mississippi City*.

PAVILION POINT In Warren and Winslow's Addition of 1853, this is the point of land overlooking the downtown skyline at the south end of Rivoli Street. This patch of woods offers unofficial walking paths where the intrepid urban traipser may encounter chance chats with congenial chaps.

PAYNE AVENUE Rice W. Payne (1818–84) was a gentleman from Warrenton, Virginia. A member of an influential family and a successful attorney in his own right, Payne visited St. Paul in 1856 to experience what was then the Far West. While here, he invested $1,000 in some lots (Borup and Payne's Addition) on the East Side, returning soon after to Virginia, where he later served as a major in the Confederate Army. According to family lore, Payne's lots in St. Paul were confiscated after the Civil War because Payne was a rebel, and after his death a lawsuit was filed to recover damages for the appropriated St. Paul lots.

PAYNE TRIANGLE This small park with a tree or two and some bushes at Payne Avenue and North Street was acquired as street right-of-way.

PAYNE-PHALEN Taking its name from Payne Avenue and Lake Phalen, this East Side neighborhood is roughly between Interstate 35E and Lake Phalen, between Maryland and Larpenteur Avenues.

PEACE BRIDGE See *Sri Chin Moy Bridge*.

PEDERSEN STREET Jens Pedersen (1866–1941) was a civil engineer who worked for the city for many years before going into business on his own. He was the surveyor for many of the additions made in the 1910s and 1920s. Born in Norway, he immigrated to St. Paul with his parents after the Civil War. The city engineer's staff had a party to honor this hard-working, dedicated man in 1917 when the city named this East Side street. The 1928 Hopkins atlas

Looking south on Payne Avenue from York Avenue, about 1935. Photograph courtesy of the Minnesota Historical Society.

shows three ponds on or near Pedersen Street: one on the northeast corner of Pedersen Street and Reaney Avenue, a second pond between Reaney and Minnehaha Avenues, and a much larger pond along the route of Pedersen Street between Minnehaha Avenue and Margaret Street. See also *East Side*.

PELHAM BOULEVARD This main thoroughfare through Desnoyer Park was named in the original Desnoyer Park plat by the Union Land Company in 1887. It referred to a resort village near New York City in Westchester County, bordering on Long Island Sound. Pelham contained a number of elegant country houses, an association making it a desirable street name.

In St. Paul, a boulevard is used to connect the parks of the city; in the 1920s, the name of this street was the Como-River Boulevard for its potential connection between Como Park and Mississippi River Boulevard. The boulevard was to be extended north, parallel to Raymond Avenue, and connected to Commonwealth Avenue, and from there to Como Park. It was changed back to Pelham in 1940.

On the southeast corner of Beverly Road and Pelham Boulevard (383 Pelham Boulevard), hidden from view, is a house built by the well-known artist Edward Brewer and his wife, Ida Kueffner Brewer. The first floor, originally a lock-keeper's house, was hauled up the hill in 1918 from an abandoned lock and dam site near the Marshall–Lake Street Bridge—Brewer facetiously called his home "Not By A Dam Site." The fetching tale can be found in the *St. Paul Pioneer Press*, March 18, 1962, Woman's Section, page 2. See also *Commonwealth Avenue, Desnoyer Park, Grand Rounds*.

PENNOCK AVENUE A man of considerable literary and musical ability, Pennock Pusey (1825–1903) was a real-estate dealer and friend of the Tatum family who platted this Midway addition in 1885. He moved to St. Paul in 1854, served as assistant secretary of state, and later as private secretary to Governor Pillsbury. In 1888, he returned to his family home at Wilmington, Delaware. Another street, now named Howell, was originally called Pusey. See also *Midway Heights, Tatum Street*.

PENNSYLVANIA AVENUE Part of DeBow, Risque and Williams' Addition in 1857, this street was named for the state. There were ten developers of this addition; perhaps one of them had connections with Pennsylvania.

As early as 1922, Pennsylvania Avenue was to be part of a truck route from Highway 12, through the East Side, across the railroad tracks, and thence to the Northern Route (now Pierce Butler Route). It would direct trucks into the Midway industrial area, removing them from downtown, as well as University Avenue, which was then the busiest street in St. Paul. See also *East Side, Minnesota Transfer Yards, Pierce Butler Route*.

PEOPLE'S PARK Before Castillo and Carty Parks were formally named, they both were informally known as People's Park. See also *Carty Park, Castillo Park*.

PETERSON POINT In the 1960s, Bill and Bernice Peterson, who lived at 309 Pelham Boulevard, posted a sign on their front gate identifying their triangle of land at Pelham Boulevard and Otis Avenue as Peterson Point. For over thirty-five years the sign has served as a landmark to, among others, pizza delivery drivers.

On the southeast corner of Beverly Road and Pelham Boulevard is the Brewer house, which was nicknamed "Not By A Dam Site." Photograph courtesy of the Minnesota Historical Society.

PETIT STREET *Petit* means "small," an appropriate name for this twenty-foot-wide East Side street named in 1852. See also *Fred Street*.

PHALEN BOULEVARD This much-ballyhooed road, also called the "Phalen Corridor," represents one of St. Paul's most expansive and expensive examples of partnerships between government, business, and the community. In the 1980s, the impetus took shape as factories on the East Side closed down, some 2,500 jobs were lost, housing foreclosures soared, and the social fabric of the East Side was in serious decline. The initiative includes a new swath of road, Phalen Boulevard, linking Lake Phalen to downtown. The broader goal of cleaning up 135 acres of polluted land along the Burlington Northern Santa Fe railroad is to attract new businesses, schools, housing development, parks, and recreational paths. It is reckoned the resulting value of the land will be $24 million compared with $2.5 million before the project began. More than $260 million of public and private money have been invested in this corridor, and it is said 2,100 new jobs have been created, along with 1,100 new housing units. However, some critics of the plan claim no substantial cost-benefit analysis of the enterprise has ever been made, and that over the long run, the value of this project will not justify the expense.

Phalen Boulevard is part of the larger Phalen Corridor project, responsible for reclaiming Ames Lake. Photograph by Kathleen M. Vadnais.

PHALEN CORRIDOR See *Phalen Boulevard*.

PHALEN CREEK This creek, which ran from Lake Phalen to the Mississippi River, was one of the landmarks of early St. Paul. The name is that of Edward Phalen (or Felyn) born in Londonderry, Ireland, about 1811. He immigrated to New York City, where he enlisted in the army in 1835 and was assigned to Fort Snelling. He was discharged from the army at the end of his three-year term, whereupon he made a claim in what is now downtown St. Paul. Six feet, two-and-a-half inches tall, with brown hair and gray eyes, he was a commanding figure, but his character was lacking. He boasted of the lawless and criminal life he had led before the army, and neighbors here reported him immoral, cruel, revengeful, and unscrupulous. Phalen soon sold his first claim and took another in the area today between Case and Minnehaha Avenues, between Edgerton Street and the railroad tracks. A creek flowing near this claim became Phalen's Creek, and by extension, the lake drained by this creek became known as Phalen's Lake, even though he did not live near its shores. William Dugas purchased this second claim in 1844 for seventy dollars. Phalen was later tried for the murder of his partner, acquitted and reindicted, whereupon he fled toward California. In 1850 it was reported he had been killed in self-defense by traveling companions.

In 1899, the newspaper wrote:

In order to make East Seventh Street passable and to maintain a grade that would be easy for teams and other traffic, it was necessary to fill across the valley of Phalen Creek, and the pavement of the street is ninety feet above the creek.

Today the creek is routed through the sewer. See also *McLeod Creek, Phalen's Landing, Trout Brook.*

PHALEN DRIVE This was named as one of the streets within Phalen Park by the city council in 1967. See also *Phalen Creek.*

PHALEN HEIGHTS This neighborhood takes its name from Lake Phalen, and its boundaries are, roughly, between Maryland Avenue, Arcade Street, and Phalen Park. See also *Phalen Creek.*

PHALEN PARK It took most of the last decade of the nineteenth century to acquire the beginnings of what is today this lovely oasis within the city, the 494-acre Phalen Park at Wheelock Parkway and Arcade Street. The only swimming lake in the city—along with good fishing—is within the park. Among other amenities, there are an eighteen-hole golf course and hiking, biking, and cross-country skiing trails. The name is that of Edward Phalen. The intrepid

In 1936, the crew was building the Phalen Creek sewer in Swede Hollow just north of East Seventh Street. Photograph courtesy of the St. Paul Department of Public Works.

urban traipser living in the western portion of the city might find a day at Phalen Park and vicinity full of delightful surprises. See also *East Shore Drive, Ivy Avenue, Lake Phalen, Phalen Creek, Poetry Park*.

PHALEN VILLAGE This neighborhood takes its name from a shopping center formerly on the site of what is today Ames Lake. The boundaries are roughly between Maryland and Ames Avenues, between Clarence and Kennard Streets. There is presently a calculated effort to have at least part of this area rechristened as the Ames Lake neighborhood. See also *Ames Lake*.

PHALEN'S LANDING Edward Phalen lived for a short time on the top of the bluff above a St. Paul steamboat landing near the foot of Chestnut Street, later called the Upper Landing. In the book *Minnesota Beginnings*, the landing is mentioned several times in testimony taken by Justice of the Peace Joseph R. Brown in the 1839 murder of James Hays. John R. Irvine later purchased Phalen's claim. See also *Phalen Creek, Upper Landing*.

PIEDMONT STREET Applied in 1888 in Burlington Heights, this was a popular name of the eighteenth century, meaning literally "foot of the mountain." Suggesting height and having a foreign sound, it was a romantic name, which, rather than any local significance, would account for its choice. Before the automobile, one route to Burlington Road from the train station ascended the bluff on Piedmont and Mystic Streets. This route remains a public right-of-way—"ghost street"—but it is no longer marked or used. See also *Burlington Heights, Ghost Streets, Mystic Street*.

PIERCE BUTLER ROUTE Conceived as a truck route into the Midway industrial area (the third largest trucking terminus in the United States), the road was first planned beginning in 1922—six years before the first Model A Ford. The concept of the road, which varied slightly over the years, was to reroute truck traffic from Highway 12 and bring it through the East Side of St. Paul, over Pennsylvania Avenue and Arch Street, and along the course of the Great Northern Railway tracks into the Midway. This route would bypass downtown and also University Avenue, the most crowded street in St. Paul. Like much of St. Paul planning, it was a long time between conception and realization, and it was not until 1955 that this four-lane road opened as the Northern Route. Although city-planning engineer George Herrold campaigned passionately to use this Northern Route as the course of Interstate 94, he was unsuccessful.

The East Side portion of the route never materialized, and Interstate 94 marginalized the Northern Route, leaving it a four-lane highway to nowhere. The eventual

Pierce Butler Jr. in uniform, circa 1913. Photograph courtesy of the Minnesota Historical Society.

uselessness of the road did not deter the city council from changing the name in 1961 to honor Pierce Butler Jr. (1893–1957), attorney and civic leader. Born in St. Paul, the son of Pierce Butler, a U.S. Supreme Court justice, he graduated from Princeton University in 1914 and Harvard Law School in 1917. Outside his law practice, he was active in the United World Federalists, St. Paul United Improvement Council, and many other organizations. During the last years of his life, he also served as Mexican consul in St. Paul. See also *Arch Street, Pennsylvania Avenue*; see also "A Folding Throne for Queen Victoria."

PIERCE STREET Franklin Pierce (1804–69) was U.S. president at the time this street was named in 1856 in the Roseville Addition. There was once a Pierce County in Minnesota, but Pierce's respect for states' rights (a pro-slavery stance) and his opposition to Lincoln made him unpopular after the Civil War, and the county name was changed. See also *Roseville*.

PIGS EYE Before 1841 when Father Galtier built his log chapel on the bluffs where downtown is today and named it St. Paul, there was an earlier settlement on the Mississippi River floodplain near the shore of Pigs Eye Lake, named for Pierre "Pig's Eye" Parrant. This very historic—and often overlooked—area of the city was noted as "Grand Marais" (big swamp) by Zebulon Pike when he passed the area in 1805. According to historian J. Fletcher Williams, a number of Canadian voyageurs settled on this riverbank in the summer of 1839, where they cultivated small farms, and by 1849 there were about forty families living here. This small village, variously called Pigs Eye, or La Point Basse, or Point LeClaire, was the source of some of the first inhabitants of the city of St. Paul as it developed on the bluffs. The 1847 surveyor's notes mention a road from Pigs Eye to St. Paul.

Over the years, Parrant has been given a very bad name by historians who continue to repeat the same imprecations. However, a recent book of old records, *Minnesota Beginnings*, dating from the years Parrant resided here, indicates that Parrant engaged in the civic life of the community. Rather than the outlaw he has been depicted, we find Parrant voted, served on juries, brought court actions, and even applied for—and received—licenses to sell liquor. One of the affidavits in that book illustrates something of Parrant's nature. When asked what process naturalized him as an American citizen, Parrant replied:

> I went before Judge Doty and told him I wished to become naturalized. The Judge inquired how long I had been in the United States; I answered about 16 years. He told me I was already a citizen. I told the Judge I would like to be certain, and would pay for it, and enquired what it would cost. The Judge answered, that if I would absolutely be naturalized, it would cost five dollars. I gave him five dollars, and he took down my name, and I left the court.

See also *Riverside Park, St. Paul*.

PIGS EYE ISLAND #1 This small island, about eleven acres, is across from Pigs Eye Lake, and legally described as Government Lot 4, Section 9; and Government Lot 1, Section 16, T28, R22. See also *Islands*.

PIGS EYE ISLAND #2 This small island, about ten acres, is across from Pigs Eye Lake and legally described as Government Lot 3, Section 23; and Government Lot 3, Section 22, T28, R22. See also *Islands*.

PIGS EYE LAKE Named for Pierre "Pig's Eye" Parrant, who, with a group of Canadian voyageurs, lived near this shallow lake before it became part of the city. Lynn Johnston, a life-long resident of the Highwood neighborhood, remembers trapping muskrat and mink and fishing on Pigs Eye Lake in the 1930s when it abounded in large sunfish and at least one seventeen-pound northern pike. His recollection of the lake back then is that it averaged about five feet deep, had a sandy bottom, and powerful springs that broke the surface. As a youth, he heard stories of the Ojibwes' annual three-day powwow in an oak savanna on Houlton's Slough just south of the lake, and of a Dakota—a discharged scout from the Army—who lived on the lake, trapping in the winter and gathering ginseng root with his dugout canoe in the summer. If the intrepid urban traipser can get to the lake by canoe without being swamped by the larger boats, a picturesque Minnesota Scientific and Natural Area (Pig's Eye Island Heron Rookery) awaits. However, a permit may be necessary at certain times of the year. See also *Highwood, Lakes/Ponds, Pigs Eye*.

PIGSEYE LAKE ROAD This road was sold to the city in 1926 by the Chicago, Milwaukee, and St. Paul Railroad. See also *Pigs Eye Lake*.

PIKE ISLAND Lieutenant Zebulon Montgomery Pike (1779–1813) journeyed up the Mississippi River in 1805 to the mouth of the Minnesota River. On this island, in a treaty with the Dakotas on September 23, 1805, Pike bought 155,520 acres of upper Mississippi River land for $200 worth of gifts and sixty gallons of whiskey—with a promise of $2,000 later. See also *Islands, Minnesota Street*.

PILLSBURY STREET Originally Main Street, the name was changed in 1886. This new name may refer to Charles F. Pillsbury (1828–88), an attorney. Born in Maine, he moved to Minneapolis in 1854 and engaged in business with Allan and Eustis, real-estate dealers in this Midway area.

Pillsbury Street is a good indication of a problem in the naming of St. Paul streets. Pillsbury is a one-block-long street off University Avenue in the Midway area. But a careful perusal of the map shows there is another one-block-long piece of Pillsbury Street (previously named McPartlen Place) about four blocks away in Desnoyer Park. For the past seventy-five years, the city has worked at having the same street name applied to any portion of that street following (more or less) the same line. However, when two portions of that same street are widely separated, the city's purpose of making it easier to find an address does not seem fulfilled.

For example, if you told a cab driver you wished to go to Pillsbury Street, the driver would have to inquire exactly which portion of Pillsbury Street you were bound for. On the other hand, in the old days, you could tell the driver you wished to go to Pillsbury Street or McPartlen Place, and the location would be immediately evident. See also *Midway*.

PINE COULEE See *Battle Creek Park*.

PINE STREET It is written that in 1851 when this downtown street was named, there was a steam sawmill at the foot of nearby Olive Street, and the pine logs sawed there inspired this name. Pine is the eleventh most popular street name in the United States according to the Census Bureau. There are 6,170 other occurrences of the name in the United States.

PINE VIEW COURT This Highwood street overlooked a clump of pines when it was named in 1965. Why are there no Box Elder View street names?

PINEHURST AVENUE Hurst is an Anglo-Saxon word revived in the nineteenth century meaning "wooded hill," and it was often coupled with tree names, such as Oakhurst, Lynnhurst. This Highland Park street name, designated in 1919, has a fashionable sound but no particular significance. See also *Highland Park*.

PLATO AVENUE Originally called Flint Street and Fay Street, this West Side street name was changed in 1883. Plato was a popular name for railroad stations of the day because it is short and easy to spell, advantages that also apply to its use as a street name. The name has subsequently become *Plato Boulevard*.

PLEASANT AVENUE This early avenue below the bluff was named in Rice and Irvine's Addition in 1851, most likely for its favorable connotation. There are over one thousand places with this name in our country.

Once an imposing street, Pleasant is no longer pleasant: only a small fragment of it remains today, but the street once ran from the edge of downtown west past Jefferson Avenue to Highland Parkway, and then along the course of what is today Lexington Parkway to West Seventh Street—along what is today the route of Interstate 35E.

PLUM STREET This street was named in 1857 for the fruit in Lyman Dayton's Addition. The adjacent street is called Cherry.

POETRY PARK Near the shore of Lake Phalen, in the southwest part of Phalen Park at Ivy Avenue and Earl Street, Poetry Park exemplifies the integration of art and literature in a garden. The park contains a "poetry pylon" with written verse by local poets, "marimba" benches designed by a local artist, and a landscaped "sleeping dragon" guarding masonry book benches. The East Side Arts Council initiated the project in the late 1990s.

POINT DOUGLAS ROAD Named for American politician Stephen A. Douglas (1813–61), Point Douglas, now a ghost town, was a significant community in early Minnesota because it was located at the confluence of the St. Croix and Mississippi river trading routes. There were two roads by this name: the first road followed along the riverbank to Red Rock (Newport), while the present road took the higher ground, a route later followed closely by Highway 61. Point Douglas Road originated in the East Side of St. Paul, where it was first named in the Suburban Hills plat in 1856.

Point Douglas Road took its name from its destination: the village of Point Douglas on the St. Croix River across from Prescott, Wisconsin. This photograph was taken about 1900; today the village has disappeared. Courtesy of the Minnesota Historical Society.

POINT OF VIEW PARK This one-half-acre, unimproved "ghost park" was dedicated to the public in 1888 in the Summit Court Addition. It is on the southeast corner of Grand Hill and Lawton Street, at the top of the Lawton Steps. See also *Ghost Parks, Lawton Steps.*

PONDS/LAKES There were a number of lakes and ponds in earlier St. Paul, many of which have since been drained or filled. See *Ames Lake, Beaver Lake, Boxmeyer Bay, Brickyards Lake, Cozy Lake, Crosby Lake, Dayton Avenue Lake, Dead Horse Lake, Dew Drop, Frost Lake, Great Northern Pond, Hare's Lake, Hastings Pond, Kahout's Ponds, Lafond Lake, Lake Como, Lake Elizabeth, Lake Hamline, Lake Iris, Lake Mennith, Lake Phalen, Lake Sarita, Lamprey Lake, Langford Lake, Larpenteur Lake, Loeb Lake, Mackubin Lake, Millett Outlet, Nigger Lake, Pacific Lake, Pigs Eye Lake, Rifle Park Lake, Roger Puchreiter Pond, Snake Lake, St. Albans Lake* (1), *St. Albans Lake* (2), *Suburban Pond, Upper Lake, Weber's Pond, Wiggins Pond, Willow Reserve.*

PORTLAND AVENUE With its somewhat stately tone, this was a popular name of the nineteenth century that ultimately derived from the Isle of Portland in England, which has a sixteenth-century castle and other romantic associations. This street was named in the Woodland Park Addition in 1870.

In 1985, Garrison Keillor, internationally famous writer, humorist, and host of the radio show *A Prairie Home Companion*—probably the most celebrated man in all of St. Paul—had just purchased a new home at 498 Portland Avenue. Already sensitive to his lack of privacy, he became enraged when the *St. Paul Pioneer Press* published the address and price of his new home. He soon thereafter escaped to Denmark, the birthplace of his wife. Within two years, he was back in this country, living in New York City, where he began a new radio program. By 1993, he was back in St. Paul and again hosting his radio show *A Prairie Home Companion*. The *St. Paul Pioneer Press* never again published his home address.

PORTLAND PARK See *Nathan Hale Park*.

POST SIDE TRACK This railroad stop in the 1870s and 1880s served, among other businesses, the St. Paul Plow Works. It was on the north side of East Seventh Street between Earl and Frank Streets. The name is said to be that of a Dr. Post.

POWERS AVENUE A longtime Democratic state leader, Winn Powers (1861–1939) was mayor of St. Paul from 1914 to 1916. Born and educated in Ohio, he moved to St. Paul in 1884, where he established the Odd Fellows Review, one of the most influential fraternal publications in the country. Powers remained editor and publisher of the magazine throughout his life, while serving five terms as city councilman, and then as mayor. This street near Battle Creek was named in 1959 by the city council. See also *Dawson Park, Edmund Avenue, Kittson Street, Larry Ho Drive, McDonough Park, Nelson Street, Olmstead Street, Otis Avenue, Prince Street, Smith Avenue, Stewart Avenue, William Mahoney Street*.

PREBLE STREET Edward Preble (1761–1807) was an American naval officer well remembered when this East Side street was named in 1857 in Irvine's Second Addition. Preble ran away to sea at the age of sixteen, was active in the Revolutionary War, and worked in the merchant service. He was a commander in the Barbary Wars in charge of the assault on Tripoli. Other streets named in this plat were for Matthew Maury, Stephen Decatur, James Lawrence, and Thomas Truxton, all famous naval officers of the early nineteenth century. See also *East Side, Truxton Street*.

PRESCOTT STREET This West Side street was named in 1874, most likely for Charles A. Prescott, an early settler in the area who owned a farm above Wabasha Street on what is today Prospect Boulevard but was then called Prescott's Point. He, with his sons and wife, ran a pawnbroker's shop in the city and platted some lots in this vicinity. See also *Prospect Terrace, West Side*.

PRESCOTT'S POINT See *Green Stairs, Prescott Street*.

PRINCE STREET Originally Third Street, the name of this downtown street was changed in 1862. "A good and very popular public officer," John S. Prince (1821–95) was five times mayor of St. Paul in the 1860s. Born in Cincinnati, he came to St. Paul in 1854 as the agent of a fur trading company. While here, he supervised an early sawmill near the street now bearing his name. Prince held a number of offices, both public and private, and was accounted one of the leading citizens of the day. See also *Dawson Park, Edmund Avenue, Kittson Street, Larry Ho Drive, McDonough Park, Nelson Street, Olmstead Street, Otis Avenue, Powers Avenue, Smith Avenue, Stewart Avenue, William Mahoney Street.*

PRINCETON AVENUE This was named in 1883, like the other streets within Macalester Park, for a college, in this case Princeton University in New Jersey. See also *Macalester Park.*

PRIOR AVENUE Charles Henry Prior (1833–1921) was born in Connecticut, moved to Ohio in 1837, was educated in Cleveland, and traveled to Minnesota with the railroads in 1858. A civil engineer by profession, he held many posts with several railroad companies before joining the Chicago, Milwaukee and St. Paul Railroad. In 1879, while laying out the track between Minneapolis and St. Paul (Short Line), he, with John L. Merriam, bought and platted Merriam Park alongside the tracks, naming this street in 1882. Besides his activity in railroad construction, he was a founder of the streetcar, electric light, and telephone companies of Minneapolis. Prior Lake in Scott County is also named for him. See also *Merriam Park, Short Line Road.*

PRISCILLA STREET Priscilla Mullens was the wife of John Alden (adjacent Brewster Street was originally named Alden). Their names are immortalized in *The Courtship of Miles Standish* by Henry Wadsworth Longfellow, a popular poem when this street was named in St. Anthony Park in 1885.

PROSPECT BOULEVARD See *Prospect Terrace.*

PROSPECT TERRACE Named in West St. Paul in 1855 for its location on top of the bluff, this street, now known as *Prospect Boulevard*, offers a dramatic prospect, or view. Originally, Prospect Boulevard was a narrow street between Hall Avenue and Bidwell Street, varying in width between the edge of the bluff and the property lines. As early as 1914, $25,000 was appropriated to widen this street by taking certain properties and extending the boulevard along the edge of the bluff to Bellows Street, where a lookout was designed. The boulevard was also to extend farther west, connecting with Cherokee Heights Boulevard via a bridge over Ohio Street. This has not happened.

Presently Prospect Boulevard runs between Hall Avenue and Bidwell Street. Houses on this section face Prospect Boulevard and have even house numbers. However, between Bidwell and Bellows Streets, there is no Prospect Boulevard graded and paved, but yet the houses on the north side of Delos Street continue to have even-numbered Prospect Boulevard house numbers and mailing addresses, much to everyone's confusion. Might you envision a grim prospect for the letter carrier? See also *Prescott Street, Prospect Terrace Park, West Side.*

PROSPECT TERRACE PARK This approximately one-acre park at Bellows and Delos Streets was acquired in 1937. See also *Prospect Terrace.*

PROSPERITY AVENUE This East Side street was named in 1884 for the dictionary definition of success, good fortune, etc. A bisecting street (now Barclay) was named Amity, meaning "peace and friendship." Check the city map for the road to prosperity. *Prosperity Road* brings the same good fortune. See also *East Side.*

PROSPERITY HEIGHTS This neighborhood seems to take its name from the street. This is a high part of the city, but the descriptive term *heights* was also very popular in the 1910s and 1920s. The neighborhood is roughly between Hazelwood Street and White Bear Avenue, between Maryland and Arlington Avenues. There seems to be the typical number of banks in the neighborhood.

PUCHREITER, ROGER, POND See *Roger Puchreiter Pond*.

PUTNAM PARK This Midway "ghost park," acquired by the state in 1979, can be reached by traveling south on Beacon Avenue, turning west on Shields Avenue, and south into the alley behind Beacon Avenue. Presently this park overlooking Fairview Avenue seems to be used primarily for overflow parking. It takes its name from Donald and Joyce Putnam, who lived in the home at 407 Beacon Avenue and lovingly tended to the trees and a garden in the park. See also *Ghost Parks*.

Looking northeast from Prospect Terrace toward downtown around 1920. Photograph by Charles P. Gibson; courtesy of the Minnesota Historical Society.

QUIRNIA AVENUE This Highland Park street was named in 1927 as part of the estate of Peter Bohland, a pioneer farmer of the area. Quirnia and Xina (now Hampshire Avenue) were designated at this time; both seem to have been chosen for their singular sound. See also *Bohland Avenue, Highland Park, Xina Park.*

R

RABBIT HOLE This is a warm, fuzzy nickname for the Kellogg Viaduct. As you head north on Kellogg Boulevard past St. Peter Street, there is an exit to the left down the hill through a tunnel to Exchange Street: the Viaduct. As early as 1922, there was a traffic plan to extend Cliff Street east to Wilkin Street, thereby using the Viaduct to create an alternative route to West Seventh Street. As objections to that downtown plan multiplied, hopping down the Rabbit Hole became a carrot to avoid traffic congestion at Seven Corners. See also *Cliff Street, Seven Corners.*

RACE STREET This 1881 West End street name most likely indicates a personal name. See also *West End.*

RAILROAD ISLAND This early neighborhood, immediately west of Swede Hollow and about one mile northeast of downtown St. Paul, is called Railroad Island because three railroad corridors surrounded it. Before the railroads came in the 1870s and 1880s, this area contained the homes of some wealthy residents of the city, but during the latter quarter of the nineteenth century, it was inhabited by Swedes, and later Irish and Italian immigrants. The neighborhood is also known as Lower Payne Avenue, and its boundaries are Payne Avenue, Edgerton Street, East Seventh Street, and the railroad tracks on the east and north. Hopkins, Petit, Brunson, and Woodward Streets are the main streets. See also *Bilanski Point, Brunson Street, Hopkins Street, Swede Hollow.*

RALEIGH STREET Sir Walter Raleigh (1552?–1618), an English military and naval commander who made several early explorations of North America, was a popular figure when this St. Anthony Park street was named in 1885. See also *St. Anthony Park.*

RAMLOW PLACE William G. Ramlow (b. 1885) was a civil and mining engineer as well as a registered land surveyor when this street was platted in 1946. After a stint in the U.S. Army Corps of Engineers during World War II, he started his own engineering firm and worked with Kenneth Bordner in platting this Highland Park addition. Audrey Street in West St. Paul is named for his daughter. This street marks a section line on the land survey. See also *Bordner Place, Highland Park.*

RAMSEY HILL HISTORIC DISTRICT The oldest National Historic District in Minnesota, the boundaries are between Summit Avenue and Interstate 94, between Dale Street and the Cathedral of St. Paul. See *Cochrane Park.*

RAMSEY STREET Alexander Ramsey (1815–1903) was territorial governor of Minnesota and an enthusiastic land speculator when this street was named in Leach's Addition in 1849. Much has been written about Ramsey's many successes; perhaps the secret lies in one description of him:

> He is exceedingly cordial in his ways; makes everybody think he is a personal friend; avoids any remark which might give offense, and in case of a sudden rumpus you will always find him missing. When he does get into trouble, however, he is like a steamboat, backs out gracefully.

See also Burnquist Street, Clough Street, Gorman Avenue, Hubbard Avenue, Johnson Parkway, Marshall Avenue, Merriam Lane, Scudder Street, Sibley Street.

RAMSEY TRIANGLE Acquired in 1908, this small West End property at Grand Avenue and West Seventh Streets is now the site of Fire Station No. 1. See also West End.

RAN/VIEW The boundaries of this West End neighborhood are roughly south of Randolph Avenue and east of View Street. See also West End.

RANDALL AVENUE (Fairgrounds) Secretary of the Minnesota State Agricultural Society from 1895 to 1907, during the period of its greatest development, Eugene Wilson Randall (1859–1940) was also at various times a farmer, an editor, and dean of the University of Minnesota Department of Agriculture. Honored by this street name within the fairgrounds, Randall was born in Winona but later lived in Morris and St. Paul. At the beginning of Randall's administration, bicycle tricks and races were all the rage; at the end of his administration, automobile performances were among the most popular events.

RANDALL STREET Considered "the biggest man in town" when this East Side street was named in 1853 in Warren and Winslow's Addition, William H. Randall (1806–61) was born in Massachusetts but moved to St. Paul in 1846 with considerable money, which he invested in real estate. Although the property he owned was later worth millions of dollars, the severe depression of 1857 and Randall's death a short time later prevented him from realizing any profit on his investments. This is probably the oldest unimproved, unmarked "ghost street" in the city—one block long, near Minnehaha Avenue and Phalen Boulevard. See also Ghost Streets.

RANDOLPH AVENUE This street is said to have been named in 1857 for the Virginia family descended from William Randolph (1651–1711). Members of this influential family served in the Continental Congress and early U.S. Congresses, as well as holding other important posts in federal and state governments. Thomas Jefferson, for whom Jefferson Avenue was named, was related by marriage to the Randolph family. This street marks a one-half section line on the land survey.

For a few years in the first part of the twentieth century, there were two orphanages on Randolph Avenue. The Crispus Attucks Orphanage, located in a house at 1537 Randolph

Looking north on Snelling Avenue from Randolph Avenue, about 1934. The children are on their way to Mattocks School. Photograph courtesy of the Minnesota Historical Society.

Avenue from 1908 to 1916, served the black community. St. Joseph's German Catholic Orphan Asylum occupied thirty-seven-and-one-half acres on the southeast corner of Warwick Street and Randolph Avenue.

RANDOLPH HEIGHTS This neighborhood lies roughly between Snelling Avenue and Lexington Parkway, between Randolph and Summit Avenues. It takes its name from the public school of that name at Hamline and Jefferson Avenues. See also *Macalester-Groveland*.

RANKIN STREET Rhodes B. and Lizzie K. Rankin of Louisville, Kentucky, owned extensive property around lower Randolph Avenue when this West End street was named in 1872. See also *Magoffin Avenue*.

RASPBERRY ISLAND It appears under this name on the first map of St. Paul in 1851, but in 1949 the U.S. Navy established a small training base on the island, and it became known as Navy Island. In 1968, the Navy facility closed, and shortly thereafter the city council changed the name back to Raspberry Island, although the change has yet to be completely reflected in common usage. There is a legal question whether St. Paul had the authority to name the island in the first place because it is in a federal waterway. See also *Islands*.

RAVOUX STREET Augustin Ravoux (1815–1906) was a Roman Catholic priest when this street was named in 1871. Born in France, he traveled to this country in 1836, was ordained in

1840, and embarked on missionary work among the Dakotas the following year. From the departure of Father Galtier in 1844 until the arrival of Bishop Cretin in 1851, Father Ravoux was in charge of the entire Catholic Church in this area. In his later years, Father Ravoux was arranging some drapery in the church and had his mouth full of pins. He fell and some of the pins passed into his windpipe and stuck in his throat. Needless to say, this affected his preaching. This Summit-University street name was discontinued for a short time, but at the urging of the Ravoux grand assembly of the Knights of Columbus, the name was restored in 1958. See also *Cretin Avenue, Galtier Street, John Ireland Boulevard, Summit-University*.

RAYMOND AVENUE Bradford P. Raymond (1846–1916) was a college president when this street was named in St. Anthony Park in 1885. Born in Connecticut, he was a student at Hamline University after the Civil War. He was elected president of Lawrence University, Appleton, Wisconsin, from 1883 to 1889 and was later president of Wesleyan University in Middletown, Connecticut. Charles H. Pratt, the individual most responsible for the development of St. Anthony Park, lived at 1181 Raymond Avenue. *Raymond Lane* and *Raymond Place* take their names from the same source. See also *St. Anthony Park*.

Raspberry Island, also known as Navy Island, July 1948. Photograph by the *St. Paul Dispatch and Pioneer Press*; courtesy of the Minnesota Historical Society.

REANEY AVENUE Master of many steamboats, Captain John H. Reaney (1836–82) was born in Pittsburgh, moved to St. Paul with his father in 1852, and at an early age began steamboating with Louis Robert. Remembered as a very kind and congenial man, Reaney was honored by this East Side street named for him in 1872. See also *Robert Street*.

RED ROCK ROAD The city accepted this street within the Red Rock Industrial District from the Port Authority in 1969. Both the district and the street take their name from the Red Rock, a large granite stone that was located on the bank of the Mississippi River at what is now Newport. This boulder, a sacred shrine of the Dakotas, is now on the grounds of the Newport Methodist Church.

RESERVE BOULEVARD By 1907, after two decades of effort, the park board commissioners were able to report that Mississippi River Boulevard had been extended from the Minneapolis boundary line to the Fort Snelling Bridge. Full of satisfaction, the commissioners broached the further extension of Mississippi River Boulevard southeast into the city, stretching along the river bluff to the Smith Avenue High Bridge. They vowed:

> The preservation and improvement for public use of this picturesque river front in its entirety is a sacred duty to the Board of Park Commissioners and shortsighted greed or other obstacles thrown into the way of progress will only delay, but not defeat the project.

Supported by many citizens under the name Reserve Boulevard, some property was purchased for the bluff road, but the difficulties proved too great. The land acquired by the parks department was sold in 1937, and it was not until Shepard Road was built in the 1960s that some semblance of this early plan was fulfilled. See also *Mississippi River Boulevard, Reserve Township, Shepard Road*.

RESERVE STREET Platted as Minnesota Street, the present name of this East Side street comes from proximity to what was in the 1850s a large tract of land known as McLean's Reservation. Lying between Mound and Griffith Streets, between Burns Avenue and Interstate 94, this sixty-three-acre tract with a lake in its center belonged to Nathaniel McLean. See also *McLean Avenue*.

RESERVE TOWNSHIP The western area of St. Paul, between Marshall Avenue and the Mississippi River, between the Mississippi River and Dale Street, was incorporated in 1858 as Reserve Township. Much of the area had previously been land reserved for the exclusive use of the Fort Snelling military. In 1860, the population of the township was 249, almost all farmers. By the 1880s, with the growth of St. Paul, land developers were platting building lots in Reserve Township, and in 1887, St. Paul annexed the last bit of Reserve Township. For more information, see the author's article "Highland–Groveland–Macalester Park: The Old Reserve Township." See also *Hidden Falls Park*.

RETURN COURT Opened in 1946 on an easement from the adjacent railroad, this Highland Park street apparently takes its name from the circle route it completes. See also *Highland Park*.

REV. DR. JAMES W. BATTLE STREET   This co-name for Central Avenue between Dale Street and Western Avenue was conferred by the city council in December 1997. Dr. Battle faithfully served the Mount Olivet Baptist Church congregation at 451 Central Avenue for twenty-five years until his retirement in 1997.

REV. DR. MARTIN LUTHER KING JR. BOULEVARD   In 2002, most of Constitution Avenue in the Capitol complex was changed to honor Rev. Dr. Martin Luther King Jr. (1929–68), Nobel laureate, one of the principal leaders of the American civil rights movement, and a prominent advocate of nonviolent resistance to racial oppression. See also *Constitution Avenue*.

REV. WALTER L. BATTLE STREET   This co-name for Grotto Street between Carroll and Marshall Avenues was bestowed by the city council in December 1997. According to the council resolution, Rev. Battle was a man of great vision who founded the Gospel Temple Church at 247 North Grotto Street in St. Paul and dedicated his life to helping youth. In 1989, to honor his forty years of service, Battle received a letter from President George H. W. Bush thanking him for helping "people draw closer to their creator and to one another." He died December 14, 1995, at age seventy-four.

RICE PARK   Rice Park was dedicated as a nameless public square in (Henry) Rice and Irvine's Addition to St. Paul in 1849. Over the years, it has been the site of a number of public gatherings. On July 18, 1894, three thousand workers assembled in Rice Park to accompany the body of Charles Luth to Oakland Cemetery. During the bloody Pullman Strike of 1894, Luth, a railroad switchman, was murdered at 364 Rosabel (now Wall) Street by Charles Leonard, chief clerk to the superintendent of the Omaha Railroad. Leonard was registering scabs at the hotel when Luth objected. A fight ensued, and Leonard shot Luth four times at close range. He was later found not guilty.

During the bitter streetcar strike of 1917, public works commissioner Oscar Keller was indicted by a Ramsey County grand jury for supporting the workers in a "disloyal" speech in Rice Park. See also *Armstrong Avenue, Boyd Park, Energy Park Drive, Kilburn Street, Sherburne Avenue, William Mahoney Street.*

RICE STREET   Tall and slender, with a fine head upon his shoulders, and a commanding presence, Henry M. Rice (1816–94) was born in Vermont. He journeyed to Fort Snelling in 1839, where he engaged in the fur trade and negotiated several American Indian treaties. A decade later, with his family, he paddled a birch-bark canoe from Mendota down the Mississippi River to St. Paul, where he later built the first residence on Summit Avenue.

Here he traded heavily in real estate and vigorously promoted both St. Paul and Minnesota. A contemporary admirer wrote of him:

> Mr. Rice wins friends by his exceedingly courteous manner. He has a swaying motion when he walks; is dignified, pleasing, cautious; somewhat retiring in his nature; a fine conversationalist; adverse to publicity; a lover of home, and an honorable, upright, manly citizen.

Of course, contemporaries on the other side of the political spectrum may not have been so kind in their assessments.

The north-south portion of this street, named in Rice and Irvine's Addition in 1851, marks a section line on the land survey. The first surveyor noted the area today along Rice Street between Van Buren Avenue and Wayzata Street was marshland and tamarack swamp. To the north of today's Wayzata Street all the way to Larpenteur Avenue, the area along Rice Street was comprised of oak barrens interspersed with marshes. See also *Lafond Lake*.

RICE'S BROOK In the 1850s, there was a creek called Rice's Brook that drained at least two lakes. Larpenteur's Lake was between Dale and St. Albans Streets, between Carroll and Marshall Avenues. The second unnamed lake was between Central and Aurora Avenues, between St. Albans and Grotto Streets. The brook ran east along the route of what is today Interstate 94, then into a swamp. The drainage continued southwest, turned, and ran alongside Exchange Street in a southeast direction, then down Chestnut Street through a ravine to the river. The ravine, shaped by this brook eroding through the bluff, created the Upper Landing for steamboats.

The creek took its name from the Rice brothers, Henry and Edmund, who owned property in the area. Harriet Bishop mentions the creek in her book *Floral Home*. Writing in the 1879 *St. Paul Illustrated* magazine, T. M. Newson recounts:

> A brook ran across the street [Fort Street], from which we drank water in 1854, especially at a time when the Typhoid fever was eating out our existence, and it was supposed by our friends that we could not live. It was only this water, from this brook, we then thought, which gave us hope, and—we did not die.

See also *Chestnut Street, Cornmeal Valley, Larpenteur Lake, St. Albans Lake (1), St. Albans Lake (2), Upper Landing.*

RICHMOND STREET Thomas Daly, a well-to-do young man from Canada named three West End streets in 1856: Canada (since changed to Colborne Street), Duke, and Richmond. The inference is they honored the Fourth Duke of Richmond, Governor General of Canada in 1818–19, who died from the bite of a pet fox. See also *West End.*

RICKETTY HILL Once a favorite sliding hill for youngsters living in the area, this bluff at the east end of Goodrich Avenue (now blocked by Interstate 35E) ascends to Grand Avenue. Before Interstate 35E, there was a stairway between Goodrich Avenue and Grand Avenue. See also *Oakland Avenue.*

Edmund Rice was known as a man of "a most generous nature and a kind heart." Photograph by Fredericks and Koester; courtesy of the Minnesota Historical Society.

RIDDER CIRCLE Bernard Ridder (1916–2002) was publisher of the *St. Paul Pioneer Press*, which had its production facility on this street in the Riverview Industrial Park when this street was named in 1990.

RIDGE STREET This Highland Park Street name was chosen in 1881 to reflect the street's position on the hill. See also *Highland Park*.

RIDGEWOOD PARK A railroad suburb platted in 1887, its boundaries were roughly between St. Clair and Palace Avenues, between Lexington Parkway and Victoria Street. The main street was Ridgewood Avenue, since changed to Benhill Road. The railroad station, on the Short Line, was at the foot of Benhill Road where Victoria Street crossed the railroad tracks. The south part of the suburb, between Milton and Oxford Streets, between the railroad tracks and Pleasant Avenue, was planned as a public park, and the park board even went so far as to acquire some land. This larger park was never completed, but the Ridgewood Park plat depicts a small park in the northeast corner, between Deubener Place and Victoria Street, that has become part of Linwood Park. For more information, see the author's article "John Ayd's Grist Mill and Reserve Township History." See also *Haldeman Park, Linwood Park, Short Line Road*.

RIFLE PARK LAKE Rifle Park was a private park on Dayton's Bluff between what is today Hancock and Conway Streets, between Griffith and Earl Streets. Much of that area was filled with a lake fifteen to twenty feet deep, according to the first grading records of Third Street. In the Sacred Heart Church Diamond Jubilee (1881–1956) commemorative book, there is a sentence: "Rifle Lake and Rifle Park . . . was the scene of many a parish picnic and also several unfortunate drownings." See also *Dayton's Bluff, Lakes/Ponds*.

RIVER PARK PLAZA This West Side waterfront street was named in 1993 in the River Park Plaza Addition.

RIVERSIDE PARK (neighborhood) Platted in 1889 by Charles and Lizzie Dickerman, Riverside Park was a unique residential peninsula along the Mississippi River between the south end of Pigs Eye Lake and the Mississippi River. According to a newspaper column written by Oliver Towne in the *St. Paul Dispatch*, April 3, 1959, this floodplain suburb flourished around the period of 1900–1915, but eventually spring inundations and the lack of roads discouraged the residents from remaining. The author visited the site around 1962 when the shells of several homes remained, and my erudite guide, Grover Singley, pointed out an early log cabin with the logs notched—in the French way, he observed—the remnant of an earlier village, Pigs Eye. Much, if not all, of this ghost town was washed away during the flood of 1965. The exact location of Riverside Park can be determined by drawing a line one-and-one-half miles due west of the section corner at Boxwood Avenue and McKnight Road. See also *Dickerman Park, Pigs Eye, Pigs Eye Lake*.

RIVERSIDE PARK Acquired in 1906 between West Seventh Street, Albion Avenue, and Lexington Parkway, this West End public park was subsequently used for the Riverside public school and playground. The name comes from the Riverside Addition to the south. See also *West End*.

RIVERVIEW Originally designated as the west side of the Mississippi River, in 1918 the residents of the West Side officially adopted Riverview as their new name—a less geographically confusing reference. The telephone exchange, post office, and branch public library were renamed accordingly. However, this newer name has not prevailed, and most people today continue to call it the West Side. See also *West Side*.

RIVERVIEW AVENUE This West Side street was named in 1874. See also *West Side*.

RIVERVIEW CEMETERY One of eight cemeteries remaining in St. Paul, Riverview is an alternate name for the West Side, where this cemetery is located at Annapolis Street and Brown Avenue. Princess Seneca (1870–1930) and Chief White Cloud (1870–1957), both full-blooded Ojibwes, are buried here. See also *Cemeteries, Riverview, West Side*.

RIVERWOOD PLACE Originally part of Ashland Avenue, this street name near the University of St. Thomas was changed in 1922 as part of a general renaming in the area. See also *Shadow Falls Park*.

RIVOLI STREET Rivoli is a town in Italy at the foot of the Alps in the province of Torino. An old castle distinguished this nineteenth-century tourist village when this street was named in 1853 in Warren and Winslow's Addition. The developer, John E. Warren, was a literary man and inveterate world traveler. At the south end of Rivoli Street is Pavilion Point. See also *Mt. Ida Street, Pavilion Point*.

ROBBINS STREET Daniel M. Robbins (1830–1905) was a leading businessman in St. Paul when this street was named in 1885. He had large investments in real estate and was very active in the organization of the Minnesota Transfer Yards near the street bearing his name. Robbins was also president of the Northwestern Elevator Company, which owned more than a hundred elevators along the Great Northern Railway tracks. See also *Minnesota Transfer Yards*.

ROBERT STREET This is one of the original fifteen street names of the city, named in 1849 on the plat St. Paul Proper, on which the street was only fifty-five feet wide. A tall, muscular man of great energy, with strong features and decided convictions, Captain Louis Robert (1811–74) was a fur trader on the Missouri River before moving to St. Paul in 1844 with his wife, Mary, where he purchased part of the original town site and named this street in 1849. The owner of several steamboats he piloted, Robert also dealt heavily in real estate, ending life with considerable money and a reputation for generosity and public spirit. Because Robert was French-Canadian, his name was originally pronounced "Row-bear." On the West Side, Robert Street was known as the Capitol Highway. See also *Lamprey Avenue, Reaney Avenue*.

ROBIE STREET Originally Oak Street, this West Side street name was changed in 1876. Robie is possibly a surname. See also *West Side*.

ROBLYN AVENUE Originally part of Rondo Avenue (obliterated by Interstate 94), this street was renamed Roblyn in 1913. This street name and the Roblyn Park Addition in which it appears are a combination of the names Orlando A. Robertson and Frederick B. Lynch

Removing snow on the West Side Robert Street hill, February 1952. Photograph by F. R. Arver; courtesy of the St. Paul Department of Public Works.

(1866–1934), developers of the subdivision. Robertson was president of the U.S. Farm Lands Company; he moved to Sacramento, California, in 1913. Lynch, born in Madison, Wisconsin, graduated from college at Yankton, South Dakota, and moved to St. Paul in 1897, where he was president of the Southern Colonization Company. Lynch was chairman of the executive committee of the National Democratic Committee and once mentioned as a candidate for a cabinet post under President Wilson in 1912. (An article in the August 31, 1912, *Saturday Evening Post* named him Minnesota's Mighty Man.) In 1918, he moved to New York and later to Orlando, Florida, where he died. See also *Old Rondo Avenue*.

ROCKWOOD AVENUE George E. Rockwood platted this West End street in 1884. He came to St. Paul about 1874 and was associated with the St. Paul branch of a Chicago clothing firm. He left the city about 1886. See also *West End*.

ROGER PUCHREITER POND This fenced pond on Ivy Avenue between Germain and Kennard Streets is a detention pond used by the sewer department to contain the overflow from the storm sewer at peak flow times. Roger Puchreiter, who designed this pond in the early 1970s, subsequently served for more than two decades as the sewer utility manager for the city of

St. Paul. There are a couple dozen of these detention ponds throughout the city; most of the sites are wetlands that have been unbuildable. See also *Devil's Ditch, Hillcrest Knoll, Lakes/Ponds, Stillwater Avenue, Willow Reserve.*

ROGERS PARK In an 1883 plat, Josias and Belle Rogers dedicated this three-acre park near Lake Como on the southeast corner of Arlington Avenue and Grotto Street. Forty-five years later, in the 1928 Hopkins atlas, the park is not noted on what is depicted as a swampy lot. Today there are houses on the old park site.

In the 1880s, before the park board was established, there were no funds to purchase park property. In response, legislation was passed requiring every developer to donate some of his addition as parkland. Most of the developers chose either to ignore the ordinance or to donate the most unbuildable lots as parkland.

ROGERS STREET Edward G. Rogers (1842–1910) was an attorney and a representative in the state legislature when this West End street was named in 1887. Born in Michigan, he graduated from law school there and moved to St. Paul in the early 1870s, where he became prominent in Republican politics. At the time of his death, he was a member of the city council. According to the first surveyor's notes, this area between (today) Lexington Parkway and West Seventh Street was swampy. See also *West End.*

ROME AVENUE Rome A. Schaffner was president of the Highland Park Company when this street was platted in 1925. During most of his residence here between 1906 and 1930, he was chief clerk for a construction company. See also *Highland Park.*

RONDO AVENUE See *Old Rondo Avenue*

RONDO SQUARE This triangular piece of public park at Rondo Avenue and Dunlap Street was sold to the state for $18,000 as part of Interstate 94. See also *Old Rondo Avenue.*

ROSE AVENUE This street was named in 1857 for the flower by the developers Harwood Iglehart, William Hall, and Charles Mackubin. See also *Iglehart Avenue, Mackubin Street.*

ROSE TOWNSHIP Incorporated in 1858, this township embraced the area between (today) Marshall Avenue and County Road D, between Rice Street and the boundary with Minneapolis. It took its name from Isaac Rose and his wife, Mary, who settled in the southwest corner of the township in 1843, purchasing 170 acres of land. He later lived near (today's) intersection of University and Snelling Avenues. Rose was born in New Jersey in 1802, worked as a land agent selecting farms for immigrants, and died of consumption in Traverse des Sioux, Minnesota, in February 1871. Within thirty years, the township had been annexed to the St. Paul city limits.

ROSEDALE PARK This is the first Rosedale, platted as an addition between Fairview, Cleveland, Summit, and Goodrich Avenues in 1876 by Bishop Thomas L. Grace. See also *Grace Street, Groveland.*

ROSEN ROAD Milton Rosen (1893–1970) was a member of the city council for thirty years, during which time he held the post of public works commissioner. Born in the slums of

The paving of Rome Avenue in 1927. The Highland Water Tower is under construction in the background. The houses at left are all on Hillcrest Avenue: numbers 1726, 1720, 1706, 1701, 1700, 1690, 1672, 1665, 1661, 1660. Photograph by K. L. Fenney Company; courtesy of St. Paul Department of Public Works.

Chicago, Rosen moved to St. Paul as a child. In 1915 he established the Milton Rosen Tire Company, which he managed until 1962. Opinionated, sometimes cantankerous, Rosen engaged in countless civic, charitable, and public service activities in his long residency in St. Paul. (The author remembers a spirited and controversial debate held at the University of Minnesota in the early 1960s between Milton Rosen and Professor Milford Q. Sibley on the virtues of the Soviet Union.) This street was named in 1957, but—going the way of the Soviet Union—was vacated in 1983 with the development of Energy Park. See also *Energy Park*.

ROSEVILLE Not the Roseville we know today, this was a village platted in 1856 at what is now the area approximately between University Avenue and Interstate 94, between Snelling Avenue and Pierce Street. This village was the origin of the names Snelling Avenue and Pierce Street, which then intersected with Floral Avenue and Hope Street. A hotel, the Roseville House, was on the northwest corner of St. Anthony Road and Snelling Avenue. The name for both this early Roseville and the present-day Roseville comes from the name of Rose Township. See also *Pierce Street, Rose Township, Snelling Avenue*.

ROSS AVENUE William H. Ross was in business with John Weide, a brother of one of the developers of this 1872 East Side street in Arlington Hills. Ross may have invested in the property. See also *Arlington Hills, Ross Island*.

ROSS ISLAND Named thus on the 1874 map of St. Paul included in the Andreas atlas, this is the location (no longer an island) of the Island Station power plant presently being converted into condominiums. Built in 1924 and decommissioned by Northern States Power in 1975, the plant off Shepard Road near Randolph Avenue has sheltered mostly pigeons, struggling artists, and houseboat dwellers over the past several years. The island also appears on the 1884 Hopkins atlas as Government Lot 5, Section 12, T28, R23. It was about six acres on the original government survey. See also *Islands*.

ROUND ABOUT WAY See *About Round Way*.

ROWE PLACE This East Side street was platted in 1953 by Herbert J. Rowe, of the firm Rowe and Knudson, which dealt in real estate and insurance. See also *East Side*.

ROY STREET Frank and Charlotte Holstrom named this short street with parts in the Midway and Highland Park in 1909, most likely for Roy Holstrom, a surveyor.

RUM TOWN See *Old Rum Town*.

RUSSELL STREET This street was laid out about 1890 on land adjacent to Phalen Creek. The identity of Russell is neither recalled nor recorded.

RUTH STREET Ruth was the daughter of Angier and Luella B. Ames, the developers of this East Side street in 1890. She taught briefly at the Harrison School, where her mother was principal, but by the time of her mother's death in 1915, she had married Waldo F. Kelly of Providence, Rhode Island. This street marks a one-half section line on the land survey. The 1928 Hopkins atlas shows a large pond (500 feet by 200 feet) between Hazel and Ruth Streets, between Fifth and Margaret Streets, just south of Eastern Heights Elementary School. This same atlas also shows a good-sized pond just east of Ruth Street between Clear and Ivy Avenues. See also *Ames Avenue, Hazel Park*.

RYAN AVENUE Previously Franklin Street, the name of this downtown street was changed in 1940 to avoid duplication. Harry, Richard, and Emmett Ryan were officers of the St. Paul Milk Company located on this street.

RYAN PARK This one-and-one-fifth-acre park in Frogtown at Thomas Avenue and Avon Street was previously the site of the Benjamin Drew Elementary School. When the school closed in 1974, the city bought the property to build single-family homes. By the early 1980s, the neighbors wanted a park on the site, and in 1983 the city agreed to consider the request. On Feb 15, 1984, local businessman Dennis Patrick Ryan, age fifty-one, was shot and killed during a robbery at his plumbing store at 811 University Avenue. The local community then contributed funds toward the park, requesting it be named for Ryan. See also *Frogtown*.

RYDE STREET Ryde is a city in Lancaster County, England. The street was named in 1885, when English names were in vogue. See also *Colne Street, Kilburn Street*.

S

SACKETT RECREATION CENTER On May 22, 1970, St. Paul police officer James T. Sackett, responding to a bogus late-night call of a woman in labor, was killed by an unseen sniper.

SAMUEL H. MORGAN REGIONAL TRAIL Extending along Shepard Road between Minnesota Highway 5 and Chestnut Street in downtown, this five-mile pedestrian and bicycle trail was named by the city council in January 2002. Sam Morgan (1911–2000) was well known for his leadership in protecting, promoting, and establishing parks and trails. He graduated from St. Paul Academy in 1929 and Harvard Law School in 1936, and practiced law for five decades. He led the battle for creation of Afton State Park, expansion of William O'Brien State Park, and establishment of the Gateway Trail and many other parks and trails, leaving a bountiful legacy. Morgan's great-granduncle was Henry Mower Rice, one of St. Paul's early political leaders.

SANDRALEE DRIVE Sandralee (b. 1947) was the daughter of Ralph and Emily Peterson, who platted their twenty-nine-acre hobby farm in 1960. An adjacent Battle Creek street was already named Darlene, the name of one Peterson daughter; this coincidence prompted the name of the second daughter.

SANDY LAKE See *Lake Como.*

SARATOGA STREET This street was named in 1874 by John Wann, an Englishman, at the instigation of his wife, an American. She felt some redress was needed for the many British names (Avon, Oxford, Milton) and suggested this name in honor of the battle of Saratoga—the turning point of the Revolutionary War—in which the Americans soundly defeated the British. See also *Lexington Parkway.*

SARGENT AVENUE Edwin and Electa Sargent were the developers of this Macalester-Groveland street in 1883. He was born in Vermont about 1823 and moved to St. Paul about 1883, where he engaged in the real-estate business. His wife was born in New York about 1826. They moved to Redlands, California, in 1895.

In the 1920s, William T. Francis, Minnesota's first black attorney to be admitted to the bar, purchased the house at 2092 Sargent Avenue. There were numerous episodes of racial harassment by area residents who wanted him to move, including an effort by the Cretin Avenue Improvement Association to buy his home. In 1927, he moved to Liberia. See also *Macalester-Groveland.*

SARITA WETLAND Lake Sarita is first noted on the surveyor's notes in 1847 as a small lake about eighty yards in length; it was first mapped and named on the Plan of St. Anthony Park by Horace W. S. Cleveland in the 1870s.

In 1909, the state fair board, seeking a new attraction, excavated the (by then) swampy lake to create a lagoon and canal that would carry passenger boats on short excursions. Because of the difficulty in maintaining an adequate water level, this feature was abandoned in 1916, and the lagoon eliminated. (There is an excellent depiction of the lagoon in the 1916 Hopkins atlas.) The Sarita Wetland was at the northeast corner of Cleveland and Como Avenues. A remnant of the lake is still visible adjacent to the University of Minnesota busway. The word *Sarita* is a Spanish diminutive for Sara. See also *Lakes/Ponds*.

SAUNDERS AVENUE The Saunders family owned an eighty-acre estate between Bohland and Montreal Avenues, between Fairview and Cleveland Avenues. Edward N. Saunders (1845–1913) came to St. Paul in 1870, where he conceived the idea of shipping coal to Minnesota through the Great Lakes. With James J. Hill, he founded the highly profitable Northwestern Fuel Company. Edward N. Saunders Jr. (1877–1953) graduated from Yale with a Ph.D. in 1899 and returned to St. Paul, where he took over the family business, one of the largest in the north-central region. This Highland Park street was named in 1924 when the Saunders estate was subdivided into building lots. See also *Highland Park*.

SCENIC PLACE Previously Suburban Place, the name of this East Side street was changed in 1957 to avoid confusion with Suburban Avenue, one block adjacent.

SCHEFFER AVENUE Originally Snelling Street, the name was changed in 1886. Albert Scheffer (1844–1905) was born in Germany, immigrated to St. Paul in 1859, and soon after became a teller in a Stillwater bank owned by his brother. After the Civil War, he became a banker, served in the state senate, and was an active school board member. He was interested in civic affairs and well regarded by most, and his son-in-law, William Hamm, was a city councilman.

In 1878, on what would today be the west side of Snelling Avenue near its intersection with Scheffer Avenue, a few of the far-sighted citizens of Reserve Township—as it was then known—erected an observatory. The sum of seventy-five dollars was collected by subscription to build a tower fifty feet high, from which five counties were visible. With a telescope, a point seventy-five miles distant could be discerned. People from all parts of the county visited the "look-out," as it was known. See also *Reserve Township, Union Park*.

SCHERERS LANE Part of a development by A. J. Scherer about 1888, this small East Side street, fifteen-feet wide, on the northeast corner of Prosperity and Maryland Avenues is an unmarked, unimproved "ghost street." Despite this lack of any identification, there are actually four houses on Scherers Lane: 1242, 1250, 1256, and 1264, all of which appear to be oddly angled on Maryland Avenue. Scherer apparently never lived in St. Paul. See also *Ghost Streets*.

SCHEUNEMAN AVENUE This one-block-long street off Ayd Mill Road and Hague Avenue was platted in 1883 by Anna Ramsey, the wife of onetime Governor Ramsey, but it was not named at that time. See also *Ramsey Street*.

SCHLETTI STREET This North End street was platted in 1916 by Elizabeth, the widow of Christian Schletty. The Schletty family moved to St. Paul from Red Wing in the 1870s and over the years acquired a good deal of property northwest of Maryland and Western Avenues. They built the family home, which is at 503 West Orange Street, high on the bluff overlooking their property. Another Schletty family home remains at 1275 Mackubin Street. Christian's son Fred was a veteran nurseryman and state fair official. The change of the last letter from "y" to "i" was apparently a whim of Elizabeth.

SCHROEDER DRIVE The city council named this street in 1956 for Alfred H. Schroeder (1901–74), city architect at the time. Graduating from St. Thomas College in 1921 with a degree in civil engineering, he worked for private firms until becoming an assistant engineer for the city in 1935. When he returned to St. Paul after World War II, he was hired to modernize the city building codes. Alas, fame is fleeting; this street was vacated in 1982 with the development of Energy Park. See also *Energy Park*.

SCOTT ROAD This street is said to be named in 1958 for Scott, son of Grege Beckett, plat commissioner at the time, and/or Scott, the grandson of Hyman J. Goldberg, office engineer in the public works department. This street was vacated in 1997.

SCUDDER STREET Reverend John L. Scudder was pastor of the First Congregational Church of Minneapolis when this street was named in St. Anthony Park in 1885. He most likely had a financial interest in the property. Andrew A. McGill was the tenth governor of Minnesota; his home, built in 1887, remains at 2203 Scudder Street. See also *Burnquist Street, Clough Street, Gorman Avenue, Hubbard Avenue, Johnson Parkway, Marshall Avenue, Merriam Lane, Ramsey Street, Sibley Street*.

SEAL STREET One of several streets named in 1887 in St. Anthony Park South, this was probably inspired by a personal name. See also *St. Anthony Park*.

SEAMER STREET Leonard C. Seamer (1888–1959) was city valuation engineer at the time the city named this street in 1956. Born in Cincinnati, he came to St. Paul as a youth and began his career with the city in 1911 as a clerk in the public works department. He subsequently served as assistant land commissioner, chairman of the city technical committee, and after 1928, assessment and valuation engineer. He also brought the National Majorette championship to St. Paul in 1941, where it became part of the Winter Carnival. This street was vacated in 1980.

SEARLE STREET Olaf and Dagmar Searle platted this street near Lake Phalen in 1887. He was born in Norway and immigrated to St. Paul in 1881; two years later, with Andrew E. Johnson, he formed a company to aid Norwegian immigrants' settlement in this country. In one year alone, his company arranged the sale of 25,000 acres of Minnesota land to new arrivals. Olaf is last listed as a resident of Minneapolis in 1926.

SECOND STREET Originally Bench Street because of its position halfway up the bluff, the name of this downtown street was changed in 1872. It is the second street from the river, a narrow turning road dwarfed by the piers supporting the railroad tracks. Second Street is, according to the U.S. Census bureau, the most common street name in the United States, with 10,866 occurrences.

SELBY AVENUE Reckoned as "industrious, economical, and thrifty," Jeremiah W. Selby (1812–55) traveled to St. Paul in 1849 for his health and purchased a forty-acre farm on St. Anthony Hill where the Cathedral of St. Paul now stands. On this farm, for which he paid fifty dollars an acre, Selby built a house and made a comfortable living raising potatoes and vegetables. This street, part of his homestead, was named in Dayton and Irvine's Addition in 1854.

In the fall of 1982, there was an effort by city councilman Bill Wilson to change the name of the street to honor Roy Wilkins (1901–81), longtime head of the National Association for the Advancement of Colored People. See also *St. Anthony Hill*.

SELBY AVENUE TUNNEL In 1906, the streetcar company, unable to surmount the 16 percent grade on the hill rising from Pleasant Avenue to Selby Avenue, reconciled to tunneling through the hill. The 1,500-foot subway was 15 feet high, 23 feet across, and 50 feet underground at its greatest depth, and afforded a 7 percent grade. With the dismantling of the streetcar system in the 1950s, the tunnel was no longer used for transportation. For some

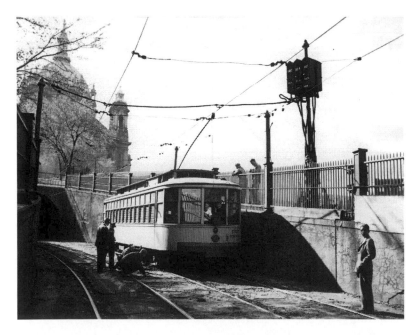

A streetcar about to enter the Selby Avenue tunnel in April 1948. It appears that a few of the riders have disembarked to look for loose change along the tracks, while others within the car urge them on. Less than a decade later, the tunnel would be closed. Photograph by the *St. Paul Dispatch and Pioneer Press;* courtesy of the Minnesota Historical Society.

years after, it served as a shelter for the homeless and various underworld purposes. The sealed entrance can be seen adjacent to Cathedral Square, a short distance from the corner of Old Kellogg Boulevard and College Avenue. See also *Cathedral Square*.

SELMA LANE Previously Grace Lane, the name of this West End street was changed in 1940. See also *West End*.

SEMINARY AVENUE In 1899, the Lutheran Seminary moved from Robbinsdale, Minnesota, to the west end of this Midway street—then named Ireland—constructing a large brick building for their school facing on Englewood Avenue and Horton Park. The following year Ireland Street was renamed Seminary Avenue. In 1917, the Lutheran Seminary united with two others and formed the present-day Luther Theological Seminary on Como Avenue in St. Anthony Park. In 1973, the site of the original seminary was bought by the St. Paul Housing and Redevelopment Authority, which demolished the old buildings and constructed public housing for the elderly.

SEMINOLE AVENUE Named in 1855, as one of a series after American Indian tribes, this West Side street refers to the Seminole tribe, which lived in what is now Florida. Osceola was one of their revered chiefs. See also *Osceola Avenue, West Side*.

SEVEN CORNERS A bustling intersection on the west edge of downtown where West Seventh Street passed through the intersection (two corners), Third Street passed through the intersection (two corners), and Eagle Street, Main Street, and Fourth Street ended at the intersection. Today the intersection is, more or less, the site of the Xcel Energy Center. See also *Cliff Street, Rabbit Hole*.

SEVEN HILLS OF ST. PAUL The early notion that St. Paul was built on seven hills probably has more to do with a flattering comparison between Rome and St. Paul

Luther Seminary at the west end of Seminary Avenue has been replaced by senior citizen housing. Photograph courtesy of the Minnesota Historical Society.

than it does with geography. What were the seven hills? *Baptist Hill, Capitol Hill, St. Anthony Hill, Mt. Airy, Mt. Ida (Pavilion Point), Dayton's Bluff,* and *Williams Hill* are the most likely.

SEVENTH STREET The seventh street from the river, this is one of the original fifteen street names of the city on the 1849 plat, St. Paul Proper. While the original sequence of numbered streets was orderly, numerous downtown reconfigurations have realigned these numbered streets so the present arrangement is incomprehensible. Currently you can travel east on Seventh Street (which is actually Ninth Street) and run into Eighth Street.

West Seventh Street is co-named Fort Road, acknowledging the fact that in the 1870s the street led to Fort Snelling. *Seventh Place* is a part of the previous location of Seventh Street. Seventh Street, approximately eleven miles long, appears to be the longest street in the city. See also *Cliff Street, Fort Road, Stewart Avenue.*

SHADOW FALLS PARK An eighteen-acre, deep, rugged, and very picturesque gorge along Mississippi River Boulevard at the end of Summit Avenue, this park features a spring-fed stream that is particularly beautiful in the winter. After viewing the river from this lookout park, the intrepid urban traipser will discover an unmarked trail on the south side of the gorge leading back to the falls and the spring.

Archbishop John Ireland, who platted the Shadow Falls Park addition adjacent to the ravine, intended to donate the falls to the city. The park board responded:

Looking toward downtown on West Seventh Street from Ramsey Street about 1917. Fire Station No. 1 has replaced the Liberty Bond billboard. Photograph courtesy of the Minnesota Historical Society.

It was doubtless from a broad and intelligent view of his own business interests as the owner of the land, as well as from those motives of local patriotism ... that Archbishop Ireland has indicated his personal willingness to donate Shadow Falls and boulevard to the city.

In the end, however, the park board had to purchase the falls property from Ireland.

In the park, there is a memorial to the soldiers and sailors of World War I designed by Thomas Holyoke and financed by the Daughters of the American Revolution. On the 1839 map of the Fort Snelling Reservation, Shadow Falls is named "Spring Leap." See also *Groveland*, *John Ireland Boulevard*.

SHADOW FALLS PARK (neighborhood) This residential district between Marshall and Summit Avenues, between Mississippi River Boulevard and the University of St. Thomas, was platted by Archbishop John Ireland in 1911. Today it contains a diverse collection of 1920s homes. See also *John Ireland Boulevard*.

SHELBY PLACE Anna N. Shelby was the mother of Beriah and Samuel Magoffin, who owned property in this Highland Park vicinity. She was a granddaughter of Governor Isaac Shelby of Kentucky. See also *Magoffin Avenue*.

SHELDON STREET This street near Como Park was named in 1881 for N. E. Sheldon, one of the developers, who apparently was never a resident of the city.

SHEPARD ROAD The St. Paul City Council named this street in 1949 to honor George N. Shepard (1889–1973), chief engineer of the department of public works from 1922 to 1927 and 1932 to 1956. During those years he designed the Ford Parkway and Robert Street bridges as well as the riverfront road that today bears his name. Toward the end of his career, a staunch advocate of Interstate 94, he served as the liaison between the city and the Minnesota Highway Department.

Around 1900 there were concerted efforts to extend Mississippi River Boulevard along the river bluff from Fort Snelling to the Smith Avenue High Bridge, but the project was finally abandoned in the 1930s, only to be replaced a decade later with Shepard Road along the river's edge. See also *Reserve Boulevard*.

SHERBURNE AVENUE Remembered as "a real judge—calm, cool, decided, clear-headed, dignified," Moses Sherburne (1808–68) was one of the developers of this 1857 street near the Capitol in Ashton and Sherburne's Addition. Born in Maine, he came to St. Paul in 1853 when President Franklin Pierce appointed him a judge of the U.S. District Court. He moved to Orono in Sherburne County (also named for him) in 1867.

Charles James, member of a pioneer St. Paul African-American family and a national leader of the Boot and Shoe Workers Union, was living at 419 Sherburne Avenue in 1902 when he was elected to the first of three terms as president of the St. Paul Trades and Labor Assembly. See also *Armstrong Avenue*, *Boyd Park*, *Energy Park Drive*, *Kilburn Street*, *Rice Park*, *William Mahoney Street*.

The lower end of Sherburne Avenue was once a classy address: the George Benz residence at number 5, circa 1915. Photograph by Charles P. Gibson; courtesy of the Minnesota Historical Society.

SHERIDAN AVENUE William Davern named this Highland Park street in 1891, most likely for Richard B. Sheridan (1751–1816), English playwright, orator, and statesman. Davern, a one-time schoolteacher, would certainly have been aware of his writings. See also *Davern Street, Wordsworth Avenue*.

SHERMAN STREET Originally Pine Street, this West End street was renamed in 1872. It is said to honor William T. Sherman (1820–91), a Civil War general who conducted "the march to the sea" through Georgia in 1864. There may also have been a thought for Marshall Sherman (1822–96), a St. Paul painter who in the course of the Civil War became St. Paul's first Medal of Honor winner. See also *West End*.

SHERWOOD AVENUE Orrin and Mary Sherwood platted this street near Lake Phalen in 1887. He came to St. Paul about 1883 and engaged in the real-estate business until moving to Minneapolis in 1898.

SHIELDS AVENUE General James Shields (1810–79) was born in Ireland and immigrated to the United States when he was sixteen, where he earned military rank in the Mexican War. He was subsequently governor of Oregon Territory, U.S. senator from Illinois, and U.S. senator from Minnesota. He served in the Civil War as a soldier from California and was later U.S. senator from Missouri. James and Sarah Shields platted this Midway street in 1873. See also *Midway*.

SHORT HILL This is a reference repeated hundreds of times a day by St. Paul taxicab dispatchers. The "Short Hill" identifies a pickup in the part of the city roughly between Pierce Butler Route and St. Clair Avenue, between Lexington Parkway and the State Capitol. See also *Long Hill*.

SHORT LINE ROAD Officially designated by the city in 1965, the street takes its name from the adjacent railroad tracks of the Chicago, Milwaukee, St. Paul and Pacific Railroad, known locally as the Short Line because it ran only from St. Paul to Minneapolis. Upon its construction in 1880, this was one of the major commuter trains connecting the (then) suburbs of the city. Stations were at Victoria Street (Ridgewood Park), Marshall Avenue (Macalester Park), Holton Street (Hamline Village), Prior Avenue (Merriam and Union Parks), and Pelham Boulevard (Desnoyer Park). Trains ran every half hour. However, the expansion of the streetcar system in the 1890s supplanted the railroad as a commuter network. This street name was changed to Ayd Mill Road in October 1987. See also *Ayd Mill Road, Desnoyer Park, Hamline Village, Macalester Park, Merriam Park, Ridgewood Park, Union Park*.

SHORT STREET Because this East Side street was only a block long in the original 1856 plat of the Suburban Hills addition, this name was applied in a short spurt of longing.

SIBLEY MANOR See *Maynard Drive*.

SIBLEY STREET This is one of the original fifteen streets of the city named on the 1849 plat, St. Paul Proper. Described as "a really good man—an honest man—a moral man—an able man—an upright man—a worthy man—a man whose name will long live in the history of the Northwest," Henry Hastings Sibley (1811–91) was born in Michigan, arrived at Mendota in 1834 as a partner in the American Fur Company's Western Outfit, and built the first private, stone dwelling in 1837—which remains today. He was Minnesota Territory's delegate to the U.S. Congress when, as one of the developers, he named this downtown street in 1849. In 1858 he was elected the first governor of Minnesota. That year he moved to St. Paul, where he bought a fine house on Woodward Street in the original Lowertown. Although he fathered a daughter with a Dakota woman, he led an army against the Dakotas in 1862.

The Noel Transfer Company shows off its fleet in 1965 on the Short Line Road, before it was renamed Ayd Mill. Photograph by Norton and Peel; courtesy of the Minnesota Historical Society.

With Alexander Ramsey and Henry M. Rice, he was probably one of the most politically influential of Minnesota pioneers. For further information, see *Henry Hastings Sibley* by Rhoda Gilman. See also *Burnquist Street, Clough Street, Gorman Avenue, Hubbard Avenue, Johnson Parkway, Lowertown, Marshall Avenue, Merriam Lane, Ramsey Street, Scudder Street*.

SIDNEY STREET Sidney D. Jackson was one of the developers of this West Side street about 1855. He was here only here from 1855 to 1857—when the financial panic hit and land values plummeted. See also *West Side*.

SIGURD STREET Sigurd Bertelsen (1899–1989) was St. Paul postmaster from 1955 to 1972; before that, he was assistant land commissioner for the Northern Pacific Railway. Bertelsen was well regarded, and upon his retirement the city council declared February 7, 1972, as Sig Bertelsen day. The name was given to the street in 1969 by his friend Grege Beckett, plat commissioner at the time.

SIMCOE STREET Originally Hazel Street, the name of this North End street was changed in 1872. A lake, county, and village in Ontario, Canada, bear this name; perhaps one of these served as the inspiration. In any case, the name was short and simple to pronounce and remember.

SIMON AVENUE In 1904, several investors from Stillwater named this short diagonal street in Ware and Hospes Addition near Lake Como. Who Simon was and what he said remains a mystery. See also *Edgar Avenue*.

SIMPSON STREET Matthew Simpson (1811–84) was, like Francis Asbury and Leonidas Hamline, a bishop of the Methodist Episcopal Church. A onetime printer, law clerk, and physician, Simpson became a Methodist when he was twenty-five. Beginning as a circuit rider, he quickly advanced to become "the best known and most influential Methodist of his day in the United States; a counselor of statesmen and a public speaker of international repute." Much of his success was due to his extraordinary power over audiences. This street near Hamline University was named in 1881. See also *Asbury Street, Hamline Avenue*.

SIMS AVENUE One possibility for the origin of this 1872 East Side name in the Arlington Hills Addition could be John Sims, a carpenter from Canada who may have invested in the property. He died the following year on October 13 of typhoid fever, age twenty-nine. See also *Arlington Hills, White Bear Avenue*.

SINNEN STREET Bernard and Anna Sinnen platted this East Side street as part of their farmstead in 1872. Bernard died in 1887; Anna, in 1891. At least one descendant still lives in that general area. See also *Arcade Street*.

SIXTH STREET The sixth street from the river, this is one of the original fifteen street names of the city named in the 1849 plat, St. Paul Proper. For several decades in the early part of the twentieth century, this was the main retail street in downtown St. Paul.

SKIDMORE PARK This one-third-acre park, east of Earl Street on Fourth Street, was dedicated to the public in 1886 in Skidmore and Cassidy's Addition. Today it is little more than a vacant

Sixth Street looking east from Wabasha Street about 1920. The hill in the foreground marks the division between what used to be Lowertown and Uppertown. Photograph courtesy of the Minnesota Historical Society.

lot, a "ghost park." Edwin and Emma Skidmore, along with Abram and Margaret Cassidy, were residents of Newburgh, New York. Skidmore, who apparently had friends or relatives here, invested in several downtown buildings, including the Skidmore Block at Fifth and Minnesota Streets. See also *Ghost Parks*.

SKYLINE OAKS PARK This one-acre-plus West Side park is on the east side of Concord Street at Belvidere Street.

SKYWAY DRIVE Previously Dilworth Avenue, this Highwood street name was changed in 1957 at the instigation of one of the six residents of the street who discovered his mail was being delivered to Dilworth, Minnesota.

SLOAN STREET All the streets in this development were first names: Agnes, Tina, Mary, Emma. This short North End street appears on the plat as Sloane, also a first name. See also *North End*.

SMITH AVENUE The first Smith Avenue—which is now Forbes Avenue—was named in 1849 in Leach's Addition. Charles K. Smith, probably an investor, was the territorial secretary, who came here from Ohio in 1849 and returned to that state in 1851.

Thirty-six years later, in 1887, with the building of the High Bridge, the city switched Forbes and Smith streets. The long street extending over the High Bridge into the West

Side—which should have been Forbes—became instead Smith Avenue, honoring Robert Armstrong Smith (1827–1913), longtime mayor of St. Paul and real-estate developer on the West Side. Born in Indiana, Smith came to Minnesota in 1853 as private secretary to his brother-in-law, Willis A. Gorman, territorial governor of Minnesota. He was subsequently territorial librarian, Ramsey County treasurer, city alderman, state legislator, city council-man, and mayor 1887–92, 1894–96, and 1900–1908. He also served as postmaster and county commissioner. See also *High Bridge, Gorman Avenue, Dawson Park, Mohawk Park; Edmund Avenue, Kittson Street, Larry Ho Drive, McDonough Park, Nelson Street, Olmstead Street, Otis Avenue, Powers Avenue, Prince Street, Stewart Avenue, William Mahoney Street.*

EQUATING YOUR HOUSE WITH ITS NUMBER

$$N = \frac{\frac{[(H - L) + 1] \times D}{2}}{B} \times 2 + L$$

Here is the official formula used by the St. Paul Public Works Department to calculate a house number in St. Paul. N signifies the required house number, H stands for the highest established corner number, L means the lowest established corner number, D is the distance from the door of the house to the lowest established number, and B denotes the length of the block.

If you do not find this formula elucidating, perhaps you would prefer to use former employee Darlene Hagen's "Numbering Guide," a one-of-a-kind ruler scaled at one inch to eighty feet and correlated to the plat maps. It is that simple!

Well . . . maybe it is not quite that simple. In fact, the formula notwithstanding, very few people in St. Paul—probably no more than ten—understand the whole system, and even they often awake in the night plagued with doubts. Linda Murphy, chief supervisor of Maps and Records, has been responsible for assigning house identifications for the past twenty years and made a valiant effort at running the numbers for us.

The first ordinance dealing with the numbering of buildings in St. Paul was Number 42, approved July 29, 1874. It had two parts: the first part specified that every 25 feet of street front (the minimum lot size) should have a number assigned to it, and the second part specified where the house numbering should begin. So, for example, on all streets running parallel to the Mississippi River, the house numbers would begin east and west from Wabasha Street.

Ordinance Number 42 was repealed six years later and replaced with Ordinance Number 205, approved on April 7, 1880. The new ordinance defined more precise boundaries between the east and west, and between the north and south, numbering. It specified that odd house numbers should be on the west and north sides, and even numbers on the east and south sides of the street. It declared the numbers on parallel streets should match at the cross streets. It added the caveat that owners and occupants should obtain the correct number for their buildings and display them within sixty days. Although repealing the previous ordinance (which had specified a house number for every 25 feet), the new ordinance neglected to specify a minimum lot size per house number.

A year later, a newspaper article reported on the implementation inroads:

> There are still a good many houses in the city without number plates. This ought not to be. A man may as well be without a given name, as without a number on his house. When number plates can be bought for 25 cents each, the man who does business in a store or lives in a house that is not numbered has got some kind of a shaky kink in him. He is altogether too economical to have right good sense.

Over the years public-spirited employees, seemingly without benefit of city ordinance, have informally modified the 125-year-old system. At some point in the past beyond anyone's recollection, the minimum lot size per number was dropped to 20 feet; that is to say, the house numbers, reckoned on a minimum lot size of 20 feet, provide a potential house number for every 20 feet of street front.

Here is how it works. Subtracting the feet used for cross streets leaves 4,800 feet of street front per mile, divided by 20-foot lots, equals 240 potential house numbers per mile on each side of the street, or 480 potential house numbers per mile. Thus, the house number on Summit Avenue at Dale Street is 623; one mile farther west at Lexington Parkway, the house number on Summit Avenue is 1103 (623 + 480). On Edgerton Street, the house number at Case Avenue is 950; one mile north at Arlington Avenue, the house number is 1430 (950 + 480). Because there are very few, if any, consecutive 20-foot lots with houses on them, rarely will every possible house number be used within a mile. Lots are more commonly around 40 or 50 feet wide, so only every second or third number will be assigned. Thus, you might have, on the south side of one block, the numbers 620, 628, 632, 634, 638, 646.

To keep the numbering consistent, the city tries to make sure that at every cross street, the house numbers on parallel streets match up. So if the number on Summit Avenue at Milton Street is 922, then the parallel streets Grand Avenue, Lincoln Avenue, and so on are also numbered 922 at their intersection with Milton Street.

Today the dividing line between east and west house numbers in St. Paul is roughly along the line of Wabasha Street projected north and south to the city boundaries. The dividing line between north and south house numbers is roughly along the line of Summit Avenue projected east to the city boundary.

All orderly and predictable. That is the way it is supposed to work. But this is a river city with irregular angles and contours. What happens when you have a curved street? A circle street? A street like Osceola that runs both north–south and east–west? Linda Murphy ruefully admits that there are a great many exceptions to the rules. For example:

- On Mound Street, house numbers run opposite to parallel Bates Avenue, a block away. The sequence of numbers on the two adjacent streets is quite different, and the odd numbers are on the east side of one of the streets.
- The house numbers on Edgcumbe Road ascend correctly as it runs west from Lexington Parkway, but they soon run amuck as the road meanders through Highland Park.
- West Seventh Street, a diagonal street, has its own unique set of house numbers.
- Smith Avenue from downtown crossing to the West Side has a completely incomprehensible set of house numbers.

- Hancock, a short street on Dayton's Bluff, was originally considered an east–west street, but then another short street, Terry, was tacked onto Hancock, and the whole became a north–south street. Now the house numbers do not seem to fit the rules for either direction.
- And so on.

Out-of-town visitors—especially those from the numerically ordered Mill City—have been heard to grumble in a plaintive sort of way: Why don't you change to a more logical house numbering system? But you, the gentle reader, will have to admit that if the system were simplified and completely consistent, any stranger—however unwelcome—could easily find the way to your door. You wouldn't want that, would you?

SMITH PARK See *Mears Park.*

SNAKE LAKE See *Hazelwood Street.*

SNELLING AVENUE This street was named in 1856 in the Roseville Addition for Colonel Josiah Snelling (1782–1828), commander of the military post that was given his name. Snelling Avenue follows roughly an early path—and before that, an American Indian trail—running from Fort Snelling to Little Canada. Few people know that mighty Snelling Avenue at its southern end turns into a narrow country road winding down a heavily wooded bluff to West Seventh Street. *Snelling Place* takes its name from the same source. Snelling Avenue marks a section line on the land survey. See also *Davern Street, Roseville.*

SNOWSHOE LANE When confronted with a telephone call from the city in 1956 requesting an immediate name for the street on his plat, Dr. David French asked his secretary for an idea. Noticing a pair of snowshoes on top of a bookcase in the office, she suggested Snowshoe Lane, which was conveyed to the city and accepted on the plat. The plat was named Lewiston Heights, taken from the Lewiston bluffs in New York State near Niagara Falls.

SONS OF ABRAHAM CEMETERY This small Jewish cemetery near Lake Phalen, on the east side of Barclay Street just north of Maryland Avenue, is indicated on the 1928 Hopkins atlas. On both sides of this cemetery is the West Side Hebrew cemetery, a separate entity. See also *Cemeteries.*

SONS OF JACOB (MOSES) CEMETERY Established in 1878, this small Jewish cemetery near Lake Phalen is on the east side of Parkway Drive, just north of Idaho Avenue. See also *Cemeteries.*

SPAGHETTI JUNCTION The epithet dished up for the tangled interchange between Interstate 94 and Interstate 35E, in which drivers must suck it up while weaving across several lanes in order to pasta through. This nickname has boiled up at a number of highway intersections throughout the world.

SPENCER ROAD Charles Langford Spencer (1855–1941) was a nephew of Amherst H. Wilder and president of the Amherst H. Wilder Charity from 1922 until his death. The Amherst H. Wilder Foundation, one of St. Paul's largest, was a major contributor to the development of Energy Park, in which this street name occurs. See also *Energy Park.*

SPRING CAVE See *Fountain Cave*.

SPRING LEAP See *Shadow Falls Park*.

SPRING STREET This formerly obscure street on the edge of downtown was named in 1849 in Rice and Irvine's Addition probably because of the springs bubbling from the bluff. Abandoned with the floods of 1952, this street has been resuscitated with the development of the Upper Landing urban village. See also *Upper Levee, Upper Landing*.

SPRINGFIELD STREET This West End street was most likely named in 1872 for the capital city of Illinois by the developer Charles A. B. Weide of that state. See also *Weide Street, West End*.

SPRINGSIDE DRIVE Previously Garden Avenue, the name was changed in 1948 as part of a general reorganization of street names within the Highwood area. The springs from which the street takes its name are on the east side of the street a short distance up from the intersection with Point Douglas Road. Today the outflow from the springs drops into the sewer system after a short spill down the hillside. See also *Highwood*.

SPRUCE STREET Previously Baldwin Street, this street near downtown was renamed for the tree in 1872. Today it is industrial blah.

SPRUCE TREE AVENUE This street was added in 1987 when Spruce Tree Place was built on the southwest corner of University and Snelling Avenues. The road was to facilitate left turns into the neighborhood behind Spruce Tree Place.

SRI CHIN MOY BRIDGE Also known as the Peace Bridge and the Marshall Avenue–Lake Street Bridge, this name was bestowed by resolution of the city council. Born in 1931 in Bangladesh, Sri Chin Moy is internationally known as a musician and advocate for world peace. During the past decade, this bridge has become the site of many peace and antiwar demonstrations. See also *Bridges*.

ST. ALBANS LAKE (1) This Summit-University area lake (named by the author) is mentioned by Josiah Chaney. It also appears on the 1853 plat, Smith and Lott Subdivision. The lake occupied most of the block between Marshall and Iglehart Avenues, and between Grotto and St. Albans Streets. It was about twenty feet deep, according to the first grading records for St. Albans Street. See also *Dale Street, Dayton Avenue Lake, St. Albans Lake* (2), *Lakes/Ponds*.

ST. ALBANS LAKE (2) This Summit-University area lake (named by the author) is mentioned by Josiah Chaney. It also appears on the 1853 plat, Smith and Lott Subdivision. This lake occupied most of the block between Carroll and Iglehart Avenues, between Grotto and St. Albans Streets. The lake was about twenty-five feet deep according to the first grading records for St. Albans Street. See also *Dale Street, Dayton Avenue Lake, St. Albans Lake* (1), *Lakes/Ponds*.

ST. ALBANS PARK See *Carty Park*.

ST. ALBANS STREET Platted as Prairie Street in 1871, this Summit-University street was renamed the following year. St. Albans is the site of one of the oldest Roman towns in England. See also *St. Albans Lake* (1) and (2), *Weber's Pond*.

ST. ANTHONY AVENUE Although the first instance of this street name occurred in the 1849 plat by Rice and Irvine, it has been applied to several streets within the city at various times, most notably that portion of Kellogg Boulevard that ran from St. Peter Street to the Cathedral of St. Paul. This early street and its continuations westward were named because they were part of an early road between St. Paul and St. Anthony Falls. The present street of this name, the north frontage road of Interstate 94, was designated in 1964. The early oxcart route between St. Paul and Pembina, North Dakota, followed roughly the course of this street. See also *Doane Avenue, St. Anthony Hill*.

ST. ANTHONY HILL In the early days of the city, the road from downtown St. Paul to St. Anthony Falls (Minneapolis) through the Midway area was known as the St. Anthony road and, later, St. Anthony Avenue. The neighborhood on top of the hill near the Cathedral of St. Paul in what is today the Summit-University area was known as St. Anthony Hill because St. Anthony Avenue accessed it. See also *Iglehart Avenue, Laurel Avenue, Oakland Avenue, Selby Avenue, St. Anthony Avenue*.

An advertisement proclaims the virtues of St. Anthony Park. From *Northwest Magazine*, April 1886.

ST. ANTHONY PARK This railroad suburb of the 1880s encompasses the area roughly between Hoyt Avenue and Territorial Road, and between Eustis and Cleveland/Raymond Avenues. The name was adopted from the village of St. Anthony (named for the falls), a small town long since integrated into southeast Minneapolis. The St. Anthony Park Company, incorporated in 1885, spent over $300,000 in the next five years improving the property and building homes in their two plats: St. Anthony Park North and South St. Anthony Park. It was designed as a middle-class community, and, typical of that period, the irregular lots and blocks were laid out according to the topography. Over the years, the park has been influenced and affected by the industrial area on the south and west, the University of Minnesota St. Paul campus on the east, and the adjacent Minnesota State Fairgrounds. Quite a bit has been written about this desirable residential enclave. See also *Alden Square, Breda Avenue, Doris Square, Everett Court, Sarita Wetlands*.

ST. CHARLES STREET This downtown street appears on George Nichols's 1851 map of St.

Paul as a street between Third and Bench (Second) Streets, just west of Jackson Street. After a lengthy trial in 1866, the Minnesota Supreme Court decided there was no public street in that location.

ST. CLAIR AVENUE Charles Willis (1819–98), the developer, grew up on the banks of Lake Erie and named this street in 1851 for Lake St. Clair, between Lakes Huron and Erie. Adjacent streets were Michigan, Superior, Ontario, Erie, and Huron. St. Clair Avenue, a section line on the land survey, marks the course of the first east-west road in Reserve Township, laid out in December 1858. See also *Reserve Township*.

ST. DENNIS COURT See *Upper St. Dennis Road*

ST. DENNIS TRIANGLE Acquired as part of the Highland Park street, these two triangle parks, one east and one west of Snelling Avenue, are at the juncture of Upper St. Dennis Road and Lower St. Dennis Road.

ST. JOSEPH'S LANE Named at the request of St. Joseph's Hospital, this street was the result of yet another downtown street reshuffling for commercial purposes in 1977. St. Joseph's is said to be the oldest hospital in the state.

ST. PAUL In 1841, the Reverend Lucian Galtier built a small log chapel, establishing a mission at what would become downtown St. Paul. In his own words, he explained the name he picked:

> On the first of November, in the same year [1841], I blessed the new *basilica* and dedicated it to "St. Paul, the apostle of nations." I expressed a wish, at the same time, that the settlement would be known by the same name, and my desire was obtained. I had, previously to this time, fixed my residence at Saint Peter's [Mendota], and as the name of PAUL is generally connected with that of PETER, and the gentiles being well represented in the new place in the persons of the Indians, I called it Saint Paul. The name "Saint Paul," applied to a town or city, seemed appropriate. The monosyllable is short, sounds well, and is understood by all denominations of Christians.

The City of St. Paul was originally established as the Town of St. Paul by an act of the Legislative Assembly of the Territory of Minnesota in November 1849. The initial town site consisted of two plats: The first plat, "Town of Saint Paul" (sometimes referred to as the "St. Paul Proper"), surveyed by Ira B. Brunson, was filed on February 28, 1849, in St. Croix County, Wisconsin Territory. The second plat, "Irvine & Rice's Addition," surveyed by Benjamin W. Brunson, was filed on May 16, 1849, as "Rice and Irvine's Addition to Saint Paul," in St. Croix County, Minnesota Territory. These two plats, comprising approximately 280 acres, formed the original town boundaries: Elm Street on the west, Smith Avenue and East Seventh Street on the north, Wacouta Street on the east, and the left bank of the Mississippi River on the south.

Saint Paul remained a town until March of 1854 when it became the "City of Saint Paul, Minnesota Territory." In May 1858 when Minnesota became a state, the city became known as

"The City of Saint Paul, State of Minnesota." Saint Paul went through fourteen boundary expansions between the years 1849 and 1887, when its present boundaries were attained.

In 1903, at the great Paris Exposition, St. Paul was selected as the "Healthiest City in the World," and awarded a gold medal.

There are approximately 850 miles of street, 250 miles of alley, and over 1,000 miles of sidewalk within the city. See also *Brunson Street, Galtier Street, Xees Phaus.*

ST. PAUL AVENUE Over the years, there have been many St. Paul Avenues. In 1925, this street was opened from West Seventh Street near Snelling Avenue, west to Edgcumbe Road and northwest to Cleveland Avenue. This diagonal route was to eliminate the trucks from the residential streets between Montreal and Randolph Avenues by providing a wide commercial road—with a minimal grade for truck traffic—to and from the Ford Motor Company plant and its corollary industries on Ford Parkway. See also *Ford Parkway, Highland Parkway.*

ST. PAUL DOWNTOWN AIRPORT (Holman Field) Established in 1926 on the West Side of St. Paul, the airport was constructed on the site of Lamprey Lake along the Mississippi River. According to the custom of the day, the airport was named for a famous aviator, in this case Charles Holman. Today the official name of the airport, which is now owned and operated by the Metropolitan Airports Commission, is the St. Paul Downtown Airport, but common usage still refers to it as Holman Field.

Charles "Speed" Holman, 1898–1931, raised on a Minnesota farm, first raced motorcycles under the nickname "Jack Speed." Later, his father, watching daredevil parachute jumps in a flying circus, was amazed to discover the parachute jumper was his son. In return for a promise never to jump again, his father bought him his first airplane. His name became a household word when the newly organized Northwest Airways hired Speed as its first operations manager, and he pioneered airmail routes across Wisconsin and North Dakota. Considered one of the country's top acrobatic pilots, Holman set a looping record that stood for many years, and his airline career was punctuated by wins in national air races. He died during an impromptu performance at the dedication of the Omaha Airport. A hundred thousand people turned out for his funeral. See also *Lamprey Lake.*

Charles "Speed" Holman, one of the country's top acrobatic pilots, circa 1930. Photograph by Robert R. Blanch; courtesy of the Minnesota Historical Society.

ST. PETER STREET This is one of the original fifteen street names of the city, named in 1849 on the plat St. Paul Proper for the St. Peter's, or Minnesota, River. The river was first designated as the St. Peter's River in 1689, and French and English explorers had known it by that name for more than 150 years. In 1852, to provide an American Indian name for the state, the appellation was officially changed to the Minnesota River. In the original plat and for a couple of decades after, the street was spelled as St. Peter's.

In the early days of the city, before there were water pipes, the fire department built and maintained cisterns collecting water for dousing fires downtown. It was one job of the street commissioner to ensure that the "cistern covers are loosened each day during the cold weather" so the covers did not freeze shut. According to the 1864 city council minutes, one of these cisterns at St. Peter and Ninth Streets was estimated to cost $544.

STAIRWAYS Like any city built in a river valley, St. Paul has a number of pedestrian stairways, although as the amount of pedestrian traffic goes down, so does the number of stairways. The most notable flights are *Bancroft Stairs*, *Green (Wabasha) Stairs*, *Grotto Steps*, *Lawton Steps*, and *Walnut Steps*.

STANDISH STREET Miles Standish (1584–1656), whose romance involving John Alden and Priscilla Mullens was recorded in Henry Wadsworth Longfellow's poem *The Courtship of Miles Standish*, served as the inspiration for this 1885 St. Anthony Park street name. See also *St. Anthony Park*.

STANFORD AVENUE This street was originally extended west as Grace Street—which name it retains east of Lexington Parkway; the new name was substituted in 1913. This was done, no doubt, at the wish of the developer of the Macalester Villas Addition, who wanted his street names identified with the desirable residential enclave of Macalester Park. *Stanford Court* takes its name from the same source. Over eighty years later, this futuristic home remains:

ELECTRIC HOME OPEN SOON

St. Paul's first electrically equipped home, which will open one week from today, has been constructed at 1774 Stanford Avenue, by the Abbott Miller company, local realtors.

The kitchen arrangement represents the latest innovations in electrically equipped labor saving devices for the housewife. The electric range will be equipped with an automatic time switch for long or short, intense or mild cooking periods.

The electric refrigeration plant provides dry cold that permits long storage of ordinary perishable food.

The kitchen equipment includes an electric dishwasher, service utensils, beaters and other conveniences.

The electric home is being sponsored here by the St. Paul Electrical League as merely an educational feature. It will be open for free public inspection for two weeks. Attendants will be in charge of the house during the exhibit hours.

Three essay contests have been announced and are open to competition by children attending the grade schools, high school students and adults. Prizes will be offered to the winners of the three contests announced.

St. Paul Pioneer Press, November 5, 1922.

See also Macalester Park.

STANFORD WALK Platted as a twelve-foot right-of-way between Mt. Curve Boulevard and Stonebridge Boulevard, it has since been vacated. See also Macalester Walk.

STARKEY STREET Originally part of Concord Street, this West Side street was renamed in 1883. Remembered as a prolific writer, a poet, and a good speaker, James Starkey (1818–92) devised the sewer system for St. Paul in 1873. Born in England, he immigrated to America in 1849 and journeyed to St. Paul the following year. He was active in the territorial government of the state, a captain in the local militia, and a county commissioner of Anoka County, and he did extensive railroad surveying. See also Childs Road, West Side.

STATE STREET First named Bertha Street, this West Side street had its name changed in 1883. There is a well-known State Street in Chicago. See also West Side.

STELLA STREET This street was named in 1885 in the original St. Anthony Park plat. See also St. Anthony Park.

STELLAR STREET Stellar means, in the dictionary definition, "of or pertaining to the stars," a reach for this short North End street dubbed in the 1880s. See also North End.

STERK ROAD Adolph Sterk (1867–1953) was born in Freiburg, Germany, where as a youth he studied horticulture. Leaving Germany to avoid the draft, he immigrated to St. Paul in

Adolph Sterk in his Como Park office. Photograph by A. F. Raymond from the collection of the St. Paul Parks Department; courtesy of the Minnesota Historical Society.

the 1890s and worked for the parks department from about 1897 until his death. He served over thirty years of his career as principal clerk, with occasional stints as assistant superintendent. He was married to Anna, daughter of Frederick Nusbaumer, a longtime parks superintendent. Before 1967, when this street in Como Park was officially named, the road was informally known as the "Banana Valley Road" from the custom of transporting banana plants from the greenhouse to the outdoors in the spring. Alas, Sterk Road was peeled away as part of the realignment of Lexington Parkway. See also Nusbaumer Drive.

STEVENS STREET This West Side street was platted in 1857 by William H. Stevens, who was apparently never a state resident. The first surveyor of this area in 1853—before there were any streets—noted a road from the American Indian village of Kaposia near what is now South St. Paul to the Upper Ferry (where the High Bridge is now) that crossed the section line of Hall Avenue at Stevens Street. See also *West Side, Wilkin Street.*

STEVENS STREET (Fairground) The first white man to settle in Minneapolis, John H. Stevens (1820–1900) began farming upon his arrival here, gaining a reputation as an agricultural authority. Stevens was a charter member of the Hennepin County Agricultural Society, and from 1893 to 1894 he served as president of the Minnesota State Agricultural Society, the organization responsible for naming this street within the state fairgrounds. It is reported that in 1853 Stevens and an associate imported the first full-blooded Devon cow and bull ever brought into Hennepin County; the animals cost them $2,000, four years of typical wages.

STEWART AVENUE Originally Old Fort Road and Bluff Street, the name was changed in 1872 to honor Dr. Jacob Henry Stewart (1829–84), three-term mayor of St. Paul. Born in New York, he came to St. Paul in 1855, where, at various times, he served as surgeon general of Minnesota, state senator, member of the St. Paul Board of Education, postmaster, U.S. congressman, and surveyor general. He was noted in his younger years for his red hair and bright, gleeful, boyish air. Stewart Avenue follows generally the course of the first road between Fort Snelling and the fledgling hamlet of St. Paul. See also *Cliff Street, Emma Street, Fort Road, Stewart Park, Dawson Park; Edmund Avenue, Kittson Street, Larry Ho Drive, McDonough Park, Nelson Street, Olmstead Street, Otis Avenue, Powers Avenue, Prince Street, Smith Avenue, William Mahoney Street.*

STEWART PARK This one-and-one-third-acre North End park on the northwest corner of Westminster Street and Jessamine Avenue was given by Edmund Rice to the city in August 1884 in memory of his friend Dr. Jacob H. Stewart, who died that month. It was noted as an attractive grass-covered hill with a great view of the Trout Brook valley. The park was confiscated in 1957 to build the exit ramp off Interstate 35E to Maryland Avenue. See also *Edmund Avenue, Stewart Avenue.*

STICKNEY STREET Alpheus Bede Stickney (1840–1916) was an attorney and railroad official when this West Side street was named in 1885. He is best known for his role as organizer and builder of the St. Paul Union Stock Yards and packinghouses, and as president of the Chicago Great Western Railway Company. See also *West Side.*

STILLWATER AVENUE There were a number of significant streets bearing this destination name in the early history of St. Paul, but only one of them remains. The present Stillwater Avenue is the result of renaming several streets; most of its length before 1940 was known as Phalen Avenue. The first surveyor's notes in 1847 record that the east-west road between Stillwater and St. Paul crossed what is today Johnson Parkway where Stillwater Avenue intersects.

There are two "detention ponds" between Stillwater and Bush Avenues on the west side of Hazel Street, which are wetlands modified to contain the overflow from the storm sewer that runs between the two ponds. There are more than two dozen of these detention ponds throughout the city; most of them occupy former wetlands or lakebeds that were unbuildable.

Across Hazel Street on the east side is another detention pond. On the 1867 L. G. Bennett township maps, however, a lake almost half the size of Beaver Lake occupies this whole area east of Hazel Street. This former lake—also noted on the first surveyor's records in 1847— was fed by a creek from Beaver Lake flowing into its southeast corner, and it was drained by Ames Creek flowing out of it, northwest to Ames Lake, and hence into Phalen Creek. See also *Ames Lake, Arcade Street, White Bear Avenue; Beaver Lake, Devil's Ditch, Hillcrest Knoll, Howard Street, Phalen Creek, Roger Puchreiter Pond, Willow Reserve.*

STINCHFIELD STREET This Highwood street was named for J. H. Stinchfield, secretary of the Bachman Realty Company. Henry Bachman bought about 250 acres, based on the rumor a bridge would be built across the Mississippi River in this area, greatly increasing the value of his purchase. Because the bridge was not built, the land lay idle for many years until platted in 1926 by the Bachman Realty Company. This street was recently improved and opened in the Oaks of Highwood plat.

Henry Bachman, first in the dynasty of Richfield–Twin Cities florists, later moved to Long Beach, California, where he had an opportunity to purchase Signal Hill before oil was discovered on it. His wife insisted on his retirement, however, and the chance to make millions of dollars passed by. See also *Bailey Street.*

STINSON PARK The original Stinson Park, dedicated to the public in 1884 in Stinson's Rice Street Addition, was on the southeast corner of Maryland Avenue and Park Street. About 1910, it became Sylvan Playground, but today we have a second Stinson Park on the southwest corner of Chatsworth and Stinson Streets that was acquired as tax-forfeit land in 1953. Both parks take their name from James Stinson. See *James Avenue.*

STINSON STREET James Stinson (1828–1917), one of the developers, named this street in 1883. There is also a street in Superior, Wisconsin, named for him. See also *James Avenue.*

STONE ARCH BRIDGE Yes, Saint Paul has its own unique stone arch bridge on the National Register of Historic Places. Technically known as the Seventh Street Improvement Arches, this bridge, built in 1884, carried East Seventh Street over the now-abandoned railroad tracks between Kittson Street and Payne Avenue. Masonry enthusiasts and intrepid urban traipsers could park their cars in a small lot above the bridge on the east side of the intersection of East Seventh Street and Payne Avenue. Follow the asphalt Bruce Vento Regional Trail a short distance down the hill until the bridge comes into view. Once you experience this memorable span and the inside of the railroad tunnels, you will swoon over its classification as a "skewed, double-arched, limestone highway bridge constructed according to the helicoidal, or spiral, method." The bridge has been characterized as "the most important piece of masonry in the city." See also *Bridges.*

STONE, TONI, FIELD See *Toni Stone Field.*

STONEBRIDGE BOULEVARD Named in 1928, the street takes its name from the estate of Oliver Crosby, titled "Stonebridge." This estate originally occupied twenty-eight acres between Jefferson and St. Clair Avenues, between Mississippi River and Mt. Curve Boulevards. The estate contained a large, sumptuous, twenty-four-room house built in 1915–16, a nine-car garage, a large greenhouse, and numerous outbuildings, and was landscaped with two artificial lakes. Water flowed from a lake at the top of the hill through waterfalls and reflecting pools to Lake Elizabeth, a city-block-sized lake in front of the residence. The water drained riverward through a small ravine spanned by a stone bridge, which remains on private property.

Oliver Crosby (1856–1922), owner of the estate, was a founder and president of American Hoist and Derrick Company. After his death, his wife, Elizabeth, and eventually his son Frederick lived in the mansion until 1935, when it became vacant. In 1944, the residence was tax-forfeited to the state. The house was considered for the governor's residence during many legislative sessions but was finally demolished in 1953, a sad ending for a beautiful estate. The Stonebridge main gate was moved to the Midway Parkway entrance at Como Park in 1937. The ornamental iron gates are located near the pavilion at Lake Como. Jay Pfaender has written a complete history of the property, "The Story of a Lost Estate and Oliver Crosby, the Inventive Genius Who Created It." See also *Lakes/Ponds*.

STONEBRIDGE OVAL The Stonebridge Oval is a fifteen-foot circle serving as a traffic island at the intersection of Stanford Court and Woodlawn Avenue. It was dedicated in 1929 to public use forever. To the residents, it has been known by various names, including the "doughnut." See also *Stonebridge Boulevard*.

Stonebridge, the estate of Oliver Crosby, circa 1930, before it was forfeited for back taxes. Photograph by Sigmund Leet Studio; courtesy of the Minnesota Historical Society.

STROH DRIVE This street was named by the city council in 1984 for the Stroh Brewery, which occupied the area at that time. For over a century, this complex was home to Hamm's Brewery, at one time one of the largest breweries in the Midwest, providing employment for generations of East Side residents. See also *Hamm Park*.

STRYKER AVENUE John L. Stryker of New York State was one of the developers of this West Side street in 1855. Stryker was a gentleman, that is to say, he did not have to work for a living. John is not recorded as a resident of St. Paul, but his son, John E. Stryker (1862–1940), moved to St. Paul in 1887 as an attorney.

The first survey of this area in 1853 notes a stream, three-and-a-half-feet wide, flowing northeast, crossing the line of Delos Street between Winslow and Stryker Avenues. See also *West Side*.

STURGIS STREET Charles E. Sturgis, his wife, Louisa, and their son William platted this West End street in 1857. They apparently never lived here. See also *West End*.

SUBURBAN AVENUE This East Side street was named in 1882 in Suburban Hills. See also *East Side*.

SUBURBAN POND This lake and its shoreline on the East Side of St. Paul at Suburban and White Bear Avenues is a thirty-two-acre Ramsey County Open Space that has evolved into a big sediment pond collecting storm-water runoff. However, in the original survey of this land in 1847, the surveyor James Marsh made note of a round lake approximately one-quarter mile in diameter. Given the fact the lake has existed at least for 150 years, long before there was any Suburban Avenue in the area, perhaps the lake deserves a more creative name. See also *Lakes/Ponds*.

SUE STREET James and Sue Fry, both of Bloomington, Illinois, platted this Highland Park street in 1886. *Sue Place* takes its name from the same source. See also *Highland Park*.

SUE'S PARK Emily Slowinski, who named this compact park at the corner of Payne and Rose Avenues about 1988, was a social worker with Lutheran Social Services at the corner of Payne and Maryland Avenues. Seeking a pleasant outdoor place to eat her lunch, she was attracted to this small city lot. Using a gift of $10,000 from her parents, Willard and FloraBel Dayton (transplants from the East Coast), and another $3,500 designated for neighborhood beautification, she initiated the planting of trees and flowers and the installation of a picnic table and bench, and a water fountain. When the new park was completed, Emily was given the honor of naming it. She picked the name of her deceased sister, Sue Dayton Price (1932–81), who had been a community activist in Arlington, Virginia, where she lived. According to local lore, the largest evergreen tree in the park was planted in recognition of a penmanship teacher at the Phalen Park School, which had previously occupied the site.

SUMAC STREET Previously Bowdoin, the name of this one-block-long street off Shepard Road was changed in 1940. In the first half of the twentieth century, according to an article in the *St. Paul Dispatch*, October 14, 1959, this was called Patterson Hill. See also *Butternut Avenue*.

SUMMIT AVENUE Platted in 1854 in Farrington and Kinney's Addition, this elm-lined boulevard, St. Paul's showplace, was named because of its course along the top of the bluff. Summit, like other names indicating height, is a common street name. For over a century, this was the most prestigious address in St. Paul; perhaps it still is. On the public boulevard in front of 1347 Summit Avenue are vestiges of sidewalk created with marble said to be left over from the construction of the State Capitol. In the alley between Summit and Portland Avenues, between Lexington Parkway and Dunlap Street, is the only remaining (as far as we know) pavement of wooden blocks in the city. *Summit Court* and *Summit Lane* take their names from the same source. See also *Chatsworth Street, Edgcumbe Road, Evergreen Place, Grand Rounds, Griggs Street, Hersey Street, Lake Mennith, Laurel Street, Lawton Steps, Long Hill, Park Place, Ramsey Hill Historic District, Rice Street, Summit-University, Walnut Steps, Wheeler Street, Woodland Park.*

SUMMIT LOOKOUT PARK In an 1873 address to the St. Paul City Council, Horace W. S. Cleveland, the famous landscape architect who designed the park system of St. Paul and Minneapolis, lamented that homes had been built on the bluff side of Summit Avenue, obscuring the view of the river valley and downtown. He vowed that his priority would be to set aside at least one place along the hilltop for a public view.

This small, one-half-acre triangle at the corner of Summit Avenue and Ramsey Hill was acquired by condemnation in 1891 for the extravagant price of $35,000. In the early days of Summit Avenue, this had been a private lot, Carpenter's Lookout, with an observation tower used by residents of Carpenter's Hotel across the street.

The 115-year-old statue of an eagle in the park, created by Louis Saint-Gaudens in 1889, is a one-ton bronze sculpture that served as a symbol of protection for the New York Life Insurance Company building in downtown St. Paul. The work depicts the bird with a twelve-foot wingspan sheltering its nest of eaglets, a snake in one talon. After the building was torn down in 1967, the sculpture was saved from a salvage pile for $800 and installed nearby at ground level at Fourth and Jackson Streets. After nearly thirty years of neglect, the eagle was donated in 1999 with the stipulation it be moved. Summit Lookout Park was selected, creating a cluster of sculptures in nearby parks. The decorative railing in the park came from the old Selby Avenue bridge over Ayd Mill Road. See also *Merle Harris Bridge.*

SUMMIT PARK This park, between Marshall and Dayton Avenues, is just west of John Ireland Boulevard. A part of the park was purchased as early as 1883; since then a number of buildings have been demolished, expanding the park almost to Louis Street.

SUMMIT-UNIVERSITY The Summit-University Planning Council is the District 8 community council covering the area of St. Paul known as the Summit-University neighborhood. It extends between Summit Avenue and University Avenue, between Lexington Parkway and Marion Street, Kellogg Boulevard, John Ireland Boulevard, Summit Avenue, and Irvine Avenue on the east. See also *Central Village, Cornmeal Hill, Oatmeal Valley, Old Rondo Avenue, Ramsey Hill Historic District, Short Hill, St. Albans Park, St. Anthony Hill, Woodland Park.*

SUMNER STREET This is a fairly common place and family name, chosen here most likely for its faintly English sound. Other Highland Park streets in this 1886 plat were named Norwich, Beverly, Salem, and Woodview. See also *Highland Park*.

SUNNY SLOPE LANE Originally part of Itasca Avenue, this Highland Park street was renamed in 1955 at the request of the residents to avoid confusion between the west and east segments of Itasca Avenue, which were widely separated. See also *Highland Park*.

SUNSHINE PLACE This is the place to visit in the winter. Go north on Chatsworth Avenue from Front Street about five blocks: on the corner of Van Slyke Avenue between Chatsworth Avenue and Como Boulevard, you will find a small point of land extending into Chatsworth Avenue. This point is the west side of a triangle (the remainder has been incorporated into Como Park) named Sunshine Place. The name no doubt dawned on the developer because it is on the east border of the village of Warrendale. See also *Ghost Parks, Warrendale*.

SUPERIOR STREET Charles Willis (1819–98), the developer, grew up on the banks of Lake Erie and named this West End street in 1851 for Lake Superior. Adjacent streets were Michigan, St. Clair, Ontario, Erie, and Huron. See also *West End*.

SUPORNICK LANE Lieutenant David Supornick was killed in the Normandy invasion in 1944, during World War II. As a testimonial to all the U.S. soldiers killed in that war, Supornick's name was offered by his brother-in-law, Sidney Goff, secretary of the Housing and Redevelopment Authority, who platted this East Side public housing development in 1951. See also *East Side*.

SURREY AVENUE Previously Van Buren Place, the name of this short East Side street was changed in 1940. See also *East Side*.

SUSAN AVENUE Susan was the daughter of Leonard Bisanz, one of the brothers who developed this Highland Park area in 1951. See also *Colette Place, Dorothea Avenue, Matterhorn Lane*.

SWEDE HOLLOW At its peak, Swede Hollow, a ravine carved by Phalen Creek, was a world of its own, with sixty homes, a grocery store, a saloon, and a Catholic chapel. Occupied by successive waves of newly arrived Swedish, Polish, Irish, Italian, and Mexican immigrants, the Hollow received no city services such as running water, sewers, or paved streets. As public health standards in the city increased, the Hollow began to look increasingly ramshackle and unsanitary. The last fourteen houses in Swede Hollow were burned on December 11, 1956.

However, those tempted to become too nostalgic about these vanished neighborhoods should read (and see the photographs) in a report on housing conditions in the city of St. Paul in 1917 sponsored by the Amherst H. Wilder Charity. With a certain prescience, the 1917 report wrote: "Phalen Creek and the banks of this stream are ideal for park purposes, while in their present state they constitute a menace to the health of the residents and to the community at large." Swede Hollow was dedicated as a nature center in October 1976. The interested reader can find much that has been written on this community. See also *Badlands, Barton-Omaha Colony, Bohemian Flats, Connemara Patch, Upper Levee, West Side Flats*.

"Swedes, Irish, Italians, Pole, Mexican—each nationality helped amplify the congestion and unsanitary conditions to a point which finally brought drastic action." Photograph courtesy of the Minnesota Historical Society.

SWEDE HOLLOW PARK See Swede Hollow.

SYCAMORE STREET This North End street was named for the tree in 1856. Some of the narrowest building lots in the city, twenty-five feet wide, are found on the north side of Sycamore Street between Sylvan and Rice Streets. A twenty-foot-wide lot was considered the absolute minimum in early St. Paul. See also *North End*.

SYLVAN STREET *Sylvan* means "abounding in woods, groves, or trees." As such it was a popular name, even though this particular area may not have been so distinguished when this North End street bordering Oakland Cemetery was named in Ashton and Sherburne's Addition in 1857. See also *North End, Oakland Cemetery*.

SYNDICATE PARK This one-acre park on the northeast corner of Syndicate Street and Summit Avenue takes its name from the street. See also *Syndicate Street*.

SYNDICATE STREET The St. Paul Real Estate Syndicate was the developer of this Midway area in 1882. See also *Midway*.

T

TAINTER AVENUE Captain Andrew Tainter (1823–99) and his wife, Bertha, were investors in the St. Anthony Park addition when this street was named in 1885. Born in Salina, New York, Tainter settled at Menomonie, Wisconsin, in 1846, where he later became a partner with John H. Knapp in what developed into one of the largest lumbering concerns in the world. The Tainters built a lavish, 313-seat theater for their daughter, Mabel, in Menomonie, which is undergoing restoration. See also *St. Anthony Park*.

TANGLE TOWN A nickname for the sinuous streets of Macalester Park, the area between Grand and St. Clair Avenues, between Snelling and Fairview Avenues. See also *Macalester Park*.

TATUM PARK See *Tatum Street*.

TATUM STREET Samuel C. Tatum and his wife, Eleanor, of Cincinnati, Ohio, were partners with Hannah Tatum of Philadelphia in developing this Midway Heights addition in 1885. They invested in this property at the instigation of Pennock Pusey, a real-estate dealer in St. Paul. *Tatum Place* takes its name from the same source. See also *Midway Heights, Pennock Avenue*.

TAYLOR AVENUE William G. and Charlotte F. Taylor platted property including this Midway street named in 1881. The following year, they platted additional property west of Snelling Avenue, adding Charlotte Street to the city. Neither of the Taylors, who sold their property six years later, was a resident of the city. See also *Charlotte Street*.

TAYLOR PARK This four-acre park in the Highwood area at Howard and Oakridge Streets is the namesake of two earlier Taylor Public Schools. The first was built in the late 1880s; the second was built in 1924 on this park site. Samuel S. Taylor (1835–89) graduated from Dartmouth College in 1859 and settled in St. Paul in 1866, where he became a teacher in the public school system. See also *Highwood*.

TEDESCO STREET In July of 1980, at the request of the Payne-Minnehaha Community Council and District 5 Planning Council, Collins Street was changed to honor Victor Tedesco, a longtime city councilman, community activist, and musician, whose parents once owned property near this street. See also *Aida Place, Antonio Drive, Collins Street*.

TELL STREET Named by Adam Gotzian in 1883, this East Side street name is probably a personal name. See also *East Side*.

TEMPERANCE STREET One of downtown's most obscure avenues, this block-long street was named in Joel Whitney's Addition in 1851 for the virtue of abstaining from alcoholic beverages. At this early date, temperance was a spirited question, and the first society for that purpose had been organized in St. Paul only three years previous. It is said that in its later years the street was disgraced by a saloon. Today, for the first time in 130 years, there are residential units on the street with, we hope, no intemperate occupants.

TEMPLE COURT This Midway street name was given in 1890; the temple area (known as the Inns of Court) is an ancient district of London in which lawyers have traditionally lived and studied. The street first occurs in the Capitol Addition, reminding us of the time when there was talk of building the new state capitol building in the Midway area. See also *Federal City*.

TENTH STREET Named in Bazil and Guerin's Addition in 1850, it was the tenth street from the river. The first dedicated city high school building was constructed at Tenth and Minnesota Streets in 1883. With its twenty-five teachers and five hundred pupils, the building was located in what was then a residential area of the city.

TERRACE COURT This street was platted in 1981 north of downtown in the Univar Addition. *Terrace* is a nineteenth-century word for "hillside."

TERRACE PARK This one-acre-plus park is on the west side of South Wabasha Street between Delos and Isabel Streets. You can access it from the east end of Delos Street by way of a stairway down to Isabel Street. It was donated in 1877, making it one of the oldest parks in the city. *Terrace* is a nineteenth-century word for "hillside." See also *West Side*.

TERRITORIAL ROAD Congress appropriated money to the War Department in 1850 for the construction of a road from Point Douglas, via Cottage Grove, Red Rock, St. Paul, and the Falls of St. Anthony, to Fort Ripley. Then, as now, good roads were justified as a necessary part of national defense. Except for an alley, all that remains of this early road between the Twin Cities can be found in the few blocks now labeled as Territorial Road. See also *Van Buren Avenue*.

TEWANNA PLACE In keeping with some of the other street names in the Beaver Lake Heights Addition platted in 1917, this is quite possibly an Ojibwe word. However, because Ojibwe is a spoken, not a written, language, it is difficult to know what sound Tewanna should have, and hence what its meaning might be. See also *Beaver Lake Heights*.

Two early street signs from St. Paul. The top, circa 1920, was at the intersection of West Seventh and Ramsey Streets. The lower, circa 1940, was in front of Ancker Hospital on Colborne Street. Photograph by Kathleen M. Vadnais.

THEODOSIA KIDD PARK This small West Side pocket park with a great view, at Prospect Boulevard and Hall Avenue, was acquired by the public works department in the 1930s to expand Prospect Boulevard. In 1978, the department declared the land surplus, and despite neighbors who wished to keep the land open space, the city council solicited bids. Theodosia Kidd of Stillwater, whose daughter lived adjacent to the parcel, offered $9,500 with a view to keeping the space undeveloped, but the Planning and Economic Development Department urged the council to accept the $6,100 bid from an architect who would build on the lot, arguing the increased taxes from a residence outweighed the higher bid. Then, in a motion that stunned the assembled city council—and drew applause from the audience—the seventy-six-year-old Kidd offered to buy the land and donate it to the city as a public park. Upon hearing this offer, Councilwoman Ruby Hunt suggested the park be named for the generous benefactress. In an ironic sequel, a number of local residents later seeded the idea of using the park as a community vegetable garden, but because the adjacent neighbors feared a horde of horticulturists, the garden idea withered on the vine. See also *Prospect Boulevard*, *West Side*.

THERESA PLACE Theresa Eisenmenger was a close friend of the Bohland family when they platted this Highland Park street in 1927; she may have been the inspiration for the name. This street was vacated in 1993. See also *Bohland Avenue*, *Highland Park*.

THIRD STREET This is one of the original fifteen street names of the city, named in the 1849 plat, St. Paul Proper. The original town site plat began numbering with Third Street; the second street from the river was Bench Street, and the street next to the river was Water Street. The present Third Street was extended from downtown, while the original portion has been renamed Kellogg Boulevard.

THIRTEENTH STREET William Dahl, a stationer born in England, immigrated to St. Paul in 1851. Seven years later, the year Minnesota became a state, Dahl built a frame house at 136 Thirteenth Street. William's son, Edward, picked chestnuts where the state capitol building was later constructed. By the 1970s, the house built in 1858—and by now placed on the National Register of Historic Places—remained as the only private single dwelling left in the downtown area. However, the state wanted the property for grander purposes, and after Governor Arne Carlson called the house "ugly," it was banished to a parking lot in 1997 to make way for a new state revenue building. Eventually the house was moved to the West End at 508 Jefferson Avenue, but having been relocated from its significant original site, the house was removed from the National Register.

THOMAS AVENUE Thomas Stinson (1798–1864) was the developer of this Midway-Frogtown street named in Stinson's Addition in 1856 by his son and agent, James Stinson. Thomas, a man of great wealth, lived in Hamilton, Ontario, Canada. Upon his death in 1864, his estate contained $45,000 worth of property in Ramsey County. His son, James, of Chicago, continued the family investments here and became probably the largest property owner in Ramsey County during the nineteenth century. See also *James Avenue*, *Lafond Avenue*, *Lafond Lake*.

THOMPSON STREET Originally part of Forbes Avenue, this West End street was renamed in 1887. The new name may have referred to Horace Thompson, an influential banker and civic leader. See also *West End*.

THORN STREET Previously Richmond Avenue, the name of this East Side street was changed in 1872. See also *East Side*.

THREE JUDGES PARK This is a proposed East Side park at Arcade and East Third Streets to honor three famous Minnesota judges who grew up in this community: Edward Devitt (U.S. District Court), and Harry Blackmun and Warren Burger (U.S. Supreme Court).

THURE AVENUE Thure A. Johnson (1886–1972) platted this Highland Park street in 1923. Born in Sweden, Johnson came to St. Paul as a young man, where he worked as a carpenter and contractor. His name was pronounced "Thurey." See also *Highland Park*.

THURSTON STREET By some sleight of hand, Hathaway Street has been transformed into honoring Howard Thurston (1869–1936), a great American magician who delighted audiences around the world with his shows of illusion. Jim Berg, whose Twin Cities Magic and Costume shop was to move to the corner of Thurston and West Seventh Streets in 2006, suggested the name.

TIGER JACK STREET Officially "Mr. and Mrs. Tiger Jack Street," this co-name was applied to Dale Street between St. Anthony and Central Avenues in 2001 to honor Tiger Jack Rosenbloom and his wife, Nurceal. Tiger Jack worked out of a little shack on a corner of Dale Street for half a century, selling candy to kids and firewood to adults, waving to the passing cars, putting a familiar face on the neighborhood, and becoming an emblem of a largely black part of the city that was mostly unknown to whites. After he died in 2001, his shack went on exhibit at the Minnesota Historical Society, along with a cardboard cutout of the man who came to personify St. Paul's black community. See also *Old Rondo Avenue*.

TILDEN PARK Near Lake Como, at the intersection of Arona Street and Almond Avenue, this nearly two-acre city park was previously the site of Tilden School, probably named for Samuel J. Tilden (1814–86), the Democratic candidate for president in 1876. He polled more popular votes than the Republican, Rutherford B. Hayes, but there were disputed electoral votes in several states, and a congressional commission of eight Republicans and seven Democrats, voting on strict party lines, awarded all the disputed states to Hayes, making him the winner by one electoral vote.

TILSEN AVENUE Edward N. Tilsen (1891–1984) is the home-building contractor and developer responsible for over two thousand "Tilsenbilt" homes. He was born in Russia, but immigrated to St. Paul in the 1930s, and named this street near Beaver Lake in 1955. See also *Lincoln Park*.

TIMBERLAKE ROAD This North End street was added to the city in 1950 in the McDonough public housing development. C. Jerome Timberlake (1923–44) was a lieutenant in the U.S.

Army, killed in the Battle of the Bulge. His name was suggested by one of the veterans associations. John J. McDonough (1895–1962), for whom the housing complex was named, was mayor of St. Paul from 1940 to 1948. See also *Biglow Lane, Klainert Street, McDonough Park, North End*.

TONI STONE FIELD Toni Stone, the first black woman professional baseball player, is remembered by this baseball stadium on Griggs Street, just north of Marshall Avenue and adjacent to Dunning Field. Born in 1931 as Marcenia Lyle Alberga and raised in St. Paul, she began her remarkable career as a teenager playing with boys' teams, and by 1949, she was making $300 a month in the Negro League minors. In later life, she recalled that most of the men shunned her and gave her a hard time because she was a woman.

> They didn't mean any harm and in their way they liked me. Just that I wasn't supposed to be there. They'd tell me to go home and fix my husband some biscuits or any damn thing. Just get the hell away from here.

She died in 1996. See also *Lexington Park Baseball Stadium, Midway Stadium*.

TOPIC LANE Previously part of McAfee Street, this street near Lake Phalen was renamed in 1955.

Toni Stone meeting boxer Joe Louis, circa 1949. He has apparently taken her baseball glove and does not seem about to return it. Photograph courtesy of Minnesota Historical Society.

TOPPING STREET This North End street was platted in 1883 in the Foundry Addition because of its proximity to the St. Paul Foundry Company, of which Herbert W. Topping (1850–1915) was general manager. Born in England, Topping came to Minnesota in 1870. He was an alderman and later president of the park board. See also *Foundry Park*.

TORONTO STREET Alexander Vance Brown, the developer of this short West End street in 1856, was a native of Canada. He is listed as a resident here in 1860, but he apparently did not remain long. See also *West End*.

TOTEM ROAD Previously part of Burlington Avenue in the area, the street was renamed in 1948 during a general reorganization of street names within the Highwood area. On this street is Boys Totem Town, a Ramsey County residential treatment facility. This name, which has been in use for at least sixty years, was derived from totem poles carved by the boys, which once graced the grounds. The institution moved to this location about 1913 as a boy's farm and industrial school for habitual truants and incorrigibles. See also *Highwood*.

TOWER STREET Officially known as the McKnight Road Standpipe, the water tower—2.3 million gallon capacity—at the south end of this East Side street was built in 1955, one year before the street was named.

TOWN SQUARE PARK Opened in 1980 with much fanfare, this two-acre indoor park in the downtown skyway system, noted for its glass roof, trees, tropical plants, and fountains, was a popular spot for workday lunches, high school proms, private parties, corporate events, and downtown day-care workers who brought children to the park on winter days. However, park usage began to fall in the late 1980s, then the Mall of America opened in 1992, and many retail shops in Town Square closed. Cafesjian's Carousel, an antique 1914 merry-go-round, was moved to the park from its former home at the state fairgrounds in 1990 in an effort to boost attendance but closed in 1996.

For many years the park's expenses were paid by area business owners through a downtown assessment, but that ended in the mid-1990s, and the full maintenance cost of $400,000 a year was passed on to city taxpayers. Meanwhile, the use of the park continued to decline as the composition of Town Square changed from retail to offices. In 2000, the park was closed as a budget measure, but at least one patron was dismayed: "It's the only spot of real sunlight you can find in the area."

TRANSFER ROAD This new Midway street was named in 1973 by city council resolution. It is near the Minnesota Transfer Yards. See also *Midway, Minnesota Transfer Yards*.

TRI AREA A North End neighborhood of small lots and narrow streets, it is an aggregation of three smaller neighborhoods divided by Oakland Cemetery. The boundaries are roughly between Maryland Avenue and Sycamore Street, between Rice Street and Interstate 35E. See also *North End*.

TRIANGLE The informal name for a neighborhood on the northeast side of Lake Phalen, between East Shore Drive, Larpenteur Avenue, and English Street. The neighborhood is also known as East Phalen. There are the remnants of a few early lakeshore cottages in the neighborhood.

TRILLIUM PARK Presently an undeveloped parcel, this public land is along the west side of Interstate 35E, south of Maryland Avenue. After a good deal of neighborhood persuasion, the city purchased the land as part of the Trout Brook Greenway, where it will serve as an environmental learning center. The name—it is not what you might think—comes from the Glacier Park Trillium Corporation, a holding company that used to sell properties for the Burlington Northern Railroad. The name was plucked off an older plat of the area. See also *Trout Brook*.

TROUT BROOK In early St. Paul, Trout Brook was one of the most prominent geographic features. Originating in McCarron's Lake, and fed by Loeb Lake, it flowed southeast into the

The scenic Trout Brook of early St. Paul flowed through Edmund Rice's estate, which was approximately west of Whitall and Westminster Streets. Photograph courtesy of the Minnesota Historical Society.

downtown area, where it followed the west side of Kittson Street. There the brook met up with Phalen Creek, and both combined to flow the short remaining distance to the Mississippi River. Edmund Rice built a country estate alongside the brook, and Henry Sibley lived downtown on its banks. By 1900 the railroads, requiring a gradual incline, had taken over most of the streambeds in St. Paul, including that of Trout Brook. What had once been a scenic pastoral setting became a noisy industrial corridor.

Today the brook—fed largely by wastewater from the city water utility—is part of the Trout Brook County Trail. The intrepid urban traipser can find it running above ground from Larpenteur to Arlington Avenues. St. Paul is acquiring land beginning at Arlington Avenue and Jackson Street to continue along the old streambed with a Trout Brook Greenway. The greenway would run southeast along a rail bed west of Interstate 35E, connect to the regional Gateway Trail and planned trail on the new Phalen Boulevard, continue south through the broad rail corridor to Fourth Street in Lowertown, and then to the Bruce Vento Nature Sanctuary site and on to the Mississippi River. See also *Bruce Vento Nature Sanctuary, Edmund Avenue, Fourth Street, Gateway Trail, Loeb Lake, Lowertown, Phalen Creek, Sibley Street, Trillium Park.*

TROUT BROOK CIRCLE When we first heard this street name, we had visions of a shady grove, a picnic spot with old Trout Brook babbling in the sunshine. What we actually found was a large concrete manufacturing facility with nary a glimpse of the brook. Platted as part of the Arlington Industrial Park in 1980, this street was named for Trout Brook, now incarcerated in a sewer. See also *Trout Brook.*

TROUT BROOK SEWER Built in the first decades of the twentieth century, this large storm sewer combined both Trout Brook and Phalen's Creek. Downtown, at Fourth Street east of John Street, the sewer opening was so large that during a heavy rainstorm Fourth Street was inundated with water, sweeping a hapless Volkswagen into the sewer. See also *Fourth Street, Trout Brook.*

TRUXTON STREET This East Side street was named in Irvine's Second Addition in 1857 for Thomas Truxton (1755–1822), born on Long Island. An active officer in the American Revolution, Truxton first went to sea at age twelve and became a ship commander when he was twenty. Other streets named in this plat were for Matthew Maury, Stephen Decatur, James Lawrence, and Edward Preble, all notable naval officers of the early nineteenth century. See also *Preble Street*.

TURNER STREET Hamlin Turner was in Minneapolis real estate and probably owned shares in the St. Anthony Park Company; his brother William, the first settler in Price County, Wisconsin, was a sometime logging contractor and proprietor of the hotel in Fifield, Wisconsin. This street was vacated in 1977. See also *St. Anthony Park*.

TUSCARORA AVENUE The Tuscarora Indian tribe prompted this West End street name in 1881. An adjacent street, since renamed Watson, was originally Iroquois. See also *West End*.

TWELFTH STREET This, the twelfth street from the river, was named in 1852.

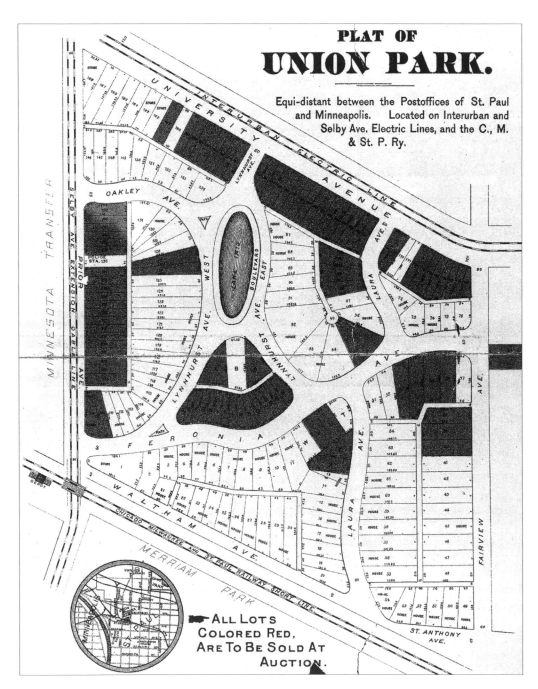

The dark-colored lots in this Union Park plat were to be sold at auction, according to this 1892 advertisement. Notice the police station, the lots with houses and stores on them, the tiny triangular parks, and the railroad depot. Poster from the collection of the Minnesota Historical Society.

U

UNDERWOOD STREET (Fairgrounds) Named by the Minnesota State Agricultural Society, this street honors Joseph Merritt Underwood (1844–1922), who was active in the management of the society and served as its president in 1910. Underwood, born in Palmyra, New York, came to Minnesota shortly after the Civil War, settling on a farm in Lake City.

UNION PARK One of the railroad suburbs on the Short Line, this Midway site had been Union Park, an amusement destination with a large dance pavilion, refreshment stands, a merry-go-round, a bowling alley, and an observation tower. The admission was twenty-five cents for adults, ten cents for children. Railroad service on the Short Line to the amusement park began November 15, 1880, with a round-trip fare of fifteen cents to either St. Paul or Minneapolis.

In 1884, the park was subdivided into building lots, continuing to use the name Union Park. The boundaries were between University and St. Anthony Avenues, between Prior and Fairview Avenues. The railroad depot, shared with Merriam Park, was at Prior and St. Anthony Avenues; the police station building remains at 502 North Prior Avenue. The winding streets and exotic street names were considered part of the charm. The intrepid urban traipser, wishing a muse on the past, might like to sit by Lake Iris in Union Park and listen for the children's laughter on the merry-go-round.

A flyer issued in September 1892 for the purpose of selling lots at auction said:

> Union Park is noted for its natural beauty and great attractiveness, possessing unusual advantages in the midway interurban district. All tourists and others that have visited it regard this Paradise of Natural Beauty as the most delightful place for a family home, second to none, between the cities.... Union Park is admired for its romantic and picturesque scenery, together with its artistic and beautiful winding avenues and streets, and fine shade trees. The lake, with fountain, is under the control of the St. Paul park system.... Over sixty beautiful houses of different designs, several having cost from $10,000 to $15,000, with their beautiful lawns, adorn Union Park.... Many of the business lots front on University and Prior avenues, and are suitable for every class of business. University avenue is the great coming business street between the twin cities....

See also *Iris Park*, *Lake Iris*, *Merriam Park*, *Scheffer Avenue*, *Short Line Road*; see also "St. Paul's Railroad Suburbs."

UNIVERSITY AVENUE Because this street initially ran between the University of Minnesota and Hamline University, it was given its name in 1874. The establishment of the Minnesota Transfer Yards, however, blocked the street, and it was necessary to shift the eastern end of the avenue one-half mile south. University Avenue appropriated the name of what had been Melrose Avenue, and the original University Avenue became part of Minnehaha Avenue.

In 1889, University Avenue was first paved with tree trunks about six to eight inches in diameter, cut to half-foot lengths, and set in the street on a cement base, the space between the blocks being filled with asphalt and cement grout. In the first half of the twentieth century, University Avenue was the busiest street in the city.

This street marks a one-half section line on the land survey. See also *Dickerman Park, Frogtown, Kittsondale Sewer, Minnesota Transfer Yards, Pierce Butler Route, Roseville, Ryan Park, Union Park*; see also "The Bedraggled Harlot."

UNIVERSITY GROVE Tucked in a quiet, wooded corner next to the University of Minnesota St. Paul campus, this neighborhood, northeast of Fulham Street and Hoyt Avenue—just outside the northern boundary of St. Paul, in Falcon Heights—is a showcase of midwestern residential architecture. The 103 single-family homes built by professors and administrators over a sixty-year period on land leased from the university had to be designed by an architect within a limited price range. No two houses are the same, and every one was specifically designed for its site; the cap on costs made it impossible for any new arrival to build a house appreciably larger or more luxurious than its neighbors.

Setting aside land in the 1920s for faculty and staff housing was the brainchild of University of Minnesota Vice President (and onetime Grove resident) William Middlebrook. He reasoned the availability of such housing would be a great asset in the recruitment and retention of topflight teachers and administrators. When landscape architects planned the area, originally four blocks long and only one-and-a-half blocks wide, they emphasized the natural land contours, tree clusters, and vistas. By the 1960s the old Grove neared capacity, and the university added more lots to the east, making the Grove eight blocks long.

UPLAND AVENUE Height is the single most popular element in street names, hence the appeal of this common name applied to this Highwood area in 1888. See also *Highwood*.

UPPER AFTON ROAD Constructed before the Civil War, this county road from St. Paul ran along the top of the bluffs toward Afton on the St. Croix River. *Upper Afton Terrace* takes its name from the same source. See also *Lower Afton Road*.

UPPER LAKE This is one of the two lakes within Crosby Regional Park. See also *Crosby Lake, Lakes/Ponds*.

UPPER LANDING In the earliest days of the city, there was a lower (downriver) steamboat landing at the foot of Jackson Street and an upper (upriver) steamboat landing at the foot of Chestnut Street where Rice's Brook had eroded through the steep river bluffs. See also *Chestnut Street, Hidden Falls, Lowertown, Rice's Brook*.

The Upper Levee in 1959, near the end of its existence. Shepard Road is on the right, and downtown is in the distance. Photograph courtesy of the Minnesota Historical Society.

UPPER LANDING (neighborhood) A new "urban village" on the site of the Upper Levee (east of the High Bridge) provides $160 million dollars worth of seven hundred housing units divided into thirteen low-rise buildings. The four-acre *Upper Landing Park* on the floodplain features four mounds with stones marking water levels from past floods. The Upper Landing resident can, by glancing out their window at the park and observing the rising water level on the mounds, judge whether an evacuation would be expeditious. See *Chestnut Street, Upper Levee.*

UPPER LEVEE The Upper Levee was a community, largely Italian, on the Mississippi River floodplain between Wilkin and Elm Streets, below the High Bridge. A 1904 newspaper article described it as "a village of southern Italy transported as if by magic from the wild mountains of Abruzzo and Molise and placed on the banks of the Father of Water." The area was first settled (or squatted) in the 1870s, and in 1965 the last resident left the neighborhood, which was often deluged by spring floods. At its peak, the area had close to five hundred residents, one hundred homes, two grocery stores, a community center, and two saloons. One connection with the rest of the city was a steep stairway up to the High Bridge; the automobile access was on Chestnut Street. Many of the residents have warm memories of growing up in this tight-knit community with its large gardens and easy river access.

Upon the demise of the community, the site became the home of a large scrap metal and recycling plant, which in turn has been replaced by a new "urban village" with the name Upper Landing. Much has been written about this community, but one of the best articles, based on firsthand accounts, is in *A Knack for Knowing Things*, by Don Boxmeyer. See also *Badlands*, *Barton-Omaha Colony*, *Bohemian Flats*, *Connemara Patch*, *West Side Flats*.

UPPER ST. DENNIS ROAD Den E. Lane (1881–1952) was one of the most active St. Paul real-estate men in the 1920s and 1930s, and a foremost developer in Highland Park and the Lake Phalen area. Born in Ireland, Lane moved to St. Paul as a child and began his real-estate ventures when yet a student at St. Thomas College. Known as "The Own Your Home Man," Lane estimated that in the 1920s he had designed, laid out, and named 50 percent of the St. Paul streets in the preceding decade. By 1925, he claimed to have handled more than ten thousand property transactions. This Highland Park street, platted in 1945, was named for his patron saint, Dennis. St. Dennis Court takes its name from the same source. See also *Elsie Lane*, *Lane Park*, *Lower St. Dennis Road*.

UPPER SWEDE HOLLOW A neighborhood rich with history, it includes the Dayton's Bluff Historic District and older housing stock roughly southeast of Swede Hollow Park.

UPPERTOWN The area around the downstream landing at the foot of Jackson Street took the name Lowertown, and the area around the upstream landing at the foot of Chestnut Street took the name Uppertown. Too much can be made of these informal names, but generally—depending on the time period—the term was sometimes applied to the area west of Wabasha Street as far west as Randolph Avenue. Today there exists the Uppertown Preservation League, whose West End boundaries are slightly different. See also *Lowertown*, *West End*.

URBAN PLACE Previously Lizzie Street, the name of this East Side street was changed in 1905. The word *urban* implies a city or town; this street occurs in the Suburban Hills addition. One of St. Paul's oldest elm trees, more than 102 years old, was at 155 Urban Place. Denoted with an historic marker, the tree died from Dutch elm disease and had to be removed in 1974.

UTICA AVENUE Originally Wabasso Avenue, the name of this East Side street was changed in 1940. See also *East Side*.

VALENTINE AVENUE Platted as Pierce Street in 1885, this St. Anthony Park street was renamed in 1940 to avoid duplication. See also *St. Anthony Park*.

VALLEY A wooded ravine above Lexington Parkway in the southeast corner of Highland Park where generations of local teenagers have gathered to escape parental guidance and law enforcement authority. See also *Devil's Ditch, Grotto*.

VALLEY STREET This street was named in 1856 in Dewey, Bass and Rohrers Addition because it used to come down the hill from Jackson Street to intersect University Avenue at Broadway. The name reflects the steep terrain originally in this part of the city, resulting in the nickname Badlands. See also *Badlands*.

VALLEY VIEW PLACE The view down into the Mississippi River valley prompted this Highwood street name in 1965. See also *Highwood*.

VALLEYSIDE DRIVE This street near Battle Creek was named in 1970 because, the proprietor said, "It just sounded nice."

VAN BUREN AVENUE Martin Van Buren (1782–1862) was the eighth president of the United States. This Midway-Frogtown street took his name in 1871. Within the block between Blair and Van Buren Avenues, between Wheeler and Aldine Streets, there is a diagonal alley following the course of the early territorial road running from St. Paul to St. Anthony (now southeast Minneapolis). This short stretch of alley is one of the few remnants of the first road between the two cities. This aberrantly angled alley offers the intrepid urban traipser a short walk in the footsteps of the pioneers—before everything became square. See also *Lafond Lake, Mt. Eudes, Territorial Road*.

VAN DYKE STREET James W. Van Dyke was the developer of this East Side property in 1887. Unmarried at the time, a carpenter by profession, he was listed as a resident of the city only from 1887 to 1889. See also *East Side*.

VAN SLYKE AVENUE Recalled as a man who made two blades of grass grow where there was but one, William A. Van Slyke (1833–1910) was called the founder of our present park system because of his efforts on the city council as chairman of the committee on parks. Born in New York State, he moved to St. Paul in 1854 as a store clerk; by 1857 the business was his. Active in many public affairs, he was "the man above all other men who has transformed our dirty, somber, dark, forbidding parks into gems of loveliness." Upon his death, the park board moved a boulder, the only remaining relic of Baptist Hill, from Smith (Mears) Park to

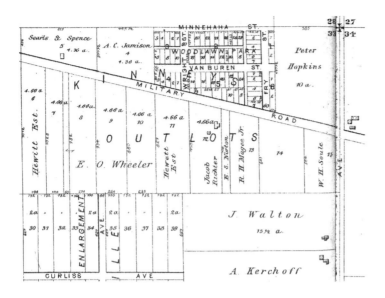

The course of the old military road as it was in 1886. Today, a short portion of the road remains as a diagonal alley off Van Buren Avenue. From *Atlas of the Environs of St. Paul*, 1886.

Van Slyke's grave in Oakland Cemetery. His name was selected for this street because of its proximity to Como Park. See also *Baptist Hill*, *Mears Park*, *Van Slyke Triangle*.

VAN SLYKE TRIANGLE This small, one-acre park at Van Slyke Avenue and Churchill Street was dedicated to the public in 1885 in the Warrendale plat. See also *Van Slyke Avenue*, *Warrendale*.

VANCE STREET Alexander Vance Brown was a Canadian real-estate speculator during the 1850s in the West End. He was also one of the more prophetic voices in the city, warning against the building of homes in Lowertown because of future railroad incursions. He was right. See also *Lowertown*.

VANDALIA STREET This was a popular and common name when this Midway street was platted in 1881. See also *Midway*.

VENTO, BRUCE See *Bruce Vento*.

VENTO TRAIL See *Bruce Vento Regional Trail*.

VERNON STREET Originally Witherspoon Avenue, the name was changed in 1890. George H. Vernon, an attorney, developed some property near St. Clair and Snelling Avenues; perhaps his name was the source.

VICTORIA CROSSING The name of this shopping complex at the corner of Grand Avenue and Victoria Street seems to have been extended to the adjacent neighborhood.

VICTORIA PARK This new sixty-five-acre West End development southwest of Otto Avenue and Victoria Street occupies what was once a gasoline tank farm and before that a stone quarry. After much controversy about the environment, the site is being converted into 850 new housing units, making it one of the larger housing developments in St. Paul's history. See also *West End*.

VICTORIA STREET Victoria was queen of England when this street was named in 1871 by a former British subject, John Wann, who built his house on the northwest corner of Victoria Street and Summit Avenue.

On the northwest corner of Victoria Street and Orchard Avenue, where the Orchard Recreation Center is today, there was a German Lutheran Cemetery in the nineteenth century. The poor condition of the cemetery is lamented, and its deplorable condition illustrated in an article in the *St. Paul Pioneer Press*, August 9, 1903. Victoria Street marks a one-half section line on the land survey. See also *Cemeteries, Chatsworth Street, Mt. Eudes*.

VICTORY PARK Never technically a city park, this was the downtown block between Wabasha and Cedar Streets, between Fourth and Fifth Streets. In 1933, the old Ramsey County courthouse and St. Paul city hall were demolished, and the block was not rebuilt until the 1950s. The name comes from the Allied victory in World War II; today the Victory Parking Ramp occupies part of the block.

VIEW STREET This West End street was named in Stinson, Brown and Ramsey's Addition in 1854 apparently for the pleasant associations of the word, because there does not seem to be any striking view on the street. View Street is, according to the U.S. Census Bureau, the sixteenth most popular street name in the United States, with 5,202 other occurrences of the name.

VILLAGE LANE (private) In a promotional article in the *St. Paul Pioneer Press* of October 8, 1939, this unusual, million-dollar apartment complex, named "Highland Village," was headlined "As New As Tomorrow." The article continued:

Let's live in Highland Village ... the Apartment City of tomorrow that is available to you today. Let's live out under God's blue sky and sunshine ... let's live where we can grow. [In 1939, this area was on the outskirts of the city.] Apartments were "unfur-

The northwest corner of Grand Avenue and Victoria Street circa 1930. Today the building remains as part of Victoria Crossing. Photograph by Charles P. Gibson; courtesy of the Minnesota Historical Society.

nished, but completely equipped with Venetian blinds, gas range, floor cabinets, wall cabinets, electric refrigerator, bathroom accessories and an abundance of electrical fixtures and outlets. . . . Another important feature is the fact that the buildings are well insulated with brick walls, clay tile roofs and weather stripping for comfort all year around."

Besides the apartment buildings, there were also six storefronts. The building that abutted the intersection of Ford Parkway and Cleveland Avenue housing the stores was torn down in 1960 to make way for a Powers department store. This is the first use of the name Highland Village; the name has since been expanded to include much of the area around Cleveland Avenue and Ford Parkway. See also *Ford Parkway, Highland Park*.

VILLARD AVENUE Henry Villard (1835–1900) was a journalist, railway promoter, and financier when this Highland Park street was platted in the Hiawatha Park Addition in 1890. Born in Germany, he came to the United States at age eighteen, where he studied law and edited a newspaper in Illinois. For the following fifteen years, he worked as a journalist until one of his investigations led him into a career as railroad promoter. He became president of the Northern Pacific Railroad in 1881 and completed the line to the West Coast in 1883, making it a transcontinental railroad, a feat for which he is honored by this street name. *Villard Court* takes its name from the same source. See also *Hiawatha Park*.

VIRGINIA STREET State names are always popular; this one in the Summit-University area was applied in 1854 in Dayton and Irvine's Addition. Virginia Street between Summit and Western Avenues is one of the few remaining brick-paved streets in the city. See also *Kenwood Parkway, Maiden Lane, Summit-University*.

VISTA AVENUE This West End street name was chosen in 1881 to give, no doubt, the suggestion of a striking view. See also *West End*.

VIVIAN LANE Vivian was the daughter of Arthur and Helen Werthauser, two of the developers of this 1983 Oakville Heights Addition in *Highwood*.

VON STEUBEN PARK Once a tiny West Side park at Cesar Chavez and Isabel Streets, the Public Works Department gave the property to the Parks Department in 1931. Friedrich Von Steuben (1730–94) was a German officer who served the cause of U.S. independence by molding the revolutionary army into a disciplined fighting force so they could more efficiently kill the bad guys. See also *West Side*.

WABASH AVENUE The river that forms the border between Illinois and Indiana most likely prompted this Midway street name in 1881. Today, Wabash Avenue between LaSalle Street and Vandalia Street is closed to the public; it has become a private street. Somehow that does not seem right.

WABASHA FREEDOM BRIDGE This bridge, connecting Wabasha Street across the Mississippi River, was dedicated as the Wabasha Freedom Bridge on September 11, 2002, as a memorial to those who died in the attack on the World Trade Center in New York City. More than seventy-five American flags were placed permanently on the bridge as a constant reminder of the freedoms and liberties we Americans (and many others in the world) enjoy. See also *Bridges, Peace Bridge*.

WABASHA STREET One of the original fifteen street names of the city, named in the 1849 plat, St. Paul Proper, the name honored three hereditary Dakota chiefs. The first Wabasha ruled his area under the French and, after 1759, the British. His son, Wabasha the second, succeeded about the time of the American Revolution, during which he went East to fight on the side of the British. His village stood near the town of Rolling Stone in Winona County. The third Wabasha succeeded his father about 1837, negotiated treaties with the whites, fought in the Dakota Conflict, and died on an Indian reservation in Nebraska in 1876. All three chiefs were highly respected men.

On the west side of South Wabasha, south of Plato Boulevard, there is a retaining wall constructed in 2004–5, replacing an earlier wall built in the 1930s. This piece of public art, containing the word for *home* in twelve languages (the nationalities of those living on the West Side), serves as a gateway to the West Side. See also *District del Sol, West Side*.

WACOUTA COMMONS Between Sibley and Wacouta Streets, between Eighth and Ninth Streets, this new downtown park features a playground, with other amenities due to be added. A block-long gravel "dog walk" is adorned with long-suffering Japanese lilac trees that patiently endure canine calls of nature.

WACOUTA STREET Named in 1849, this was one of the first street names of the city. Wacouta, an Indian chief and the son of Red Wing, became chief just as the whites were coming into the state in numbers, and he was forced into signing unwise land treaties and joining in the Dakota Conflict. Like Wabasha, he died on the Santee Indian reservation in Nebraska.

At the foot of Wacouta Street was the Union Depot. A union depot was a single train station that served the passengers of all the railroad companies. The alternative—common in

The first Union Depot on Wacouta Street in the 1880s. Photograph by Joel Emmons Whitney; courtesy of the Minnesota Historical Society.

the early days of railroading—was every railroad having its own depot, in which case the passenger wishing to change from one railroad company to another in the course of his journey had to carry his luggage from one train station to another, possibly several blocks away. While the union depot was a convenience for passengers, most railroad companies continued to maintain their own separate freight depots.

The first Union Depot in St. Paul opened in 1881. By 1895, there were eight railroad companies using the depot. In that year, 109,625 passenger cars came into the depot, 110,295 passenger cars left, and 640,029 pieces of baggage were handled. Every day, an average of 78.5 tons of mail passed through the depot. The daily average number of tickets sold was 759. It is hard to imagine today the influence of the railroads in the nineteenth century: almost everything and everybody entered and left the city via the railroad.

WADENA AVENUE Previously Arlington Avenue, the name of this East Side street was changed in 1940 to avoid duplication. To descend Wadena was to travel back a century. This unpaved street dropped into Swede Hollow to a dead end surrounded by three or four old and somewhat ramshackle houses with colorful inhabitants. Today the houses have been demolished, and most of the street bulldozed to make way for Phalen Boulevard. See also *Phalen Boulevard*.

WAGENER STREET John and Susan Wagener platted this East Side street in 1886. He came to St. Paul in 1873, where he had a coal, wood, and brick store in this area. Active in public affairs, he served as Ramsey County commissioner, and their son of the same name was several times sheriff of Ramsey County. A native of Luxembourg, John died in 1888. Susan, a native of Alsace-Lorraine, died in 1895. This street was vacated in 1998. See also *Culvert Street*.

WAKAN OR WAUKON ISLAND See *Harriet Island Park.*

WAKEFIELD AVENUE Originally Birch Street, the name of this East Side street was changed in 1892 to honor William Wakefield (1825–1906) and his wife, Harriet. Born in Rhode Island, he moved to St. Paul in 1856, where he worked in the dry goods business. In 1860, he purchased four acres on Dayton's Bluff for about $300; today this property lies between Wakefield and Wilson Avenues, between Forest and Cypress Streets. On his land he built a house and planted trees, making it, as a contemporary said, "a very lovely and desirable home" and "one of the beautiful residences of the city." The house remains at 963 Wakefield Avenue, but the estate, with the intriguing Rhode Island name, "What Cheer Lawn," has long since been subdivided into building lots. The Wakefield house is askew to the present street because it had been aligned with a previous road.

WALES STREET Originally Warren Street, the name of this East Side street was changed in 1940.

WALL STREET Designated as Rosabel Street in 1849, one of the first and most historic downtown streets, the name was changed in 1970 at the request of the North Central Life Insurance Company. At the time, the company had purchased the Wall Street Mutual Fund, and they wished to have a Wall Street address. This street has remnants of St. Paul's 1890s warehouse district, which was located conveniently close to the railroad freight depots. See also *Hunting Valley Road.*

WALNUT STEPS This obscure bluff shortcut will intrigue the intrepid urban traipser. A series of 157 steps follows the course of Walnut Street up to Summit Avenue alongside the James J. Hill house. In the late nineteenth century the city agreed to vacate this part of Walnut Street to James J. Hill; in return Hill promised to construct a suitable stairway for the public, ten feet wide, "without any expense to the city." This clause has been the source of considerable discussion between the city and the adjacent property owners over the years. See also *Stairways.*

WALNUT STREET It is said a grove of walnut trees standing where United Hospital is today prompted this name in Rice and Irvine's Addition in 1849.

WALSH PARK This small "ghost park," between Edgcumbe Road and Lexington Parkway, just south of the cul-de-sac on Edgcumbe Place, was dedicated to the public in 1884 by Vincent D. Walsh as part of the West End Addition—long before there was any development in this area. It appears on the current city map as Old Walsh Park. At one time, access to the park was by means of a thirty-foot bridle path descending the hill from Edgcumbe Road, but today public access to this rugged hillside is by way of an unmarked alley. The intrepid urban traipser can follow the uphill course of Deer Park street (on the west side of Lexington Parkway, across from Albion Avenue) and continue west across the grass to the fence gate. See also *Dawson Park, Deer Park, Ghost Parks, Walsh Street, West End.*

WALSH STREET Vincent D. Walsh was one of the developers of this East Side street in the Arlington Hills Addition in 1872. Living in New Orleans, Louisiana, he made substantial investments in St. Paul real estate, and his name appears on many plats and deeds. At his death in 1899, his estate held $135,670 worth of property in Ramsey County. See also *East Side, Walsh Park.*

WANDA STREET Previously Highland Street, the name of this North End street was changed in 1940 to avoid duplication.

WARBLER LANE This street near Battle Creek was so named, in 1970, because, as the developer put it, "the name just sounded nice."

WARNER ROAD The city council named this riverfront road in 1937 for Richmond Perez Warner (1871–1936), chairman of the St. Paul Port Authority and the Upper Mississippi and St. Croix River Improvement Commission. Born in St. Paul, he was educated at home and abroad. Beginning as a stock clerk with a shoe company, he worked his way up to become vice president of Griggs, Cooper, and Company. Warner was deeply committed to the improvement of the upper Mississippi River as a major transportation route, with the nine-foot channel one of his goals. Upon his death, the city hall flag was flown at half-mast for fifteen days. Anne Warner French, a well-known author around the turn of the century, was Warner's sister.

WARREN STREET The city named this street near Battle Creek in 1959 most likely for Henry E. (Ned) Warren (1893–1965), city councilman and public safety commissioner. In 1934 and 1935 he was instrumental in ridding the city of gangsters. Born in Canada, he moved to St. Paul as a boy, where he graduated from Central High School. He entered the automobile sales business in 1918 and continued in that occupation the rest of his life, with the exception of his years on the city council.

WARRENDALE Once promoted as "a beautiful suburban village growing up within ten minutes ride of St. Paul," Warrendale is today well within the city limits, between Lexington Parkway and Chatsworth Street, between Jessamine Avenue, West Como Boulevard, and Como Park. An article in the *Northwest Magazine*, March 1885, has a long, detailed description of this new railroad community.

The fifty-two-and-one-half acres for this suburban development had been the Aldrich farm, which contained a hotel on Lake Como dating from the early days of the city. The developers were Cary I. Warren of Louisville, Kentucky, and George W. Cross and F. D. Hager, both of St. Paul. The development was arranged by Horace W. S. Cleveland and Kilvington of Minneapolis, "who will make use of all the natural advantages of the site to create the framework, in streets, avenues, parks, boulevards, and squares of as beautiful a suburb as can be planned." Cary Warren's house, built in 1886, remains at 1269 North Como Boulevard. See also *Leroy Triangle, Sunshine Place, Van Slyke Triangle;* see also "St. Paul's Railroad Suburbs."

WARWICK STREET William and Mary Brimhall platted this Macalester-Groveland street in 1886. Warwick is a county and city in England; the other street names in this vicinity were Berkeley (now Palace), Rothley (Jefferson), and Wilford (Stanford). British names were popular at this time.

ST. PAUL'S RAILROAD SUBURBS
Nineteenth-Century Urban Sprawl

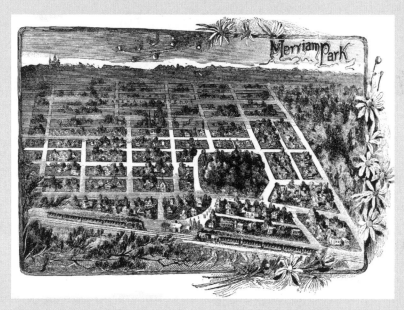

Merriam Park is one of the railroad suburbs completely integrated into the city today. This view was printed in *Northwest Magazine* in April 1886 to help sell the lots.

Urban sprawl created St. Paul. Thousands of settlers migrated west to escape the crowded cities and lack of opportunity in the East. Once settled in downtown St. Paul, the residents continued to sprawl out: east of downtown into the original Lowertown. The first "suburb" in name was Suburban Hills on the East Side, platted in 1856.

Within thirty years of St. Paul's founding, the expansion of the railroad in the 1880s added a completely new dimension to the word *suburb*. No longer was the commuting distance from downtown to a residential district on the outskirts of a city limited to what a person might walk or the distance a horse-drawn wagon might travel. For the first time in history, a commute of three or four miles—made in a half hour or less—was possible from downtown to a country residence. Developers were quick to realize the possibilities, and within a decade, a dozen railroad suburbs were built along the tracks, widely separated from the central city.

But just as these railroad suburbs were being established miles away from the central city, St. Paul was booming with hundreds of new residents every month. Within only a few years, by 1887, all these suburban railroad villages had been annexed by the rapidly expanding city. Today some of these early suburbs remain as residential neighborhoods, retaining their original identity: St. Anthony Park, Merriam Park, Macalester Park, Desnoyer Park, and Hazel Park. Others have lost their unique identity over the years: Burlington Heights, Warrendale, and Union Park are names no longer recognized.

Would you be surprised to know the reasons for living in one of the railroad suburbs of the 1880s are remarkably similar to those given in favor of living in today's automobile suburbs?

Presently one of the forces fueling urban sprawl is the fact the price of a lot is reduced in direct proportion to the distance of the commute. This was also true in the 1880s. An article on Merriam Park in the *Northwest Magazine* of April 1886 made the argument of price:

> Sensible people soon discovered the superior advantages of a swift ride of twelve minutes to Merriam Park, in a warm [railroad] car with a comfortable seat, and also the opportunity to purchase large lots, 50 × 150, at a cost of about one-fifth of city prices. A good lot, with a comfortable house upon it, can be had at Merriam Park for about the cost of a bare lot in St. Paul or Minneapolis.

A common argument in favor of moving out of the city, then and now, was the "restfulness" of the country. Getting away from the noise and bustle and traffic of the urban areas and reposing in the bucolic countryside present an idyllic incentive for suburbia. Another cogent reason often advanced for moving out to the suburbs is the larger lot size available. Today three- to five-acre lots are driving urban sprawl, but our ancestors required a little less space. One hundred twenty-five years ago, they observed:

> There are always a large number of people whose ideal of comfortable living is the village, with its shaded streets, its gardens, its sociable inhabitants, its freedom from dust and smoke, its vistas of green landscapes stretching off to distant horizon lines and its general air of neatness and repose. These sensible people want more elbow room than the narrow building lots of the city afford—room for lawn and flower beds, for a barn where they can keep a horse for driving and, perhaps, a few chickens; space and margin enough, in short, around their houses to enable them to feel a pleasant sense of ownership in the soil.

Then, as now, people moved to the country to escape a certain class of "city people." One of the railroad suburbs of the 1880s, Merriam Park, noted in promotional literature that its "residents are refined, intelligent people, owning their homes and having well established business relations in one or the other of the neighboring cities." Union Park at University and Prior Avenues made the same claim: "Society of a select character is an important feature in securing a permanent place of residence for your family."

The suburban developers wanted homeowners, not land speculators or renters, and most of the railroad suburbs specified that a house of a minimum value must be built on the newly purchased lot within a year or so. In Merriam Park and Burlington Heights, the value of the house was to be at least $1,500; in Warrendale by Lake Como, the necessary cost was $2,000. As one writer quite simply put it, "Nice houses mean nice people."

These railroad suburbs also incorporated amenities lacking in the central city: winding streets following the contours of the terrain were common, parks and parkways were often included, and consideration was paid to the relationship between residents, houses, and the land.

The railroad suburbs of St. Paul—on the Short Line Railroad—were Ridgewood Park with a train depot at Victoria Street, Macalester Park with a train depot at Marshall Avenue,

Hamline Village with a train depot at Holton Avenue, Merriam Park and Union Park with a train depot at Prior Avenue, and Desnoyer Park with a train depot at Pelham Boulevard. St. Anthony Park had two depots: one on the St. Paul, Minneapolis & Manitoba Railway and one on the Northern Pacific Railroad. Hazel Park was laid out in 1886 with a train station at Hazel Place along the tracks of the Chicago, St. Paul and Omaha Railroad. Burlington Heights was a commuter suburb in the northeast part of the city with two stations—Highwood and Oakland—along the tracks of the Chicago, Burlington and Northern Railroad.

The reasons driving urban sprawl have remained constant for the past 125 years. Will we someday have a light-rail transit system creating in the farm fields of today the "railroad suburbs" of the twenty-first century?

WASECA STREET Originally Sophia Street, the name of this West Side street was changed in 1883. *Waseca* is a Dakota word meaning "fertile land." There are also a county and city by that name.

WASHINGTON STREET This downtown street was named in 1849 in Rice and Irvine's Addition for George Washington, first president of the United States. Forty years later, Washington Street was infamous as the location of Nina Clifford's brothel.

WATER STREET Using a common name in river towns, this 1858 West Side street is best known for its natural caves, used over the years for storing beer, aging cheese, and growing mushrooms.

The intrepid urban traipser will want to wander Water Street, a country lane following the Mississippi River, from Harriet Island Park west to Lillydale. Along the way, the traipser will happen upon Pickerel Lake, one of the unknown gems of the West Side. See also *Joy Avenue*.

WATERLOO STREET Recalling the defeat of Napoleon, this West Side name was given in 1885.

WATERMELON HILL A name given to the location of the Catholic Infants Home at 341 Dale Street (corner of Rondo Avenue), where unwed Catholic girls were sent to wait out their pregnancies and deliver their babies—who were then given up for adoption. The name comes from the observation that the young pregnant mothers looked like they carried a watermelon under their dress. See also *Mt. Eudes*.

WATSON AVENUE John J. (1850–1925) and Joanna B. Watson platted this West End street in 1886. A native of Ulster County, New York, he left school at age eleven, subsequently learned the watchmaker and jeweler trade, and later worked as a clerk. In 1869 he moved to Chicago, where he worked for a fire insurance company, but the Chicago fire of 1871 bankrupted the company, and in 1875 he came to St. Paul. Four years later he began making real-estate investments, including the development of Lexington Park. Watson is said to have originated the idea of selling houses on the installment plan, and he is remembered as a man of enterprise and boldness. See also *Lexington Park*.

WAUKON AVENUE Applied in 1917 in Beaver Lake Heights, this is a Chippewa word meaning "spirit." See also *Harriet Island Park, Carver's Cave*.

The intrepid urban traipser will be immersed in the hydrology exhibit between Howard Street and Waukon Avenue, between Stillwater Avenue and East Seventh Street. Between the two alleys is a swampy ditch, the remainder of Ames Creek, which once carried water from Beaver Lake southwest to eventually join up with Phalen Creek by way of Ames Lake. The first grading profile of Stillwater Avenue confirms the four-foot-deep natural channel through which the water flowed from Beaver Lake into this creek. See also *Ames Creek, Ames Lake, Beaver Lake, Phalen Creek, Stillwater Avenue.*

WAVERLY PLACE William H. Jarvis of St. Paul named this East Side street in 1851, probably for the village of Waverly in his native New York State. In the 1880s, this street off Lafayette Road was in an area of fine homes and mansions. It was vacated in 1970, and today the Minnesota Department of Natural Resources building occupies the space. See also *Lowertown.*

WAY ROUND ABOUT See *Round About Way.*

WAYZATA PARK Created out of a vacated portion of Wayzata Street on the east side of Albemarle Street, this North Side city park next to the Lewis Park multistory apartments provides a path for residents to travel to and from Rice Street. Jerry Gammel, a local resident master gardener, was the guiding force behind this peaceful passageway.

WAYZATA STREET Both Wayzata and Litchfield, Minnesota, were stops along the St. Paul and Pacific Railroad in 1872 when this street was named. See also *Atwater Street, Litchfield Street.*

This wishing well with mosaic inlays representing the seasons inspires those walking the path through Wayzata Park to make a wish. Photograph by Kathleen M. Vadnais.

WEBER'S POND In the 1884 Hopkins atlas, this appears to be a shallow pool of water; today it would be between Grotto and St. Albans Streets, between Front and Hatch Avenues. Henry Weber was a gardener living on the east side of Grotto Street north of Front Avenue in 1904. In his recollections of the Junior Pioneers, "A Collection of One-Page Articles on the History of St. Paul," Max Winkel mentions the pond. See also *Lakes/Ponds*.

WEBSTER PARK This one-and-one-quarter-acre West End park—which dated from the 1880s—at the intersection of Webster Street and Pleasant Avenue was sold in 1926 for $1,000.

WEBSTER STREET Originally Second Street in 1856, the name of this West End street was changed in 1872. It most likely commemorated Daniel Webster (1782–1852), American statesman and orator.

WEIDE STREET Charles A. B. Weide (1833–92) was a real-estate dealer when this street was named in the Arlington Hills Addition in 1872. Born in Germany, Weide came to the United States with his parents, moving to St. Paul in 1853, where he worked in a store on Third Street. He later sold real estate, in which he did well, and declared himself "the happiest man in the state."

WELD'S BLUFF According to local historian Steve Trimble, what is today known as Dayton's Bluff was previously called Weld's Bluff, after Eben Weld, one of its first white residents. Weld, born in New Hampshire in 1815, came to Minnesota in the early 1840s and traded with American Indians. In 1848, he purchased Charles Mousseau's claim on the bluff; two years later he sold his farm and left for the California gold fields, along with Edward Phalen and others. After Lyman Dayton bought much of the land on the bluff, it came to be known as Dayton's Bluff. See also *Dayton's Bluff, Phalen Creek*.

WELLESLEY AVENUE Platted as Sloan and Lansing Streets, the name was changed in 1913. This was done, no doubt, at the wish of the developer of the Macalester Villas Addition, who wanted his street names identified with the desirable residential enclave of Macalester Park. Before it was improved and graded, the area between Fairview and Snelling Avenues, between St. Clair and Randolph Avenues, was low and marshy, the genesis of a stream running northwest to Finn's Glen. See also *Finn's Glen, Macalester Park*.

WELLS STREET Like several streets in this addition, the origin of this name is uncertain. Designated in 1872 in the Arlington Hills Addition, it could refer to George Wells, a bus driver for Cook's St. Paul Omnibus Company. Built into a hillside between Greenbrier and Walsh Streets, Wells was once divided into a lower, eastbound lane and an upper, westbound lane. With one lane twenty-four feet above the other, it was no place for a U-turn. Unfortunately this street, one of the most unique in the city, has been dramatically changed as part of the Phalen Boulevard project. Sometimes it seems like the city administration, having no new lands to conquer, masticates the old city neighborhoods, spitting out new beige townhouses, wide boring streets, and utterly predictable blandness. In the process, they destroy the colorful and funky streetscapes that make the city singular and intriguing. See also *Arlington Heights, Phalen Boulevard, Wadena Avenue*.

The east lane of Wells Street was much higher than the west lane, making a U-turn precipitous indeed on this unique drive of the past. Photograph courtesy of the Minnesota Historical Society.

WEST END In delineating locations of the streets in this book, we have defined the West End as the area below the bluff and west of downtown along the length of West Seventh Street, including the area between Interstate 35E and the Mississippi River. See also *Barton-Omaha Colony, Bohemian Flats, Kipp's Glen, Ran/View, Uppertown, Victoria Park.*

WEST GATE DRIVE Named in the West Gate Addition, this Midway street was platted by the St. Paul Port Authority in 1989.

WEST SEVENTH STREET This neighborhood stretches along West Seventh Street, between downtown and the Interstate 35E bridge across the Mississippi River, between the river on the south and Interstate 35E on the north. See also *Uppertown.*

WEST SIDE This neighborhood is directly across the river from downtown St. Paul, the area on the south side of the river. Yes, the West Side is really south of downtown, but the Mississippi River runs north and south; therefore (when ascending the river) the bank on the right is considered the east side of the river, and the bank on the left is considered the west side of the river.

In 1858, this area was incorporated as the city of West St. Paul in Dakota County; in 1874, it was annexed by the City of St. Paul and became part of Ramsey County. Today, a new city of West St. Paul lies just south of the West Side.

This area of the city is unique in its hilly topography, its diverse ethnic mix, and its public art. See also *Cherokee Heights, District del Sol, Riverview, West Side Flats.*

WEST SIDE FLATS This now-vanished neighborhood on the West Side was below the bluff, east of Robert Street to the airport. Today the Riverview Industrial Park and the Lafayette freeway occupy most of the area.

The neighborhood was a large residential district, with hundreds of homes, shops, bars, public schools, churches, grocery stores, and Neighborhood House, a community center. It was ethnically diverse, with Jewish, Mexican, Irish, Russians, and Lebanese among the many nationalities represented. However, those tempted to become too nostalgic about vanished neighborhoods should read—and see the photographs—in a report on housing conditions in St. Paul in 1917 sponsored by the Amherst H. Wilder Charity. With a certain prescience, the 1917 report wrote:

> The "Flats" if properly treated would afford a splendid opportunity for the development of an industrial zone accessible to rail and river transportation instead of being what they are today, a slum of the worst character.

The picture was not presented as much better in a Depression-era 1930s report on housing conditions in St. Paul:

> District "B" [as it was called] is composed of one and two room shacks literally in the shadow of industrial plants. Those homes that did possess some merit at the time of erection have suffered from their environment and from the first attracted a type of tenant or owner that seemed not to realize the importance of maintaining their home, or felt it hopeless to do so in face of surrounding conditions, or simply lacked knowledge as to what should be done. There are also in this district homes inhabited by squatters; homes built from salvaged materials that present hopeless living conditions.

The river community was plagued with spring flooding, and after a series of disastrous floods in the 1950s, the St. Paul Port Authority purchased the land, demolished the homes, and built an industrial park. Then, after the neighborhood was eliminated, the city built a flood wall to protect the industrial park. Much has been written about the "Flats," but one of the best articles, based on firsthand accounts, is in *A Knack for Knowing Things* by Don Boxmeyer. See also *Badlands, Barton-Omaha Colony, Bohemian Flats, Connemara Patch, Upper Levee.*

WEST SIDE HEBREW CEMETERY This small Jewish cemetery on the east side of Barclay Street just north of Maryland Avenue dates from the turn of the twentieth century. In the middle of this cemetery is the Sons of Abraham cemetery, a separate entity. See also *Cemeteries.*

WEST ST. PAUL PARK This was to be a public park on the West Side between Robert Street and Gorman Avenue, between Elizabeth and Morton Streets. The potential park was surveyed for the parks department in 1889, but in the end the land was not purchased, and houses were built on it. See also *Hiawatha Park, Lincoln Park, Mohawk Park.*

WESTERN AVENUE On the 1854 plat of Dayton and Irvine's Addition, this street was the western boundary. One of the most splendid old buildings remaining in St. Paul, on the northeast corner of Western and Marshall Avenues, was St. Joseph's Academy, a Roman Catholic school for girls. The oldest portion was built about 1863 with yellow limestone from local quarries.

In its earliest days, the school was located such a distance from the residential districts of the city that day students had difficulty attending. In the 1850s this had been the location of a Catholic cemetery. Western Avenue marks a one-half section line on the land survey. See also St. Anthony Hill.

WESTERN SCULPTURE PARK This four-and-one-half-acre park at Marion and Ravoux Streets was acquired by the parks department in 1966 as part of an urban renewal project. In 1995, the Fuller-Aurora Neighborhood Association obtained a capital improvement grant of $350,000 to develop the space as a vital place for the community. In 1998, the park opened with a children's play area, volleyball court, and a rotating exhibition of twenty large-scale outdoor sculptures.

It is said—although difficult to verify—this prairie above downtown was where the Red River oxcarts regrouped for their six-hundred-mile return trip to Manitoba. See also *Doane Avenue*.

WESTMINSTER JUNCTION Once a busy railroad junction just north of downtown where over one hundred trains a day crowded through a narrow ravine in a weave of tracks and four tunnels, it is today the site of a twenty-five-acre business center and a new city bridge. The name was taken from the adjacent street. See also *Bridges*.

WESTMINSTER STREET John E. Warren named this street in 1853 in Warren and Winslow's Addition, most likely for Westminster, London, the site of Westminster Abbey.

Edmund Rice's estate was west of Westminster Street and south of York Avenue. Titled "Trout Brook Farm" and encompassing forty-five acres, the estate had a plum orchard, a summer house, an ice house, a barn, and a large mansion built in 1862 with eight bedrooms and three bathrooms. Trout Brook, running through the grounds, was dammed to create an artificial lake. Financially hard-pressed, Rice sold his estate to the railroad in 1883, and the grounds and house were destroyed. Because they require a 4 percent grade or less, the rail-

This whimsical writers' block is one of the clever art pieces in the Western Sculpture Park. Photograph by Kathleen M. Vadnais.

roads would, whenever possible, follow a streambed; therefore, almost every stream in St. Paul was supplanted by railroad tracks. This street marks a section line on the land survey. See also *Edmund Avenue, Trout Brook*.

WHEELER STREET Rush B. Wheeler (1844–1930) was a prominent St. Paul real-estate dealer. Born in New York State, graduating from Yale University, he came to Austin, Minnesota, where he studied law with his brother. He moved to St. Paul in 1883 and became active in the Chamber of Commerce, Real Estate Board, and YMCA.

Working with the Summit Avenue Improvement Association, Wheeler, who at the time resided at 749 Summit, negotiated with all the property owners from Lexington Parkway west to the river, persuading them to donate enough land on each side of the street so Summit Avenue could be widened from 100 to 200 feet. The land thus obtained was placed into a central strip separating the driving lanes, planted with trees and shrubs, and appointed as a bridle path. See also *Summit Avenue*.

WHEELER WALK Originally named Fredericka Walk on the 1925 Highland Park plat, a remnant exists as Wheeler Walk, an eleven-foot right-of-way between Saunders Avenue and Montreal Avenue, midway between Davern Street and Fairview Avenue. Although not marked, you can see the open space between 1756 and 1762 Saunders Avenue, and between 1756 and 1762, and 1757 and 1763 Rome Avenue. In the 1920s, these public walks were popular with developers because a walkway, instead of a cross street, allowed for very long blocks, which left more footage for salable lots. See also *Burg Street, Ghost Streets, Macalester Walk, Stanford Walk*.

WHEELOCK PARK This is a neighborhood roughly defined as between Arcade Street and Interstate 35E, between Arlington and Larpenteur Avenues.

WHEELOCK PARKWAY Joseph Albert Wheelock (1831–1906) was born in Nova Scotia and came to St. Paul in 1850 searching for better health. Eleven years later he founded the *St. Paul Pioneer Press*, remaining its editor until the end of his life. Active in civic affairs and politics, Wheelock was postmaster for five years, and in 1893 he was appointed president of the park board, a position he held for thirteen years. Named in 1908, three years after his death, this parkway, which links Lakes Como and Phalen, commemorates Wheelock's prodigious efforts to complete the St. Paul park system. *Wheelock Avenue, Wheelock Drive, Wheelock Lane,* and *Wheelock Ridge Road* all derive their names from the parkway. See also *Grand Rounds*.

WHITALL STREET Remembered for her "bright, beautiful countenance with black hair and black eyes," Matilda Whitall (1827–1906) was the wife of Henry M. Rice and sister-in-law to the developer Edmund Rice, who platted this street in 1855. Born in Rome, New York, Matilda moved to Richmond, Virginia, when she was seven. She met Henry Rice in Washington, DC, where she was attending school, and later married him in 1849. See also *Edmund Avenue, Matilda Street, Rice Street*.

WHITE BEAR AVENUE Laid out as a county road between Hudson Road and Larpenteur Avenue in 1886, this street was renamed White Bear Avenue two years later. The first surveyor's notes

Looking northeast on Wheelock Parkway from Cohansey Street about 1915. The two houses
to the left of the automobile remain at 1501 Western Avenue and 1458 Cumberland Street.
Photograph courtesy of the Minnesota Historical Society.

record that in 1847 the east-west road between Stillwater and St. Paul crossed the line of
White Bear Avenue at about the intersection with (today's) York Avenue, and a creek crossed
the street about where (today's) Sims Avenue intersects. This street marks a section line on
the land survey. See also *Arcade Street, Stillwater Avenue*.

WIGGINS POND Located behind 466 Burlington Road, this Highwood pond was named for
Edward and Minnie Wiggins, who owned a farmhouse at 448 Burlington Road in the 1940s.
This pond inspired the name Pond Street, which continues in adjacent Maplewood but has
been renamed as part of Burlington Road in St. Paul. See also *Lakes/Ponds*.

WIGGINS ROAD Edward Charles Wiggins Jr. and Etta L. Wiggins were the developers of this
Highwood street in their 1979 plat Wiggins Oak Hills. Edward was the son of Edward and
Minnie. See also *Wiggins Pond*.

WILDER STREET Helen N. Wilder (1835–1915) was the second wife of John L. Merriam, the
developer of this Merriam Park street in 1882. Her brother, Amherst H. Wilder (1828–94),
was a onetime business partner of the Merriams. Born in Vermont, Amherst moved to St. Paul
about 1859, where he worked with several different firms in the transportation of goods, including the railroads. He was very active in the business community, amassing a good deal of
money in the process, and several charitable institutions throughout St. Paul bear his name.
See also *Energy Park, Merriam's Overlook, Merriam Park*.

WILDVIEW AVENUE Previously Springfield Avenue, the name of this Highwood street was changed in 1940 to avoid duplication. See also *Highwood*.

WILKIN STREET Weighing no more than one hundred pounds and known as the "Little Captain" because of his small stature, Alexander Wilkin (1820–64) was born in Orange County, New York, where he studied law with his father. After earning the rank of captain in the Mexican War, he moved to St. Paul, where he practiced law and dabbled in real estate, naming this West End street in Leach's Addition in 1849. He was U.S. marshal for Minnesota and a founder of the St. Paul Companies, and later fought and died in the Civil War. There is also a Minnesota county named for him.

At the south end of Wilkin Street, extended to where it would enter the river under the High Bridge, there was a ferry—known as the Upper Ferry—in the earliest days of the city, as shown on the plat of Kinney, Bond and Trader's Addition in 1855. See also *Stevens Street*.

WILLIAM MAHONEY STREET This new downtown street co-name was bestowed by the city council in 2002 on Main Street at the urging of labor groups within the city. William Mahoney (1869–1952) came to St. Paul in 1905, a young Irish Socialist printer with a law degree. Throughout his life, he worked tirelessly and shrewdly to organize the efforts of St. Paul workers. Active with the Nonpartisan League and a staunch promoter of the Farmer-Labor party, he was mayor of St. Paul from 1932 to 1934. He nearly succeeded in obtaining municipal ownership of the public utilities, triggering a desperate campaign against him by Northern States Power Company, which cost him his reelection. He was editor of the *Union Advocate* newspaper and president of the St. Paul Trades and Labor Assembly. His home remains at 1852 Dayton Avenue.

His name was given to this particular street because the offices of the St. Paul Trades and Labor Assembly are located at 411 Main Street. For more information on Mahoney, see *Claiming the City* by Mary Wingerd. See also *Armstrong Avenue, Boyd Park, Energy Park Drive, Kilburn Street, Rice Park, Sherburne Avenue; Edmund Avenue, Kittson Street, Larry Ho Drive, McDonough Park, Nelson Street, Olmstead Street, Otis Avenue, Powers Avenue, Prince Street, Smith Avenue, Stewart Avenue*.

WILLIAM TELL ROAD The mother of the developer was born in Switzerland, making this an appropriate Highwood street name in his Swiss Meadows Addition. William Tell was a legendary Swiss patriot of the fourteenth century.

Matilda Whitall Rice, namesake for Whitall Street and wife of Governor Henry M. Rice, could be quite snide when the occasion warranted. Photograph courtesy of the Minnesota Historical Society.

William Mahoney, a Socialist (gasp) at heart. Photograph courtesy of the Minnesota Historical Society.

WILLIAMS HILL There was until about 1990 a hill where the Williams Hill Business Center is today, just northeast of downtown.

Beginning in the 1870s, the Broadway-Mississippi horse-car line ended here, and the hill was a favorite picnic spot. In the next decade it became residential property; by 1884, there were close to one hundred relatively small single-family and boarding houses on the hill, served by three winding streets: Williams Street (named for Brook B. Williams, one of the developers in 1857), DeBow Street, and St. Paul Street. At this period, the hill stretched about 1,000 feet on the east-west axis, and about 1,200 feet on the north-south axis, encompassing about twenty-seven acres. The topography was irregular, but the hill was maybe 40 feet at its highest point.

In the early 1900s the railroad, which by then encircled the hill, began actively acquiring the land and houses, planning to level the hill and build maintenance shops. By 1927, only about twenty houses remained; by the 1950s, fewer than five were left.

When the author visited the hill about 1963, he drove over the railroad tracks on a rickety wooden bridge off Mississippi Street. The streets were still paved, the fire hydrants were in place, and there were abandoned houses. It was a true ghost town.

In the following decades, the hill was systematically mined for its gravel; at one point the remains of bodies were found—evidence of an early cemetery—and collectors combed the diminishing hill for fossils and old bottles. It was a depressing ending for one of the touted seven hills of St. Paul: Williams Hill had become Williams Depression. See also *Seven Hills of St. Paul*.

WILLIUS STREET Originally platted as College Street in 1852, this street near downtown was renamed in 1872 to avoid duplication. Ferdinand Willius (1830–1916) and his brother, Gustav (1831–1924), were born in Germany and immigrated to St. Paul in the 1850s, where they opened a bank, which prospered under several names in the following years. Ferdinand was a member of the city council at the time the street name was changed. Both brothers were considered "cool, careful, calculating, cautious, conservative, industrious, and financially shrewd." They were also wealthy. Today this street is enjoying a revival, with new buildings along its length, but there remains an old classic limestone and brick building on the northwest corner of Willius and East Seventh Streets. See also *Lowertown*.

WILLOW BROOK See *Fish Hatchery Road*.

WILLOW RESERVE This is a five-and-one-half-acre conservancy district in the North End on the northeast corner of Maryland Avenue and Arundel Street. The former owner brought willow trees from Austria to plant in the wetland; in the spring he cut stems for florists to use in their bouquets. The property was acquired by the sewer department in 1977 after the League of Women Voters (who were doing a water-quality study), ornithologists, and the neighborhood exerted pressure on the city to buy the land before it was developed. Now used as a detention pond taking the occasional overflow from the storm sewer, the reserve has continued to host a vast array of birds, using this marshy site on their flyway. An adjacent neighborhood is sometimes known by this name as well. See also *Lakes/Ponds*.

WILMOT AVENUE At one time Caulfield Avenue, the name of this "ghost street" between St. Paul and Field Avenues was changed in 1940. See also *Ghost Streets*.

WILSHIRE PLACE Formerly River Street, the name of this East Side street was changed in 1940. See also *East Side*.

WILSON AVENUE Previously Hudson Avenue, the name of this East Side was changed in 1940 to avoid confusion with Hudson Road. See also *East Side*.

WINCHELL STREET Phillip D. Winchell platted this short street near Lake Phalen in 1888 with his wife, Martha. A carpenter on the West Side, Phillip died in 1912.

WINDMILL STREET Born in Baden, Germany, Michael Strub (1817–97) traveled to Minnesota in 1857 by way of Sandusky, Ohio. He lived at Sixth and John Streets for a while, then purchased a farm between the present-day limits of Westminster and Windmill Streets, between

"Swedish Castle" on Williams Hill at the corner of Williams and Pine Streets. Built in 1880 by Andrew M. Carlson, a St. Paul patent attorney, the thirty-seven-room house offered accommodations to newly arrived Scandinavian immigrants. Photograph courtesy of the Minnesota Historical Society.

Arlington and Clear Avenues. When the railroad dissected his farm, he platted the east half in 1888. The surveyor told Michael he needed some street names; Michael replied he didn't care, so the surveyor picked Strub (now Clear Avenue), and Residence Street (since vacated) because it ran by the house. The surveyor must also have looked around and seen a windmill, prompting this street name. The one-and-a-half-story farmhouse stood on what is now the west bank of Interstate Highway 35E, just south of Arlington Avenue. When Michael and his wife, Katherina, died, the remainder of the farm was subdivided in 1926. Alas, this street with the interesting name was vacated in 1997.

WINIFRED STREET Originally Harriet Street, the name of this West Side street was changed in 1876 to signify the daughter of William P. Murray, president of the city council at this time. She married Richard Demming, was widowed about 1894, taught school, and lived in the city until 1916, when her name was no longer listed in the directory. See also *West Side*.

WINNIPEG AVENUE The "dean of St. Paul real estate men," Robert P. Lewis (1835–1934) named this North End street in 1882. He came to St. Paul from Pennsylvania in 1859 as a law school graduate, and after the Civil War he went into real estate. Manitoba and Winnipeg Avenues were named together. Both were stations on the St. Paul and Manitoba Railroad. See also *North End*.

WINONA STREET Once Julia Street, the name of this West Side street was changed in 1883. *Winona* is a Dakota word meaning "firstborn daughter." There is a county by this name in Minnesota.

Part of an early 1980s boom in innovative, energy-efficient homes, the compact two-bedroom home at 425 Winona Street is the only earth-sheltered residence in St. Paul. Attractive inside and out, the well-planned concrete home has a pleasant greenhouse and a back door heading to a cleverly landscaped yard tucked below street level. See also *West Side*.

WINSLOW AVENUE Remembered as a man who "measured his words as a clerk measures molasses in cold weather," James M. Winslow (1810–85) was one of the developers of this West Side street in 1855. Born in the East, he ran a large stagecoach business in Vermont before coming to St. Paul in 1852. Here he built several hotels, all of which bore his name, plus the Winslow Mill on Trout Brook. He also introduced telegraph service to the city, running a line from Dubuque, Iowa, to St. Paul. He later moved to California, but his body was returned to Oakland Cemetery for burial.

In 1853, when the first survey of this area was made, the surveyor noted a road heading southeast from St. Paul to Traverse des Sioux, the famous treaty site in Nicollet County, where two years before the Dakota had signed away most of their land in southern Minnesota. This road ran through what is today approximately the property at 875 Winslow Avenue. See also *Trout Brook*, *West Side*.

WINSTON STREET Mary and Edgar C. Long, who lived near Hewitt and Snelling Avenues, platted this Midway street in 1885. The city directory for that year lists Eunice Winston as boarding with them; she may have been a sister or some other relative. See also *Midway*.

WINTER STREET While this North End street was named in 1858 for the season and remains under its original name, a nearby Summer Street has since been changed to Sherburne Avenue. It was a goal of the planning board in the late 1940s to open and extend Winter Street from Jackson Street to Como Avenue to permit traffic coming from the northwest to reach the downtown warehouse district without driving through the central business district. See also *North End*.

WINTHROP STREET The Union Land Company borrowed this name from a town near Boston and applied it to this Highwood street in 1888 in the Burlington Heights Addition. *Winthrop Court* and *Winthrop Lane* take their name from the same source.

If you travel south on Winthrop Street from Larpenteur Avenue, you will come upon one of the few unpaved streets in the city, a couple of old houses, and on your left, the Hillcrest Reservoir for the St. Paul water utility. (There is a second underground reservoir in Highland Park.) See also *Highwood*.

WITHAM AVENUE Previously Wilder Avenue, this West Side street name was changed in 1888. It was vacated in 1972, but part of it ended up as Barge Channel Road. See also *West Side*.

WOLSEY STREET This unimproved, unopened "ghost street" is just off Edgcumbe Road, a little east of Snelling Avenue. See also *Ghost Streets*.

WOOD STREET "A large man, with large brain, and large heart, and large sympathies," Edward H. Wood (1836–1907), a native of Kentucky, arrived in St. Paul in 1856, where he helped survey building lots around Lake Como. He subsequently engaged in real-estate speculation, was admitted to the bar in 1860, served in the Civil War, and settled on the West Side in 1867. See also *West Side*.

WOODBRIDGE STREET This North End street was named in 1876 in Cone and Ryder's Addition, most likely for the sound of the word; at any rate there is no evidence of a bridge in the area. One of the most interesting churches in St. Paul is the 1914 St. Mary Romanian Orthodox Church at 854 Woodbridge Street. The onion-shaped dome is typical of orthodox churches everywhere. See also *North End*.

WOODBURY STREET Dwight Woodbury (1800–1884) owned extensive property in the area and platted Woodbury and Case's Addition on the West Side in 1874. Born in Charlton, Massachusetts, he moved to Minnesota in 1855 and settled in the Anoka area, where he was an active community leader. See also *Charlton Street*, *West Side*.

WOODCREST DRIVE This street near Battle Creek was named in 1964 in the Bacchus St. Paul Hills Addition.

WOODLAND PARK This 1870 plat divided the area between Summit and Marshall Avenues, between Dale Street and Western Avenue, into building lots. It was within this plat that Summit Avenue changed from its course along the bluff and headed due west across the prairie. This was done, no doubt, by the developers, who wished to extend the aura of Summit Avenue to as much adjacent property as possible. The list of Woodland Park developers included William Dawson, Alexander Vance Brown, James Burbank, William Wright, John Merriam, Horace Thompson, James Stinson, Henry Rice, Stella Selby, Robert Smith, and Warren Carpenter, many of whom owned or had an interest in property that would increase in value as a result of the westward course of Summit Avenue. Today Woodland Park is an Historic District. See also *Dawson Park, James Street, Mears Park, Merriam Park, Ramsey Hill Historic District, Rice Street, Selby Avenue, Summit Avenue, Summit Lookout Park, Vance Street.*

WOODLAWN AVENUE Applied here in 1913, *wood* is always a popular component of place and street names, implying trees, shade, and calm.

There are at least two notable houses on this street: 151 South Woodlawn, built in 1923, is one of the best examples of the Prairie Style; and the Metal Experimental House at 265 South Woodlawn was built as part of an experiment following the Chicago Century of Progress Exposition of 1933.

WOODLAWN OVAL This small Highwood park between Blocks One and Two in the Oakland Addition to Burlington Heights is now part of Highway 61. See also *Highwood.*

WOODWARD STREET Now covered with railroad tracks and commercial buildings, Woodward Street was once, in the 1880s, a most exclusive address. Location of the Thompson, Sibley, and Wilder mansions, each with its own large grounds and extensive private driveways, the street had at its east end picturesque Trout Brook. The whole area, entirely residential at that

This elegant neighborhood looking down Woodward Street from the corner of Lafayette Road and Woodward Street was overrun by the railroads. Engraved by the Photo Engraving Company (New York); courtesy of the Minnesota Historical Society.

time, was known as Lowertown. Absolutely nothing of it remains today. Woodward was named in 1852 in Brunson's Addition for an avenue in Detroit, Henry Sibley's birthplace. See also *Lowertown, Sibley Street, Trout Brook.*

WORCESTER AVENUE Worcester, a county of England, prompted this Highland Park street name in 1912. See also *Highland Park.*

WORDSWORTH AVENUE William Davern, who named this Highland Park street in 1891, was a onetime schoolteacher well acquainted with the poetry of William Wordsworth (1770–1850). See also *Highland Park.*

WRIGHT AVENUE (Fairgrounds) This street honors Kindy C. Wright, architect for many of the buildings presently gracing the fairgrounds. Born in St. Paul in 1893, Wright began an association with the fair in 1933. In his early years with the fair he supervised the many Emergency Relief Administration (ERA) and Works Progress Administration (WPA) building projects on the fairgrounds. Among these were the Conservation Building (now the Natural Resources Building) built by the ERA in 1934, the Horse Barn and Poultry Buildings in 1937, the half-mile dirt track in 1939, and the 4-H Buildings—for which Wright personally obtained the funding from the WPA—in 1939. Wright's private firm also designed in the late 1940s and early 1950s the Agriculture Building, the Food Building, and the Hippodrome (now the Coliseum).

WYCLIFF STREET Part of St. Anthony Park, this street was named in 1885 for John Wycliff (1320?–84), an English religious scholar who by his criticism of the Roman Catholic Church sowed the seeds of the later Reformation. See also *St. Anthony Park.*

WYNNE AVENUE Platted west of Fairview Avenue in 1885 in St. Anthony Park, this street now exists only east of Fairview Avenue. See also *St. Anthony Park.*

WYOMING STREET Originally Judith Street, the name of this West Side street was changed in 1883 to acknowledge the state. See also *West Side.*

X

XEES PHAUS This is the Hmong name for St. Paul, which has become a center of Hmong culture in the United States. Because the Hmong, most of whom relocated from Laos as a result of the Vietnam War, are spread throughout the world, there is probably a wider international use of this Hmong name for St. Paul than the English version. See also *Oakland Cemetery, St. Paul*.

XINA PARK Platted in 1927, this large triangular park with several trees is at the intersection of Howell Street and Hampshire Avenue. When the park was named, Hampshire Avenue was Xina Avenue. The meaning of Xina is clouded in obscurity. See also *Bohland Avenue, Quirnia Avenue*.

Xina Park is typical of many of these public triangles throughout St. Paul. Photograph by Kathleen M. Vadnais.

YACHT CLUB ROAD Named by the parks department, this road is in proximity to the St. Paul Yacht Club.

YORK AVENUE Platted as Douglas Street, this East Side street was changed in 1872. The present name is very common and was chosen probably because it was short and easy to pronounce and remember. See also *White Bear Avenue*.

YORKSHIRE AVENUE This Highland Park street was named in 1948 in Hampshire Park. Both Yorkshire and Hampshire are counties in England; the developer did not recall the significance. *Yorkshire Court* takes its name from the same source. See also *Highland Park*.

YOUNG STREET John Young, the developer, owned six-and-a-half acres in the vicinity when this Midway street was named in 1887. See also *Midway*.

YOUNGMAN AVENUE Christopher W. Youngman, a native of Indiana, named this West End street in 1886. He moved to St. Paul about 1882, where he first managed a piano and organ store downtown. Later he went into the real-estate business and bought the forty-acre West Seventh Street stone quarries. See also *Butternut Avenue, Maynard Drive, Victoria Park, West End*.

Z

ZIMMERMAN PLACE This is a small subdivision on the southwest corner of East Seventh Street and Bates Avenue. It is noteworthy as the only entry in this book beginning with the letter Z.

A NOTE ON SOURCES

WITH A FEW RECENT EXCEPTIONS, there is no record, official or otherwise, of why any street name was selected. It is almost always necessary, therefore, to determine or infer the significance of any name from the shreds of evidence that can be gathered.

Any serious research must begin with the original plat on file in the Register of Deeds office in the county courthouse. The plat must be examined for the original sequence of street names, many of which may have since been changed. The name of the developer should be determined, as well as the names of the surveyor, notary public, or any other individuals associated with the plat.

If none of these individuals seems related to the street name, and subsequent biographical research cannot make any connection, then a check of the ownership of the property before the platting will often prove successful. In the case of more recent plats, a telephone call to the developer will usually clarify the meaning of the street names.

If the plat does not provide a useful clue, then research must be extended. Early atlases, maps, probate and district court records, city directories, genealogical data, newspapers, census records, histories of the city, manuscripts, periodicals, and (depending on the street name) a variety of other usual and unusual reference sources will often supply the missing information.

I spent many hours studying the plats of Ramsey County, which can be found in the county recorder's office; copies of all the St. Paul plats are also in the St. Paul Public Works Department. I looked at a number of original deeds, particularly when preparing the first edition of this book. They can be found in the Ramsey County Register of Deeds office. (It is helpful to know whether the property is abstract or torrens.) Grading records for the streets of St. Paul are on microfiche in the St. Paul Public Works Department. If not otherwise credited in the text, original documents were found in the St. Paul Public Works Department.

The origin of street names changed by the city itself—such as those renamed in 1940—is difficult to identify, and as a class the significance of these new street names presents an often impossible problem. Sometimes the street names simply have no significance; they were chosen because they sounded nice or seemed to have some promotional value. This is particularly true if the name is bestowed by a large company, a corporate entity, or a large-scale developer who, like the old woman in the shoe, has become oblivious to the delight of bestowing a name.

PREVIOUS WRITING ON STREET NAMES

The only previous detailed information on the street names of St. Paul appeared in a volume by Warren Upham, *Minnesota Geographic Names: Their Origin and Historic Significance*. This book, containing thirty-one pages of research on the street and park names of St. Paul, was published in 1920 by the Minnesota Historical Society, which reprinted the book in 2001 as *Minnesota Place Names: A Geographical Encyclopedia*. Much of the data gathered by Upham was featured in an extensive newspaper article in the *St. Paul Daily News* on March 1, 1925.

From time to time, an article has been printed in the newspaper listing some of the obvious street name derivations, such as Ramsey Street or Sibley Street. Examples of this type of feature appeared in the *St. Paul Pioneer Press* on April 15, 1894, and in the *St. Paul Globe* on August 17, 1902.

The St. Paul Department of Public Works has, for many years, maintained a volume recording the street name changes in the city. This book, which is by no means complete and not always accurate, was copied as a WPA project, and a carbon typescript is cataloged in the library of the Minnesota Historical Society under St. Paul Department of Public Works, *Guide to St. Paul Street Names before 1937*.

A useful guide to early street name changes is found in Everett S. Geer's *New Guide for Citizens and Strangers to the Location and Numbers of Streets and Avenues in the City of St. Paul ...*, published in St. Paul by Everett S. Geer in 1884.

BIBLIOGRAPHY

Altshuler, Alan A. *The City Planning Process: A Political Analysis.* Ithaca, NY: Cornell University Press, 1965.

Andreas, A. T. *An Illustrated Historical Atlas of the State of Minnesota.* Chicago: A. T. Andreas, 1874.

Andrews, C. C. *History of St. Paul, Minn.; with Illustrations and Biographical Sketches of Some of Its Prominent Men and Pioneers.* Syracuse, NY: D. Mason & Co., 1890.

Aronovici, Carol. *Housing Conditions in the City of Saint Paul: Report Presented to the Housing Commission of the St. Paul Association.* St. Paul: Amherst H. Wilder Charity, 1917.

Atwater, Isaac, ed. *History of the City of Minneapolis, Minnesota.* New York: Munsell & Co., 1893.

Bass, Patrice. "The Early History of the St. Paul Park System, 1872–1907." Manuscript prepared for the St. Paul Division of Parks and Recreation, 1997.

Bennett, L. G. *Map of Ramsey County, Minnesota, 1867.* Chicago: 1867?

Bessler, John D. *Legacy of Violence: Lynch Mobs and Executions in Minnesota.* Minneapolis: University of Minnesota Press, 2003.

Bliss, Frank C. *St. Paul: Its Past and Present.* St. Paul: F. C. Bliss Publishing Company, 1888.

Board of Park Commissioners of the City of St. Paul. Annual Reports of the Board of Park Commissioners of the City of St. Paul. 1895–1913.

Boxmeyer, Don. *A Knack for Knowing Things: Stories from St. Paul Neighborhoods and Beyond.* St. Paul: Minnesota Historical Society Press, 2003.

Brick, Greg A. "St. Paul Underground: What Happened to Fountain Cave, the Real Birth Place of St. Paul?" *Ramsey County History* 29, no. 4 (Winter 1995).

———. "Stairway to the Abyss: The Diverting Story of Cascade Creek and Its Journey under St. Paul." *Ramsey County History* 33, no. 1 (Spring 1998).

"A Brief History of the Irvine Park District: The People and Architecture of an Extraordinary Neighborhood." St. Paul: Irvine Park Association, 1986?

Business Directory for the City of St. Paul, Minnesota Territory. St. Paul: Goodrich & Somers, 1856.

Chaney, Josiah. *Early Bridges and Changes of the Land and Water Surface in the City of St. Paul. Collections of the Minnesota Historical Society,* vol. 12. St. Paul: Minnesota Historical Society, 1908.

City of Edmonton. *Naming Edmonton: From Ada to Zoie.* Edmonton: University of Alberta Press, 2004.

Congress of American Road Builders. *Modern Road Building: Being Reports of the Transactions of the First Congress of American Road Builders Held at Seattle, Washington, July 4, 1909.* New York: 1909?; St. Paul: West Publishing Company.

"Downtown St. Paul: A Plan for Its Development by the Organizing Committee of the City of St. Paul Central Business District Authority." Harry G. Clemans, secretary. August 1943.

Dunn, James Taylor. "Whatever Happened to the Oxford Club?" *Grand Gazette* 1, no. 4 (December 1973).

Empson, Donald. "Highland–Groveland–Macalester Park: The Old Reserve Township." *Ramsey County History* 10, no. 2 (Fall 1973).

———. "The History of the Mississippi River Boulevard in St. Paul, for the Mississippi River Boulevard Association." St. Paul: The Mississippi River Boulevard Association, 1975.

———. "John Ayd's Grist Mill and Reserve Township History." *Ramsey County History* 11, no. 2 (Fall 1974).

———. "Portrait of a Neighborhood: A History in Tour Form of the Cliff Street ITA, the Neighborhood between West Seventh Street and the Mississippi River, between Smith Avenue and Richmond Street, St. Paul, Minnesota." St. Paul: 1980.

———. "William Nettleton and the Highland Park Spring Water Company." *St. Paul Dispatch*, Neighborhood section, March 4, 1975.

Fairbanks, Evelyn. *The Days of Rondo.* St. Paul: Minnesota Historical Society Press, 1990.

Gilman, Rhoda. *Henry Hastings Sibley: Divided Heart.* St. Paul: Minnesota Historical Society Press, 2004.

Goodman, Nancy, and Robert Goodman. *Joseph R. Brown, Adventurer on the Minnesota Frontier, 1820–1849.* Rochester, MN: Lone Oak Press, 1996.

A Guide to Minnesota's Scientific and Natural Areas. St. Paul: Minnesota Department of Natural Resources, Section of Wildlife, Scientific, and Natural Areas Program, 1995.

Hatfield, Marshall. "Lafayette Park and the Vanished Houses of St. Paul's Elite." *Ramsey County History* 29, no. 2 (Summer 1994).

Hennessy, W. B. *Past and Present of St. Paul, Minnesota.* Chicago: S. J. Clarke Publishing Company, 1906.

Herrold, George H. "Disruption, Long Chaos Seen in Proposed Twin Cities Freeway." *Northwest Architect* 20 (1956).

Hiebert, Gareth D. *City on Seven Hills: Columns of Oliver Towne.* St. Paul: Pogo Press, 1999.

———. *Once upon a Towne.* St. Paul: North Central Publishing Company, 1959.

———. *St. Paul Is My Beat.* St. Paul: North Central Publishing Company, 1958.

"Historic St. Paul Buildings: A Report of the Historic Sites Committee, a Special Citizens Group Named by the St. Paul City Planning Board." St. Paul: St. Paul City Planning Board, 1964.

History of Ramsey County and the City of St. Paul. Minneapolis: North Star Publishing Company, 1881.

Hoffmann, Alexius. "Frogtown." Manuscript, 1925. St. Paul: Minnesota Historical Society.

Hopkins, G. M. *Atlas of the City of St. Paul, Minnesota.* Philadelphia: G. M. Hopkins, 1884.

———. *Atlas of the Environs of St. Paul, Including the Whole of Ramsey County, Minnesota.* Philadelphia: G. M. Hopkins, 1886.

Hopkins, G. M., Co. *Plat Book of St. Paul, Minn. and Suburbs.* Philadelphia: G. M. Hopkins Company, 1916.

———. *Plat Book of the City of Saint Paul, Minn. and Suburbs, from Official Records, Private Plans and Actual Surveys. Compiled for and under the Direction of the St. Paul Real Estate Board. . . .* Philadelphia: G. M. Hopkins Company, 1928.

"The House of the Good Shepherd in St. Paul; A Retrospect of Fifty Years." *Acta et Dicta* 5, no. 2 (July 1918).

Hummel, Mary Benton. "Sleeping on the Hill: The Cemeteries of Ramsey County, Minnesota." Master's thesis, Hamline University, 1991.

The Kom-mu-ter. A newsletter of the Highwood Commercial Club, October 1921–May 1924, including a history of Highwood. Privately owned.

Lanegran, David A. *St. Anthony Park: Portrait of a Community.* St. Paul: District 12 Community Council, St. Anthony Park Association, 1987.

Lincoln Park Improvement Association. Loose-leaf binder containing handwritten and typescript materials pertaining to the Lincoln Park Improvement Association, 1954–57. Privately owned.

Luecke, John. *Dreams, Disasters, and Demise: The Milwaukee Road in Minnesota.* Eagan, MN: Grenadier Publications, 1988.

Bibliography

"The Memoirs of Lillian E. Gilbertson: Pig's Eye's Great-Great-Granddaughter." As told to Janell Norman, April 2004. Typescript privately owned.

Minnesota Beginnings: Records of Saint Croix County, Wisconsin Territory, 1840–1849, Including Minutes of the Board of Commissioners, Treasurer's and Tax Assessor's Records, Deeds, Justice of the Peace Records, Road Surveys, and the Miscellaneous County Records, with Brief Biographies of Citizens Mentioned. Stillwater, MN: History Network of Washington County, published by the Washington County Historical Society, 1999.

Mischke, Michael. *Here's Highland: Your Guide to Highland Park.* St. Paul: Villager Communications, Inc. Published for the Highland Business Association, 1989.

Nason, George L. *Visiting around St. Paul Parks.* St. Paul: St. Paul Dispatch, 1932. Extracted from *St. Paul Dispatch*, July 4–December 1, 1932.

Nelson, Paul D. "Lost Neighborhood: The Life and Death of Central Park." *Ramsey County History* 39, no. 3 (Fall 2004).

Newson, Thomas, ed. *Illustrated Saint Paul and Fireside Companion.* Vol. 1, no. 4. April 1879.

Parks and Public Places in Ramsey County. St. Paul: Friends of the Parks and Trails of St. Paul and Ramsey County, 1994.

Pfaender, Jay. "The Story of a Lost Estate and Oliver Crosby, the Inventive Genius Who Created It." *Ramsey County History* 40, no. 3 (Fall 2005).

"Plan of Saint Paul, the Capital City of Minnesota." Edward H. Bennett and William E. Parsons, consultant city planners. George H. Herrold, city plan engineer. Submitted to the Citizens of Saint Paul by the City Planning Board. St. Paul: Commissioner of Public Works, 1922.

"Planning St. Paul for Better Living: Report of the City Planning Board of Saint Paul, Minnesota." St. Paul: 1946.

Protz, George. *Pocket Edition of the Original Plats of the City of St. Paul.* St. Paul: 1883?

Przybylski, Anna. "It Truly Is a Village: An Analysis of the Central Village Neighborhood of Saint Paul, Minnesota." 2002. Privately owned.

Ramsey County League of Women Voters. *The City of St. Paul: A Civic Handbook.* St. Paul: 1926.

Rondo Avenue, Inc. *Remember Rondo . . . Celebrating the People, Their Lives and Times. July 1, 2, 3, 1983. History of Rondo Avenue.* St. Paul, 1983.

Saint Paul, a Comprehensive Industrial Survey of Saint Paul and the Great Northwest. Industrial Department, the Saint Paul Association of Commerce. St. Paul, 1926.

St. Paul Labor History Map. www.workdayminnesota.org. Accessed April 2005.

St. Paul, plaintiff. *City of St. Paul vs. the Chicago, Milwaukee & St. Paul Railway Company. Levee case. Evidence and pleadings.* Globe Job Office, D. Ramaley and Son, Printers, 1888.

"A Survey of Housing Conditions in Older Areas of Saint Paul, Minnesota, Made under the Supervision and Direction of the City Planning Board, for the Citizen's Housing Committee." Written and edited by Marc. V. Sullivan. WPA, 1937. Mimeograph.

Thornley, Stew. *Six Feet Under: A Graveyard Guide to Minnesota.* St. Paul: Minnesota Historical Society Press, 2004.

Upham, Warren. *Minnesota Place Names: A Geographical Encyclopedia.* 3d. ed. St. Paul: Minnesota Historical Society Press, 2001.

Vadnais, Kathleen. *High Bridge Highs: A Goodbye.* St. Paul: Low End Press, 1984.

Vogt, James. *Desnoyer Park: A History of the Neighborhood.* St. Paul: Desnoyer Park Improvement Association, 1990.

Williams, J. Fletcher. *History of the City of Saint Paul to 1875, and the County of Ramsey, Minnesota.* St. Paul: Minnesota Historical Society Press, 1983.

Bibliography

Wing, Frank. *We Present: A Collection of Seventy-five Sketches of St. Paul Citizens.* St. Paul: Perkins-Tracy, 1925.

Wingerd, Mary Lethert. *Claiming the City: Politics, Faith, and the Power of Place in St. Paul.* Ithaca, NY: Cornell University Press, 2001.

Winkel, Max. "A Collection of One-Page Articles on the History of St. Paul, Its Streets, Buildings, Parks, etc., Prepared by Max Winkel for the Junior Pioneer Association, St. Paul." St. Paul, 1955–61.

Woodruff, Mark W. *Facts about the City of St. Paul, Minnesota, Compiled from Records of City of St. Paul and Minnesota Historical Society.* St. Paul: Printed at St. Paul Vocational School, 1939.

INDEX

Street names where they appear in alphabetical sequence in the text are not indexed.

DONALD L. EMPSON

was born and has spent much of his life in St. Paul, where he worked as a librarian at the Minnesota Historical Society, as a freelance writer and researcher, and as an antique clock and watch repairman. He currently enjoys semi-retirement in Stillwater, Minnesota, with his wife, Kathleen M. Vadnais.

DON BOXMEYER

wrote for the *St. Paul Dispatch* and *St. Paul Pioneer Press* for more than thirty-five years. He is the author of *A Knack for Knowing Things: Stories from St. Paul Neighborhoods and Beyond.*